D1745183

Th.

THE ECONOMICS AND POLITICS OF INTERNATIONAL TRADE

The post-World War II period has seen a marked increase in liberalization of trade. Despite this, freedom of trade is, only now, returning to the level it reached in the period following the repeal of the Corn Laws, and arguments for trade control continue to influence thinkers on policy. This collection of essays by leading economists and political thinkers provides a timely evaluation of the current debates concerning the value of free trade.

The contributions range over a wide field, offering complementary perspectives on the theme of freedom and trade. Frank Hahn explores the fragility of the simple model of comparative advantage. Paul Krugman explains why this simple idea remains so poorly understood and distrusted by many policy-thinkers. Christopher Bliss re-examines the original Corn Laws debate from the perspective of modern economic theory. Martin Wolf reflects on the Cobdenite theme that free trade promotes peaceful coexistence between nations. Ippei Yamazawa provides an insight into the Osaka action agenda of the Asia Pacific Economic Cooperation forum. John Baldwin and Richard Caves present new evidence of the ability of trade to enhance efficiency through competition.

The studies in *The Economics and Politics of International Trade* provide a rich and varied perspective on the feasibility and desirability of free trade.

Gary Cook gained his Ph.D. in Economics from the University of Manchester and has taught at Manchester Business School and the University of Derby. He has published in the area of industrial economics and has been consultant to *Cambridge Econometrics* for several years.

ROUTLEDGE STUDIES IN THE MODERN WORLD ECONOMY

THE ECONOMICS AND POLITICS OF INTERNATIONAL TRADE

Freedom and trade
Volume II

Edited by
Gary Cook

Proceedings of a conference to commemorate the 150th anniversary
of the repeal of the Corn Laws

General editors
Geraint Parry and Hillel Steiner

R
ROUTLEDGE

London and New York

First published 1998
by Routledge
11 New Fetter Lane, London EC4P 4EE

Simultaneously published in the USA and Canada
by Routledge
29 West 35th Street, New York, NY 10001

Editorial matter © 1998 Gary Cook
Individual contributions © 1998 individual contributors

Typeset in Garamond 3 by Keystroke, Jacaranda Lodge, Wolverhampton
Printed and bound in Great Britain by TJ International Ltd, Padstow, Cornwall

British Library Cataloguing in Publication Data
A catalogue record for this book is available from the British Library

Library of Congress Cataloging in Publication Data
A catalogue record for this book has been requested

ISBN 0–415–15525–8

CONTENTS

CONTENTS

CONTENTS

FIGURES

viii

TABLES

TABLES

x

CONTRIBUTORS

John R. Baldwin is Director, Micro-economic Studies and Analysis, Statistics Canada.

Alvin Birdi is Lecturer in Economics at Middlesex University.

Christopher Bliss is Nuffield Professor of International Economics at Nuffield College, Oxford.

Richard E. Caves is Professor of Economics at Harvard University.

K. Alec Chrystal is Professor of Monetary Economics at City University, London.

Anthony Cockerill is Director of Durham University Business School and Professor of Economics.

Gary Cook is Senior Lecturer in Economics at the University of Derby.

Jarko Fidrmuc is Research Assistant at the Institute of Advanced Studies in Vienna.

Harald Gruber is Senior Economist at the European Investment Bank and Professor of Economics at the University of Siena.

Frank Hahn is Professor of Economics at the University of Siena and Professor Emeritus at the University of Cambridge.

Christian Helmenstein is Head of the Department of Finance at the Institute for Advanced Studies in Vienna.

Peter Huber is Research Assistant at the Institute for Advanced Studies in Vienna.

Parmjit Kaur is Senior Lecturer in Economics at Leicester Business School.

Jacob Kol is Professor of Economics at Erasmus University, Rotterdam.

Paul Krugman is Professor of Economics at the Massachusetts Institute of Technology.

Lynden Moore is Senior Associate Member of St Anthony's College, Oxford and formerly Lecturer in Economics at the University of Manchester.

Robert O'Brien is Lecturer in International Relations at the University of Sussex.

George A. Petrochilos is Senior Lecturer in Economics at the University of Coventry.

Erik S. Reinert is Research Director at the Norsk Investorforum.

Magdolna Sass is Economist at the Institute of Economics of the Hungarian Academy of Sciences.

Hylke Vandenbussche is a Postdoctoral Researcher at the University of Antwerp, Research Affiliate of the Centre for Economic Policy and Research and External Fellow of CREDIT, University of Nottingham.

David Williams is Senior Lecturer in Economics at the University of Derby.

Martin Wolf is Associate Editor and Economics Editor at the *Financial Times* and is a past winner of the Wincott Foundation senior prize for excellence in financial journalism.

Ippei Yamazawa is Professor of Economics at Hitotsubashi University and was Japan's representative to the Eminent Persons Group of APEC.

GENERAL EDITORS' PREFACE

Geraint Parry and Hillel Steiner

The three volumes of *Freedom and Trade* consist of papers arising from a multi-disciplinary international conference held at the University of Manchester in 1996 to commemorate the 150th Anniversary of the Repeal of the Corn Laws in 1846. The papers, along with commentaries, are published in three volumes, each self-contained and each devoted to one or more of the disciplines represented at the conference. One volume, edited by Andrew Marrison, is devoted to *Free Trade and its Reception 1815–1960*, a second, edited by Gary Cook, to *The Economics and Politics of International Trade* and the third to *The Legal and Moral Aspects of International Trade*, for which the editors are Asif Qureshi, Hillel Steiner and Geraint Parry. Professor Frank Hahn's plenary address to the conference appears in the volume on *The Economics and Politics of International Trade*. The volume on *The Legal and Moral Aspects of International Trade* also includes chapters by a panel of distinguished scholars representing each of the major disciplines involved who were invited to speak on 'The Feasibility and Desirability of Global Free Trade'.

The repeal of the Corn Laws in 1846 was an event of enormous significance in the history of international trade, in the development of institutions of international regulation, in the realignment of political parties and interests in Britain and in the emergence of new modes of political action through mass politics and single-issue interest groups. It remains an event which promptly conjures up the economic, political and moral sentiments surrounding the idea of free trade and its confrontation with the policy of protection. This significance can safely be affirmed even though, as so many chapters in these volumes attest, the nature of this significance remains hotly debated by leading world scholars in every intellectual discipline which is touched by this still controversial measure. Was the real impact of the repeal substantive or symbolic? It would clearly be mistaken to dismiss it as merely symbolic since symbols can be of the utmost importance, not merely in history and politics but also in economics. No measure to regulate trade has ever given rise to so much contention at the time and since. It is also a suggestive indicator of the contemporary geopolitical situation that this was not an international agreement such as the General Agreement on Tariffs and Trade (GATT) but a unilateral legislative action by one economically hegemonic state.

A return to the subject of 'Freedom and Trade' in 1996, 150 years after the repeal and as the new world economic order faces the uncertainties of the twenty-first century, is an intriguing experience. History never exactly repeats itself, either as tragedy or farce. Nevertheless many of the claims and counter-claims of the repeal period can readily be recognized in new guises in the present era. The campaign for free trade stemmed in part from a recognition of the growing interdependence of nations and the emergence of an ever more global market. This has now become the phenomenon which dominates not only international politics but also the domestic politics and economies of nations large and small. The international and the domestic are intertwined as never before. Within this new order economic liberalization may be the dominant ideology but many arguments, familiar from debates surrounding the repeal, make a reappearance. Is liberalization a policy which in reality is designed to promote the interests of the present-day economic hegemon? Is free trade of genuinely mutual benefit or is it a cloak for exploitation of various kinds? Will the new trading blocs and the new political communities which they have begun to create seek to revert to forms of protection? A distinctively new concern, not at the forefront of minds in the optimistic period of the repeal, is whether free trade is compatible with protection of the global environment.

These concerns have given new urgency to the search for authoritative institutions of international regulation. The emergence and influence since World War II of such institutions and agencies as the World Bank, International Monetary Fund (IMF) and GATT must be counted among the most striking developments in the history of international politics and international law. The range and scope of these bodies have grown steadily and they have increasingly assumed political responsibilities in promoting policies which are of considerable future significance. It is not surprising therefore that, alongside these developments, there has been a growing interest among political theorists in the moral underpinnings of international economic and political policies. Many have turned from discussing the justice of domestic policy to examining the issues of fairness between nations, the legitimacy of interventions in the affairs of foreign countries and the proper limits to free international exchange.

The conference, which was entitled '1846 Freedom and Trade 1996: A Commemoration of the 150th Anniversary of the Repeal of the Corn Laws', together with these volumes, sought to address this range of issues from the perspective of economic and political historians, international economists, international lawyers and political theorists. While the repeal itself is the subject of many of the chapters, in others it serves as the peg upon which to hang discussions of the contemporary state of the international political economy. Moreover the conference was, it should be noted, a 'commemoration' and not a 'celebration' of the repeal. As many contributions indicate, the event still engenders strong views as to its intentions and its consequences. In each of the disciplines represented there have been important developments in the ways in which the repeal and later issues of freedom and trade are analysed. Innovations in the study of political parties and interests have permitted new examinations of the coalitions of groupings behind the repeal. Subsequent experience of mass politics allows scholars to see the campaigns of the Anti-Corn Law League as forerunners of the techniques of contemporary single-issue politics. In international economics we are, as Cook says in the Introduction to the volume on *The Economics and Politics of International Trade*, still experiencing 'Corn Laws' debates that may be conducted in different economic languages but which can produce results just as paradoxical in terms of winners and losers as occurred 150 years ago. The remarkable revival in political theory over the last thirty years is now bringing new insights to questions of international justice, while lawyers are refining the instruments of international regulation in an arena traditionally dominated by the interplay of power politics. Finally, 150 years which have experienced decades of imperial rivalry, two world wars and forty years of Cold War tension have inevitably increased scepticism about the cherished beliefs of Cobden and other campaigners that free trade would usher in an unprecedented era of world peace and harmony. Cobden was President of the International Education Society, which sought to promote the cause of European peace by establishing international schools in Britain, France and Germany. His views on trade were inextricably linked to his ideas on morality and education. Cobden and the free traders might therefore take some comfort if they could learn that, despite the intervening periods of scepticism and disillusionment, scholars are rediscovering the Cobdenite thesis and beginning to explore whether there is indeed a link between liberalization, democratization and peace between nations.

The conference and the volumes of *Freedom and Trade* have sought to address the range of issues raised by the original repeal of the Corn Laws, not only for its own time but in ways which have seemed of continuing interest and relevance. The conference was initiated and convened by Hillel Steiner and Geraint Parry of the Department of Government of the University of Manchester which was the main sponsor of the event. Andrew Marrison of the Department of History, Asif Qureshi of the Faculty of Law of the University of Manchester and Gary Cook, initially of the Manchester Business School and currently at the University of Derby, were the convenors of the academic specialisms into which the conference and these volumes were divided. Professor Michael Rose of the Department of History at the University of Manchester and Professor Keith Tribe of the University of Keele made major contributions to the conference Steering Committee. The editorial team is also grateful to Routledge for its support and, in particular, to Alan Jarvis whose involvement extended to active participation in the conference.

That Manchester was the most appropriate venue for this event can hardly be doubted. The 'Cottonopolis' was where the Anti-Corn Law League was founded. The ideology and the interests of the major manufacturing interests of the city entirely coincided. Indeed the statues of Richard Cobden and John Bright still prominently adorn the city centre. The movement's salience has been perpetuated in the name of the Free Trade Hall which has been Manchester's chief venue for political and cultural events until, somewhat ironically, it closed in 1996 to reopen as an hotel and conference centre. Perhaps this too has its symbolic quality since the closure and reopening can be seen as part of the city's reinvention of itself as a different kind of commercial centre, responding to new terms of international trade in a global economy more complex than existed in 1846 but still one exercised by fundamental issues of freedom and protection.

ACKNOWLEDGEMENTS

During the gestation and organization of the conference '1846 Freedom and Trade 1996' and the preparation of the three volumes of *Freedom and Trade* we have incurred many obligations. There is space only to acknowledge some of these debts. The Department of Government of the University of Manchester and its Manchester Centre for Political Thought sponsored the event. We are grateful for their support. The Dean of the Faculty of Economic and Social Studies, the Department of Economics and Professor Martin Harris, Vice-Chancellor of the University of Manchester, were instrumental in arranging for the crucial seed money to enable the conference to be organized. The Faculty of Law and the Department of History at Manchester provided funds and administrative facilities, as did the University of Derby. On behalf of the History and Policy Section, Andrew Marrison gratefully acknowledges the support of the Conferences and Initiatives Fund of the Economic History Society for a grant towards administrative and travel costs.

Mrs Rebecca Naidoo was an outstanding administrator in the preparatory period leading up to the organization of the conference. Ms Bernadette McLoughlin of the Department of Government provided invaluable administrative backing at all stages and particularly during the immediate conference period.

Hillel Steiner acknowledges the support of the Economic and Social Research Council for the award of a grant to study issues of international justice which formed one of the conference's prime themes. Geraint Parry acknowledges the support of the Leverhulme Trust for an award to undertake research into nineteenth- and twentieth-century political thought.

Geraint Parry and Hillel Steiner
Department of Government, University of Manchester

1

INTRODUCTION

Gary Cook

The conference '1846 Freedom and Trade 1996' was convened to commemorate the repeal of the Corn Laws in 1846, an event of outstanding symbolic significance in the history of free trade. The history of the Corn Laws in England has been a long one and subject to three phases:

- the early period prior to 1660 when most regulation was of trade within the country and the emphasis was on protection of the consumer;
- the period from 1660 to 1814 when the emphasis, if anything, was on regulation of the exportation of grain and the aim was to maintain a balance between the interests of producers and consumers;
- the period from 1814 when the emphasis shifted firmly to the control of imports and the promotion of the interests of the landed classes.

There were two significant Acts which laid the basis for the shift to the third phase which generated such fierce debate. The Act of 1814 removed restrictions on the exportation of grain as well as removing a system of bounty payments on exports once prices fell below specified levels. Much more odious to its opponents was the Act of 1815 which imposed a ban on imports until the domestic price reached 80 shillings in the case of wheat. While this was relaxed by an Act of 1828 to a sliding scale of duties (the lower the price of grain, the higher the duty) and further relaxed by Peel's Budget of 1842 through a reduction in the level of duty, this protection was anathema to many outside the landed classes.

The chief objection of Richard Cobden and the Anti-Corn Law League, who represented the interests of manufacturing, was that the raising of the price of wheat had a knock-on effect in raising the subsistence wage of manufacturing labour. This placed English manufacturers at a disadvantage to overseas rivals who had access to cheaper labour by dint of having to meet a lower subsistence wage (see Chapter 15 by Bliss for a more formal analysis of these arguments). While being primarily motivated by a narrow class interest, the Anti-Corn Law League appear genuinely to have believed that repealing the laws would be widely beneficial not only to themselves but also

1

manufacturing and agricultural labourers and indeed the period following the repeal appears to have been one of general prosperity (Barnes 1965). The counter-arguments for protection were various and have a familiar ring: fear of over-reliance on foreign sources of food supply; the overwhelming of the domestic agriculture sector by cheap imports leading, among other things, to large-scale unemployment.

It is fitting in 1996 to reconsider the issue of free trade in the light of the Corn Laws debate. For one thing, we are still having fierce 'Corn Laws' debates as witnessed during the tortuous discussions on reduction of agricultural protection during the Uruguay Round of GATT. One of the paradoxical conclusions is that one of the chief beneficiaries from the reductions agreed will be the EU which has been a major exponent of protection. Second, there has been a clear trend of post-war trade liberalization yet there are both forces urging further progress and fresh arguments for protection, thus it is timely to take stock. Third, as suggested above, while the repeal of the Corn Laws brought in a period of free trade and the principle appeared firmly established in the second half of the nineteenth century the lesson of history is that a swift return to protectionism cannot be ruled out. Indeed Paul Krugman in his conference address suggested that there is a real danger of such an anti-free trade backlash, particularly in Europe. Nevertheless, if the case for free trade is to be forcefully presented, the validity of that case must be examined. Fourth, it is important to enquire how best to proceed if the path is to be one of increasing liberalization.

The chapters in this volume are generally supportive of free trade, either in the form of trade in goods or international movements of capital. They variously probe how confident we can be about the case for free trade (Hahn), explore ways in which we can proceed to improve international trade (Chrystal, O'Brien, Reinert), suggest how we can better advocate the case for free trade (Krugman), develop new insights into the potential gains from trade (Baldwin and Caves, Williams, Birdi, Wolf), examine the mis-guidedness of protection (Gruber, Bliss) or consider important current developments in the global trading system (Fidrmuc *et al.*, Yamazawa). The remainder of this introduction will review in a little more detail some of the important recent trends in international trade, then provide a brief introduction to the chapters.

DEVELOPMENTS IN ARGUMENTS AGAINST FREE TRADE

Until the Great Depression the main arguments against free trade centred on infant industry protection and the optimal tariff. Protecting jobs has also had a long history as an anti-free trade argument. For example, in the inter-war period Keynes changed his mind on free trade and argued trade restriction was a way to deal with unemployment, although he later came to believe that domestic reflation was superior to trade protection. Nevertheless, the Depression experience left a lingering doubt about free trade. The 1950s to 1970s were the heyday of free trade, when liberalization and income growth worked virtuously on one another. Subsequently, despite progress on liberalization, protectionist arguments have gathered pace.

The 1970s and 1980s were characterized by two phenomena. First, there was a substantial threat to free trade from the demands for protection from many developing countries which embraced extensive protection as part of their development strategy of import substitution. Second, the theory of imperfect competition undermined the belief that free markets lead to prices which reflect social cost and by association undermined free trade arguments. Chicago economists saw the threat and set out to show that the imperfections were not significant enough to warrant intervention. This did not, however, prove an effective counter. Strategic trade theory was not really used by those who attacked free trade until the 1980s. The developed countries, particularly the USA and the EU, lapsed into the use of non-tariff barriers such as voluntary export restraints, antidumping suits and countervailing duties, with economic adversity in the late 1970s and early 1980s being once more a proximate cause. Analyses of strategic trade protection met the needs of the protectionists and were quickly taken to the centre of policy debate.

While strategic trade theory has been blunted as a weapon by considerable analysis of its shortcomings, Bhagwati (1994) has identified the following more recent varieties of arguments against free trade, both of which he regards as erroneous.

Fair trade as a precondition for free trade

There have recently been calls to harmonize everything from distribution systems and technology policy to labour and environmental regulations. This has been associated with rapidly shifting comparative advantage. The effect has been in part to make companies very sensitive to sources of 'unfair' advantage.

Trade and wages

During the 1950s and 1960s the South tended to view trade with the North as a threat. It turned to protection just as the North was liberalizing. Now the North fears that trade with the South will depress wages. This fear has been underpinned by the Factor Price Equalization (FPE) theorem, which would suggest that Northern wages would be forced to the level of Southern wages. Yet at the time that it was set out, the theory was viewed as implausible. Now the FPE theory is taken as an inevitability in some quarters, despite the fact that its assumptions are extremely demanding. As Paul Krugman suggested,

3

while there is a kernel of truth, low wage competition does not explain the whole of this phenomenon.

This issue of unfair trade has led to tension between the USA and the EU on the one hand which allege increased levels of unfair practices by other countries, including methods of circumventing their countervailing measures and the other countries who allege that the USA and the EU are using current 'unfair' trade provisions to discriminate unfairly against them.

Thus, despite considerable liberalization and palpable gains from freer trade, protectionist arguments are not only alive but developing. As ever, they find a receptive audience in quarters ideologically opposed to free trade.

THE URUGUAY ROUND

Despite sometimes considerable cynicism regarding the GATT, it has not proved moribund. The recently concluded Uruguay Round, while less than ideal, provides some important lessons regarding the feasibility and desirability of free trade. The impact of the GATT Final Agreement has been assessed by Nguyen *et al.* (1993, 1995) in the authors' own calibrated global macro model. The two papers report respectively estimates of the gains from the draft final agreement (the Dunkel Text) and the Final Agreement, the latter containing more modest concessions than had previously been entertained. The effects are measured as the amount of income at today's prices which would make a person as well off with the barriers as with the changes. The more modest final agreement is estimated to bring overall gains of only 0.4 per cent of world gross product compared to 1.5 per cent in the draft final act. While any calibrated model is open to methodological objections, the results are nevertheless indicative of the magnitude of the gains from liberalization and how much may potentially be lost when the process is impeded. What is more, all participating regions appear to have gained, albeit that the gains are unevenly distributed.

Yet the bottom line figures quoted may not do the agreement justice. The Uruguay Round was significant not only for the extent of the progress made in agriculture and textiles, newly brought within the GATT, but also in the progress made in the areas of services, trade-related investment (TRIMs) and intellectual property rights (TRIPs). Flows associated with services, intellectual property and foreign direct investment (FDI) are relatively small but have become more important. Some of the gains from these measures, such as the positive spillovers of foreign direct investment (see Chapter 9 by Williams and discussion by Petrochilos) and the extra innovation which may result from better protection of intellectual property rights are hard to gauge, but real nonetheless. Moreover, the agreements reached, while modest in scope, provide a platform for future liberalization; thus their importance should not be underestimated (Baldwin 1995). The Agreement has also grappled with the thorny issue of alleged 'unfair' trade and the remedies which may be imposed, although there are substantial fears that not enough has been done to prevent substantial abuse in the future which could nullify many putative gains from the round. Finally, the Agreement also took steps forward in strengthening dispute resolution machinery and in establishing the World Trade Organization (WTO) as a permanent institution and requiring members to sign up to all except its so-called plurilateral agreements. These things bolster the institutional underpinnings of free trade.

Nevertheless substantial problems remain. Specialization in production with associated FDI flows has increased the visibility of differences in national regulatory regimes. This has led in turn to calls for deeper integration at the multilateral level ranging from coordinated application of national policies to the harmonization of regulatory regimes pertaining to product and process standards, professional certification, environmental and social policies. This is seen as necessary to provide fair trade or equality of opportunity for domestic and foreign firms. There is a problem that harmonization can be expected to be aligned on industrial country standards, with common rules likely to be enforced through countervailing trade restrictions. The experience with anti-dumping (see Chapter 17 by Gruber) and other measures to offset 'unfair' trade suggests that it is important that these measures should not be expanded to address environmental or social dumping as this is a recipe for rent seeking and protectionist capture. Given the vitality of protectionist forces and the vested interests of powerful firms this is a considerable cause for concern.

REGIONALISM IN THE WORLD SYSTEM

The growth of regional trade areas has been an important trend and one which has led some to fear that the world trading system may be in danger of fragmenting into autarkic regional trade blocs. The prime example is the post-war widening and deepening of economic integration within Europe. As Sapir (1992) argues, this has been associated with a net stimulus to trade and trade liberalization through the GATT. Brown *et al.* (1992) also suggest that the North America Free Trade Agreement (NAFTA) will be trade enhancing with relatively little effect on third parties. The Asia Pacific Economic Co-operation (APEC) does not have a comparable role within South East Asia, although in Chapter 23 Yamazawa suggests that it might. In any event, the sheer dynamism of many South East Asian economies and the strong belief that openness to trade has been an important ingredient make trade arrangements in the Asia–Pacific region of great interest. Whether and how far these regional agreements contribute to closer integration in the world economy as a whole is a much-debated issue. Henderson (1993) argues that the common belief that three inward-looking trade blocs are being created is mistaken. There is no reason why regional integration agreements should result in a reduction in trade and investment flows vis-à-vis the rest of the world. As the arrangements are now emerging they appear likely to have a net positive influence on integration with the rest of the world and there is a substantial amount of trade between the three blocs.

Potentially far-reaching developments are now underway in Central and Eastern Europe. In the wake of transition to market economies in this region, of which greater openness to trade is a dimension, there is potential for rapid increase, albeit from a small base, in trade with the Organization for Economic Co-operations and Development (OECD) (see Fidrmuc *et al.*, Chapter 21). However, Enders and Wonnacott (1996) have expressed concern that liberalization among the former centrally planned economies has proceeded on a piecemeal bilateral basis which has resulted in a distortionary and inefficient trading system. They suggest a major challenge is to work towards a European free trade area.

In sum, there has been a long history of anti-free trade arguments including: infant industry protection; countering unemployment; the optimal tariff; preventing unfair competition in various guises and defending wages. Despite the persistence and prevalence of anti-free trade arguments, substantial progress has nevertheless been made in the post-war period in liberalizing trade. Some gains have come through the GATT and others through regional agreements to liberalize trade. As liberalization extends into new areas such as services and capital flows there is the prospect of important future gains. Nevertheless there are question marks regarding not only whether we can achieve these gains but whether we can maintain progress made to date. As with the original Corn Laws debate there are concerns as to whose interests are being served both by liberalization and protection. Thus issues of freedom and trade are very much alive.

INTRODUCTION TO THE CHAPTERS

In Chapter 2 Frank Hahn puts forward a persuasive case that economists ought to be more circumspect in their arguments for free trade. Indeed, the leitmotif of his comments throughout the conference was that we ought to be candid about admitting that much of the time, despite our confident assertions in favour of free trade, we simply do not know for sure. There is some paradox in his observation that economists too often ignore the fact that there will be losers from free trade since they typically argue that the gains are too imperceptible, whereas the losses are concentrated on particular interest groups which allows lobbies to form against free trade. Yet, as he rightly points out, some of the costs are rather subtle and difficult to quantify. Greater job insecurity and the costs of excess variety are two cases in point where individuals suffer but face probably insuperable difficulties in terms of lobbying in favour of policies to mitigate these effects. Moreover, he argues that these weaknesses of the classic free trade argument need to be brought fully into the public domain in order that policy-makers can address the redistributions that free trade entails.

In Chapter 3 Paul Krugman provides an insightful analysis into why intellectuals do not understand Ricardo's idea of comparative advantage and what is more why they do not want to do so. First, he identifies that in the US cultural milieu being avant-garde is more important than being right and that since everyone loves to hate economists attacking one of their most cherished totems is a popular thing to do. Second, and perceptively, he argues that what seems to the professional economist simple and self-evident is, in fact, a sophisticated theory assuming knowledge of an interrelated set of other economic theories. In other words, the idea is more difficult than it looks, which presents a problem when people are not even disposed to try to understand it. Third he suggests that there is a popular aversion to mathematical modelling, which is an inalienable feature of economic reasoning. To combat these obstacles he suggests that as economists we need to take ignorance seriously, to adopt the stance of the rebel and not to take what seems obvious for granted. This is timely advice, since as he argued elsewhere in the conference, there is an ever-present danger of sliding back into more protectionist ways.

In Chapter 5 Alec Chrystal provides a lucid guided tour through the difficult terrain of asking what monetary arrangements would best support international trade. One of the contributions of Chrystal's chapter is to show that some well-rehearsed arguments are not as valid as is often assumed and in consequence the answer to the question is highly uncertain. For example, he argues that whether fixed or floating exchange rates are preferable, at least from the narrow interests of the national economy, reduces to the issue of whether domestic or foreign economic shocks are more important, which is not known. Furthermore, he cautions that we cannot simply rely on historical evidence regarding how different regimes performed in the past. For example, the Bretton Woods system emerges as having the best record on real growth, yet this may have had nothing to do with the system itself but rather with other post-war economic factors. One area where there does appear to be reasonably clear evidence is that real exchange rate volatility reduces the volume of trade. In addition Chrystal argues that even worse detriments to trade may arise from the distortion of price signals which real exchange rate volatility brings in its wake. He offers tantalizing suggestions that a single global fiat currency may be the best arrangement, yet concedes that, whatever the theoretical merits, it is likely to remain moribund due to political infeasibility. The theme of practical impediments to achievement of improved international monetary arrangements is taken up by Parmjit Kaur in her discussion (Chapter 6).

In Chapter 7 Baldwin and Caves present evidence on a relatively unexplored consequence of increased international competition: its effect on the degree of turbulence faced by domestic firms. Turbulence in their study is taken to be proxied by entry and exit of plants, mergers and gains and losses in employment. In general their results support their hypothesis that exposure to international competition is indeed a source of turbulence, which they see as working through two channels. The first they call the external effects channel, whereby increased exposure to imports creates greater variance of disturbances. The second they call the competitive pressure channel, whereby the turbulence producing effects of disturbances are magnified by greater intensity of competition. Their evidence suggests that the competitive effects channel is quantitatively the more important. Exposure and turbulence have both been increasing, yet in the 1980s the increase in exposure appears to have been offset by a reduction in international disturbances compared to the 1970s. The authors conclude that the welfare effects are ambiguous.

In Chapter 9 David Williams addresses the question of how we can assess the regional impact of foreign direct investment (FDI). He argues that the comparatively small amount of attention which has been paid to this may be due to the fact that this sort of activity has no privileged status in the classical theories of trade. There FDI is formally equivalent to free trade in that it brings the same results (in theory) in terms of shifting out the production possibility frontier and equalizing factor prices. Yet, as he suggests, it is by no means obvious that the production of goods is the same as the export of goods. Moreover, given that sales by multinationals now exceed the value of trade flows and given the stubborn persistence of regional economic imbalances, understanding regional impacts of FDI should be a foremost policy concern.

Williams provides a careful analysis of the type of approach which would be necessary to pursue such an endeavour. He suggests we should be more thorough in enumerating the costs and benefits of FDI, arguing that a focus on the most easily measurable direct impacts such as output and employment may be misleading since they ignore indirect impacts such as technology transfer. As George Petrochilos indicates in his discussant's remarks (Chapter 10), this is likely to be a formidable undertaking.

In Chapter 11 Robert O'Brien takes up the theme that increasing international activity, driven in part by increased activity of multinationals and in part by an increasing trend of economic liberalization in the post-war period, is likely to create both winners and losers. He argues persuasively that not only is it likely that, in particular, the interests of labour will be translated into increased international regulation of labour standards but also that it is desirable that it should. The reason is that the prospects for the trend of liberalization being continued could be worsened if civic interests mobilize at the domestic level to oppose free trade. The Uruguay Round was significant in bringing within the sphere of international regulation areas previously considered the preserve of national governments such as intellectual property rights and the regulation of services. This does not mean that international regulation of labour standards will necessarily follow, but does make it more probable. As O'Brien states, the jury will be out until a major area such as the USA or the EU is challenged on this issue. As George Petrochilos argues in his discussion (Chapter 12), concessions of sovereignty will probably only be made if the parties concerned see sufficient advantage in return.

In Chapter 13 Martin Wolf provides a cogent argument, based on Cobden's own thinking, that free trade brings the benefit of making war less likely. The kernel of the argument is that democracies are less likely to make war and very unlikely to start wars with each other and that if this tendency is made stronger, the closer are trade links. Wolf suggests a parallelism between trade and peace in democracies. In both cases the wider interests of citizens find fuller expression: both war and trade protection benefit the few at the expense of the many. Second, democracies depend on the rule of law which in turn makes it easier for international law to be effective. International law is necessary to support trade. Trade both increases trust between countries and gives them more to lose from entering into conflict. In his discussion (Chapter 14), Jacob Kol agrees but suggests that greater international regulation is desirable to secure these gains.

In Chapter 15 Christopher Bliss provides an appraisal of the arguments of Cobden and Bright that agricultural protection gave rise to a 'bread tax' by lowering the food wage of labour. This contrasts with Ricardo's view that agricultural protection primarily hurt manufacturing profits. He proceeds by using analytical frameworks of conventional trade theory, worked up generations after the actual debate. He demonstrates that the arguments of Cobden and Bright can be supported by modern trade theory depending on the characterization of the model used. The standard 2×2 Stolper–Samuelson (S–S) model shows the opposite, that the bread tax would be negative. However, using a three factor S–S model, with land as the additional factor, or an S–S model with immobile capital can yield the result of a positive bread tax. He goes on to suggest that a 'bread tax' may be the consequence of the current Common Agricultural Policy (CAP), while counselling that, despite similarities, the analogy between the Corn Laws and the CAP should not be pushed too far. Further notes of caution are sounded by Hylke Vandenbussche (Chapter 16) in her discussant's remarks.

In Chapter 17 Harald Gruber provides an analysis of the deficiencies of EU antidumping policy in the case of semiconductors, a highly politically sensitive sector. He succinctly exposes the fragility of strategic trade theory: we can never be sure when intervention is warranted, nor what form it should take. He then exposes EU policy as being both unfair and misguided. A key reason why it fails on both counts is the failure, or perhaps unwillingness, to recognize that experience curve pricing[1] is a legitimate commercial practice. The unfairness resides in the wide discretion used in constructing the 'normal

9

THE ECONOMICS AND POLITICS OF INTERNATIONAL TRADE

price' used both to prove dumping and set antidumping duties. The wrong-headedness of the policy, he suggests, relates to four factors. First, the policy does not appear to be effective in providing protection. Second, it does nothing to promote efficiency. Third, it keeps prices artificially high, harming users of chips within the EU. Fourth, the chief beneficiaries appear to be the Japanese and Korean exporters who are effectively given sanction to collect tariff revenues on their own exports. In sum, he reaches the conclusion that the policy is driven by political expediency, a point taken up in Hylke Vandenbussche's commentary (Chapter 8).

In Chapter 19 Anthony Cockerill provides an analysis of the extent of job protection in the British steel industry between 1967 and 1985, approximately the period of nationalization, through the use of subsidies. He provides a careful analysis of the extent of subsidization which occurred predominantly through subscriptions of unremunerated public capital. He further compares the extent to which jobs were protected by subsidies and by exchange rate movements. He concludes that the trend depreciation in sterling was quantitatively much more important in protecting jobs. He provides an estimate of the gross cost of job protection through subsidization as being £53,800 per job, although as he points out any such estimate is approximate and subject to qualification. This thought is extended in Lynden Moore's discussion (Chapter 20) which suggests that much of the subsidy went into modernization and therefore contributed to the large-scale job losses which occurred in the early 1980s.

In Chapter 21 Jarko Fidrmuc *et al.* provide a fascinating glimpse into the generally rapid restructuring of trade flows between Austria and its trade partners in the former Eastern bloc. As he argues, this evidence has substantial relevance for the issue of EU enlargement. The optimistic message emerging from these results is that the fears both that these economies may destroy jobs in high wage EU countries, or that they may themselves be trapped in low wage/low productivity equilibria, appear to be overstated. The key evidence is that much of the growth in trade which has occurred has been intra- rather than inter-industry. One note of caution, however, is that those countries which were not very open to trade have experienced quite substantial falls in activity. Further important qualifications are provided in Magdolna Sass' commentary (Chapter 22).

In Chapter 23 Ippei Yamazawa gives an interesting insight into the operation and aspirations of the Asia Pacific Economic Cooperation forum, in whose Eminent Persons Group he has represented Japan, with particular emphasis on its Osaka Action Agenda. What makes Yamazawa's optimistic predictions about the significance of APEC particularly interesting is a recent suggestion that statistical evidence of unusually high trade activity within APEC is a mere artefact (Polak 1996). Yamazawa provides some interesting points of comparison and contrast between APEC and the EU and also addresses some pertinent remarks as to the future relationship between them.

As he points out, APEC is second in scope as a regional trade area to the EU and has committees active in a quite broad range of areas, although they are currently on nothing like the same scale. The two regions have also comparable proportions of intra-regional trade and rates of growth. Nevertheless he also acknowledges substantial differences. He suggests that in some regards both APEC and the EU have a commonality of interest in seeking further trade liberalization, yet he points out that the relationship between the two is problematic given the mistrust of the EU within APEC. The question of how far APEC will be able to realize its aspirations and resolve its difficulties with the EU is taken up in Cook's remarks (Chapter 24).

In Chapter 25 Alvin Birdi provides an interesting and careful extension on ideas set out in Grossman and Helpman (1991) regarding the nature of specialization in high technology under general equilibrium with free trade. What is particularly welcome is that Birdi produces a model in which the hysteresis result of Grossman and Helpman, which states that a country which once has a lead in high technology will retain it, is shown to be a special case. He demonstrates that whenever basic research is important to applied research, then a country which has superior productivity in applied research can always overtake one which has a lead. He also suggests that government policy can aid the process by committing more resources to basic research and also by fostering collaboration between basic and applied research sectors. In Chapter 26 Cook discusses how these useful results could be extended.

In Chapter 27 Erik Reinert provides an explanation of why it was that both the free trader, Cobden, and the protectionist, List, agreed that the repeal of the Corn Laws would benefit Britain. In Cobden's case, notwithstanding his views that it would promote peace (see Chapter 13 by Wolf), he considered that it would make manufacturing more competitive through lowering the bread wage of labour (see Chapter 15 by Bliss). In List's view good trade consists of importing raw materials and exporting manufacturers, whereas exporting raw materials is bad trade. The reason suggested is that manufacturing, by contrast to raw material production, is able to raise prosperity through realization of increasing returns to scale and also has a dynamic ability to stimulate growth through innovation and spillover effects on the rest of the economy. He suggests that the success of the First World which specialized in trade in manufactures and the relative poverty of the Third World which exports mainly raw materials demonstrates the validity of List's case. Parmjit Kaur's comments (Chapter 28) provide important qualifications to the broad sweep of Reinert's arguments.

NOTE

1 Experience curve pricing is the practice of pricing low in order to gain market share. This results in a rapid build up of cumulative sales which as a matter of

empirical observation results in a lowering of costs through what is known as the 'experience' effect; essentially practice makes better. The quantitative importance of this effect varies from industry to industry.

REFERENCES

Baldwin, R.E. (1995) 'An economic evaluation of the Uruguay round agreements', in S. Arndt and C. Milner (eds) *The World Economy Global Trade Review*, Oxford: Blackwell.

Barnes, D.G. (1965) *A History of the English Corn Laws from 1660–1846*, New York: Augustus M. Kelley.

Bhagwati, J. (1994) 'Free trade: old and new challenges', *Economic Journal* 104: 231–46.

Brown, D.K., Deardorff, A.V. and Stern, R.M. (1992) 'North American integration', *Economic Journal* 102: 1507–18.

Enders, A. and Wonnacott, R.J. (1996) 'The liberalisation of East–West European trade: hubs, spokes and further complications', *World Economy*: 253–72.

Grossman, G.M. and Helpman, E. (1991) *Innovation and Growth in the Global Economy*, Cambridge, MA: MIT Press.

Henderson, D. (1993) 'The EC, the US and others in a changing world economy', *World Economy*: 537–52.

Nguyen, T., Perroni, C. and Wigle, R. (1993) 'An evaluation of the Draft Final Act of the Uruguay round', *Economic Journal* 103: 1540–49.

Nguyen, T., Perroni, C. and Wigle, R. (1995) 'A Uruguay round success?', *World Economy*: 25–30.

Polak, J.J. (1996) 'Is APEC a natural regional trading bloc? A critique of the "gravity model" of international trade', *World Economy*: 533–43.

Sapir, A. (1992) 'Regional integration in Europe', *Economic Journal* 102: 1491–1506.

2

RECONSIDERING FREE TRADE

Frank Hahn

I am an economic theorist and not an economic historian. So I fear that I shall not be able to say anything seriously informed concerning the Corn Laws or their repeal. Instead I propose to reconsider the question of whether on balance economic theory can make a convincing case for free trade. This may be of interest when thinking about the events of 150 years ago, but is also currently relevant given the present tide in its favour.

I start with some preliminaries. A policy is said to bring about a Pareto improvement if by it no citizen is made worse off and some have their position improved. A state of the economy is then said to be Pareto efficient if no Pareto-improving policy exists. It is clear that these concepts involve only very weak value judgements. Thus nothing is postulated concerning the distribution of well-being among citizens, so that the efficiency criterion cannot be used to discuss policies which change that distribution. Even so one might argue that given a desirable distribution it would be foolish not to pursue a Pareto-improving policy if one exists.

Although we dispose of a rather sophisticated body of economic theory,[1] many applications of the Pareto criterion are crude and often unconvincing. The free trade argument is no exception. Here is the textbook version of Ricardo's theory.

Assume that there are only two goods and two countries. Assume further that these two goods are all the citizens of the two countries care about. That is, their welfare depends only on the consumption of these two goods and thus welfare is increasing in each of them. Last, postulate that both countries can produce both goods with given fixed resources. By allocating these resources differently each country can produce the two goods in different amounts.

First, suppose that before trade each country is in a Pareto-efficient state. It must then be that the countries cannot produce more of one good (with its given resources and technology) without producing less of another. So more of (say) grain must mean less of (say) cars. So each country in every Pareto-efficient state has given a rate at which it can substitute cars for grain. If in the present pre-trade state country A can produce one more car by giving up 100 bushels of grain, while country B can produce one more car by giving up 200 bushels of wheat, then we say that A has a comparative advantage in the production of cars.

Ricardo considered the special case where comparative advantages did not depend on the composition of output (see Figure 2.1).

In each country the triangles represent the production opportunities of A and B respectively. Pareto efficiency implies that neither country will produce in the interior of the triangle. The slopes of the frontier lines give the rate at which cars can be substituted for grain.

Now suppose A and B open trade. The maximum grain they can produce together is Oa+Ob. If they now want a car it clearly will be best to let A produce it since that involves only a sacrifice of 100 bushels of grain (instead of 200 if B produced it). This can continue until A produces nothing but cars (Oc). After that if still more cars are desired they will have to be produced in B. The production opportunities for A and B together are shown in Figure 2.2.

At c both countries are fully specialized: A in the production of cars and B in that of grain. Along Cc, B is partially specialized and along cA, A is partially specialized. Next, if there is free trade and no monopoly power then the rate at which citizens of either country can substitute cars for grain in their consumption will be the same and equal to the rate at which the two countries jointly can substitute it (there is an indeterminacy at C which does not affect the argument). These substitution rates must be the same since otherwise there would remain unexploited Pareto-improving gains from trade. If we now think of the two countries together as the 'world' (W), then it is clear that the move to free trade between A and B has been Pareto improving. This result does not depend on Ricardo's special assumption that the efficiency frontiers of the production possibility set (shaded areas in Figure 2.1) are straight lines.

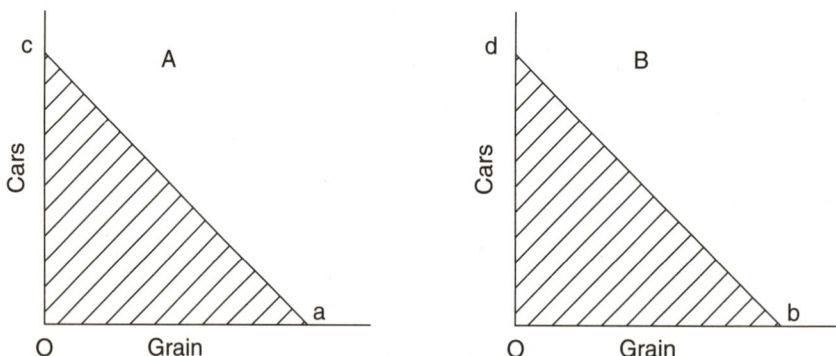

Figure 2.1 Production possibility sets of country A and country B

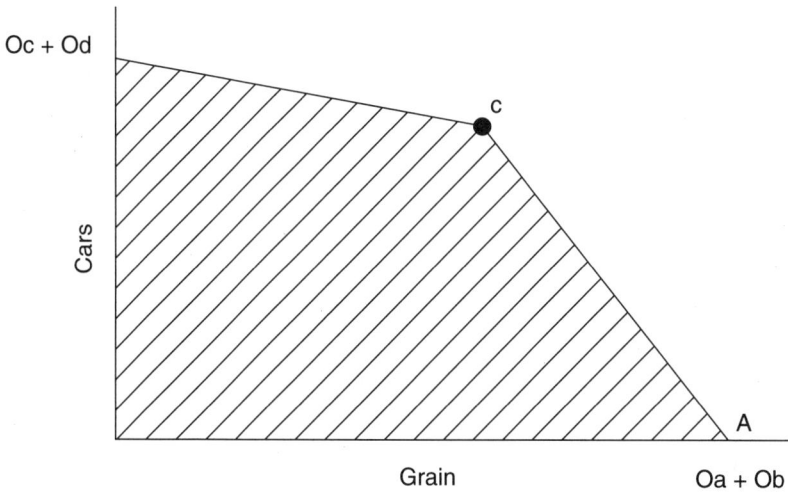

Figure 2.2 Production possibility set of country A and country B jointly

But there is a number of important assumptions and simplifications of the story which need to be firmly kept in mind. Economists often proceed on the simplest 'model' with special assumptions on the grounds that simplicity is itself desirable (they like to refer to $e = mc^2$), often provides 'insights' and in any case is needed if we are to be able to tell enquirers (e.g. politicians) anything crisp and definite. I do not deny the virtue of insight but in economics this is only a first stage in reasoning. I think that the exact conditions needed to make claims true must be known and, when policy is at stake, publicly known. Indeed I have a strong preference for showing others how one proceeds in economic reasoning so that they can put their own weight on various elements, rather than announcing conclusions while suppressing the necessary assumptions.

I shall now proceed in the manner which I favour and I shall do so schematically in order to save time and possible confusion.

THE LONG AND THE SHORT RUN

Suppose in our example A and B are not presently trading and each is producing a combination of the two goods. Assume that the goods are produced by 'labour' alone. When trade opens then to take advantage of comparative advantages the composition of output changes in A and B. But since this means that labour has to move from one occupation to another, possibly from one location to another, and acquire the skills required in new occupations, this will take time. Figure 2.1 shows long run opportunities after all transition problems have been assumed away. During the transition

15

the economy may well find itself (temporarily) on the inside of the triangle, that is, inefficient. The transition may therefore be associated with a loss in welfare.

In making our judgement we must have some idea of the length of the transition and of the loss in welfare. For instance, if only the young can move from agriculture to car production the old will suffer and that has to be weighed against the long-term gain. But such weighing is no part of the Paretian argument – it will no longer be possible to tell A and B that free trade between them will be Pareto improving. At best (and that depends on the actual situation) we may be able to tell them that it is 'potentially Pareto improving', for example, the young will be sufficiently better off to be able to compensate the old for their loss in welfare. On the other hand (speaking as an old person) I am only reassured if the compensation will actually be paid.

PRESENT AND FUTURE GOODS

Any first-year economics student knows that a car today is not valued the same as a car tomorrow – they are different goods. Indeed in proper theory we distinguish goods not only by their physical characteristics but by the date of their availability. Since our lives are not confined to a single moment it is clear that in principle a two-good model is unacceptable. There are 1996 and 1997 cars and there are, in general, possibilities of having more of the latter by giving up some of the current. Certainly citizens' welfare is taken to depend on their consumption of goods at every date in their lives.

Thus even if there are only two physically distinct goods we have very many possible comparative advantage comparisons to make. For instance, B may have (in 1996) a comparative advantage in 1996 grain versus 1996 cars, but a comparative advantage of 1997 cars versus 1996 cars, and a comparative advantage of 1997 cars over 1997 grain (pretty complicated). One can sort it all out once proper preferences are given, but recall that there are dates beyond 1997. Economists would probably proceed to look for a steady state, that is, a situation where the composition of goods remains constant over time and no Pareto improvement (taking account of dated goods) is possible. But much of the simplicity is gone – more importantly one needs to know much more of the actual possibilities before making any recommendation.

There is, however, another serious problem. In the simple Ricardian case we could argue that the market will sustain the long run efficient division of labour because all gains from trade will be exhausted. To make the same argument here we need to suppose that at any time citizens of both A and B can trade in promises to deliver goods in the future. This is a big assumption, and it is not well supported by facts. I cannot here go into this matter in detail. But to give an idea, suppose citizens in B decide to consume less grain in 1996 but more cars in 1997. If there is no market in promises, their decision – as Keynes noted – may take the form of holding money to be spent on A's cars in 1997. But A citizens do not know this and the world economy finds that there is more grain produced than demanded. All sorts of things can now happen, including a recession. Of course this is a bit of 'handwaving' but it can be made precise. The restrictions on inter-temporal trade however do pose serious problems.

UNCERTAINTY

Citizens not only care about dated goods but they are also not indifferent to uncertainty. By and large we are, I think, correct in postulating that most people would be willing to pay a premium over its expected value to avoid an uncertain prospect. But engaging in cross-country trade is likely to change the uncertainty faced by citizens. Suppose, for instance, that the comparative advantage between cars and grain depends on the weather – good (g) or bad (b). Then if resources – say labour – cannot be instantly moved between the two activities ordinary theory suggests that Pareto efficiency would not entail the Ricardian doctrine. If all citizens could insure against the weather in either country the outcome would be different, but such insurance possibilities are extremely limited for good reasons.

Apart from that, one notes that under autarchy the citizens of any one country did not care about the weather in the other. After trade they need to care. Suppose that the weather affects harvests and that the weather in A and B is negatively correlated (i.e. $g_a b_b$ and $g_b b_a$). The trade may offer insurance – that is, reduce uncertainty, provided no country is fully specialized in cars. But if it is positively correlated then there is a desire for insurance which must be met by, say, storing grain, and the Ricardian story is once again in need of more or less drastic modification.

MORE GENERAL PREFERENCES

In their better moments economists admit that a person's welfare depends on other things besides his consumption at different dates and the uncertainty faced. The argument is that these 'other things' can be taken as unaffected by the policy under consideration. But that is rarely so. For instance, if one is attached to the place in which one lives, free trade may entail moving (the transition) and that may bring a loss of welfare. Or again if A specializes completely on cars (point c, Figure 2.1), then it will have no agriculture and lose all the amenities associated with a farmed countryside. Or again if B is a very go-ahead society so that innovations are frequent as are changes in comparative advantages, citizens will face not only more uncertainty but more need to change occupation and residence. There are many more examples.

All of this reminds us that Pareto efficiency is defined in terms of citizens' welfare and not directly on goods. If more of (some) a good(s) means less of 'other things' entering in our welfare, then the doctrine requires us to take this into account. Economists very often forget to do so.

DISTRIBUTION

Many years ago Lerner and Samuelson showed that in certain circumstances the movement of goods between countries is an alternative to the free movement of 'factors'. If, for instance, labour moved between countries until (real) wages were the same, then stopping the mobility but allowing free trade in goods would have the same effect. The argument was based on the assumption that countries had the same technological know-how. A country would have a comparative advantage in the good which used its relatively abundant factor most intensively. Thus, for instance, India would have a comparative advantage in labour-intensive goods. As these get exported to a relatively capital-rich country they would displace that country's own labour-intensive production. To be reabsorbed the displaced labour must get employment in the relatively capital intensive sector and this it can only do at a lower real wage. Thus Indian exports compete directly with the importing country's labour.

There is a number of technical conditions which must be met for this argument to be valid. As usual one needs to consider states of long run equilibria under perfect competition. But it should be remembered that a very ambitious proposition is here suggested: free trade leads to the international equalization of factor prices. One ought to be satisfied with the more plausible Marshallian way of putting things: free trade sets up a tendency to factor price equalization. There can be little doubt that there is such a tendency. When workers in advanced countries view trade with 'cheap labour' countries with alarm they are not being obscurantist but self-interested.

Indeed the argument is perhaps stronger now than it once was. This is because free trade has been accompanied by greatly increased capital mobility. If one supposes that capital moves between countries to equalize its rate of return then, if the technologies are constant returns to scale, there is no joint production and labour is the only non-produced input; real wages between countries will also be equalized as will relative prices of goods. Here it is capital mobility rather than the movement of goods which brings about equalization. Once again the result should not be taken too seriously – there are lots of assumptions and one is only concerned with long run world equilibrium with constant technological knowledge. But also once again this 'pure case' points in a plausible direction. Sending capital to Thailand to produce there will involve direct competition between Thai labour and that of the capital exporting countries.

Evidently there is much more to be said and to be said more rigorously. But I hope to have indicated some slips between the cup and the lip. In particular it seems that basing an advocacy of free trade on Pareto-efficiency considerations is grossly inadequate. Any move to free trade involves redistributions between all sorts of groups including intergenerational re-distributions. In addition the Pareto line argument is rather deeply flawed by the simple fact that the conditions required are not met. One of these is the absence of adequate intertemporal insurance markets.

So far, while rather ahead of the textbook, I have argued on its terms. But I cannot leave it there without ignoring much of the world we know. However, as I have warned, it will leave us with 'on the one hand' and 'on the other' without crisp conclusions. Yet the arguments should make it easier to grasp what the essential questions are.

Let us first of all take note of what to all of us is obvious: much of international trade is not in different goods but in different varieties of the same goods. This will only be explicable with great difficulties in terms of comparative advantage although some elements may remain – for instance, differential availability in different countries of labour of a particular skill and training. But the main explanation is to be found in increasing returns and in imperfect competition. The last arises when differentiation of prod-uct allows a firm to earn some rents – at least for a time. These rents are of a pseudo-monopolistic kind since, being the only supplier of a particular differentiated product, a firm can charge a price higher than its nearest competitor without losing all of its market. Of course, as more and more firms attempt this the less differentiated the product becomes – in the limit any two of them may share almost all characteristics. But increasing returns impose a limit on the number of differentiating firms because, when the market is too small, a firm will make a loss.

The last consideration suggests that one of the benefits of free trade may simply be an enlargement of market size which allows greater exploitation of increasing returns. Citizens are thus provided with greater variety with-out having to pay the cost of lots of unexploited returns to scale. On the other hand, it is perfectly possible that even though market size is increased as a whole, competition becomes sufficiently fierce so that each firm obtains a smaller share of a larger market. Robinson (1934) and Chamberlin (1933) believed this to be so and if you consider the number of petrol stations along some stretches of road, you can see what they meant.

But when entry is difficult as, say, in the case of chip production, firms may continue to enjoy monopoly profits. There is of course some competition, but the natural reaction of competition-hating businessmen is to amalgamate and to take over potential rivals. Certainly there cannot be many economists or others who believe that matters can be left in the hands of businessmen alone, and one needs international anti-monopoly legislation. But this is easier said than done, since some countries will have an interest in protecting their own monopolies. All of this, of course, refers to cases with large increasing returns.

Indeed there is an ancient argument that a country may want to protect an industry from competition, at least for a time, until it has exploited sufficient increasing returns to be able to face foreign competition. This argument has probably more validity, at least in certain cases, than economists have been willing to grant. It needs to be recalled that increasing returns may have their source not just in large-scale fixed equipment but in the training of a larger labour force when production is greater. Such training would not be available if the industry did not operate or operated at a smaller scale. There are other policies available, for example, direct subsidies or direct training of labour. But when economists say 'available' they abstract from political and institutional constraints.

In any case the argument now is that free trade allows larger variety of goods at a lower cost than would otherwise be possible. This 'preference for variety' is a tricky idea as indeed is the question of whether markets reflect that preference. It can be shown in simple examples that the market may induce 'too much' variety – that is, less variety would be Pareto improving. But the main point to reflect upon is how an individual agent could, in a market economy, choose the amount of variety available. The answer is not only that direct choice is not possible but also that the marginal cost of variety is unknown. One could argue that a single firm by choosing to produce a straightforward standardized variety, for example, a Ford model T, would do so if by charging a low enough price it could have a large enough slice of the market. But such a strategy may mean driving out other firms and strategic issues loom and need to be studied case by case.

There is no satisfactory general theory to resolve the issue. One might agree that if, for instance, there were only one type of motor car which was very cheap there would be a market for a dearer different one. But how many different ones? These are not questions to be solved by appeals to Pareto efficiency, partly because of increasing returns which, in any case, make the usual perfectly competitive market results inapplicable and partly because it is hard to argue that any increase in variety does not have distributional consequences.

We are now a long way from Ricardo and a long way from very clinching conclusions. Special cases with special functional forms can and have been studied, but one can have no great confidence that they generalize. (There is a very good account of these in Dixit and Norman 1980). However, there is one further argument I have not yet considered.

Trade in goods is in some sense trade in knowledge. For instance trade in pottery in ancient times led to many societies learning this craft. The same is true today. A new Japanese computer gives new ideas of possibilities to the Americans or even the British. Here free trade yields benefits not too dissimilar from those claimed by academics for the free international exchange of intellectual capital. This I believe is a very important aspect of the whole debate. Albania paid the price of isolation, as did Japan, at some time past. Free trade is a kind of knowledge highway and so important. But I do not mean in a Pareto sense. New knowledge can bring great harm to those practising the old, as English economic history testifies. It is important from a long run point of view of human endeavours.

Abandoning the notion that everyone must gain from free trade seems to me a step in the right direction. Identifying the losers, whether of the temporary or permanent kind, is a first step to reducing their losses by means of policies of various kinds. So far there is rather little recognition that such policies need to be formulated and enacted if there are to be propositions like 'country A is better off under free trade'. As a current example we may take the increased job uncertainty which, we are told, is inevitable under 'global competition'. People must expect to change employer many times in their working life. Such changes have psychic and other costs. The people involved may think the price too high for the benefits reaped of free trade. We must ask not only whether those who benefit can compensate the losers but whether it is possible to do so without, for instance, damaging incentives or giving up too many advantages of free trade.

NOTE

1 By far the best account of the pure theory of international trade is to be found in Dixit, A.K. and Norman, V. (1980) *Theory of International Trade*, James Nisbet and Cambridge University Press.

REFERENCES

Chamberlin, E.H. (1933) *The Theory of Monopolistic Competition*, Cambridge: Harvard University Press.
Robinson, J. (1934) *The Economics of Imperfect Competition*, London: Macmillan.

3

RICARDO'S DIFFICULT IDEA

Why intellectuals don't understand comparative advantage

Paul Krugman

The title of this chapter is a play on that of an admirable recent book by the philosopher Daniel Dennett, *Darwin's Dangerous Idea: Evolution and the Meanings of Life* (1995). Dennett's book is an examination of the reasons why so many intellectuals remain hostile to the idea of evolution through natural selection – an idea that seems simple and compelling to those who understand it, but about which intelligent people somehow manage to get confused time and time again.

The idea of comparative advantage – with its implication that trade between two nations normally raises the real incomes of both – is, like evolution via natural selection, a concept that seems simple and compelling to those who understand it. Yet anyone who becomes involved in discussions of international trade beyond the narrow circle of academic economists quickly realizes that it must be, in some sense, a very difficult concept indeed. I am not talking here about the problem of communicating the case for free trade to crudely anti-intellectual opponents, people who simply dislike the idea of ideas. The persistence of that sort of opposition, like the persistence of creationism, is a different sort of question, and requires a different sort of discussion. What I am concerned with here are the views of intellectuals, people who do value ideas, but somehow find this particular one impossible to grasp.

My objective in this chapter is to try to explain why intellectuals who are interested in economic issues so consistently baulk at the concept of comparative advantage. Why do journalists who have a reputation as deep thinkers about world affairs begin squirming in their seats if you try to explain how trade can lead to mutually beneficial specialization? Why is it virtually impossible to get a discussion of comparative advantage, not only onto newspaper op-ed pages, but even into magazines that cheerfully publish long discussions of the work of Jacques Derrida? Why do policy wonks who will happily watch hundreds of hours of talking heads droning on about the global economy refuse to sit still for the ten minutes or so it takes to explain Ricardo?

In this chapter I will try to offer answers to these questions. The first thing I need to do is to make clear how few people really understand Ricardo's difficult idea – since the response of many intellectuals, challenged on this point, is to insist that of course they understand the concept, but they regard it as oversimplified or invalid in the modern world. Once this point has been established, I will try to defend the following hypothesis:

1   At the shallowest level, some intellectuals reject comparative advantage simply out of a desire to be intellectually fashionable. Free trade, they are aware, has some sort of iconic status among economists; so, in a culture that always prizes the avant-garde, attacking that icon is seen as a way to seem daring and unconventional.

2   At a deeper level, comparative advantage is a harder concept than it seems, because like any scientific concept it is actually part of a dense web of linked ideas. A trained economist looks at the simple Ricardian model and sees a story that can be told in a few minutes; but in fact to tell that story so quickly one must presume that one's audience under-stands a number of other stories involving how competitive markets work, what determines wages, how the balance of payments adds up, and so on.

3   At the deepest level, opposition to comparative advantage – like opposition to the theory of evolution – reflects the aversion of many intellectuals to an essentially mathematical way of understanding the world. Both comparative advantage and natural selection are ideas grounded, at base, in mathematical models – simple models that can be stated without actually writing down any equations, but mathematical models all the same. The hostility that both evolutionary theorists and economists encounter from humanists arises from the fact that both fields lie on the front line of the war between C.P. Snow's two cultures: territory that humanists feel is rightfully theirs, but which has been invaded by aliens armed with equations and computers.

YOU JUST DON'T UNDERSTAND

In scholarly discourse, it is a normal courtesy to give one's debating opponents the benefit of the doubt. If they say something that seems confused, one tries to find a charitable interpretation – although it may seem that they are saying X, which is patently wrong, perhaps they are merely badly expressing their belief in Y, which could be right in principle (although it is inconsistent with the data).

Many economists – myself included – have tried to extend this same courtesy to people who seem, on a casual reading, not to understand comparative advantage. Surely, we have argued, the problem is one of different dialects or jargon, not sheer lack of comprehension. What these critics must be trying to do is draw attention to the ways in which comparative advantage may fail to work out in practice. After all, economists are familiar with a number of reasons why the gains from free trade may not work out quite as easily as in the simplest Ricardian model. External economies may mean under-investment in import-competing sectors; imperfect competition may lead to a strategic competition over industry rents; because of distortions in domestic labour markets, imports may reduce wages or cause unemployment; and so on. And even if national income rises as a result of trade, the distribution of income within a country may shift in a way that hurts large groups. In short, there is a number of sophisticated extensions to and qualifications of the model introduced in the first few chapters of the undergraduate textbook (typically covered later in the book, for example, in Chapters 10 to 12 of Krugman and Obstfeld 1994).

Therefore one is prepared to be sympathetic after reading a passage like the following, on the first page of Sir James Goldsmith's *The Trap*:

> The principal theoretician of free trade was David Ricardo, a British economist of the early nineteenth century. He believed in two interrelated concepts: specialization and comparative advantage. According to Ricardo, each nation should specialize in those activities in which it excels, so that it can have the greatest advantage relative to other countries. Thus, a nation should narrow its focus of activity, abandoning certain industries and developing those in which it has the largest comparative advantage. As a result, international trade would grow as nations export their surpluses and import the products that they no longer manufacture, efficiency and productivity would increase in line with economies of scale and prosperity would be enhanced. But these ideas are not valid in today's world.
>
> (Goldsmith 1994: 1)

On close reading, the passage seems a bit garbled; but maybe he is just a careless writer (or the translation from the original French is imperfect). One expects him to follow with a discussion of some of the valid reasons why one might want to qualify Ricardo's idea – for example, by referring to the importance of external economies in a high-technology world.

But this expectation is utterly disappointed. What is different, according to Goldsmith, is that there are all these countries out there that pay wages that are much lower than those in the West – and that, he claims, makes Ricardo's idea invalid. That's all there is to his argument; there is no hint of any more subtle content. In short, he offers us no more than the classic 'pauper labour' fallacy, the fallacy that Ricardo dealt with when he first stated the idea, and which is a staple of even first-year courses in economics. In fact, one never teaches the Ricardian model without emphasizing precisely the way that model refutes the claim that competition from low-wage countries is necessarily a bad thing, that it shows how trade can be mutually beneficial regardless of differences in wage rates. The point is not that low-wage competition never poses a problem. Rather, what is significant is that despite ostentatiously citing Ricardo, Goldsmith completely misses one of the essential lessons of his argument.

One might argue that Goldsmith is a straw man, that he is an intellectual lightweight whom nobody would take seriously as a commentator on these issues. But *The Trap* is structured as a discussion with Yves Messarovitch, the economics editor of *Le Figaro*; Mr Messarovitch certainly took Sir James seriously (never raising any objections to his version of international trade theory), and the book became a bestseller in France. In the USA Goldsmith did not sell as many books, but his views were featured in intellectual magazines such as *New Perspectives Quarterly*; he was invited to speak to the US Congress; and the Clinton administration took his views seriously enough to send its chief economist, Laura Tyson, to debate with him on television. In short, while Goldsmith's failure to understand the basic idea of comparative advantage may seem stunningly obvious to any trained economist, other intellectuals – including editors and journalists who specialize on economic matters – regarded his views as, at the very least, a valuable addition to the debate.

Or consider the recent anti-free trade writings of James Fallows, the Washington editor of *The Atlantic Monthly* and one of the USA's most prominent intellectuals. In his book *Looking at the Sun* (1994), Fallows argues that Asian success proves the effectiveness of protectionist policies in promoting economic growth. One might have expected him to offer some intellectually cutting-edge explanation of why this might be so, of why comparative advantage is invalid in the modern world economy. But instead he claims that economists have gone astray by ignoring the nineteenth-century ideas of Friedrich List. One must assume that Fallows actually read List; in which case his praise for List shows clearly that he does not understand Ricardo. For List's old book, like Goldsmith's new one, is the work of a man who, right from the beginning, just did not get it; who could not get straight in his mind how trade between two countries could raise incomes in both. (A sample List argument: he points out that agricultural land near cities is more valuable than that far away, and concludes that tariffs on manufactured goods will help farmers as well as industrialists.)

While the ideas of both Fallows and Goldsmith have been well received in intellectual circles, they have not by any means persuaded everyone. What is striking, however, is that virtually none of the reviews of their books have pointed out that they appear not to understand comparative advantage. (Indeed, reviews of Fallows's book tended to praise his economic sophistication and question his political and cultural analysis.) The explanation, of course, is that the reviewers do not understand it either – or, in some cases, that editors who did not understand the concept refused to allow it to be mentioned in the reviews. (I speak from personal experience.)

I believe that much of the ineffectiveness of economists in public debate comes from their false supposition that intelligent people who read and even write about world trade must grasp the idea of comparative advantage. With very few exceptions, they do not – and they do not even want to hear about it. Why?

THE CULT OF THE NEW

One of the USA's new intellectual stars is a young writer named Michael Lind, whose contrarian essays on politics have given him a reputation as a brilliant *enfant terrible*. In 1995 Lind published an article in *Harper's* about international trade, which contained the following remarkable passage:

> Many advocates of free trade claim that higher productivity growth in the United States will offset pressure on wages caused by the global sweatshop economy, but the appealing theory falls victim to an unpleasant fact. Productivity *has* been going up, without resulting wage gains for American workers. Between 1977 and 1992, the average productivity of American workers increased by more than 30 percent, while the average real wage *fell* by 13 percent. The logic is inescapable. No matter how much productivity increases, wages will fall if there is an abundance of workers competing for a scarcity of jobs – an abundance of the sort created by the globalization of the labor pool for US-based corporations
>
> (Lind 1995: 35–9)

What is so remarkable about this passage? It is certainly a very abrupt, confident rejection of the case for free trade; it is also noticeable that the passage could almost have come out of a campaign speech by Patrick Buchanan. But the really striking thing, if you are an economist with any familiarity with this area, is that when Lind writes about how the beautiful theory of free trade is refuted by an unpleasant fact, the fact he cites is completely untrue.

More specifically: the 30 per cent productivity increase he cites was achieved only in the manufacturing sector; in the business sector as a whole the increase was only 13 per cent. The 13 per cent decline in real wages was true only for production workers, and ignores the increase in their benefits:

total compensation of the average worker actually rose 2 per cent. Even that remaining gap turns out to be a statistical quirk: it is entirely due to a difference in the price indexes used to deflate business output and consumption (probably reflecting overstatement of both productivity growth and consumer price inflation). When the same price index is used, the increases in productivity and compensation have been almost exactly equal. But then how could it be otherwise? Any difference in the rates of growth of productivity and compensation would necessarily show up as a fall in labour's share of national income – and as everyone who is even slightly familiar with the numbers knows, the share of compensation in US national income has been quite stable in recent decades, and actually rose slightly over the period Lind describes.

The question here is not why Lind got these numbers wrong. It takes considerable experience to know where to look and what to worry about in economic statistics, and one should not expect someone who does not work in the field to be able to get it right without some guidance. The question is, instead, why Mr Lind felt that it was a good idea to make sweeping pronouncements about this subject, when he clearly was unwilling to invest time and energy in actually understanding it.

The short answer in this case is surely that Mr Lind, who is always looking for ways to enhance his *enfant terrible* status, saw this as a perfect opportunity. Free trade is a sacred cow of economists, who are well known to be boring, stuffy types. What could be a better way to reinforce one's credentials as a radical, innovative thinker than to skewer their most beloved doctrine? (It seems not to have occurred to him that there might be a reason other than ideological rigidity that the striking fact he thought he knew has not been noticed by economists.)

This is a fairly extreme case, but by no means unique. Modern intellectuals are supposed to be daring innovators, not respecters of tradition. As any publisher will tell you, books about startling new scientific discoveries always sell better than books about known areas of science, even though the things science already knows are in many ways stranger than any of the speculations in the latest cosmological bestseller. Old ideas are viewed as boring, even if few people have heard of them; new ideas, even if they are probably wrong and not terribly important, are far more attractive. Books that say (or seem to say) that the experts have all been wrong are far more likely to attract a wide audience than books that explain why the experts are probably right. Stephen Jay Gould's *Wonderful Life* (1989), which to many readers seemed to say that recent discoveries refute Darwinian orthodoxy, attracted far more attention than Richard Dawkins' equally well written *The Blind Watchmaker* (1986), which explained the astonishing implications of that orthodoxy. (See Dennett 1995 for an eye-opening discussion of Gould.) Roger Penrose's *The Emperor's New Mind* (1989), which rejects the possibility of explaining intelligence in terms of computational processes, attracted far more attention than any of the exciting discoveries of cognitive scientists who are actually trying to understand the nature of intelligence.

The same principle applies to international economics. Comparative advantage is an old idea; intellectuals who want to read about international trade want to hear radical new ideas, not boring old doctrines, even if they are quite blurry about what those doctrines actually say. Robert Reich, now Secretary of Labor, understood this point perfectly when he wrote an essay for *Foreign Affairs* entitled 'Beyond free trade' (1983). The article received wide attention, even though it was fairly unclear exactly how Reich proposed to go beyond free trade. (There is a certain similarity between Reich and Gould in this respect: they make a great show of offering new ideas, but it is quite hard to pin down just what those new ideas really are.) The great selling point was, clearly, the article's title: free trade is old hat, it is something we must go beyond.

In this sort of intellectual environment, it is quite hard to get anyone other than an economics student to sit still for an explanation of the concept of comparative advantage. Just imagine trying to tell an ambitious, energetic, forward-looking intellectual who is interested in economics – William Jefferson Clinton comes to mind – that before he can start talking knowledgeably about globalization and the information economy he must wrap his mind around a difficult concept that was devised by a frock-coated banker 180 years ago.

A HARDER CONCEPT THAN IT SEEMS

To a trained economist, the basic Ricardian model seems almost trivial. Two goods, two countries, one productive factor, perfect competition: what could be simpler? Indeed, one of the fierce joys of being an international trade economist is that so many seemingly sophisticated tracts can be revealed as nonsense, so many self-important men unmasked as poseurs, using such a minimalist framework.

Yet if one tries to explain the basic model to a non-economist, it soon becomes clear that it really is not that simple after all. Teaching the model, to docile students, is one thing: they get the model in the course of a broader study of economics, and in any case they are obliged to pay attention and learn it the way you teach it if they want to pass the exam. But try to explain the model to an adult, especially one who already has opinions about the subject, and you continually find yourself obliged to backtrack, realizing that yet another proposition you thought was obvious actually is not.

Just before this chapter was written, I was trying to explain to an editorial writer for a major US newspaper why international trade is probably not the main cause of the country's ills. After a confused interlude, it became clear what one of the blocks was: he just did not understand, even after being told the numbers, why a situation in which productivity increases were not being shared with workers would necessarily be reflected in a decline in the labour share of income – and therefore why the stability of that share in practice is a crucial piece of evidence. Eventually I was reduced nearly to babytalk ('suppose the factory produces 10 tons of cheese, and pays out wages equal in value to 6 tons; now suppose that the workers become more productive and turn out 12 tons of cheese, but that wages haven't changed . . . '). This was not a successful conversation: he wanted to talk about global trends, and instead I was teaching him first-grade arithmetic.

That particular confusion is more common than one might expect. But even at a somewhat higher level, there are, I believe, at least three implicit assumptions that underlie the most basic Ricardian model, assumptions that are justified by the whole fabric of economic understanding but are not at all obvious to non-economists. Here they are.

Wages are determined in a national labour market

The basic Ricardian model envisages a single factor, labour, which can move freely between industries. When one tries to talk about trade with laymen, however, one at least sometimes realizes that they do not think about things that way at all. They think about steelworkers, textile workers, and so on; there is no such thing as a national labour market. It does not occur to them that the wages earned in one industry are largely determined by the wages similar workers are earning in other industries.

This has several consequences. First, unless it is carefully explained, the standard demonstration of the gains from trade in a Ricardian model – workers can earn more by moving into the industries in which you have a comparative advantage – simply fails to register with lay intellectuals. Their picture is of aircraft workers gaining and textile workers losing, and the idea that it is useful even for the sake of argument to imagine that workers can move from one industry to the other is foreign to them.

Second, the link between productivity and wages is thoroughly mis-understood. Non-economists typically think that wages should reflect productivity at the level of the individual company. So if Xerox manages to increase its productivity 20 per cent, it should raise the wages it pays by the same amount; if overall manufacturing productivity has risen 30 per cent, the real wages of manufacturing workers should have risen 30 per cent, even if service productivity has been stagnant; if this does not happen, it is a sign that something has gone wrong. In other words, my criticism of Michael Lind would baffle many non-economists.

Associated with this problem is the misunderstanding of what inter-national trade should do to wage rates. It is a fact that some Bangladeshi apparel factories manage to achieve labour productivity close to half those of comparable installations in the USA, although overall Bangladeshi manufacturing productivity is probably only about 5 per cent of the US level. Non-economists find it extremely disturbing and puzzling that wages in those productive factories are only 10 per cent of US standards.

Finally, and most importantly, it is not obvious to non-economists that wages are endogenous. Someone like Goldsmith looks at Vietnam and asks, 'What would happen if people who work for such low wages manage to achieve Western productivity?' The economist's answer is, 'If they achieve Western productivity, they will be paid Western wages' – as has in fact happened in Japan. But to the non-economist this conclusion is neither natural nor plausible. (He is likely to offer those Bangladeshi factories as a counter-example, missing the distinction between factory-level and national-level productivity.)

Constant employment is a reasonable approximation

The standard textbook version of the Ricardian model assumes full employment in both countries. But in reality unemployment is constantly a concern of economic policy – so why is this the usual assumption?

There are two answers. One – the answer that Ricardo would have given – is that international trade is a long run issue, and that in the long run the economy has a natural self-correcting tendency to return to full employment. The other, more modern answer is that countries have central banks, which try to stabilize employment around the Non-accelerating Inflation Rate of Unemployment (NAIRU); so that it makes sense to think of the Federal Reserve and its counterparts acting in the background to hold employment constant.

This is not at all the way that non-economists think about the issue. Both supporters and opponents of free trade normally claim that their preferred policies will create jobs; free traders are forever warning that the Smoot–Hawley tariff caused the Great Depression. And the alternative view does not come at all naturally. During the North American Free Trade Agreement (NAFTA) debates I shared a podium with an experienced, highly regarded US trade negotiator, a strong NAFTA suppporter. At one point a member of the audience asked me what I thought the effect of NAFTA would be on the number of jobs in the USA; when I replied 'none', based on the standard arguments, the trade official exploded in anger: 'It's remarks like that which explain why people hate economists!'

The balance of payments is not a problem

The standard textbook presentation of the Ricardian model assumes balanced trade – indeed, it is usually a one-period model in which trade must be balanced. Yet the news is full of stories about the balance of payments, of complaints about trade surpluses and deficits. Why are these absent from the story?

Again, economists have good reasons for thinking that it is a good approximation to separate balance of payments from real international trade issues. In Ricardo's case, the essential ingredient was the argument by David Hume that trade imbalances are self-correcting: a surplus country will acquire specie, leading to rising prices that price its goods out of world markets, while a deficit country will correspondingly find its goods increasingly competitively priced. In the modern world, again, the channels involve less invisible hand and more government intervention: when monetary policies target the unemployment rate, exchange rates do the adjusting.

Economists are also aware that even persistent trade imbalances are not necessarily a problem, and certainly that surpluses are not a sure sign of health or deficits one of weakness. Trade may be balanced in Chapter 2; but Chapter 13 explains that the trade balance is equal to the difference between savings and investment, and that a country may justifiably run persistent deficits if it is an attractive site for foreign investment.

Again, none of this is obvious to non-economists. The essential accounting identity, savings minus investment equals exports minus imports, is if anything a better kept secret than the concept of comparative advantage. The debate over NAFTA was entirely phrased in terms of the apparent prospect that the USA would run a trade surplus with Mexico – that was why the treaty was in our interests – and the deficit that has actually materialized is universally regarded as a bad thing.

In sum, while the concept of comparative advantage may seem utterly simple to economists, in order to achieve that simplicity one must invoke a number of principles and useful simplifying assumptions that seem natural and reasonable only to someone familiar with economic analysis in general. ('What do you mean, objects fall at the same rate regardless of how heavy they are – if I drop a cannonball and a feather . . . you're assuming away air resistance? Why would you do that?') Those principles and simplifying assumptions are indeed reasonable, but they are not obvious.

THE TWO CULTURES

I once had a very unpleasant, but ultimately useful, conversation with the editor of one of the USA's leading intellectual magazines. He was in the process of refusing to print a piece I had written at his request, and his dissatisfaction with what I had written was the main subject at hand. But along the way I somehow mentioned the need to represent economic ideas with carefully thought out models, and he responded with a mixture of bafflement and asperity. Clearly the idea that economic ideas could benefit from being modelled was new to him, even though his journal frequently publishes articles on economic affairs; and he suggested to me that in future I would do well to explain why models are sometimes useful and why they usually are not.

At the time I was fairly flabbergasted: to question the usefulness of economic models at this late date seemed rather strange. But the economist's idea that economic theory for the most part consists of models has by no means been accepted by intellectuals outside our field. In fact, if one looks at the favourite economic writers of the non-economist intellectual – Robert Reich, Lester Thurow, John Kenneth Galbraith – one realizes that they have in common an aversion to or ignorance of modelling. There are model-oriented economists, like Alan Blinder, who also write for a broader audience, and they do not put their equations in their books and articles; but the skeleton of the models that structure their thought is visible under the surface to those who know how to look. By contrast, in the writings of Reich or Galbraith what you read is what you get – there is no hidden mathematical structure to the argument, no diagram one might draw on a blackboard or simulation one might run on a computer to clarify the point.

In this the situation in economics is virtually identical to that in evolutionary theory. Ask a working biologist who is the greatest living evolutionary thinker and he or she will probably answer John Maynard Smith (with nods to George Williams and William Hamilton). Maynard Smith not only has a name that should have made him an economist; he writes and thinks like an economist, representing evolutionary issues with stylized mathematical models that are sometimes confronted with data, sometimes simulated on the computer, but always serve as the true structure informing the verbal argument. A textbook like his *Evolutionary Genetics* (1989) feels remarkably comfortable for an academic economist: the style is familiar, and even a good bit of the content looks like things economists do too.

But ask intellectuals in general for a great evolutionary thinker and they will surely name Stephen Jay Gould – who receives one brief, dismissive reference in Maynard Smith (1989). (One of my ill-advised moves in the conversation with the editor was to point out that the index to Tyson 1993 contains no references either to Reich or to Thurow.)

What does Gould have that Maynard Smith does not? He is a more accessible writer – but evolutionary theory is, to a far greater extent than economics, blessed with excellent popularizers: writers like Dawkins (1989) or Ridley (1993), who provide beautifully written expositions of what researchers have learned. (Writers like Gould or Reich are not, in the proper sense, popularizers: a popularizer reports on the work of a community of scholars, whereas these writers argue for their own, heterodox points of view.) No, what makes Gould so popular with intellectuals is not merely the quality of his writing but the fact that, unlike Dawkins or Ridley, he is not trying to explain the essentially mathematical logic of modern evolutionary theory. It is not just that there are no equations or simulations in his books; he does not even think in terms of the mathematical models that inform the work of writers like Dawkins. That is what makes his work so appealing.

The problem, of course, is that evolutionary theory – the real thing – is based on mathematical models; indeed, increasingly it is based on computer simulation. And so the very aversion to mathematics that makes Gould so appealing to his audience means that his books, while they may seem to his readers to contain deep ideas, seem to people who actually know the field to be mere literary confections with little serious intellectual content, and much of that simply wrong. In particular, readers whose ideas of evolution are formed by reading Gould's work get no sense of the power and reach of the theory of natural selection – if anything, they come away with a sense that modern thought has shown that theory to be inadequate.

Economics is not as well served by its writers as evolution. Still, the distinctive feature of the writers whose ideas about world trade play well with an intellectual audience is the same: the successful books are those that not only do not explicitly discuss mathematical models, they are not even implicitly based on mathematical reasoning. A book like Robert Reich's *The Work of Nations* (1991) not only eschews equations and diagrams, it never even tries to present the idea of comparative advantage informally. In fact, it never uses the phrase 'comparative advantage' at all, even to criticize it. As a result, books by authors such as Reich or Thurow do not make humanists uncomfortable. Unavoidably, however, they also give them no sense of the power and importance of economic models in general, or of Ricardo's difficult idea in particular. If anything, the message one gets from these books is that in the new economy nineteenth-century concepts no longer apply.

It might be worth pointing out one exception to the general intellectual aversion to mathematical models. Intellectuals do reserve, both in evolution and economics, a small pedestal for mathematical modellers – as long as their models are confusing and seem to refute orthodoxy. Call it the 'Santa Fe syndrome'. At one point in Dennett's book he reports a list of the top ten objections raised to Steven Pinker's theories about the evolution of language; one of them is 'Natural selection is irrelevant, because now we have chaos theory.' At about the same time I read this passage I had received a barrage of protests over an article that tried, without explicit mathematics, to walk through some simple models of international trade (Krugman 1994). Several of the letters insisted that because of non-linear dynamics it was impossible to reach any meaningful conclusions from simple models. ('Have you ever thought about the implications of increasing returns? You should read the work of Brian Arthur and Paul Romer.')

There are two odd things about the popularity of certain kinds of mathematical modelling among intellectuals who are generally hostile to such models. One is that the preferred models are typically far more difficult and obscure than the standard models in the field. The other is that the supposedly heterodox conclusions of these models are often not heterodox at all. To take a theme common to both evolution and economics: the idea that small random events can under certain conditions set in motion a cumulative process of change is the theme both of 'peacock's tail' accounts of sexual selection and of external economy accounts of international specialization, both familiar stories that lie well inside the boundaries of academic orthodoxy, stories that can be and are illustrated with simple models in advanced undergraduate textbooks like Maynard Smith (1989) and Krugman and Obstfeld (1994). Yet many intellectuals believe that this idea was discovered at Santa Fe and challenges the foundations of both fields.

The secret to the popularity of certain mathematical modellers, I suspect, is that they are valued precisely because they seem to absolve intellectuals from the need to understand the models that underpin orthodox views. Hardly anyone tries to understand what the Santa Fe theorists are actually saying; it is the pose of opposition to received wisdom, together with the implication that in a complicated world you cannot learn anything from simple models anyway, that is valued, because it seems to say that not knowing what is in the textbooks is OK.

A final note here: there is a new trend among people who do not like conventional economics, toward what is sometimes called 'bionomics'. The manifestos of groups like the Bionomics Institute claim that they are developing a new science of economics that abandons the mechanistic approach of the existing field in favour of a model based on ecology and evolution. (Speaker of the House, Newt Gingrich, is reported to be among those who find bionomics appealing.) The irony is that neoclassical economics, with its emphasis on modelling the interactions of self-interested individuals, is no more mechanistic than neo-Darwinian evolutionary theory – in fact, the theories are very similar to one another, down to the details of the models and the curves on the diagrams.

WHAT CAN BE DONE?

I cannot offer any grand strategy for dealing with the aversion of intellectuals to Ricardo's difficult idea. No matter what economists do, we can be sure that ten years from now the talk shows and the op-ed pages will still be full of men and women who regard themselves as experts on the global economy, but do not know or want to know about comparative advantage. Still, the diagnosis I have offered here provides some tactical hints.

1   Take ignorance seriously: I am convinced that many economists, when they try to argue in favour of free trade, make the mistake of over-estimating both their opponents and their audience. They cannot believe that famous intellectuals who write and speak often about world trade could be entirely ignorant of the most basic ideas. But they are – and so are their readers. This makes the task of explaining the benefits of trade harder – but it also means that it is remarkably easy to make fools of your

opponents, catching them in elementary errors of logic and fact. This is playing dirty, and I advocate it strongly.

2 Adopt the stance of rebel: there is nothing that plays worse in our culture than seeming to be the stodgy defender of old ideas, no matter how true those ideas may be. Luckily, at this point the orthodoxy of the academic economists is very much a minority position among intellectuals in general; one can seem to be a courageous maverick, boldly challenging the powers that be, by reciting the contents of a standard textbook. It has worked for me.

3 Don't take simple things for granted: it is crucial, when trying to communicate Ricardo's idea to a broader audience, to stop and try to put yourself in the position of someone who does not know economics. Arguments must be built from the ground up – do not assume that people understand why it is reasonable to assume constant employment, or a self-correcting trade balance, or even that similar workers tend to be paid similar wages in different industries.

4 Justify modelling: do not presume, as I did, that people accept and understand the idea that models facilitate understanding. Most intellectuals do not accept that idea, and must be persuaded or at least put on notice that it is an issue. It is particularly useful to have some clear examples of how 'commonsense' can be misleading, and a simple model can clarify matters immensely. (My recent favourite involves the 'dollarization' of Russia. It is not easy to convince a non-economist that when gangsters hoard $100 bills in Vladivostock, this is a capital outflow from Russia's point of view – and that it has the same effects on the US economy as if that money was put in a New York bank. But if you can get the point across, you have also taught an object lesson in why economists who think in terms of models have an advantage over people who do economics by catchphrase.)

None of this is going to be easy. Ricardo's idea is truly, madly, deeply difficult. But it is also utterly true, immensely sophisticated – and extremely relevant to the modern world.

REFERENCES

Dawkins, R. (1986) *The Blind Watchmaker*, New York: Longman.

Dennett, D. (1995) *Darwin's Dangerous Idea: Evolution and the Meanings of Life*, New York: Simon and Schuster.

Fallows, J. (1994) *Looking at the Sun*, New York: Pantheon.

Goldsmith, J. (1994) *The Trap*, New York: Carroll and Graf.

Gould, S.J. (1989) *Wonderful Life*, New York: Norton.

Krugman, P. (1994) 'Does Third World growth hurt First World prosperity?', *Harvard Business Review*, July.

Krugman, P. and Obstfeld, M. (1994) *International Economics: Theory and Policy*, 3rd edn, New York: HarperCollins.

Lind, M. (1995) 'To have and have not', *Harper's* 290: 35–9.

List, F. (1841) *The National System of Political Economy* [*Das Nationale der politischen Ökonomic*], Stuttgart: Cotta.

Maynard Smith, J. (1989) *Evolutionary Genetics*, Oxford: Oxford University Press.

Penrose, R. (1989) *The Emperor's New Mind*, New York: Oxford University Press.

Reich, R. (1983) 'Beyond free trade', *Foreign Affairs* 61: 773–804.

Reich, R. (1991) *The Work of Nations*, New York: Basic Books.

Ridley, M. (1993) *The Red Queen: Sex and the Evolution of Human Nature*, New York: Penguin.

Tyson, L. (1993) *Who's Bashing Whom?*, Washington: Institute for International Economics.

4

COMMENTARY ON CHAPTER 3

Jacob Kol

In Chapter 3, Paul Krugman addresses the question of why many intellectuals fail to grasp the idea of comparative advantage and even resist it. This resistance, Krugman argues, is common even among authors who are considered to be serious commentators on international trade, economic integration and globalization. To explain this resistance, Krugman presents three reasons:

1　The idea of comparative advantage is considered old and boring, not new and exciting.
2　The idea of comparative advantage is only seemingly simple, in reality it is difficult to understand.
3　The idea of comparative advantage presents an outlook on the economic world which is essentially mathematical in nature, to which many intellectuals feel opposed.

Clearly, Krugman is of the opinion that this opposition matters and needs to be exposed because: 'Ricardo's idea (of comparative advantage) is extremely relevant to the modern world.'

COMPARATIVE ADVANTAGE IS AN OLD AND BORING CONCEPT

Comparative advantage is an old idea. However, intellectuals who want to read about international trade want to hear radical new ideas, not boring old doctrines; new ideas are far more attractive, even if they are probably wrong and not terribly important (pp. 26–8).

There is much to enjoy in the two sections where Krugman portrays a series of authors being successful because they are 'making sweeping statements' on international economics but 'clearly unwilling to invest time and energy in actually understanding it'.

Krugman is also right, however, in observing: 'one can seem to be a courageous maverick, boldly challenging the powers that be, by reciting the contents of a standard textbook'.

THE IDEA OF COMPARATIVE ADVANTAGE IS ONLY SEEMINGLY SIMPLE

Krugman underlines the fact that the idea of comparative advantage is not so simple after all: 'There are, I believe, at least three implicit assumptions that underlie the most basic Ricardian model – assumptions that are justified by the whole fabric of economic understanding – but are not at all obvious to non-economists.' These simplifying assumptions are:

1   Wages are determined in the national labour markets.
2   Constant employment is a reasonable approximation.
3   The balance of payments is not a problem.

In order to understand the concept of comparative advantage properly, it is also necessary to appreciate these three simplifying assumptions.

Krugman illustrates the reasonableness of simplifying assumptions with a witty imaginary conversation on Galileo's experiments to show that the earth's gravity produces constant downward acceleration independent of the bulk of bodies: 'What do you mean, objects fall at the same rate regardless of how heavy they are – if I drop a cannonball and a feather . . . you're assuming away air resistance . . . Why would you do that?'

THE AVERSION TO MODELLING AND MATHEMATICAL THINKING

At the deepest level Krugman identifies the intellectual opposition to the idea of comparative advantage as the aversion against modelling and a mathematical way of understanding the world (pp. 31–4).

A first step in explaining this aversion follows from Tinbergen (1969) in his lecture in memory of Alfred Nobel explaining the usefulness of models: 'They force us to present a "complete" theory, by which I mean a theory taking into account all relevant phenomena and relations, and, on the other hand, the confrontation with observation, that is, reality.'

More generally, Tinbergen (1979) observes that the amazing progress made in natural sciences is due in no small degree to the continual confrontation of thinking and measuring. Furthermore, the measurement of temperature in physics shows the development of an ordinal classification in cold, cool, lukewarm, warm and hot, based on subjective sense perceptions, to a cardinal classification based on thermodynamical changes in substances embodied in a thermometer. This historical development around the measurement of temperature illustrates the vocation of science: the retreat of subjectivity and the simultaneous advance of objectivity.

When discussing 'The necessity of quantitative social research', Tinbergen (1973) observes: 'For some queer and deplorable reason most human beings are more impressed by words than by figures, to the great disadvantage of mankind.'

MODELLING UNDERMINED CREDIBILITY OF THE IDEA OF COMPARATIVE ADVANTAGE

These observations support and expand Paul Krugman's observation that aversion to modelling might be an important source of resistance to the idea of comparative advantage.

But precisely in this case of comparative advantange the argument seems to be one-sided. Arguably, the opposite holds: intellectuals far from being averse to modelling have insisted on a rigid model representing the idea of comparative advantage. This model with two goods, two countries, one productive factor, and perfect competition representing the Ricardian idea and the same model with one additional factor of production representing the Heckscher–Ohlin theorem, has served as a Procrustean bed for empirical observations and common sense.

As a result, Deardorff (1984) in his survey on testing trade theories had to conclude that 'the Ricardian theory generally lacks independent empirical support' and that: 'We need something more or different [than the factor proportions model] to address issues of the bilateral [2 countries] pattern and volume of trade. Further developments . . . will provide us with a model in which factor proportions, scale economies, and degrees of product differentiation and imperfect competition all interact to determine how much countries trade, what they trade, and with whom.'

As a second result, Balassa (1965) introduced the concept of 'revealed' comparative advantage to facilitate empirical analysis.

As a third result, in the mid-1970s new trade theories were announced to account for the simultaneous exports and imports of similar products as observed in real trade data. Economies of scale were introduced alongside non-perfect competition to explain the observed two-way trade.

Regarding these 'new' ideas and 'new' theories, however, it would have sufficed to read the relevant authors more carefully. Ohlin (1952), for instance, described 'interregional differences in factor endowment as *a* (not *the*) fundamental cause of division of labour and trade between regions' and 'that the circumstances governing the character and effects on international trade are more numerous, many sided, and difficult to describe in precise terms than was indicated in dealing with interregional trade'. With respect to economies of scale, Ohlin (1952) observes: 'It must be emphasized that the economies of large scale production and the different equipment of factors are not independent "causes" of trade; on the contrary, their effects are intermingled in several ways.'

Intellectuals who are fond of modelling and averse to empirical observation thus contributed to the notion that the idea of comparative advantage was old and irrelevant. Or, in the spirit of Krugman's chapter, it was precisely the theoretical modellers who acted as an enemy within, undermining the credibility of the idea of comparative advantage.

COMPARATIVE ADVANTAGE AND DARWIN'S THEORY OF EVOLUTION

Krugman indicates that Darwin's Theory on the Origin of Species and the idea of natural selection met opposition from the same source as the resistance to the idea of comparative advantage, namely the aversion to mathematics.

Regarding comparative advantage, the previous section indicated this to be unlikely, while with respect to evolutionary theory the situation seems to be quite different as well.

Freud (1920) explains the resistance to Darwin's idea as stemming from the hurt to human pride entailed, namely that mankind is not above the animal world but just part of it. Freud sees an analogy to the resistance to Copernicus' view of the sun as the centre of the solar system with the earth just circling around it; this disturbed the illusion of the earth (and thus mankind) as the centre of the universe.

THE TRUE NATURE OF RESISTANCE AGAINST THE IDEA OF COMPARATIVE ADVANTAGE

From the previous sections it follows that aversion to a mathematical view of reality can at best only partly explain the resistance to the idea of comparative advantage; a parallel with the opposition to Darwin's idea of evolution through natural selection is unlikely. Furthermore, the nature of this resistance to Darwin's idea, namely the hurt to human pride, seems to be far from applicable to the resistance to the idea of comparative advantage.

Yet, on second thoughts this applicability may not be so remote. To see this more clearly, it can be recalled from Krugman's chapter that the idea of comparative advantage leads to the insight that both exports and imports are of mutual benefit to the trading partners, increasing income in both nations, in principle. This places an intellectual bar on the road back to the idea of the advantages of autarky.

In this perspective it can be remembered that the idea of comparative advantage of Ricardo (as well as the idea of absolute advantage of Adam Smith) underlined that benefits of trade were mutual and that it emerged in reaction to the mercantilist view that trade was beneficial to the exporter only (and not even that for all commodities) but certainly harmful to the importer. Second, it should be recalled that the new trade theories in the 1970s deviated from the idea of comparative advantage as embodied in the factor proportions model, and led to the implication of protection in the form of strategic trade policies.

These elements illustrate that the true source of resistance to the idea of comparative advantage may well be the wish to keep open the retreat to bilateralism or even autarky in times of depression. Stressing the benefits of interdependence in trade, the idea of comparative advantage undermines the illusion of beneficial independence.

REFERENCES

Balassa, B. (1965) 'Trade liberalization and "revealed" comparative advantage', *The Manchester School of Economic and Social Studies* 33: 99–123.

Deardorff, A.V. (1984) 'Testing trade theories and predicting trade flows', in Ronald W. Jones and P.B. Kenen (1984) *Handbook of International Economics*, vol. I, Amsterdam: North-Holland.

Freud, S. (1920) 'One of the difficulties of psycho-analysis', *International Journal of Psycho-Analysis* 1: 17–33.

Ohlin, B. (1952) *Interregional and International Trade*, Cambridge: Harvard University Press.

Tinbergen, J. (1969) 'The use of models: experience and prospects', lecture in memory of Alfred Nobel, in *Lex Prix Nobel en 1969*, Stockholm: P.A. Norstedt & Söner, 244–52.

Tinbergen, J. (1973) 'The necessity of quantitative social research', *Indian Journal of Statistics* 35 (B–2): 141–8.

Tinbergen, J. (1979) 'Recollections of professional experiences', *Banca Nazionale del Lavoro Quarterly Review* 131: 331–60.

5

INTERNATIONAL MONETARY ARRANGEMENTS AND INTERNATIONAL TRADE

Does the monetary regime matter?

K. Alec Chrystal

The primary function of an international monetary system is to provide institutions through which international trade (and investment) can be transacted efficiently. What type of monetary system would provide the best environment for such international transactions?

There appears to be no well-established answer to this question. Indeed the question has rarely been posed in this form, even though there are huge literatures on what, at first sight, seem to be related questions. Four obvious strands in the economics literature spring to mind. First, there is the long literature on the issue of fixed versus floating exchange rate regimes. Second, there is a significant body of work on 'monetary regimes' with particular emphasis on the evaluation of historical episodes under the three main regimes – gold standard, Bretton Woods and floating. Third, there is the 'optimal currency area' literature which ought to ask what is the best currency structure for the world economy, but in practice has been used to ask if country X or region Y is an optimal currency area. Fourth, there is a growing literature on the impact of exchange rate volatility on trade.

The first three of the above lines of enquiry have focused almost exclusively on the macroeconomic question of which exchange rate regime is best for the macro performance of the economy. In other words, which regime is best from the perspective of stabilization policy (unemployment and the business cycle) and/or inflation? Only the last of these poses the direct question of the impact of the exchange rate regime on the level of trade. However, no one to my knowledge has attempted to draw conclusions from any of these literatures about what global regime would be best. There is a good reason for this. Such conclusions are dangerous and can almost certainly not be drawn from any amount of historical evidence. Indeed, it may be that the optimal regime is one that we have not yet experienced, for example, a global single fiat currency. All other regimes may be second best.

An alternative available conclusion is that any regime is as good as any other from the point of view of real economic activity. All that matters (maybe) is that prices should be transparent and transaction costs low. It is arguable that all of the available regimes (commodity standard, fixed rate, floating rate or global single fiat currency) combined with modern derivative markets and information systems could deliver such an efficient system. Therefore, we should choose the one which is politically cheapest to deliver. This would almost certainly be the floating system with each nation state having its own currency.

Unfortunately, perhaps, there are reasons to doubt that the system based upon floating national currencies is the best we can do. Hence we need to articulate if and why this might be true and then discuss preferred alternatives. I shall proceed by reviewing briefly each of the four lines of analysis mentioned above in order to see what light they throw on this question, before returning to the problem of how we should decide what monetary structure would be best.

FIXED VERSUS FLOATING EXCHANGE RATES

The dominant opinions for or against fixed versus floating exchange rates have oscillated periodically since the demise of the gold standard in the 1930s. A critical and influential group among those who experienced the monetary disruptions of the 1930s regarded a fixed exchange rate regime as the best way to deliver a stable monetary environment and one which would be the best available for sustaining a growth in international trade. It seemed obvious from the evidence of the 1930s that exchange rate volatility was seriously disruptive to trade. Hence, the Bretton system was designed as a pegged exchange rate regime and was, indeed, remarkably successful in delivering rapid trade growth in a low inflation environment. However, it could be argued that this was just luck because there were no major exogenous shocks until the early 1970s. Also, the Bretton Woods regime was artificial in that it was propped up by exchange controls and tariff barriers, and so did not really provide an environment of true free trade.

A theoretical case against fixed exchange rates was made by Milton Friedman (1953). This was based partly upon the fact that fixed exchange rates do not permit individual countries to run an independent monetary policy. Hence, no single country would be able to control its inflation rate independently of the world rate (or, in practice, that of the centre country – USA). Friedman also thought that floating rates would be best for avoiding government interference in trade. He was optimistic that floating rates would not be unstable and that speculation would generally be stabilizing.

In later literature, monetary freedom was interpreted as the advantage of insulating the home economy from external (aggregate demand) shocks. A positive inflation shock overseas would not affect (allegedly) the home economy as it would be neutralized by an appreciation of the domestic currency and domestic prices would stay unchanged.

Of course, the downside of floating exchange rates is that a domestic shock cannot be partially 'exported', as it could under fixed rates. Although, at least, it could be argued that under floating an extra policy tool was available in the form of monetary policy instruments (notwithstanding the weakening of fiscal policy).

The choice between fixed and floating regimes was thus perceived to come down to an issue of whether domestic or foreign shocks were the dominant form of disturbance. The general answer then has to be that we do not know. Either is possible, so there can be no presumption in favour of one or other system. We cannot settle the issue simply by looking at the shocks that arose historically because most of the shocks that economists study are themselves endogenous to the exchange rate regime. Hence, statements like 'only floating could have coped with the oil crisis' could equally be stated as: 'Oil producers would not have thought about raising the oil price if the Bretton Woods system had not already broken down with dramatic inflationary consequences.'

Another way of looking at fixed versus floating exchange rates is to ask which system promotes the greatest protectionism among nations. Fixed rates promote protectionism for 'balance of payments' reasons, while floating rates promote protectionism when there are sustained real exchange rate misalignments. In both cases, the sources of protectionist pressure could be thought of as 'temporary' (that is, something that will go away once the economy is fully adjusted). However, it is well known that temporary measures have a habit of persisting beyond the life of the cause.

From the evidence of the past it is hard to tell which regime is more supportive of liberal commercial policies. Certainly the trend towards capital account liberalization has mainly happened under floating, but this is true even of countries in regional pegged regimes, such as the exchange rate mechanism (ERM). Yet large strides in tariff reduction were taken under the Bretton Woods regime through successive GATT rounds and there was certainly a resurgence of protectionist tendencies as a result of the exchange rate misalignments of the 1980s.

In short, we cannot be confident about which of these regimes is most supportive of liberal commercial policy. The past, as always, has special features attached to it which make general conclusions for the future dangerous. What is clear, however, is that commercial policy and monetary arrangements are not entirely orthogonal. Problems caused in the monetary system can easily have commercial policy implications and vice versa.

Another important point to notice about the fixed versus floating exchange rate choice which is often not appreciated is that single countries (or even groups of countries) do not have the option of a fixed exchange rate regime so long as any significant group of countries has a floating rate. A fixed exchange rate regime can only be adopted by all countries acting together and, therefore, requires some degree of collective action and mutual commitment. Whenever some countries are floating, any one country only has the choice of pegging to one or other of the currencies. Thus it can peg one bilateral rate but it cannot peg its effective exchange rate. Hence the choice is not between a fixed and floating regime but merely to float against what.

The general presumption in this context is that, if pegging is adopted, it should be to the currency of the largest trading partner. No one is surprised that the Dutch choose to peg the guilder more or less exactly to the Deutschmark. Hence trade patterns and optimal monetary arrangements are clearly linked. The only question is what the implications are for less extreme cases, that is, more diverse trade patterns.

Most of the debate between fixed and floating has been conducted in a macro framework. One major exception is the work of Helpman and Razin (1979). They approach the choice of regimes from the perspective of an optimizing representative consumer. They conclude that flexible rates are preferable to fixed rates for the simple reason that flexible rates do not restrict the range of domestic interest rates. Hence the representative consumer in each economy can have an interest rate which equals their own time preference rate. Of course, this advantage is lost when it is realized that all consumers are different so there is no reason why one country's consumers will be any happier with their own domestic rate than with that of some other country. Also, the analysis does not take account of the fact that expected real interest rates are likely to be equalized under floating just as under a fixed rate regime. The critical characteristic is not the exchange rate regime but the degree of capital mobility. Critical factors missing from the Helpman–Razin analysis are transaction costs and price risk. Hence we must conclude that the micro case for floating is not proven one way or the other.

MONETARY REGIMES

Monetary historians have long had an interest in evaluating the regimes of the past. This has interest in its own right, but is potentially a helpful input into arguments about which regime would be best for the future. However, there are serious dangers involved in assuming that the past behaviour of economies under a specific regime is any guide at all to how it might behave in a different century. The problems are that the shocks of the past may be quite different to the shocks of the future: the entire structure of all economies is now quite different from what it was even twenty years ago, let alone a century.

An excellent survey of the comparison between regimes is provided by Bordo (1993). His data for the G7 countries show that the three major regimes of the past hundred years exhibited quite different performance by objective measures. In terms of mean inflation rate the gold standard comes out best (unsurprisingly), followed by the Bretton Woods system with floating in last place. However, the standard deviation of inflation was about the same under floating as during the gold standard and lower than under Bretton Woods (though the latter was heavily biased by the inclusion of Italy and the fact that countries were given equal weight).

In terms of average real per capita GDP growth the Bretton Woods system comes out best by a long way (with double the real growth of the next best regime), followed by floating with the gold standard in last place. Floating has the lowest variability of growth rate followed closely by Bretton Woods, with the gold standard a poor third.

Bordo (1993) does not study trade directly but he does analyse nominal and real exchange rate variability. The gold standard has the lowest nominal and real exchange rate variability. Floating undoubtedly delivers the highest real exchange rate variability. However, Bretton Woods has the greatest nominal exchange rate variability (due to several periodic large discrete changes, especially in Japan and Italy in the pre-1958 period).

A possible conclusion from this evidence is that the gold standard is good for tying down prices but is bad for real economic activity (possibly because of the inelastic supply of gold). The Bretton Woods system is best for real growth. Floating is very bad for inflation, but better for growth than the gold standard. The system which is best for growth should also be best for trade, but I will not attempt to draw that conclusion. It could be argued that growth is more important than trade. The difficulty in drawing conclusions from the Bretton Woods experience is that the post-war recovery period was an unusual one and the mere imposition of fixed exchange rates would not replicate all the other characteristics of this period.

Bordo goes further than descriptive statistics in attempting to identify the shocks which affected each system. He distinguishes endogenous (demand) and exogenous (supply) shocks by a vector autoregression (VAR) methodology. According to his results, the gold standard suffered both greater demand and supply shocks than the floating era, while the Bretton Woods system suffered least shocks of either kind. There are problems with identification here. As Manfred Neumann (1993) points out, one country's demand shock can be another country's supply shock so it is not clear what systemic shocks are truly endogenous and which exogenous. This is important because we cannot blame the system for shocks that would have happened anyway, while we can blame it for shocks which result from inappropriate 'rules of the game'. In other words, we want to find the most incentive efficient system.

Bayoumi and Eichengreen (1994) approach the regimes issue from the perspective of identifying characteristics of each regime which were responsible for its ultimate demise. They agree with Bordo that the gold standard suffered the greatest shocks but claim that its survival until World War I was due to its greater adjustment speed. The Bretton Woods system by contrast suffered only minor shocks but was brought down (by implication) because of its poor adjustment properties. Perhaps this confirms the reinterpretation of the 1960s 'international liquidity' literature which suggests that creation of new liquidity was the wrong solution (even if there was a problem) and the focus should have been on adjustment all the time (Chrystal 1996).

This suggests that even if we want to conclude that the Bretton Woods system was best while it lasted, there were clearly design problems with that system which made it vulnerable to breakdown. Who would want to buy a car that looked good in the showroom but broke down on long journeys?

OPTIMAL CURRENCY AREAS

As a matter of practical politics, nation states have evolved into the units which have their own currency, even though their economic characteristics vary enormously. The optimal currency literature is really about the question: If we could design the world currency structure from scratch on purely economic criteria, what would it look like? It is possible that the answer would be that the world itself is the optimum currency area, and I shall return to this possibility later.

Unfortunately, the seminal paper by Mundell (1961) approached the problem from a short-term macro policy perspective and came up with the conclusion that currency areas should be small and homogeneous, containing a high degree of internal factor mobility. The reasoning was that if an industry suffered a real downward shift of demand while its real wages were slow to adjust, then a currency devaluation could correct for the real market failure and restore the 'correct' real wage and, therefore, full employment. What Mundell does not point out is that exchange rate changes are just as likely to create price distortions as to correct them. In any event, Mundell was not making a case for floating exchange rates, merely for an independent devaluable currency under fixed rates.

Despite the limitations of the Mundell analysis the criterion of factor mobility, mainly labour mobility, has gone down in economists' consciousness as the key feature of an optimal currency area. This is unfortunate because it is wrong. The optimal currency structure is the one that maximizes the efficiency of all markets, especially goods and capital markets. Indeed, it is arguable that the labour market is the least important so long as factor price equalization is a serious possibility. Indeed, labour mobility is still highly regulated even where goods and capital movements are not, and labour markets may be inefficient even within existing currency areas which nobody would want to subdivide. It would be dangerous to conclude that countries with the most draconian labour and immigration laws are optimal currency areas based upon the low level of labour mobility.

If micro prices do not adjust to clear markets, it is hard to imagine a currency structure which will improve this problem. No currency devaluation can correct all of the millions of relative goods prices available in a modern economy. As McKinnon (1963) pointed out, to get the maximum informational efficiency out of monetary exchange, a currency area must be large and diverse and have a high proportion of its trade internal to the area. Money is a public good and social benefit of money is greater the more widely it is used as the medium of exchange and unit of account. According to the McKinnon criterion when taken to its logical conclusion, the optimum currency area is the world – or at least the world of liberal market economies. Of course there are political costs to setting up a single world currency, which mean that it is unlikely to happen, but aside from these costs it is possible that such a system would maximize the efficiency of the world market economy – or at least minimize the disruption generated by monetary disturbances. A good approximation to the global optimum might be achieved by large regional currency blocs, but this is highly controversial.

It could be argued that the gold standard was a global single currency system, so, not only could it happen, but it actually has. However, for present purposes, the gold standard is more like a fixed exchange rate regime with a real, rather than nominal, anchor. A genuine global single fiat currency would be very different from the gold standard as there would be no locally differentiated currency, no cross rates and no problem with reserve ratios. The case for a global single fiat currency as a long run solution to the international monetary problem has been made by Cooper (1990) and Bergsten (1993).

The case against a global single fiat currency would be the Keynesian one that it would disable independent monetary policy, and this instrument could be useful for any country or region that was at a different stage of the business cycle than any other. Recall, however, that discretionary monetary policy can be the source of disturbances as well as the cure and this was the basis for the monetarist case for rules over discretion. Those who believe in neutrality of money and rules rather than discretion in monetary policy should regard a world single currency as a good thing (so long as it can be guaranteed to deliver low and stable inflation). Curiously, on the debate about a single currency for Europe (in the UK at least) it is the Keynesians who are most in favour and the monetarists who are most against.

According to a real business cycle view of the world, of course, even the existence of business cycles is not a reason for preserving local demand management tools. Under this approach the business cycle is always an optimal response to whatever real shocks have hit the economy and there is nothing that discretionary monetary policy can do to improve the course of events. Hence the efficiency of price signals is the only thing that matters and a global fiat currency would be as good a system as any and better than most.

EXCHANGE RATE VOLATILITY AND TRADE

Since the adoption of floating exchange rates in the 1970s there has been a growing literature on the question of whether exchange rate volatility is harmful to trade. In the early days of floating there was a false expectation that exchange rate volatility would diminish over time as stabilizing speculation took over. However, this has not happened, partly because there is no pattern in forecast errors, and volatility has become a permanent feature of foreign exchange markets. It was also believed that the impact of volatility could be insignificant because risk averse traders could hedge their foreign exchange (FX) exposure through efficient forward markets.

The impression that this volatility was unimportant was reinforced by early empirical studies such as that by Hooper and Kohlhagen (1978) who found that exchange rate uncertainty did have an effect on international trade prices but not on volumes. This was partly explained by the fact that exports were dominantly invoiced in the exporters' currency so that the supplier did not suffer significant exchange risk, at least once contracts were signed.

One feature of the Hooper–Kohlhagen study which turned out to be critical (apart from their short sample of the floating period) was that they only tested for the effects of nominal exchange rate volatility. Later literature argued convincingly that it is real exchange volatility that matters, or even unexpected real exchange rate volatility. A bunch of recent studies of the impact of real exchange rate volatility on trade all find a significant negative impact of such volatility on the volume of trade. Examples include Kenen and Rodrik (1986), De Grauwe (1988) and Savvides (1992). Also Watson (1995) finds some positive (but weak) effects on trade within the EU from the reduction in exchange rate volatility associated with the ERM.

De Grauwe (1988) shows that the general presumption that real exchange rate volatility must reduce the level of trade because of risk aversion is not correct and, in fact, depends upon the balance of two effects (analogous to income and substitution effects). However, the empirical evidence as to which effect dominates is clear. Real exchange rate volatility is unambiguously welfare reducing, though there is an implicit assumption here that the volatility is a random product of the monetary system rather than an equilibrium response to volatility in tastes or technology (a highly plausible condition).

Independently of risk aversion, it is possible that real exchange rate variability is trade creating (or at least trade diverting). This is because real exchange rate changes create arbitrage opportunities in goods markets. In effect, there can be noise traders in goods markets. This could mean that the mere measurement of trade volumes may not be the appropriate measure of the costs of real exchange rate volatility. It is possible that such volatility would increase the volume of trade and yet still reduce global welfare by distorting the trade pattern away from the true underlying comparative advantage. Price signals would, in practice, be creating 'false trade'.

In short, there is good reason to believe that the high levels of real exchange rate volatility (not to mention major sustained misalignments of real exchange rates) are costly. They do have a measurable negative effect on trade levels, but even this may underestimate the true economic cost of adding such noise to price signals in the global economy. An efficient international monetary system would avoid such unnecessary noise so that the monetary system itself would add to the transparency of the market economy, not distort it.

THE BOTTOM LINE

It would be pleasing to be able to conclude that the flexible exchange rate system is the best that we have had, or could have, and we should, therefore, stick with it. However, such a conclusion is unwarranted. The accumulating evidence is that floating exchange rates are excessively volatile and this volatility is transmitted to real exchange rates. The price mechanism is thereby significantly reduced in efficiency.

Unfortunately, the Bretton Woods system and the gold standard also had problems associated with them which make them unlikely candidates for the title of 'optimal system'. The Bretton Woods system worked well for a while, but in an environment which is unlikely to be replicated in the future. An inadequate adjustment mechanism probably proved fatal. The gold standard proved robust and delivered stable prices over a long period. However, it is unlikely that the world will go back to a system based on 'that barbaric metal' which could only provide for long-term growth in real money balances by trend deflation (rise in the price of gold).

The one system we have not yet tried is a single global fiat currency. This may be the optimal system from an economic efficiency perspective but it is unlikely to arise owing to the political costs of delivery. The nearest we are likely to see for the foreseeable future is the second best of regional currency blocs. This may be able to achieve much of the efficiency gain from having each currency widely traded across a diverse economy with a high proportion of trade internalized. However, this still leaves major exchange rates floating and it is a matter of guesswork at this stage as to whether the benefits would outweigh the costs.

In order to make floating exchange rates the optimal system we would have to argue that this system minimizes endogenous protectionism and that the gains from monetary stabilization policy outweigh the costs of real exchange rate volatility. Unfortunately the destabilizing effects of independent monetary policy may reinforce the volatility costs and make floating a definitely inferior system.

An optimist might say yes, but these monetary effects are small. A pessimist might respond no, they are not small but we are going to have to live with them. We may know what the optimal commercial policy is for the world economy, but we still have no agreement on what the best monetary system would look like.

REFERENCES

Bayoumi, T. and Eichengreen, B. (1994) 'Economic performance under alternative exchange rate regimes: some historical evidence', in P. B. Kenen, F. Papadia and F. Saccomanni (eds) *The International Monetary System*, Cambridge: Cambridge University Press.

Bergsten, C.F. (1993) 'The rationale for a rosy view: what a global economy will look like', *The Economist* 328, September: 57–9.

Bordo, M.D. (1993) 'The gold standard, Bretton Woods and other monetary regimes: a historical appraisal', in *Dimensions of Monetary Policy: Essays in Honor of Anatol B. Balbach*, Proceedings of the Seventeenth Annual Economic Policy Conference, *Federal Reserve Bank of St Louis Review* 75 (2) March–April: 123–87.

Chrystal, K.A. (1996) 'The SDR and its characteristics as an asset: an appraisal', paper presented to IMF conference on the Future of the SDR, Washington DC, 18–19 March, forthcoming in conference proceedings.

Cooper, R. (1990) 'What future for the international monetary system?', in Y. Suzuki, J. Miyake and M. Okabe (eds) *The Evolution of the International Monetary System: How Can Efficiency and Stability Be Attained?*, Tokyo: University of Tokyo Press, pp.277–300.

De Grauwe, P. (1988) 'Exchange rate variability and the slowdown in growth of international trade', *IMF Staff Papers* 35: 63–84.

Friedman, M. (1953) 'The case for flexible exchange rates', in *Essays in Positive Economics*, Chicago: University of Chicago Press, pp.157–203.

Helpman, E. and Razin, A. (1979) 'Towards a consistent comparison of alternative exchange rate systems', *Canadian Journal of Economics* August: 394–409.

Hooper, P. and Kohlhagen, S.W. (1978) 'The effect of exchange rate uncertainty on the prices and volume of international trade', *Journal of International Economics* 8: 483–511.

Kenen, P.B. and Rodrik, D. (1986) 'Measuring and analysing effects of short-term volatility in real exchange rates', *Review of Economics and Statistics* 68: 311–19.

McKinnon, R.I. (1963) 'Optimum currency areas', *American Economic Review* 53, September: 717–25.

Mundell, R.A. (1961) 'A theory of optimum currency areas', *American Economic Review* 51, November: 509–17.

Neumann, M.J.M. (1993) 'Commentary', *Federal Reserve Bank of St Louis Review* 75 (2) March–April: 192–9.

Savvides, A. (1992) 'Unanticipated exchange rate variability and the growth of international trade', *Weltwirtschaftliches Archiv* 128: 446–63.

Watson, A.M.S. (1995) 'An examination of the relationship between exchange rate instability and trade within the EMS', PhD thesis, University of Dundee.

6

COMMENTARY ON CHAPTER 5

Parmjit Kaur

Alec Chrystal's chapter provides a thoughtful evaluation of the literature on various international exchange rate regimes which have existed since the gold standard. The functioning of a globally optimal exchange rate regime should be one of the fundamentally important areas in international monetary economics. However, the complexity of the area under examination does not lend itself to simple conclusions and, at best, one ends up trying to evaluate past and present international monetary regimes in an attempt to specify a future regime which would be superior. Chrystal's chapter has carried out this task, by examining the various literature themes on exchange rates. The arguments are delivered in a concise way with a degree of simplicity which aids the clarity of the discussion.

Other authors in the field such as Bordo (1993) have also undertaken significant historical and empirical evaluation on the question of whether monetary regimes matter, when evaluated on the criteria of stability and rate of growth of trade which they facilitate. Chrystal's chapter has evaluated this same area and concludes that floating exchange rate volatility does affect real variables and hence is damaging to the rate of growth of trade.

For the sake of thoroughness I shall start off by stating again the aim of an efficient international monetary system, which is to produce sustainable economic growth internationally by promoting trade in goods and services and, increasingly, the flow of capital. This definition highlights the dual aspect of trade in physical goods and capital flows, in the functioning of any international monetary system.

Chrystal's chapter starts from the assumption that what is meant by an international monetary regime is both known and understood. This is an interesting point from which to begin the discussion, since what constitutes a monetary 'regime' can also be debated. As discussed by Bordo and Capie (1993) the term regime means a system of government. From this they raise the question of whether the regime should be at the domestic national or international level. Is the regime definitely a monetary regime or just a political one? Such clarification is necessary as it allows examination of time periods that show a transition of regime has occurred, such that events

53

leading up to the transition can be documented and examined. More importantly it should be noted, as is clearly set out in the chapter, that the performance of monetary variables such as inflation will vary under different monetary regimes and hence when evaluating monetary regimes this must be acknowledged. Persistent inflation does not tend to afflict commodity money regimes such as the gold standard as much as fiat money regimes where money supply is harder to control.

An optimal international monetary regime would have three fundamental aspects of operation as stated by Lal (1980). First, there is 'the role of exchange rate adjustment, secondly there is the question of the nature and role of international reserve asset and finally the degree of control of international capital movement' (Lal 1980: 1).

In this commentary on the chapter I will seek to examine the international monetary system (IMS) under two separate but related aspects of operation. First, exchange rate stability will be considered, this being the major aim of the Bretton Woods system. Second, the globalization of international capital flows will be discussed, as the 1970s and 1980s have brought to the fore the issue of international capital movement and the increasing convertibility between the capital and current account.

Calls for reform of the current managed floating exchange rate system tend to point to its underperformance on two criteria. As noted in Chapter 5, the increased volatility of exchange rates has been detrimental to international trade and investment flows. Second, there has been significant misalignment between the value of nominal and real exchange rates for major currencies. The discussion by Mussa et al. (1994: 2) shows that 'misalignment arises when exchange rate values are not related to the economic fundamentals of the country at the time or reflect unsustainable economic policies'. As such they will eventually be subject to market readjustment, thus increasing exchange rate volatility in itself. Therefore monetary regimes with persistence of this phenomenon must be inefficient. Another aspect of efficiency of monetary regimes is discussed in the chapter with reference to McKinnon's work on optimum currency areas.

The three major industrial trading countries of USA, Japan and Germany have operated a managed system of floating bilateral exchange rates since the 1970s. There have been significant episodes of intervention since then to offset economic disturbances and it could be argued that this fluidity has been useful in providing a workable system. Thus if a new international monetary regime is to evolve with the aim of enhancing international economic stability, it would have to incorporate these major trading countries. However, it has to be noted that to date these nations have used their monetary policy primarily for sustainable growth and low inflation on a domestic level. Hence their commitment to use monetary policy for external stability has not as yet been sufficiently demonstrated. Interestingly, Chrystal points out that the case for a single global fiat currency would be supported more by

Keynesians than by monetarists, even though it would involve disabling independent monetary control for any country at different stages of the business cycle.

There is also the view that before it is meaningful to discuss monetary regime changes through commitment we must first empower the structures which will deliver these changes through pre-commitment. Manfred Neumann examines the notion of pre-commitment as 'an external mechanism which effectively ties the hands of present and future governments' (1993: 199). Pre-commitment requires the independence of central banks such that their primary aim becomes price stability which is consistent with the true fundamentals of the country, so that there is no longer any interest in defending misaligned exchange rates.

It is of value to recognize that at present economic negotiations are often not backed by enough legislative framework to allow them to come to fruition. However, if the requirement of pre-commitment was enforced we could question whether a fundamental reform of the IMS would be possible at all. To fulfil the criteria of fundamental reform this would involve a conscious attempt by the three major industrial countries to fix their exchange rates within agreed ranges. In the chapter it is noted that a fixed exchange rate regime would require collaborative action and mutual commitment. The instrument of monetary policy would have to be allocated predominantly to this function. Currently it is unacceptable for these nations to relinquish independent control of monetary policy, as would be required to formally announce pre-set targets. Given that this dilemma will not be resolved in the foreseeable future, it is likely that changes to the IMS will be more piecemeal than revolutionary.

The second area of examination is the rapid globalization of the international capital market occurring since the 1970s. Ongoing financial innovation has presented opportunities for efficiency gains and there has been a marked increase in activity of this type, as current and capital accounts become increasingly convertible. An international monetary system of the future would have to recognize the importance of these transactions and have a regulatory framework which can supervise them adequately given their increasing importance and complexity. The present international monetary system has been the subject of examination on such aspects as incidences of malpractice have highlighted the issue.

Chrystal's belief that a system of floating national currencies is not the best we can do is a point of agreement. For extreme examples of high inflation debtor countries, such as Mexico, the continual problem of capital flight illustrates that internal and external balance are fundamentally linked. However, the increasing complexity of international financial markets may raise the question of the feasibility of a fixed exchange rate regime at all. It is recognized that undoubtedly this does mean that the 'conditions under which a fixed regime could operate will become more complex and demanding, as there is a greater urgency to achieve convergence on economic policy and on the orientation of medium term policy' (Mussa *et al.*, 1994: 15). The increasing importance of capital movements in shaping the future IMS is not stressed enough in the chapter. The fact that this is a fundamental issue in examining a new international monetary order needs to be emphasized.

In conclusion Chrystal's chapter is putting forward an optimization problem, and one which is subject to many constraints, perhaps too many to be resolvable. Clearly the major players in this debate would be the three main industrial nations. However, given the global level of discussion, a new international monetary system would have to embrace the developing countries of the world in a vital manner to provide for future stability and growth. There must also be some bias in the system which places a greater emphasis on surplus countries to act towards balance of payments equilibrium, on the logic that first they could afford to do so and second that the future growth prospect of the world would depend upon this.

Alec Chrystal's chapter throws up important issues for further examination and as such is a good basis for expansion of research in an area which is often not explicitly tackled.

REFERENCES

Bordo, M.D. (1993) 'The gold standard, Bretton Woods and other monetary regimes: a historical appraisal', in *Dimensions of Monetary Policy: Essays in Honour of Anatol B. Balbach*, Proceedings of the Seventeenth Annual Economic Policy Conference, *Federal Reserve Bank of St Louis Review* 75 (2) March–April: 123–87.

Bordo, M.D. and Capie, F. (1993) *Monetary Regimes in Transition*, Cambridge: Cambridge University Press.

Lal, D. (1980) '"A liberal international economic order": the international monetary system and economic development', *Essays in International Finance* 139, October, Princeton NJ: Princeton University, International Finance Section.

Mussa, M. *et al.* (1994) 'Improving the international monetary system: constraints and possibilities', International Monetary Fund, Occasional Paper 116, December.

Neumann, M.J.M. (1993) 'Commentary', *Federal Reserve Bank of St Louis Review* 75 (2) March–April: 192–9.

7

INTERNATIONAL COMPETITION AND INDUSTRIAL PERFORMANCE

Allocative efficiency, productive efficiency and turbulence

John R. Baldwin and Richard E. Caves

The year 1846 saw the repeal of the Corn Laws, which imposed a variable levy designed to support the domestic price of grain whenever the world price fell below 72 shillings per quarter. Although Britain once again embraced a variable levy on grain by acceding to the European Union's Common Agricultural Policy, the 1846 spirit of free trade enjoyed greater success in non-agricultural commerce, where most tariffs of the industrial countries have been negotiated down to low levels. Governments have bought off the ever-present interests seeking protection by managing trade through 'voluntary' export restraints, international quota systems such as the Multifibre Agreement, and the like. Although the management of trade gets no respect from most economists, its consequence has been more to limit the growth of trade and distort its pattern than to raise the (static) marginal incidence of trade restrictions.

This shift toward freer trade and the generally sustained economic growth of the industrial countries have yielded (especially in the past three decades) much experience with the effects of international competition on national product markets. By these we mean the distinctive ways in which domestic sellers' competition and the market outcome are affected by the presence of foreign customers and/or sellers. In the first three sections of this chapter we review theory and recent empirical evidence on the effects of international competition on the performance of domestic industries in two familiar dimensions – allocative efficiency and productive efficiency. Then we present new empirical evidence on one manifestation of international competition that only recently gained recognition, its effect on turbulence or turnover within the domestic industry.

INTERNATIONAL COMPETITION: THEORETICAL APPROACHES

If international competition simply meant more rival sellers and buyers in the relevant market than in a closed economy, it would be both welcome normatively and simple analytically. For a country that is small in relation to the world economy (changes in its international excess demands have no perceptible sustained effect on world prices), its domestic producers, however few they may be, would become locked into pure competition and constrained to behave as price takers. Any international disturbance reflected in a change in the world price would cause domestic producers' output to adjust along their 'competitive' supply curve representing optimal quantity responses to a parametric price change. The adjustment works the same way whether the nation is a net importer or exporter. This model is simple and decisive, but it leaves out properties vital to the operation of most product markets. We can fortify the vintage by making either of two assumptions:

A1 Transactions across national borders encounter large natural (transport, marketing) and/or artificial (tariffs, quotas) restrictions that do not impede domestic transactions.

A2 Buyers' tastes for attributes of differentiated goods are heterogeneous and might be nationally distinctive; a large fixed cost must be incurred to produce each differentiated variety of a product.

Most analytically interesting and empirically fruitful models of international competition rest on either A1 or A2.[1] We first focus on homogeneous products and employ assumption A1, which implies that trade restrictions and international transaction costs create a wide zone of insulation around the domestic price. That zone stretches from the delivered domestic price of importables down to the net price that can be realized from exports. Trade restrictions with a tariff-equivalent incidence of 10 per cent remain common, and studies of the specific international component of transaction costs place them at least that high; since the zone of insulation is made up of the sum of domestic and foreign tariffs and transaction costs, a span of 40 per cent of the world price is quite plausible.

This potentially large zone of insulation raises the possibility that equilibrium in the domestic market depends solely on domestic cost and demand conditions, and that it reflects any imperfection due to domestic sellers being few and their mode of interaction non-competitive. Import competition sets an upper bound on domestic price (world price plus domestic tariffs and transaction costs) and limits monopoly rents from producers' domestic sales. Export opportunities set a lower bound to domestic price (world price minus foreign tariffs and transaction costs). If domestic producers can export profitably, the domestic equilibrium price might be determined in either of two ways: it might be locked by arbitrage to the lower bound net domestic price of exportables, or it might be set higher in the manner of the classical model of 'dumping'.

Assumption A2 leads to very different results from A1: the now-familiar monopolistic competition equilibrium in international trade, in which directly competing varieties might be produced either at home or abroad and consumed in both locations. Two-way or intra-industry trade takes place, and the incremental effect of international trade on welfare involves some combination of gains in utility to consumers from the opportunity to consume more varieties and from lower prices of varieties that would be produced in a closed economy (because their producers now face competition from closer substitutes, and/or because they produce at larger scales).

Models of international competition based on A1 or A2 thus predict that international competition generally enhances allocative efficiency, that is, reduces deadweight losses due to any non-competitive behaviour of domestic sellers. For models based on A1 the qualitative prediction is complex, in that it depends in an interactive way on the number of domestic rivals, their cost position (absolute advantage) vis-à-vis their foreign rivals, and the size of the zone of insulation. For models based on A2 the effect of international competition is clear and simple, but the quantification of international competition becomes problematic. It depends on the incremental effect of international rivalry on the number of product varieties offered to domestic customers and consequently the elasticity of demand faced by the typical domestic (or foreign) seller: the greater the elasticity, the lower the price–cost margin.

These models also supply predictions about productive efficiency, the degree to which domestic producers produce whatever quantities they offer at the minimum attainable social cost. With scale economies or fixed costs limiting the number of sellers who can in equilibrium serve a closed domestic market, A1 models imply that tariff protection allows too many domestic producers to occupy the market; the excess increases with the size of the zone of insulation and decreases with the aggressiveness of domestic producers' market rivalry (which limits the excess of price over minimized cost). A2 models imply that the restriction of international competition inflates the number of producers serving the domestic market and curtails their scales of operation; to the extent it does not constrict scales of operation, it reduces the number of varieties available to domestic consumers and the surplus they enjoy. Economic welfare is impaired one way or the other. If we suppose that productive inefficiency can result because utility maximizing managers who face few rivals fail to minimize costs, both A1 and A2 models suggest that inefficiency can result where the optimal number of domestic producers is small (and, for A1 models, the zone of insulation is large).

The analytical framework that we have sketched supplies empirical predictions about how international competition improves the performance of product markets in national economies. The results from empirical testing of the resulting hypotheses can now be summarized. The effect of international competition on allocative efficiency seems to be a well-settled matter. Less familiar and fully developed are empirical investigations of international competition's effect on productive efficiency.

ALLOCATIVE EFFICIENCY:
EMPIRICAL FINDINGS

The early evidence on international competition and allocative efficiency was summarized in Caves (1985). A fairly clear consensus prevails on the proposition that when markets suffer deadweight losses from too little competition, the distortion results jointly from the fewness of domestic sellers, barriers that impede entrants, and absence of close competition from imports (that is, three necessary conditions). Studies of the effects of domestic producers' opportunities to export on domestic deadweight losses have reached diverse conclusions or none at all, consistent with the theoretical prediction that the outcome depends on whether dumping occurs, something that usually the researcher cannot control.

Recent research has supplemented these earlier findings principally in two ways. First, the short-term effects of changing international competition have been isolated from the long-run equilibrium effects isolated in the earlier cross-section studies. Domowitz *et al.* (1986) showed the effect of increasing import competition on US manufacturing industries by comparing estimates of the standard model of the determinants of allocative efficiency in cross-section year by year from 1958 to 1981. The statistical fit of this model began to deteriorate in the early 1970s, and by the later 1970s its explanatory power had dried up. They showed that one substantial cause of this desiccation was the increased import competition faced by many of these industries. It was not the only cause, however: the havoc wreaked on patterns of stable oligopolistic conduct by the inflationary disturbances of the 1970s decade and the coincident (temporary) capture of substantial rents by trade unions were also important. These domestic factors proved transient and were reversed in the early 1980s (Salinger 1990; Caves 1992), but the effect of international competition held fast. Katics and Petersen (1994) exploited their panel data to confirm these findings about the impact of changes in import competition with concentrated domestic producers, and they showed specifically that the relationships continued to hold at least through 1986.

The second new element is to incorporate strategic interaction between oligopolistic producers in different producing countries. Yamawaki (1986) implicitly factored the profits of Japanese manufacturing industries into profits on their domestic and international sales. The domestic component was found to depend on Japan's domestic market structure in the usual way; the foreign component varied with the structural competitiveness of counterpart producers in the USA so as to suggest that Japanese exports are more profitable, the less competitive are their US rivals.[2] Yamawaki and Audretsch (1988) obtained results similar to Yamawaki (1986) by means of a model which assumes that US and Japanese producers are in Cournot competition with each other in each of the two national markets taken separately. Specifically, they related the Japanese share of US domestic disappearance to variables indicating the relative costs and relative competitiveness of Japanese and US producers, finding that the share increases with the cost and structural competitiveness of the Japanese and decreases with those variables for their US rivals.[3] Yamawaki (1991) demonstrated one of the avenues by which import competition operates. One factor limiting the number of competitors able to fit into a market is a substantial fixed cost or scale economy in establishing a distribution system to handle a new producer's output. Yamawaki (1991) showed that Japanese exports to the US market and investments in distribution facilities in the USA are complementary: an increase in one positively influences the level of the other.

PRODUCTIVE EFFICIENCY: EMPIRICAL FINDINGS

The theoretical models of international product market competition noted previously have no precise implications for productive efficiency. Indeed, economists have not made much headway formalizing the commonplace that external rivals (wherever located) limit sloth and inefficiency within the firm. The more competitive is a market, the lower are profits for an efficient firm, and the less inefficiency can persist consistent with the firm's meeting the opportunity costs of its inputs and keeping the coalition together. Recently more sophisticated models have explored the effect of market competition on the efficacy of governance contracts within the firm (see the summary in Nickell 1996), but some of these obtain positive, others negative relations between competition and efficiency. We turn to the evidence.

Important findings about international trade and productive efficiency have emerged from employing stochastic frontier production functions to estimate the gaps between average and best-practice plant productivity in individual national manufacturing industries. This line of research assumes that the plants or firms classified to a national industry employ a common technology or production function that determines the maximum output attainable for any given bundle of inputs. In statistical estimation of the output–input relationship the error term is assumed to be the sum of the usual random component and some one-sided distribution of inefficiencies, or amounts by which a randomly drawn unit's efficiency might lie below the attainable frontier. An estimate is obtained of both an industry's frontier production function and the average departure of its plants or firms from best-practice efficiency. Although this procedure for estimating productive inefficiency is purely statistical and does not rest on an economic model of optimizing behaviour, Torii (1992) showed that it can be given a plausible economic foundation.

Caves and Associates (1992) applied this methodology to individual industries in the manufacturing sectors of six nations, testing in cross-section what structural factors influence differences among industries' efficiency levels in each country. They found that competition in general has the expected favourable effect on efficiency. In industries with few sellers efficiency increases with competition in each of the countries, although in most of them efficiency drops off in the least concentrated industries (probably associated with high rates of gross turnover of entering and exiting units). Notably, in every country efficiency increases with international competition, measured either directly by imports' share of the domestic market or inversely by the amount of protection provided by the government. These results are strongly consistent with models of international competition based on assumption A1. So far we lack direct tests of the implications of models based on A2 – that gains from international competition should take the forms of larger scales or less diversified outputs of domestic production units. However, extensive research mostly on small countries with import-competing manufacturing sectors and traditionally high levels of protection, mainly Canada and Australia, has tended to show that international competition truncates the small-unit tail of an industry's size distribution of plants.

Other evidence reveals that international competition improves the cost and efficiency levels of individual firms. Consider the cadre of white-collar employees in a large firm. Although economists presume that the value maximizing firm employs some optimal number of administrative workers, that target surely cannot be easy for the manager to identify and implement. Non-production employees work in teams and carry out many investment type activities whose future cash flows defy accurate prediction (or indeed isolation ex post). Furthermore, white-collar employment is prone to inflation when departures from purely value maximizing behaviour occur. One such departure lies in the natural dynamics of bureaucratic expansion, which cannot necessarily be kept in check even by a skilled, value maximizing top manager without the constraint of external competitive pressure. If managers can slant the firm's input choices toward providing utility for themselves, staff perquisites and empire building could lead to inflated white-collar staffs. To explore this dimension of productive efficiency, Caves and Krepps (1993) investigated whether the squeeze-out of white-collar workers from various US industries that occurred in the 1970s and 1980s could be associated with increases in international competition. Especially in the 1980s international competition along with pressures from the market for corporate control forced significant and substantial reductions in white-collar employment. Nickell (1996) analysed the determinants of large UK firms' productivity levels and growth rates over the period between 1972 and 1986. After controlling for domestic competition (which clearly favours productivity), he found a marginally significant positive influence of international competition on productivity growth. It did not, however, prove robust when he switched to a larger but less complete data set.

These efficiency gains forced on individual firms by international competition should also appear as an association between industries' rates of productivity growth and changes in the growth of imports' share of the market. MacDonald (1994) related rates of productivity growth of US manufacturing industries for three-year periods to rates of growth of imports' shares in the preceding three-year period. He found that in concentrated industries imports' lagged growth rate exerts a significant positive influence (with the industry's growth and other structural attributes controlled). A related corollary tested by Baily and Gersbach (1995) holds that productivity differences between national branches of a given industry should reflect differences in the international competition to which they are exposed. Intensively studying nine industries in the USA, Germany, and Japan, the authors controlled (by a process that is opaque to the reader) for an extensive set of factors that might cause productivity differences: the standard neo-classical sources (including capital age, utilization, and technology) but also scale of operation, product mix, and organizational factors. New investment and efficient scales of operation are important for some industries; 'innovations in manufacturing design that involve research and development and engineering' are important, but proprietary technology generally is not. Upon classifying the firms in each industry as facing either local, national, or global competition (both trade and foreign investment), they found a positive relation between the productivity position of a sector and the globalness of its competition. Causation is not demonstrated directly, but among the 'laggard' country/industry cells they found the more productive ones to face more competition than the least productive; if low productivity attracted international competition, the relation would show the opposite sign.

Although models of international competition with differentiated products have not been tested directly, an indirect test appears in studies of industries' adjustments to changes in international competition. The focus falls on intra-industry trade, a predicted and confirmed correlate of monopolistic competition in international markets. The implications of intra-industry trade for productive efficiency can be seen in a domestic industry's response to increases in international competition. Caves (1990, 1991) studied how Canadian manufacturing industries adjusted to the substantial increases in international competition that took place during the 1970s. Increased world excess supplies of importables to Canada drove down Canadian prices relative to world prices, although those declines were retarded in concentrated industries and those offering differentiated products. The structural adjustments that followed did not match the model of contraction down the supply curve of a purely competitive domestic industry. Employment was reduced, but capital expenditures typically increased rather than declining, and Canadian exports showed a lagged positive response to exogenous increases in Canadian imports. This adjustment pattern matches the comparative statics predicted by models of monopolistic competition in international industries. Unfortunately, the adjustment process could not be pursued to the implied changes in plants' scales and product mixes, especially relevant for productive efficiency.

In conclusion, international competition supports productive efficiency just as clearly as it promotes allocative efficiency. Evidence confirms predictions from models based on both A1 and A2 characterizations of the underlying market structures.

INTERNATIONAL COMPETITION AND THE INCIDENCE OF DISTURBANCES

There remains a corollary of the models of international competition that has been little tested. Consider the A1 approach and its zone of insulation of the domestic price. The model implies that when the domestic price lies at neither boundary, any sufficiently small external disturbance to the world price will have no effect on the domestic price. Other things equal (in particular the frequency and scope of disturbances of domestic origin striking various domestic industries), the amounts of adjustment observed to occur in various industries should increase with the closeness of their international competition.

This prediction had its origin in a recent contribution by Forsyth (1995), who was investigating asset sales and purchases made by firms in various US industries during the merger wave of 1979–86. Her analysis, framed in the literature of corporate governance, addresses the ability of corporate control mechanisms to force the managers of large, diversified firms to make decisions to disgorge or acquire assets in the best interest of shareholders. Her model assumes a (potential) gap between the (random) cash flow realized by a firm from a durable asset and that asset's value from sale or liquidation prior to its ultimate demise. Real synergies might warrant the firm holding a diversified group of assets. Without synergies, however, by choosing to hold several dissimilar assets the managers can impair the firm's value, either because negative cash flows from a poorly performing asset drag down a profitable one enough to force bankruptcy, or because a profitable asset supports an underperforming one that should be sold off. A diversified firm therefore has a positive value exceeding the sum of its component assets' values only if the synergies from teaming the assets exceed the expected value losses in states of nature when the assets are inappropriately combined.[4]

Forsyth nominated the industry's exposure to international trade as the proxy for a factor increasing the divergence of value trends for assets held by a firm. That is, disturbances occurring solely within the US economy are more likely to be correlated with each other than are disturbances of mixed domestic and international origin. She validated this assumption by showing that the year-to-year variability of US industries' levels of net output increases with their exposure to international trade. Forsyth then identified mergers and acquisitions that had occurred among large firms in each narrowly defined (three-digit) US manufacturing industry during 1979–86. For each acquired firm she identified asset sales that had occurred in the four years following the acquisition and regressed their normalized value on the variability of net output charges in the firm's industry. With asset purchases by the combined firm controlled, asset sales increase with output variability which itself increases with an industry's exposure to international competition.

To summarize this mechanism, Forsyth found that trade exposure is a source of disturbances to the values of business assets and thereby a trigger for their reorganization through merger. Those changes in assets' valuations should correspond to changes in real activities of the firms owning them: favourable shocks causing businesses holding the 'right' assets to expand, those with the 'wrong' assets to contract. Forsyth's model thus implies that the turnover of market shares among an industry's incumbent firms and the entry and exit of firms should also increase with trade exposure. Her empirically validated assumption that a market's exposure to international trade increases the incidence of disturbances parallels what we have called the A1 approach to modelling trade and domestic industry competition.

Before we proceed to test that hypothesis, however, its plausibility requires closer consideration. While the A1 approach implies that some markets are exposed to international disturbances while others are sheltered, the A2 approach and practical observation combine to suggest that nearly all national industries face some exposure to world markets. Do we then expect turbulence among domestic producers to increase with exposure to international markets? Two lines of reasoning could support this prediction.

First, we might assume that the variance of the typical dollar's worth of transnational transactions is greater than that of the typical dollar's worth of domestic transactions. This assumption, which Forsyth made, can be supported by invoking the variability of the exchange rate and the caprices of governments' trade policies, which directly affect international but not domestic transactions. The a priori force of this assumption should not be oversold, however. One implication of the smallness of an open economy is that the number of domestic sellers and/or buyers regularly in the market is absolutely small. Disturbances originating with individual domestic parties then might be averaged out less fully than disturbances to comparable individual parties located abroad. Trade exposure could then actually help to reduce overall turbulence among domestic suppliers. In short, the assumption of greater variance in international transactions is plausible but not compelling.[5]

Second, implications for market turbulence and trade exposure flow from the theory and evidence previously summarized in this chapter about the favourable effect of international competition on allocative and productive efficiency. Consider the national economy that is small in the sense of the A2 approach: total domestic consumption allows only a small number of differentiated varieties to be offered. The foreign market being much the larger, probabilistically the producer faces a more elastic demand in the international market. Even if domestic and foreign buyers' reservation prices for this producer's 'brand' have the same variance, they will lead to larger changes in quantities where trade exposure is greater, because trade exposure increases the relative sizes of quantity responses to disturbances from either foreign or domestic sources.[6]

In short, we can predict that turbulence increases with trade exposure through either of two mechanisms: greater variance of international disturbances, or competitiveness increased in ways that raise turbulence. Each prediction rests on assumptions that are plausible but not obviously applicable to all product markets. Clearly, the empirical evidence must decide.

INTERNATIONAL COMPETITION AND TURBULENCE IN CANADIAN MANUFACTURING INDUSTRIES

We employed primary records from Canada's census of manufactures over the period 1973 to 1992 to test the relation between an industry's exposure to trade and its incidence of mergers and other forms of industrial turbulence. This country and time period provide an attractive site. First, over these two decades trade exposure increased substantially. In five groups of Canadian manufacturing industries the rate of import penetration (imports/domestic disappearance) grew at rates varying from 1.23 to 1.60 per cent annually. The importance of exports similarly increased: exports/total production increased at rates between 1.30 and 2.05 per cent annually. Second, in 1987 Canadian manufacturing industries were presented with the opportunity/threat of a major reciprocal reduction in protection under the North American Free Trade Agreement (NAFTA). In 1989 Canadian producers began to lose tariff protection against other North American suppliers, at the same time as they began to gain tariff-free access to (most) other North American product markets; we shall break out the period of 1989 to 1992 for comparison to the years that preceded it. Third, because of the existence of a longitudinal database that tracks Canadian plants and firms over time, detailed measures can be developed of the reorganization of narrowly defined manufacturing industries through the entry and exit of firms, the growth and contraction of firms' employment levels, and the turnover of control of business units (mergers).

The relation between turbulence and trade exposure can be tested both in cross-section and over time. While we can and will integrate them in a standard analysis of panel data, the different facets of behaviour that they expose should be kept in mind. In cross-section we should observe any long-run relation between levels of turbulence and trade exposure. A positive relationship will fail to reject one or more of the mechanisms stated previously: international disturbances on average have a greater variance, or greater competitiveness due to trade exposure amplifies the turbulence that disturbances from all sources cause for domestic producers. To isolate a cross-section relation will require care in controlling for differences in industries' structures, for these could readily affect both trade exposure and turbulence. Time series analysis allows us to compare short-run changes in turbulence and in trade exposure with industry structure held strictly constant. It will be particularly appropriate if we suspect that greater variance of disturbances in international markets may be not a constant but an occasional consequence of large shifts in exchange rates, countries' trade policies, and the like.

Measures of turbulence

Turbulence in each Canadian manufacturing industry will be measured by merger activity (Forsyth's hypothesis) and also by shifts in firms' competitive positions within industries:

1   *Entry* into an industry occurs when a new plant is created in an industry by a firm (new, or established elsewhere) that previously did not possess a plant in that industry. For each year the variable is measured by the number of total employees in such new plants divided by employees in all plants of the industry.

2   *Exit* from an industry occurs when a plant ceases to operate and its owning firm no longer possesses any other plant in the same industry. It is measured by the number of employees in the exiting plant in its last year divided by employees in all plants in the industry at that time.

3   *Gain* is obtained by dividing firms each year into those that increased their employment within an industry and those that reduced it. For each year the growth in employment of those that grow is divided by total industry employment.

4   *Loss* is obtained by summing the decreases in employment within an industry for those firms that experienced reductions in a given year, then dividing it by total industry employment in that year.

5   *Merger* is defined to occur when the ownership of a plant changes, and the variable is defined as the number of plants that have changed hands in a year divided by the total number of plants in the industry.

We also make use of *Entry and exit = Entry + Exit* and *Turnover = Gain + Loss*. Note that the census measure of a plant's employment level for 1974 (say) is an average of observations taken at various times during the year. Its change from 1973 to 1974 thus summarizes changes occurring over twenty-four months that we can regard as centred on mid-1973 to mid-1974. The 1974 value of *Gain, Loss, Entry*, and *Exit* thus will be affected by trade exposure in both 1974 and 1973. Since some delay in response seems natural, we shall lag trade exposure measures by one year when explaining these dependent variables (the problem does not arise with *Merger*).

In previous research (Baldwin 1995a: Chapter 8) these measures of turbulence were found strongly and explicably related to structural characteristics of industries such as the concentration of producers, the efficient scales of plants, advertising/sales ratios, and research and development intensity. Rather than employ a group of the standard market structure measures as controls, we made use of a classification originated by the Organization for Economic Cooperation and Development (OECD) of manufacturing sectors into five groups: natural resource; labour intensive; scale-based; product differentiated; and science-based. The effectiveness of this schema as applied to the Canadian standard industrial classification was validated by a discriminant analysis using variables such as the wage rate, labour remuneration's proportion of value added, producer concentration, estimates of scale economies, research and development intensity, and ratios of advertising to sales (Baldwin and Rafiquzzaman 1994). In previous research (for example, Baldwin 1995a: Chapter 11) this classification proved to be a strong, parsimonious tool for controlling differences in the incidence of changes in business unit control and the productivity of those changes – exactly the variables suited to testing Forsyth's hypothesis.

Panel and cross-section relationships

We began the analysis with a very simple approach based on time series. For each year we aggregated establishments to the level of the five OECD sectors and calculated each measure of turbulence at the sectoral level. We then calculated for each sector simple correlation coefficients between pairs of eighteen-year time series of turbulence and *Exports + Imports*. The results were encouraging. All correlations were positive and most statistically significant, especially those with *Exit, Loss*, and *Merger*. However, we also discovered that most turbulence measures as well as trade exposure had upward trends over the period. Was trade exposure causing turbulence, or were both rising on the tide of more fundamental changes?

We shifted to a panel of 110 manufacturing industries defined at the three-digit level of Canada's standard industrial classification. In each industry the measures of turbulence and trade exposure (*Imports* = imports/domestic disappearance, *Exports* = exports/production) are available for each year

1973–92.[7] This two-decade period is divided into three blocks – the 1973–82 period dominated by energy shocks and inflation (hereafter 1970s), the 1982–9 period centred on years of low inflation and unemployment (1980s), and 1989–92 with domestic recession and trade adjusting to the North American Free Trade Agreement (1990s).

A pattern surfaced in the association between turbulence measures and trade exposure that influenced the model specifications that we report. *Imports* and *Exports* are correlated in the panel data set, so one cannot measure their separate effects on the measures of turbulence precisely. There is a stable pattern, however, whereby *Gain* and *Entry* are better explained by *Exports*, *Loss* and *Exit* by *Imports*, and *Turnover* and *Merger* by their sum. This is highly plausible: the losers among Canadian producers are knocked out by the superior price–quality offers of imports, while the winners claim their victories in both domestic and export markets. The reported results therefore match each turbulence measure with what is revealed to be its natural partner among measures of trade exposure.

The main conclusions from the panel data appear in Tables 7.1, 7.2, and 7.3, each reporting two models of the dependence of each turbulence measure on its partner measure of trade exposure. The first model is a simplified fixed-effects treatment in which the controls are dummies for four of the OECD sectors (science-based omitted) and two of the three time periods (1990s omitted).[8] The second model estimates not a single slope coefficient on trade exposure but a separate one for industries classified to each OECD sector. Table 7.1 addresses *Turnover* and its components *Gain* and *Loss*. First of all, trade exposure exerts a highly significant positive influence on each turbulence measure. The OECD sectoral dummies prove their worth as controls: relative to the omitted science-based industries, the scale-based industries tend to show significant negative intercept shifts, and the product differentiated and labour intensive groups significant positive shifts. It is certainly plausible that product differentiated industries should exhibit high turnover due to product innovation and obsolescence. Labour intensive industries should also exhibit high turnover because of their low levels of sunk costs, just as heavy sunk costs and well-defined capacity limitations should dampen turnover in the scale-based sector.

In the second equation for each turbulence measure the positive overall relation is confined to the resource-based, product differentiated, and (with marginal significance) science-based OECD sectors. For the latter two the results obviously correspond to the expected effect on international competition when products are differentiated. But that explanation also holds for natural resource industries, which include the food and beverage sector. Trade exposure appears to reduce *Gain* for scale-based industries, consistent with world market exposure actually allowing more steady utilization where sunk costs sharply demarcate capacity.

Table 7.1 Determinants of turnover of market shares, Canadian manufacturing industries, 1973–92

Exogenous variable	Gain (1)	Gain (2)	Loss (1)	Loss (2)	Turnover (1)	Turnover (2)
Intercept	0.083 (0.003) (0.0001)	0.081 (0.005) (0.0001)	0.159 (0.006) (0.0001)	0.161 (0.009) (0.0001)	0.240 (0.007) (0.0001)	0.243 (0.010) (0.0001)
Trade intensity	0.080 (0.028) (0.004)		10.089 (0.039) (0.024)		0.102 (0.029) (0.0004)	
OECD sectors:						
Natural resources	−0.003 (0.003) (0.332)	−0.001 (0.004) (0.740)	0.012 (0.006) (0.044)	0.004 (0.009) (0.321)	0.009 (0.006) (0.165)	0.002 (0.001) (0.053)
Labour intensive	0.006 (0.003) (0.073)	0.008 (0.005) (0.075)	0.036 (0.006) (0.0001)	0.412 (0.009) (0.0001)	0.043 (0.006) (0.0001)	0.052 (0.011) (0.0001)
Scale-based	−0.014 (0.003) (0.0001)	−0.006 (0.005) (0.180)	−0.006 (0.006) (0.297)	−0.008 (0.009) (0.358)	−0.021 (0.007) (0.002)	−0.015 (0.010) (0.157)
Product differentiated	0.008 (0.003) (0.042)	0.003 (0.005) (0.530)	0.031 (0.006) (0.0001)	0.034 (0.010) (0.0004)	0.038 (0.007) (0.0001)	0.036 (0.012) (0.002)
1973–82	−0.002 (0.002) (0.393)	−0.002 (0.003) (0.380)	−0.075 (0.004) (0.0001)	−0.075 (0.004) (0.0001)	−0.076 (0.005) (0.0001)	−0.078 (0.005) (0.0001)
1982–9	0.003 (0.002) (0.206)	0.003 (0.002) (0.230)	−0.056 (0.004) (0.0001)	−0.056 (0.004) (0.0001)	−0.053 (0.005) (0.0001)	−0.054 (0.005) (0.0001)
Trade intensity in:						
Natural resources		0.104 (0.035) (0.003)		0.197 (0.078) (0.011)		0.236 (0.046) (0.0001)
Labour intensive		0.087 (0.078) (0.265)		−0.102 (0.110) (0.353)		−0.139 (0.082) (0.093)
Scale-based		−0.144 (0.065) (0.027)		0.128 (0.073) (0.079)		−0.016 (0.060) (0.795)

Table 7.1 continued

Product differentiated		0.430		0.020		0.128
		(0.115)		(0.089)		(0.071)
		(0.0002)		(0.818)		(0.071)
Science-based		0.185		0.078		0.087
		(0.142)		(0.106)		(0.094)
		(0.190)		(0.465)		(0.352)
F	14.34	11.19	60.06	39.79	65.40	43.85
	(7,2355)	(11,2355)	(7,2355)	(11,2354)	(7,2354)	(11,2354)
Prob. value of F	(0.0001)	(0.0001)	(0.0001)	(0.0001)	(0.0001)	(0.0001)
R^2	0.04	0.15	0.15	0.15	0.16	0.17

Note: For *Gain*, trade is measured by exports/production; for *Loss*, imports/domestic disappearance; for *Turnover*, sum of exports/production and imports/domestic disappearance. Standard errors appear immediately below coefficients, followed by significance probabilities (two-tail test).

Equations (1) and (2) include time-period dummies that indicate significant and substantial upward trends through the period for *Loss* and *Turnover*. Replacing the decade dummies with individual year dummies shows the upward trend in *Turnover* to be steady with minor hesitations through the whole period. What factors should account for the trend, apart from the rising trade exposure that is controlled in our analysis, is a question of great interest, especially since Davis *et al.* (1996: Table 2.1) found no such trend for the USA. If we allow the trade-exposure variable to take a different slope coefficient in each period (not shown in the table), its effect on *Turnover* is not significant in the 1970s but increasingly positive and highly significant in the 1980s and 1990s. The perception, widespread in Canada and elsewhere, of increasing international competition seems to be supported.

Table 7.2 reports models specified identically to those in Table 7.1 for *Entry*, *Exit*, and their sum. This form of turbulence also shows a significant positive dependence on trade exposure. The highly significant effect on *Entry and Exit* flows chiefly from the surprisingly strong effect of export opportunities on the entry of new units. Since exporting tends to be concentrated among an industry's larger firms, this relation might be due to the effect of exporting opportunities on new plant construction by large firms. The pattern of sectoral intercept shifts is similar to that in Table 7.1, and the upward trends over time in *Exit* and *Entry and Exit* parallel those for *Turnover*. The pattern of slope coefficients among the OECD sectors (equation 2) differs, however, with the natural resources sector showing the closest linkage. *Entry* increases with *Exports* in the labour intensive industries but decreases with

71

Table 7.2 Determinants of entry, exit and entry and exit combined, Canadian manufacturing industries, 1973–92

Exogenous variable	Entry (1)	Entry (2)	Exit (1)	Exit (2)	Entry and exit (1)	Entry and exit (2)
Intercept	0.006	0.007	0.037	0.040	0.042	0.044
	(0.002)	(0.003)	(0.007)	(0.004)	(0.006)	(0.0006)
	(0.0005)	(0.007)	(0.0001)	(0.0001)	(0.0001)	(0.0001)
Trade intensity	0.081		0.027		0.075	
	(0.017)		(0.018)		(0.027)	
	(0.0001)		(0.124)		(0.006)	

OECD sector:

Exogenous variable	Entry (1)	Entry (2)	Exit (1)	Exit (2)	Entry and exit (1)	Entry and exit (2)
Natural resources	0.007	0.005	0.009	0.004	0.018	0.010
	(0.002)	(0.003)	(0.002)	(0.004)	(0.004)	(0.006)
	(0.0005)	(0.058)	(0.0004)	(0.260)	(0.0001)	(0.064)
Labour intensive	0.015	0.014	0.023	0.019	0.039	0.037
	(0.002)	(0.003)	(0.003)	(0.004)	(0.004)	(0.006)
	(0.0001)	(0.0001)	(0.0001)	(0.0001)	(0.0001)	(0.0001)
Scale-based	0.0001	0.006	−0.0002	−0.0003	0.001	0.005
	(0.0002)	(0.003)	(0.003)	(0.004)	(0.004)	(0.006)
	(0.953)	(0.030)	(0.930)	(0.418)	(0.790)	(0.040)
Product differentiated	0.010	0.011	0.016	0.020	0.026	0.033
	(0.002)	(0.003)	(0.003)	(0.005)	(0.004)	(0.007)
	(0.0001)	(0.001)	(0.0001)	(0.0001)	(0.0001)	(0.0001)
1973–82	0.002	0.001	−0.025	−0.025	−0.023	−0.023
	(0.002)	(0.002)	(0.002)	(0.002)	(0.003)	(0.003)
	(0.311)	(0.420)	(0.0001)	(0.0001)	(0.0001)	(0.0001)
1982–9	0.008	0.007	−0.018	−0.018	−0.009	−0.010
	(0.001)	(0.001)	(0.002)	(0.002)	(0.023)	(0.003)
	(0.0001)	(0.001)	(0.0001)	(0.0001)	(0.0004)	(0.0001)

Trade intensity in:

Exogenous variable	Entry (1)	Entry (2)	Exit (1)	Exit (2)	Entry and exit (1)	Entry and exit (2)
Natural resources		0.052		0.122		0.182
		(0.021)		(0.035)		(0.026)
		(0.0001)		(0.0005)		(0.0001)
Labour intensive		0.120		0.031		0.064
		(0.047)		(0.050)		(0.047)
		(0.011)		(0.530)		(0.174)

Table 7.2 continued

Scale-based		−0.164		0.036		−0.038
		(0.039)		(0.033)		(0.034)
		(0.0001)		(0.270)		(0.261)
Product differentiated		0.017		−0.080		−0.034
		(0.069)		(0.040)		(0.040)
		(0.798)		(0.040)		(0.176)
Science-based		0.062		−0.018		0.041
		(0.089)		(0.047)		(0.053)
		(0.464)		(0.690)		(0.442)
F	25.39	21.18	46.82	31.35	44.85	32.50
	(7,2355)	(11,2355)	(7,2355)	(11,2355)	(7,2355)	(11,2355)
Prob. value of F	(0.0001)	(0.0001)	(0.0001)	(0.0001)	(0.0001)	(0.0001)
R^2	0.07	0.09	0.12	0.12	0.12	0.13

Note: For *Entry*, trade is measured by exports/production; for *Exit*, imports/domestic disappearance; for *Entry and exit*, sum of exports/production and imports/domestic disappearance. Standard errors appear immediately below coefficients, followed by significance probabilities (two-tail test).

them in the scale-based sector (probably due to the slow growth and established export positions of Canada's wood, paper, steel, and automobile plants). *Exit* and *Imports* are related in natural resources but only weakly overall. There is not much direct relation between these variables, although the relation of *Loss* to *Imports* implies an indirect link.

Before evaluating Table 7.3's findings on *Merger* we must make an important point about its construction. Unlike the other turnover variables, *Merger* takes zero values in a number of industry/year cells of the data set. Probably that is because the forms of control changes identified in this database miss many of the control changes that occur in small businesses, when individual proprietors sell or closely held corporations are reorganized. We elected therefore to analyse the relation between measured control changes and trade exposure only in those industries and years with strictly positive amounts of acquisition occurring. This procedure, while not the only plausible choice, has the advantage of alignment with Forsyth's hypothesis, which pertains to public corporations with widely traded securities.[9] With this property noted, we observe in Table 7.3 that changes in plants' control also depend significantly on trade exposure, confirming Forsyth's result for the USA. The intercept shifts show that control changes were particularly extensive during 1982–9 and in the scale-based and natural resources sectors. The dependence of control changes on trade exposure, however, is apparent in

Table 7.3 Determinants of proportion of establishments subject to control changes, Canadian manufacturing industries, 1973–92

Exogenous variable	*(1)*	*(2)*
Intercept	0.040	0.036
	(0.007)	(0.009)
	(0.0001)	(0.0002)
Trade intensity	0.075	
	(0.027)	
	(0.006)	
OECD sector:		
Natural resources	0.010	0.015
	(0.006)	(0.009)
	(0.096)	(0.099)
Labour intensive	−0.007	−0.008
	(0.006)	(0.010)
	(0.238)	(0.936)
Scale-based	0.010	0.017
	(0.006)	(0.009)
	(0.081)	(0.074)
Product differentiated	0.004	0.005
	(0.006)	(0.010)
	(0.553)	(0.657)
1973–82	−0.008	−0.008
	(0.005)	(0.005)
	(0.111)	(0.112)
1982–9	0.009	0.009
	(0.004)	(0.005)
	(0.063)	(0.063)
Trade intensity in:		
Natural resources		0.064
		(0.041)
		(0.120)
Labour intensive		0.029
		(0.088)
		(0.740)
Scale-based		0.041
		(0.060)
		(0.480)

Table 7.3 continued

Product differentiated		0.128
		(0.062)
		(0.040)
Science-based		0.137
		(0.089)
		(0.120)
F	8.44	5.53
	(7,1715)	(7,1715)
R^2	0.033	0.035

Note: Trade intensity is measured by sum of exports/production and imports/domestic disappearance. Standard errors appear immediately below coefficients, followed by significance probabilities (two-tail test).

the product differentiated and science-based industries. That finding is interesting because these are also the sectors in which Baldwin (1995a: Chapter 11) found control changes during the 1970s to be both more prevalent and more favourable in their effects on productivity in the affected business units. Exposure to international competition seems to speed the reorganization of business assets just where reorganizations on average create the most value.

Relationships over time

The effects of trade exposure on turbulence measured so far are obtained from fixed effects models that are partial with respect to both industries and years. Hence, the key regression coefficients represent some mixture of cross-section effects, time series effects, and uncontrolled systematic disturbances. Recall the two channels identified by which trade exposure enlarges turbulence: either it 'imports' a greater variance of disturbances from abroad (the external disturbances channel) or it inflates the turbulence producing effect of whatever disturbances are occurring (the competitive pressure channel). Evidence already presented supports the competitive pressure channel by locating the effect of trade exposure in the OECD sectors most prone to product differentiation and innovation (and least tied down by sunk plant capacities). The external disturbances channel was not specifically supported; for example, the sensitivity of turbulence measures to trade exposure was greater in the tranquil 1980s than in the 1970s, which were roiled by wide swings in countries' inflation rates and nominal and real exchange rates. Can the external disturbances channel be isolated in time series?

Despite the richness of the underlying data, our leverage on intertemporal effects is limited. As we have seen, common upward trends exist in turbulence and trade exposure. Analysis of time series for the individual three-digit industries would face this problem while introducing a great deal of random noise. A relationship in first differences is the natural choice, but it also elevates the importance of random disturbances.

We settled on a simple approach based on a cross-section of first differences keyed to the shifts in the overall incidence of international disturbances that apparently occurred during 1973–92. We divided the period into the same three segments used in Tables 7.1, 7.2 and 7.3. The first period, 1973–82, runs from a recession year to a recession year and covers the inflationary disturbances that succeeded the 'energy shock' caused by the Organization of Petroleum Exporting Countries (OPEC). The second interval, 1982–9, embraces an expansionary economic period free from major domestic macroeconomic disturbances. The third period, 1989–92, coincides with the first part of the gradual phase-in of multilateral tariff reductions under NAFTA. Although reductions continued after 1992, it is reasonable to assume that business managers promptly set about making their long-run adjustments: the member countries' commitments were widely regarded as credible, and managers making investment decisions naturally seek to anticipate conditions prevailing over a capital project's lifetime (this antici-patory adjustment was noted in the original formation of the European Common Market).[10] In effect we are taking NAFTA as the prototype of a large international disturbance. Each trade exposure and turbulence measure defined previously as an annual observation was summed over the years within each of the three time intervals. Changes were calculated in each industry's turbulence and trade exposure measures from 1973–82 to 1982–9, and from 1982–9 to 1989–92. Correlations were calculated across industries between changes in turbulence and trade exposure from the first period to the second (reported in Table 7.4) and from the second to the third (reported in Table 7.5).

Tables 7.4 and 7.5 show that the relation between changes in turbulence and in trade exposure differed appreciably between the two pairs of time periods. Between 1973–82 and 1982–9 no significant relationships appear, except that changes in mergers are correlated with changes in trade flows in a pattern that is regular but below standard levels of significance. The 1970s were (for Canada, like other countries) a period of macroeconomic turmoil both at home and abroad. The variance of international disturbances decreased from the 1970s to the 1980s while the average industry's level of trade exposure went up, so it is not surprising that the 1973–82 to 1982–9 changes analysed in Table 7.4 offer next to no support for the turbulence–trade hypothesis in general or the external disturbance channel in particular.

In Table 7.5 the growth of trade associated with NAFTA's tariff changes apparently did significantly affect turbulence and industrial reorganization.

Table 7.4 Correlations between changes in trade exposure and industrial turbulence measures, Canadian manufacturing industries, 1973–82 to 1982–9

Turbulence measure	Imports	Exports	Imports + exports
Entry	0.16 (0.11)	−0.03 (0.75)	0.09 (0.34)
Exit	0.11 (0.28)	−0.05 (0.58)	0.05 (0.63)
Entry and exit	0.16 (0.11)	−0.05 (0.60)	0.08 (0.39)
Gain	−0.07 (0.47)	−0.13 (0.21)	−0.11 (0.24)
Loss	−0.04 (0.70)	0.07 (0.47)	0.01 (0.92)
Turnover	−0.01 (0.88)	−0.13 (0.19)	−0.08 (0.49)
Mergers	0.14 (0.15)	0.10 (0.32)	0.15 (0.13)

Note: Significance probabilities appear in parentheses.

The increase in gross trade exposure is positively and significantly correlated with changes in *Entry and exit* as well as in *Exit* taken separately. The association is due to changes in imports and not in exports, and the association between the growth of exports' share and *Exit* changes from negative for 1973–82 to 1982–9 to positive for 1982–9 to 1989–92 (though neither is significant). Changes in *Merger* continue positively related to the total change in trade, a result that corresponds to Forsyth's (1995) finding for the USA, but once again fall short of standard significance levels. The association between changes in trade exposure and the turnover of incumbent businesses between 1982–9 and 1989–92 parallels that with *Entry and exit*: the change in imports (and, through it, the change in total trade exposure) is strongly related to *Turnover* mainly through its association with *Loss*, echoing the pattern found in Table 7.1. NAFTA's implementation did increase turbulence, mainly through the obvious mechanism of inflicting share losses and exit decisions on some domestic producers.

Table 7.5 Correlations between changes in trade exposure and industrial turbulence, Canadian manufacturing industries, 1982–9 to 1989–92

Turbulence measure	Imports	Exports	Imports + exports
Entry	0.09 (0.35)	−0.11 (0.29)	−0.00 (0.97)
Exit	0.28 (0.004)	0.10 (0.35)	0.21 (0.03)
Entry and exit	0.30 (0.002)	0.01 (0.85)	0.18 (0.06)
Gain	0.05 (0.59)	0.11 (0.28)	0.01 (0.88)
Loss	0.22 (0.02)	0.03 (0.75)	−0.11 (0.26)
Turnover	0.25 (0.01)	0.04 (0.67)	0.17 (0.09)
Mergers	0.10 (0.31)	0.15 (0.14)	0.14 (0.17)

Note: Significance probabilities appear in parentheses.

In summary, the test based on changes in individual manufacturing industries provides only limited evidence that short-run changes in exposure to international commerce increase turbulence within a domestic industry. However, the significant associations with NAFTA's inception is consistent with the external disturbances mechanism.[11]

One last empirical point bears on the normative significance of turbulence, considered in the next section: the various types of turbulence are related to productivity growth in the industry. Substantial productivity improvements are associated with the transfer of market share from units that are losing market share to those that are gaining; Baldwin (1995b) found that over six-year periods the gainers on average start out a little less productive than those destined to lose, but they wind up 26 to 33 per cent (depending on the period) more productive. Similarly, Baldwin (1995a: Chapter 11) found that changes in the control of business units on average raise their productivity appreciably, and the productivity of control changes varies strongly among industries in ways that tie the gains to better use of lumpy, heterogeneous assets (especially intangibles).[12] Turnover from entry and exit is not so directly productive: Baldwin (1995b) found that units destined to exit during a six-year period begin it one-fifth less productive than the survivors, but entrants suffer high infant mortality, and the survivors need a decade to match the productivity of continuing units (also Davis *et al*. 1996: 52).

Causation: turbulence and exports

In formulating this study we saw no general reason to treat import competition and export opportunities asymmetrically: competition from foreign suppliers should, to a first approximation, affect Canadian producers the same whether it occurs in Canada or abroad. However, the traditionally import competing status of Canadian manufacturing suggests that a particular asymmetry might be involved. Caves (1990, 1991) traced a sequence whereby reduced trade barriers in the 1970s lowered Canadian domestic prices but raised capital expenditures, induced productivity raising reorganizations, and ultimately caused Canadian producers facing more import competition also to become more substantial exporters.

This adjustment process, the 'comparative statics' behind intra-industry trade, implies that causation runs from turbulence in producers' market shares to the extent of industry exports: firms making a run for an internationally efficient scale expand at the expense of those retreating before imports' fire. Indeed, despite the general empirical symmetry between effects of *Exports* and *Imports* found in Tables 7.1, 7.2, 7.3, 7.4 and 7.5, we noticed some patterns pointing to this direction of causation. Using the panel data set of Tables 7.1, 7.2 and 7.3, we regressed *Exports* in each year on *Turnover* in the year preceding, including dummies for the OECD sectors. We obtained the coefficient (standard error) of 0.053 (0.017), significant at the 0.2 per cent level. Adding time controls left the relation significant at the 1 per cent level. We allowed this slope coefficient to vary among time periods, discovering that for the 1970s the coefficient increases to 0.158, thrice the magnitude for the whole period. Thus, the relation was strongest and most significant in the 1970s and trailed off through the remaining years.

We do not attempt an elaborate dissection of the apparent two-way causation between turbulence and exports, but we note a satisfying consistency in the simple evidence: The strength of the effect of lagged *Turnover* on *Exports* was greater early in our period, when a number of Canadian manufacturing industries were first graduating from purely import competing status. The strength of the effect of lagged *Exports* on *Turnover* was greater late in the period, once that shift had occurred. Both directions of influence appear 'real'.

CONCLUSIONS

In this chapter we have reviewed empirical evidence on three effects of international competition on the performance of domestic industries. Two of these are familiar. First, exposure to international trade, especially import competition, tends strongly to limit domestic industries' departures from 'ideal' price–cost margins, and trade restrictions correspondingly rob this discipline of its effectiveness. The second is less familiar but well supported by evidence: international competition limits the amount of productive inefficiency that is viable in domestic firms, and trade barriers again relax this pressure for efficiency.

The third effect of international competition – on turbulence within domestic industries – has only recently been detected. In this chapter we report tests for the effect using primary data on the plants and firms operating within the manufacturing industries of Canada. The analysis was conducted on variations in turbulence and trade exposure within a large panel data set: 110 industries over 1973–92. Turbulence, measured by the entry and exit of firms, the turnover among incumbents, and the frequency of changes in control of business units, pervasively increases with trade exposure after controlling (partially) for industry and time fixed effects. The only exception is that exits by domestic producers are not significantly related to import competition. The closeness of the relationship varies among broad industry groups in a way consistent with the model of international competition that rests on trade in differentiated products. We also sought to isolate (with cross-sections of first differences) a pure short-run association. None was found between the 1970s and 1980s, but the North American Free Trade Agreement in 1989 apparently provided just the disturbance needed to kick off increased turbulence.

With this effect of trade on turbulence supported empirically, we should consider its welfare significance. Unlike the effects of trade on allocative and productive efficiency, the effect on turbulence has ambiguous benefit. Consider the negative elements first. Even without invoking subjective costs to risk-averse agents, disturbances inflict costs of adjustment that would be avoided in their absence. The uncertainty surrounding irreversible investments increases with ambient disturbances, and with it the chances that projects will be undertaken that their sponsors will later regret. Other projects will, of course, exceed mean expectations, but these can be expanded when a propitious state of nature has been revealed.

Turbulence from international disturbances also has welfare benefits, best seen in the light of continuous economic change, with international disturbances serving to deliver innovations in products, services, their qualities and varieties, and in ways of doing business and organizing activities. International disturbances then serve in part as innovations whose value is not fully appropriated by their originators, and which therefore bestow net positive benefits within a country as they are picked up from external sources of origin. To avoid disturbances, then, is to pass up opportunities or to delay their seizure.

The idea that international disturbances convey benefits can be put in other ways as well. With products differentiated, a disturbance that lowers the cost of international transactions makes it possible to cover the fixed costs associated with importing or exporting product varieties not previously traded. This benefit can be regarded as simply another component of classical equilibrium gains from trade (Romer 1994), but given the continual appearance of commodity innovations around the world it also implies a benevolent association between trade and the turbulence of the domestic consumption set. Exporting activities are similarly linked to the expected payout of new products, practices, and varieties. Insofar as innovations' costs are fixed, and international commerce enlarges the potential market beyond the nation's boundaries, the expected return is increased to innovative activities broadly defined.

Still another benevolent link between international commerce and turbulence harks back to the ability of trade to make markets more competitive. The heart of that effect lies in making individual domestic producers face more elastic (excess) demands than they otherwise would. In addition, disturbances communicated through international commerce can also increase competition by making collusion less feasible. Several models of collusion imply that its sustainability declines with the incidence of random disturbances, and empirical evidence for Canada has indeed supported this proposition (Spence 1978). Whether due to disrupted collusion or more directly to international disturbances, increases in turbulence (exit of low productivity units, turnover of share to higher productivity incumbents, and improvement in units' productivity levels through changes in control) clearly contribute to an industry's productivity level (growth). Empirical evidence was noted in the preceding section.

These cross-cutting considerations keep any prudent economist from regarding the turbulence effects of international commerce as a clear source of net welfare gains. However, they certainly undermine any belief that clear gains in national tranquillity could stem from excluding the world's Cobdens from the forum of public policy or its Commodore Perrys from the nation's harbours.

NOTES

1 Here we ignore the many issues that arise when the country is 'large' and can exert monopoly power or strategic leverage internationally.

2 Pugel (1980) earlier showed that, while the rents of US producers decrease with the share of the market held by competing imports, the import share also increases with the concentration of the domestic producers.

3 They controlled for the share of US domestic disappearance held by third-country exporters, finding that its statistical influence is consistent with these exports injecting (Cournot) competition additional to that due to the US and Japanese producers.

4 She showed that, given the lock-in of diversified assets, separate debt contracts conditioned upon the outcomes of individual assets will not solve the problem. If two assets of initially equal values are pooled and their values move in opposite directions, the less likely are they optimally liquidated at the same time. A decrease in the covariance of the assets' cash flows increases the likelihood of either inefficient liquidation or inefficient failure to liquidate.

5 Davis et al. (1996: 47–9) assumed that no presumption exists, and they found no effect of international exposure on employment turnover in US markets.

6 If the A2 approach predicts that turbulence increases with international competition, the same does not necessarily follow from other models of imperfect competition. Indeed some empirical research on industrial organization suggests that international exposure could increase turbulence when it increases competition from 'little' to 'moderate', but reduce it when the change is from moderate to strong. See Caves and Porter (1978) and other literature on biases toward non-price competition in moderately collusive industries.

7 Trade flows were matched comprehensively to production related data for these industries. The trade data come from the International Trade Division, Statistics Canada.

8 In previous research on job creation and destruction, concepts closely related to turnover as measured in this chapter, Baldwin (1995a: 139–47) (in collaboration with Timothy Dunne and John Haltiwanger) found that they are significantly related to import competition in Canada, although not when industry fixed effects are included. For export intensity the results are erratic. A parallel analysis for the USA also turned up a significant positive influence of import competition on job turnover that is not sensitive to industry or year fixed effects.

9 Recall also that *Merger* is based on counts of plants, not weighted by size or value.

10 This assumption is supported by the findings of Clausing (1996) about the prompt and substantial adjustments of Canadian trade flows in response to the tariff reductions.

11 An intriguing parallel result was reported by Lansbury and Mayes (1996). In a panel data analysis of productive efficiency in UK industries during the 1980s, they found that efficiency increases significantly with the sum of import and export exposures. However, when the variables were first-differenced, the sign reversed to negative, consistent with increases in trade exposure producing short-run increases in turbulence.

12 This finding has been reported from US data as well. For example, McGuckin and Nguyen (1995) observed that large plants in the food-processing industry that undergo changes in corporate control start out less productive than average (small ones begin more productive, however), and subsequently their labour–productivity growth is significantly faster than for plants continuing with no control changes.

REFERENCES

Baily, M.N. and Gersbach, H. (1995) 'Efficiency in manufacturing and the need for global competition', *Brookings Papers on Economic Activity: Microeconomics*, Washington DC: Brookings Institution, pp.307–47.

Baldwin, J.R. (1995a) *The Dynamics of Industrial Competition*, Cambridge: Cambridge University Press.

—— (1995b) 'Productivity growth, plant turnover and restructuring in the Canadian manufacturing sector', Research Paper Series no. 87, Analytical Studies Branch, Statistics Canada.

—— and Rafiquzzaman, M. (1994) 'Structural change in the Canadian manufacturing sector, 1970–1990', Research Paper Series no. 61, Analytical Studies Branch, Statistics Canada.

Caves, R.E. (1985) 'International trade and industrial organization: problems, solved and unsolved', *European Economic Review* 28, August: 377–95.

—— (1990) *Adjustment to International Competition: Short-run Relations of Prices, Trade Flows, and Inputs in Canadian Manufacturing Industries*, Ottawa: Economic Council of Canada.

—— (1991) 'Trade liberalization and structural adjustment in Canada: the genesis of intraindustry trade', in C. W. Reynolds, L. Waverman and G. Bueno (eds) *The Dynamics of North American Trade and Investment*, Stanford CA: Stanford University Press, pp.44–69.

—— (1992) 'Technical efficiency, rent-seeking and excess profits in US manufacturing industries, 1977', in D.B. Audretsch and J.J. Siegfried (eds) *Empirical Studies in Industrial Organization: Essays in Honor of Leonard W. Weiss*, Dordrecht: Kluwer Academic, pp.187–206.

Caves, R.E. and Associates (1992) *Industrial Efficiency in Six Nations*, Cambridge MA: MIT Press.

Caves, R.E. and Krepps, M.B. (1993) 'Fat: the displacement of nonproduction workers from U.S. manufacturing industries', *Brookings Papers on Economic Activity: Microeconomics 2*, Washington DC: Brookings Institution, pp.227–43.

Caves, R.E. and Porter, M.E. (1978) 'Market structure, oligopoly, and the stability of market shares', *Journal of Industrial Economics* 26, June: 289–313.

Clausing, K.A. (1996) 'Essays in international economic integration', PhD dissertation, Harvard University.

Davis, S.J., Haltiwanger, J.C. and Schuh, S. (1996) *Job Creation and Destruction*, Cambridge MA: MIT Press.

Domowitz, I., Hubbard, R.G. and Petersen, B.C. (1986) 'Business cycles and the relationship between concentration and price–cost margins', *Rand Journal of Economics* 17, Spring: 1–17.

Forsyth, J.G. (1995) 'Leverage and restructuring: theory and application to corporate control in the 1980s', PhD dissertation, Harvard University, pp.57–83.

Katics, M.M. and Petersen, B.C. (1994) 'The effect of rising import competition on market power: a panel study of US manufacturing', *Journal of Industrial Economics* 42, September: 277–86.

Lansbury, M. and Mayes, D. (1996) 'Shifts in the production frontier and the distribution of efficiency', in D.G. Mayes (ed.) *Sources of Productivity Growth*, Cambridge: Cambridge University Press, pp.66–88.

MacDonald, J.M. (1994) 'Does import competition force efficient production?', *Review of Economics and Statistics* 76, November: 721–7.

McGuckin, R.H. and Nguyen, S.V. (1995) 'On productivity and plant ownership change: new evidence from the longitudinal research database', *Rand Journal of Economics* 26, Summer: 257–76.

Nickell, S.J. (1996) 'Competition and corporate performance', *Journal of Political Economy* 104, August: 724–46.

Pugel, T.A. (1980) 'Foreign trade and U.S. market performance', *Journal of Industrial Economics* 29, March: 119–30.

Romer, P. (1994) 'New goods, old theory, and the welfare costs of trade restrictions', *Journal of Development Economics* 43, February: 5–38.

Salinger, M.A. (1990) 'The concentration-margins relationship reconsidered', *Brookings Papers on Economic Activity: Microeconomics*, Washington DC: Brookings Institution, pp. 287–321.

Spence, M. (1978) 'Tacit co-ordination and imperfect information', *Canadian Journal of Economics* 11, August: 490–505.

Torii, A. (1992). 'Technical efficiency in Japanese industries', in Caves and Associates, *Industrial Efficiency in Six Nations*, Cambridge MA: MIT Press, pp.31–119.

Yamawaki, H. (1986) 'Exports, foreign market structure, and profitability in Japanese and U.S. manufacturing', *Review of Economics and Statistics* 68, November: 618–27.

—— (1991) 'Exports and foreign distribution activities: evidence on Japanese firms in the United States', *Review of Economics and Statistics* 73, May: 294–300.

Yamawaki, H. and Audretsch, D.B. (1988) 'Import share under international oligopoly with differentiated products: Japanese imports in U.S. manufacturing', *Review of Economics and Statistics* 70, November: 569–79.

8

COMMENTARY ON CHAPTER 7

Lynden Moore

Baldwin and Caves consider the benefits from trade in two types of market. First, one in which the product being produced is homogeneous and there are more barriers to international trade in the form of transport cost, etc. than domestic trade; in that case increased trade reduces the monopoly power of domestic producers. The producer is operating between the price at which he can export and the price at which imports can enter. The second is one in which products are differentiated and a fixed cost is required to produce each type of differentiation; trade then increases the choice available to consumers or reduces the cost of producing a wide choice. Trade increases allocative efficiency and productive efficiency. Efficiency appears to be considered in terms of labour productivity, and there is some discussion about the reduction in the number of white-collar workers. However, it appears to the discussant that much of this is due to the subcontracting of activities such as designing and market research to consultancies.

Implicit in the whole argument is the assumption that the domestic producers are first supplying only the home market. However, due to the repeal of the Corn Laws this was not generally Britain's position; its manu-facturing industry grew up from the outset orientated towards exports. Even in the 1950s one-third of its manufactures were exported. Small firms even in risky markets may export 60 to 80 per cent of their output. Furthermore most large British firms are multinationals and thus may always produce abroad rather than export. The shock to the British system occurred when we abandoned Commonwealth preference and joined the EC and the British home market was invaded by exports from other EC countries.

9

THE REGIONAL IMPACT OF INWARD DIRECT INVESTMENT

Some reflections on the issue of measurement

David Williams

INTRODUCTION

Attitudes to foreign direct investment (FDI) vary throughout the world – from those countries who perceive it as an aid to regional development and, thus, something to be encouraged to those who regard it as a process which will retard economic growth and displace indigenous industry. The European Union (EU) provides a good illustration of how divided countries are on this issue.

Many economists are more interested in trade matters than investment – despite the growth which has occurred in worldwide FDI flows over recent years. There is a voluminous literature on strategic trade policies which examines the effects of tariffs or subsidies on traded goods and production. In contrast, there has been little analysis of the strategic implications of FDI. What there is has been limited to the rivalrous behaviour of oligopolistic firms. This is all the more surprising when one considers that in 1992 the global sales of the affiliates of multinational enterprises (MNEs) were estimated to be $5.2 trillion, compared with world exports of goods and non-factor services of $4.9 trillion (UNCTAD 1995). Thus, it could be argued that FDI has eclipsed the role of trade flows in the world economy.

Traditional general equilibrium trade theory has little to say about the MNE since the pure version of the Heckscher–Ohlin–Samuelson (HOS) model would indicate that trade is induced by differences in factor endowments and that factor prices are equalized through the process of free trade. Thus, there is no FDI at all. Even when the model is extended to allow for international factor movements, it does not include FDI determinants other than factor proportions.

The new international economics has relatively little to say about the effect of MNEs on the determination of trade patterns (Gray 1992). There is, however, a well-developed, although less formal, theoretical literature to be found which has attempted to explain why MNEs should exist in spite of the costs of operating across international frontiers. This became firmly established in the international production literature through the seminal work of Dunning (1977, 1981).

POTENTIAL BENEFITS AND COSTS OF FDI

Although there is a substantial literature which seeks to determine the impact of FDI, much of it is concerned with the macroeconomic implications. From this perspective, it is difficult to argue with the assertion of Georgiou and Weinhold (1992) that FDI is likely to increase international integration and interdependence by facilitating the trade of goods, services and knowledge, allowing countries to specialize more effectively and thereby to increase the benefits of comparative advantage based on trade and economies of scale. Thus, it is common to assess the overall national effects without examining the implications for regional economies.

The arguments for and against FDI which are most commonly encountered are neatly summarized in Giese et al. (1990). One of the principal arguments against is the charge that FDI will result in domestic overcapacity in conditions of stagnant or declining demand. Many would argue that the car manufacturing industry could be placed in this category.

Another argument against FDI is that foreign firms obtain an 'unfair' advantage when they produce in the domestic economy. This arises from any direct or indirect subsidies which might be given to the foreign firm. Examples would include government grants and the propensity to use foreign component suppliers over indigenous firms. The latter has often been used to criticize the quality of much Japanese manufacturing FDI. Anti-FDI arguments also normally point to the potential for a loss of economic control and are illustrated with images of Hood and Young's (1976) branch plant syndrome or the hollow corporation of Giese et al. (1990) where the foreign-owned subsidiary carries out relatively low level value-added activities with strategic decisions being made by a distant parent organization.

The arguments which are mounted in favour of FDI revolve around the idea that it will improve competitiveness and, thus, create employment and increase the welfare of the host nation. This is a result of inward investment increasing the number of entrants in the indigenous industry which forces all competitor firms in the industry to become more competitive by reducing costs and improving efficiency and quality. This should result in lower prices and more efficient levels of consumer service. Benefits may accrue from cooperation as well as competition. Much FDI activity is achieved by way of a joint venture between a foreign company and an indigenous company. Perlmutter and Heenan (1986) point to advantages which this sort of corporate collaboration may bring – such as risk diversification, capital requirement reductions and lower start-up costs. This may particularly apply to R&D, high technology industries where the opportunity for technology transfer will be considerable.

In order to study the impact which FDI makes, it is useful to think of the regional economic effects which are produced by the activities of MNE subsidiaries in terms of spatial units of account. The use of different economic space will obviously have a profound effect upon the welfare of a regional economy. Moreover, the fact that today's MNEs are integrating production capabilities at a global level by transferring factor inputs across international frontiers, means that their potential for impacting upon the economies of these countries will be considerable. When decisions are made to modify the nature of international investment flows, then the balances of the spatial units of account will also be changed.

It is because of this that any effective analysis of the impact of FDI must be based at the regional level. Impact analysis at a macroeconomic level will produce a net statement of costs and benefits and fail to reveal the regional losers and gainers. In addition, it is necessary to realize that FDI is not an homogeneous phenomenon (Pigozzi and Bagchi-Sen 1995). MNEs will use different entry modes when they participate in foreign markets. This chapter will argue that the study of regional impact may best be achieved through an analysis of the mode of entry which the MNE chooses in order to gain access to a foreign market. The entry mode will greatly influence the nature of the subsidiary which is set up by the MNE – for instance entry by some sort of contractual arrangement is unlikely to produce the sort of spillover effects which could potentially result from some form of direct ownership. To proceed, it is necessary to examine the concepts of entry mode and subsidiary type in further detail.

MNE ENTRY MODES AND SUBSIDIARY ROLES

A firm which seeks to operate outside its domestic market must select the most appropriate mode of entry into the foreign market. An international market entry mode may be defined as: 'an institutional arrangement that makes possible the entry of a company's products, technology, human skills, management, or other resources into a foreign country' (Root 1987).

Economists have normally viewed the entry mode variable as a simple choice between market entry based on trading relationships (i.e exporting) and direct investment in the host country economy. However, much corporate strategy literature in this field has highlighted the various contractual relationships which may be formulated in order to provide an intermediate entry mode between exporting and direct investment.[1] It is common practice (for example, Hill *et al.* 1990) to classify foreign market entry modes as follows:

- exporting – direct or indirect;
- contractual – such as licensing or franchising;
- joint ventures – equity or non-equity based;
- wholly owned – either greenfield or acquisition.

Exporting is unlikely to have any significant impact since it merely involves the transfer rather than the production of goods. While the contractual mode is capable of producing an impact upon the host economy, the nature of this impact will be principally limited to balance of payments effects, although it is possible for contractual modes to stimulate indigenous production.

Investment entry modes are said to exist where an international company possesses a total or partial production capability in a different country from that in which the parent company is domiciled. Sole ventures will involve full ownership and control by the parent organization and may be achieved by means of a greenfield investment or through the acquisition of a company or plant in the host country; joint ventures will be characterized by owner-ship and control being shared between the parent company and one or more (sometimes local) partners. The structure of collaborative agreements will vary considerably and this has the effect of making the study of the investment entry mode particularly difficult.

Joint ventures and strategic alliances are a comparatively new form of entry mode and one which has been increasing both in terms of frequency and strategic importance (Geringer and Hebért 1991). There is evidence to suggest that many MNEs would prefer the joint venture type of entry mode even when the government of the host nation does not require it as a condi-tion of entry (Beamish 1984). Harrigan (1985) noted the large number of US companies which favoured joint ventures and Contractor and Lorange (1987) found that all types of cooperative venture outnumbered wholly owned subsidiaries by a ratio of 4 to 1. Morris and Hegart's (1987) work shows that alliances are found in many different types of industrial sector. Not only has this increasingly influential entry mode been recognized empirically, but Beamish and Banks (1987) demonstrate how it may be incorporated into the theory of the MNE, using the transaction cost paradigm of Williamson (1975). The choice of an appropriate entry mode will be the result of a number of factors. International companies will often combine a contractual entry mode with that of an exporting or investment entry mode. The precise combination of entry modes is also likely to be a dynamic phenomenon and will change according to the variation in the influencing factors.

The corporate strategy literature has produced many subsidiary typologies,[2] principally designed for the purpose of producing a framework for the analysis of organizational decision-making. One of the most useful typologies which may be adapted for the analysis of regional impact is that devised by White and Poynter (1984). They used it to examine the impact of MNEs on the Canadian economy and it was also applied later by Young *et al.* (1988) to assess the type of MNE subsidiary which was present in the Scottish economy. Williams (1995b) has further developed this typology, redefining and renaming the ideal types to facilitate the capture of a wider range of subsidiary types, for use in impact analysis. The business of defining more and more categories of subsidiary types is, however, of limited operational significance.

The constraints of obtaining sufficiently disaggregated data are likely to result in a less ambitious classification. Even so, with information on the range of value added activities which the subsidiary undertakes and the amount of strategic autonomy which is given to the subsidiary, it is relatively easy to distinguish subsidiary types. In terms of the Williams (1995b) typology these may range from the transplant assembler type of subsidiary which will simply carry out low-level assembly and manufacturing activities to the global marketer, responsible for carrying out additional value added activities but only over a limited product range, or the global strategist which would be able to develop product lines for global markets.

Williams (1995b) also suggests that it is necessary to examine concepts such as the degree of control which the parent organization exerts over the subsidiary, the degree of networking which is undertaken, the contribution which the subsidiary makes to the value added chain and the degree of internalization which the activities of the subsidiary exhibit. These features may be thought of as the behaviour which shapes the organizational configuration of the MNE subsidiary.[3] This, in turn, will determine what sort of impact an MNE subsidiary will make. Participation in additional value added activities follows from the greater involvement by the subsidiary in downstream processes such as marketing and services. The opportunities for and the need to network will increase as the subsidiary develops further strategic relationships with suppliers and other firms.

The mode of entry selected by the MNE will have a significant influence upon the organizational characteristics of MNE subsidiaries. This will result in different types of MNE subsidiary and these will produce a differential level of impact on the regional economy in which they are located. The interrelationship between mode of entry and subsidiary type and the resultant effect upon the regional economy is particularly well illustrated in the case of an acquisition.[4]

The effect of an acquisition on regional employment will depend upon whether or not there is likely to be a net loss or gain of functions in the acquired firm as well as the extent to which suppliers in the parent company's country are used in preference to local suppliers. The transfer of functions and the use of suppliers in the home country could result from the desire to reap economies of scope and scale in the purchase of inputs. Should there be a gain in functions, then additional staff could either come from the internal labour market of the merged company, from the local external labour market or by immigration from other regions. If there should be a loss of functions and local supplier linkages then the displacement of key staff might see them migrating to other positions within the merged company or securing jobs with other companies. If this takes place within the regional economy others will be displaced.

There are additional explanatory variables which should be taken into account in the assessment of regional impact. One of these is MNE ownership. There is a considerable literature on the limited research and development (R&D) capability and local procurement activities of the subsidiaries of Japanese MNEs. The proliferation of routinized, low-level, value added activities is documented in Morris (1988) in respect of the UK and Milkman (1991) for the USA. Although these conclusions were contradicted by the work of those such as Garrahan and Stewart (1992), there is still considerable support for the assertion that the relatively low level of local decision-making among Japanese MNE subsidiaries severely limits the impact which they are able to make upon regional economic development. The fact that it remains an area of some controversy makes it a worthy subject of future research.

Another factor which could help to explain differential impact is that some MNEs possess a unique corporate culture which helps to shape the impact which they make upon the host economy. Ohmae (1990) illustrates the importance of this point when he refers to what Sony's Akio Morita describes as global localization. This results in a greater use of indigenous managers and suppliers, a recognition of local traditions, more strategic autonomy and, at the same time, an emphasis on customer care at the expense of the nationality of the parent firm.

There is also evidence to suggest that MNEs choose different entry modes for different national markets. For instance, Japanese MNEs have used acquisitions and joint ventures, to a significantly higher degree, when entering the US market than the European market (Yamawaki 1994). Yamawaki (1994) also produces some interesting analysis on sectoral differences in entry patterns between the USA and Europe. Kenney and Florida (1995) also illustrate how sectoral differences may lead to different employment effects.

DEVELOPING A MODEL TO ASSESS REGIONAL IMPACT

An operationally useful way of measuring the regional economic impact of FDI is to consider its effect on key economic variables such as employment, technology, linkages and spillovers, competitiveness, entrepreneurial capacity and the balance of payments. The nature of the impact which FDI has upon these factors will vary. It is important to differentiate between types of impact since the precise nature of the impact will have different consequences for the host economy. Specifically, FDI may have a direct, indirect and dynamic impact upon the economy. A direct impact will result in changes in factors such as employment, output, enterprise and the balance of payments, whereas the indirect impact will manifest itself in the creation of spillovers and linkages – typically in suppliers and customers. Finally, the dynamic impact will affect the competitive environment. Although the direct impact is the easiest to observe and measure, the indirect and dynamic impact could be just as, if not more, significant in terms of long run impact.

The employment effects and the linkages are those which are easiest to quantify and this is illustrated by the empirical work which has been completed in the past. The dynamic effects would need to be studied by means of a more qualitative approach such as structured interviews. Work which has been completed to date (for example, Bagchi-Sen 1991; Pigozzi and Bagchi-Sen 1995) to test whether the regional impact of FDI may be differentiated by entry mode suffers from a relatively unsophisticated conceptual framework and a reliance upon official data which have considerable shortcomings.

In order to overcome these conceptual and empirical problems it is necessary to collect firm-specific data via a fieldwork survey.[5] While it is acknowledged that there are difficulties with obtaining firm-specific data by a survey method, it is the only way of obtaining data which would allow one to construct a model of sufficient intricacy. Respondent companies could be asked to provide data about employment on entry, or another appropriate benchmark date and data which would pertain to their current situation. The danger of not comparing like with like is ever-present, but this method has the advantage of allowing the explanatory variables to become sector and region specific and of making the dependent variable a more accurate measure of the change in employment brought about by the regional FDI activity. Some proposals for constructing appropriate regression models to measure the direct and indirect effects are presented in Williams (1996). Briefly, these may be summarized as: direct effects and indirect effects.

Direct effects

Two of the most influential variables to examine would be employment and output. The former could be defined as the change in company employment which has taken place over the impact study period. Thus, we shall obtain a direct measure of the impact which foreign manufacturing investment has made over time. Following the conceptual framework which has been developed above, it is suggested that the model should test whether the mode of entry, the type of foreign subsidiary and the ownership of that subsidiary explain regional impact as measured by changes in employment. Therefore dummy variables would be included for these.

In constructing the model, however, it is important to identify additional variables, other than those connected with foreign investment, which might explain the change in company employment. Thus, it is suggested that the model should also include other explanatory variables which are not specifically connected with FDI. Because the demand for labour is a derived demand, these should include a measure of relative factor prices as well as the change in the level of sales turnover. Since the ability of firms to adjust their demand for labour depends, to a great extent, upon supply constraints, an attempt should be made to include a proxy in the regression model for labour market structure, as illustrated by Fair (1969). The regional unemployment rate could typically be used in this context. We have noted the potential for industrial sector in which the firm operates to influence employment and, thus, this variable should also be included in the model. The regression equation could be specified as follows:

$$\triangle CE = \triangle LMS, \triangle STO, SEC, \triangle WAGES, MOE, SUB, OWN$$

where:

$\triangle CE$ = Change in company employment
$\triangle LMS$ = Local Labour Market Structure (e.g. regional unemployment rate)
$\triangle STO$ = Change in company sales turnover
SEC = Industrial sector
$\triangle$Wages = Change in Regional Wage Level
MOE = Mode of Entry
SUB = Subsidiary Type
OWN = Ownership (Japanese, US or other)

The employment equation assumes that sales or output are exogenous in the short run and that output rates are determined in order to maximize profits at a given set of prices.[6] However, a more realistic long run perspective would be characterized by the endogeneity of sales turnover. Since sales turnover is likely to be a key determinant of company employment, a separate regression model could be constructed to determine whether sales/output are entry mode specific. It is suggested that the regression equation take the following form:

$$\triangle STO = \triangle PRICE, \triangle INC, FA, MOE, SUB, OWN$$

where:

$\triangle STO$ = Change in company sales turnover
$\triangle PRICE$ = Unit price index for sector
$\triangle INC$ = Weighted European/OECD GDP
FA = Firm Age (Current – Entry)
MOE = Mode of Entry

SUB = Subsidiary Type
OWN = Ownership (Japanese, US or other)

The sales turnover/output regression model will contain the mode of entry, subsidiary type and ownership explanatory variables as the change in employment model. Since sales turnover/output is expected to be a key determinant of any employment change, it would be appropriate to determine whether or not it is entry mode and ownership specific. It would be prudent not to restrict the analysis of the direct effects to employment for with substantial movements towards automation the employment equation may not be sufficiently sensitive to measure the direct effects of FDI. Output will not suffer from this potential problem and it could be further argued that the direct effects could also be measured by the inclusion of a profitability model. This could also produce additional problems since one would have to obtain further information, some of which may be regarded as confidential by potential respondents.

Additional explanatory variables have been added to the equation in order to capture that part of the change in sales turnover which is not explained by foreign market entry. Thus, the unit price index for the sector has been included since sales turnover movements may simply be a function of price changes within the sector. For the same reason, a measure of European GDP is included since sales changes could simply be reflecting general movements in income. Firm age is also included in the equation to measure the 'maturation effect'. Once a firm has gained entry into a foreign market, one would expect it to increase its ability to penetrate further and generate higher volumes of sales, ceteris paribus.

Indirect effects

These are mostly concerned with spillovers and linkages. Scott (1983) and Ó hUallacháin (1986) provide summaries of impact studies which indicate that the character of the local economy greatly influences the nature of linkage effects. These studies and more recent research conducted on the Scottish economy by Ashcroft and Love (1989) and Schachmann and Fallis (1989) in Germany demonstrate that the impact of FDI on the process of regional development is not consistent. Foreign owned firms which depend upon just-in-time (JIT) production methods appear to cultivate closer relationships with local suppliers.[7] Thus, Japanese firms which employ such techniques might prove more likely to develop local linkages. Ó hUallacháin (1986) notes that intra-regional linkages will tend to be sensitive to country of ownership, as well as product line and production technology.

Thus, it is appropriate to investigate the factors which might explain the development of linkages in the regional economy. Dummies would again be included for the entry mode, subsidiary type and ownership variables.

Drawing on the model developed by Barkley and McNamara (1994), linkages may be measured as the proportion of non-labour inputs which are purchased in the local region, the UK and the EU. Additional control variables could be specified such as firm size, firm age, industrial sector and the proportion of inputs which are purchased from the firm's largest supplier. Thus the linkages equation could be specified along the following lines:

Link = FS, FA, SEC, INCONC, MOE, SUB, OWN

where:

Link = per cent of non-labour input purchases from regional suppliers
FS = Firm size
FA = Age of firm (Current − Entry)
SEC = Industrial sector
INCONC = per cent Inputs acquired from the largest supplier
MOE = Mode of Entry
SUB = Subsidiary Type
OWN = Ownership (Japanese, US or other)

No analytical framework can eliminate the problems associated with the measurement of the dynamic effects of FDI. However, once data have been gathered on the type of subsidiary (in terms of its value added activities and strategic autonomy) which is operating in the host economy, a more qualitative approach (perhaps in the form of company case studies) could be taken to identify the dynamic impact. The measurement of dynamic impact, such as technology transfer and competitive effects, is necessarily complex and does not lend itself to a postal questionnaire approach. The inclusion of questions on such topics would lead to difficulties of quantification and almost certainly reduce the response rate. The analysis could be staged in an incremental manner with the strategy of the case study element being planned after the analysis of the direct and indirect effects. Although this involves a considerable research effort, it remains the most effective way of adding to our understanding of this most important subject. It should enable much more authoritative statements to be made about the impact of FDI upon the UK economy.

CONCLUSION

The study of the regional impact of FDI reveals obvious implications for regional economic development policy. Although there have been impact studies which seek to analyse the effect on localities or regions, the larger issue of long-term structural adjustment is one which has been relatively neglected.

It would be naive to suggest that the global ambitions of successful corporations will coincide with the need to influence regional development. Indeed the two factors could easily conflict – particularly if such corporations seek to extend their sphere of influence. However, until we have studied the impact of FDI projects with a greater degree of objectivity, it is not possible to be prescriptive. Application of the above framework would provide such objectivity.

Given the potential which FDI has to influence regional economic development, it is rather surprising that more research has not been carried out to investigate its regional effects. Much of the work which has been done in this area has tended to be empirical rather than analytical. This often produces interesting results but does not provide a framework for analysis. The above framework will provide the basis for analysis and prediction. Its derivation is eclectic and this explains its power.

Progress in the study of the regional impact of FDI demands that more rigorous and ambitious conceptual frameworks are developed in order to facilitate a more sophisticated empiricism. Entry modes, subsidiary types and regional development have been analysed from different academic perspectives. The appraisal of regional economic impact may be considerably strengthened by using some of the conceptual apparatus which has been assembled by the corporate strategists. The cost of this more rigorous approach is the effort of gaining firm-specific data. Realistic assessments of entry mode choice and subsidiary type will be almost impossible to make unless one mounts a fieldwork programme.

The benefits of such enquiry will be the development of a regional impact model which has considerable explanatory power. The process of regional development is necessarily the result of a complex interplay between indigenous and foreign investment and the environmental factors which shape the direction of such investment. Any model which attempts to explain such behaviour will, of necessity, include entry mode, subsidiary type and ownership variables which are influential in shaping the behaviour of MNEs in the host economy and, therefore, the impact which such firms make upon that host economy.

NOTES

1 See Williams (1995a) for a survey of the entry mode literature.
2 See Williams and Smith (1996) for a brief account of the more influential of these.
3 In general, as the subsidiary matures the amount of value added activities and the degree of networking will increase, whereas the degree of control and internalization are reduced. The latter follows from the fact that the subsidiary is likely to become more like indigenous firms over time and, thus, the need to internalize firm-specific advantages will diminish. The extent to which this happens will

depend upon the nature of the problems encountered by the subsidiary and the degree of development which is allowed by the parent company.

4 Ashcroft and Love (1993) use the Scottish economy to provide a comprehensive study of the effect of takeovers on the regional economy and illustrate the insight gained when mode of entry and subsidiary type are emphasized.

5 The author is currently engaged in such a survey and the results of the investigation should be available during 1997.

6 This is based on the well-established empirical and theoretical literature centred around the seminal work of Brechling (1965).

7 This is analysed in Mair *et al.* (1988) and Kenney and Florida (1995).

REFERENCES

Ashcroft, B. and Love, J.H. (1989) 'Evaluating the effects of external takeover on the performance of regional companies', *Environment and Planning A* 22: 197–220.

—— (1993) *Takeovers, Mergers and the Regional Economy*, Edinburgh: Edinburgh University Press.

Bagchi-Sen, S. (1991) 'Employment in foreign-owned manufacturing firms in the United States – the impact of modes of entry', *Tijdschrift voor Economische en Sociale Geografie* 82: 282–94.

Barkley, D.L. and McNamara, K.T. (1994) 'Local input linkages: a comparison of foreign-owned and domestic manufacturers in Georgia and South Carolina', *Regional Studies* 28 (7): 725–37.

Beamish, P.W. (1984) 'Joint venture performance in developing countries', Ph.D. thesis, University of Western Ontario.

Beamish, P.W. and Banks, J.C. (1987) 'Equity joint ventures and the theory of the multinational enterprise', *Journal of International Business Studies* 18: 1–16.

Brechling, F. (1965) 'The relationship between output and employment in British manufacturing industries', *Review of Economic Studies* 32: 187–216.

Contractor, F. and Lorange, P. (1987) *Cooperative Strategies in International Business*, Lexington MA: D.C. Heath.

Dunning, J.H. (1977) 'Trade, location of economic activity and MNE: a search for an eclectic approach', in B. Ohlin, P.-O. Hesselborn and P.M. Wilkman (eds) *The International Allocation of Economic Activity*, London: Macmillan.

—— (1981) 'Explaining the international direct investment position of countries: towards a dynamic or developmental approach', *Weltwirtschaftliches Archiv* 117: 30–64.

Fair, R.C. (1969) *The Short-run Demand for Workers and Hours*, Amsterdam: North-Holland.

Garrahan, P. and Stewart, P. (1992) *The Nissan Enigma: Flexibility at Work in a Local Economy*, London: Mansell.

Georgiou, G. and Weinhold, S. (1992) 'Japanese direct investment in the US', *World Economy* 15 (6): 761–78.

Geringer, J.M. and Hebért, L. (1991) 'Control and performance of international joint ventures', *Journal of International Business Studies* 20: 235–54.

Giese, A.S., Kahley, W.J. and Riefler, R.F. (1990) 'Foreign direct investment: motivating factors and economic impact', *Regional Science Perspectives* 20: 105–27.

Gray, H.P. (1992) 'The interface between the theories of international trade and production', in P.J. Buckley and M. Casson (eds) *Multinational Enterprises in the World Economy: Essays in Honour of John Dunning*, Aldershot: Edward Elgar.

Harrigan, K.R. (1985) *Strategies for Joint Ventures*, Lexington MA: D.C. Heath.

Hill, C.W.L., Hwang, P. and Kim, W.C. (1990) 'An eclectic theory of the choice of international entry mode', *Strategic Management Journal* 11: 117–28.

Hood, N. and Young, S. (1976) 'US investment in Scotland – aspects of the branch factory syndrome', *Scottish Journal of Political Economy*, XXIII (3): 279–94.

Kenney, M. and Florida, R. (1992) 'The Japanese transplants: production organisation and regional development', *Journal of the American Planning Association* 58: 21–38.

—— (1995) 'The transfer of Japanese management styles in two US transplant industries: autos and electronics', *Journal of Management Studies* 32 (6): 789–802.

Mair, A., Florida, R. and Kenney, M. (1988) 'The new geography of automobile production: Japanese transplants in North America', *Economic Geography* 64: 352–73.

Milkman, R. (1991) *Japan's Californian Factories: Labour Relations and Economic Globalisation*, Los Angeles: University of California, Institute of Industrial Relations.

Morris, D. and Hegart, M. (1987) 'Trends in international collaborative agreements', *Columbia Journal of World Business* 22: 15–21.

Morris, J. (1988) 'The who, why and where of Japanese manufacturing investment in the UK', *Industrial Relations Journal* 19: 31–40.

Ohmae, K. (1990) *The Borderless World*, London: Collins.

Ó hUallacháin, B. (1986) 'The role of foreign direct investment in the development of regional industrial systems: current knowledge and suggestions for a future American research agenda', *Regional Studies* 20: 151–62.

Perlmutter, H.V. and Heenan, D.A. (1986) 'Cooperate to compete globally', *Harvard Business Review* March–April: 78–86.

Pigozzi, B.W. and Bagchi-Sen, S. (1995) 'Impacts of acquisitions and new plants on the employment in US affiliates of foreign manufacturing firms', *Tijdschrift voor Economische en Sociale Geografie* 86: 328–38.

Root, F.R. (1987) *Entry Strategies for International Markets*, Lexington MA: D.C. Heath.

Schachmann, K. and Fallis, P. (1989) 'External control and regional development within the Federal Republic of Germany', *International Regional Science Review* 12: 245–61.

Scott, A.J. (1983) 'Location and linkage systems: a survey and reassessment', *Annals of Regional Science* 17: 1–39.

United Nations Conference on Trade and Development, Division on Transnational Corporations and Investment (UNCTAD) (1995) *World Investment Report:*

Transnational Corporations and Competitiveness, Geneva and New York: United Nations.

White, R.E. and Poynter, T.A. (1984) 'Strategies for foreign-owned subsidiaries in Canada', *Business Quarterly* Summer: 59–69.

Williams, D.A. (1995a) 'International market entry mode policies: a taxonomy and analysis of decision-making and its consequences for the performance of multi-national enterprises', *Economia, Societa' e Istituzioni* VII: 583–99.

—— (1995b) 'Entry mode decisions of multinational enterprises and their impact upon host economies: a framework for analysis', *British Review of Economic Issues* 17(43): 27–52.

—— (1996) 'Analysing the regional impact of foreign manufacturing firms', *Tijdschrift voor Economische en Sociale Geografie* 87: 259–65.

Williams, D.A. and Smith, D.J. (1996) 'Entry mode decisions of multinational enterprises and their impact on regional economic development', in S. Hill and B. Morgan (eds) *Inward Investment, Business Finance and Regional Development*, London: Macmillan.

Williamson, O.E. (1975) *Markets and Hierarchies: Analysis and Antitrust Implications – A Study in the Economics of Internal Organisations*, New York: Free Press, Macmillan.

Yamawaki, H. (1994) 'Entry patterns of Japanese multinationals in US and European manufacturing', in M. Mason and D. Encarnation (eds) *Does Ownership Matter? Japanese Multinationals in Europe*, Oxford: Oxford University Press.

Young, S., Hood, N. and Dunlop, S. (1988) 'Global strategies, multinational subsidiary roles and economic impact in Scotland', *Regional Studies* 22: 487–97.

10

COMMENTARY ON CHAPTER 9

George A. Petrochilos

David Williams is interested in the impact that inward foreign direct investment has on a regional level. He believes that the study of regional impact may best be achieved through an analysis of the mode of entry which multinational enterprises choose in order to gain access to a foreign market, and proposes to develop a model to assess the regional impact of their operations.

The chapter tends to be economical with analysis, explanation and examples and provides a number of statements which readers are expected to accept at face value. For instance, we are told that the EU provides a good illustration of how divided countries are on their attitudes to FDI, without providing any evidence to back up this assertion. On the contrary, the EU members are not equivocal on direct investment. The Treaty of Rome regulates for freedom of capital and subsequent directives have provided practical substance to this principle, so that today complete liberalization of capital flows of any kind has been achieved among the fifteen EU member states. This is to be expected, since one of the characteristics of common markets and economic unions is the explicit encouragement of capital flows, providing one of the dynamic economic benefits to the participants. Member states of the EU are free to control or liberalize both inward and outward direct investment from third countries, and such investment flows have, in general, been encouraged by all concerned (Burgenmeier and Mucchielli 1991).

The statement that 'FDI has eclipsed the role of trade flows in the world', because the sales of multinationals in 1990 reached $5.2 trillion worldwide as against exports of goods and non-factor services of $4.9 trillion, is like comparing apples with oranges, since not all output of the multinationals is traded internationally. The right comparison is between FDI flows and trade flows. While FDI flows have been increasing from an annual average of $77 billion in the period 1983–7, to $177 billion in 1988–92, to $210 billion in 1993 and $226 billion in 1994 to reach $314 billion in 1995, they represent a tiny percentage of total trade (*Financial Times* 1996; UNCTAD 1996).

One is also uneasy with the statements that 'there has been little analysis of the strategic implications of FDI', what there has been 'is limited to the rivalrous behaviour of oligopolistic firms', but that there is a well-developed theory 'which has attempted to explain why MNEs should exist in spite of the costs of operating across international frontiers'. In the past thirty-five to forty years a voluminous literature has appeared, which has turned the subject of foreign direct investment and its vehicles, the multinationals, into a separate area of economics. This literature has, among others, analysed the determinants and the role of FDI. In particular, the impact of multinationals on both the home and host countries has received and is still receiving considerable attention, as browsing through some of the recent surveys shows, for example, Dunning (1993) and Caves (1996). As far as theories of FDI are concerned, they have ranged from Hymer's market power paradigm and the role of ownership advantages, to the internalization hypothesis, to Dunning's 'eclectic' theory – incorporating ownership, locational and internalization (OLI) elements, to the competitive industry approach, to the macroeconomic developmental model, and, finally, to the international division of labour theory. In addition, the literature has examined the rise of multinational companies domiciled in less developed countries and has tried to explain it in terms of the product cycle model and the theory of localized technological change. In terms of the economic effects of multinationals on the host countries, the literature has considered, mostly, effects on output, employment, balance of payments, productivity, technology, training, management, interindustry linkages and also effects on competition and market structure. Various writers have looked at such effects both from a national macroeconomic and a regional perspective. By and large, the positive effects of foreign direct investment on output, employment, technology, training, productivity, trade and financial flows have been well documented in the literature, and explain why countries are eager to attract such investment. Additionally, multinationals help significantly in the process of integration of the recipient countries in the international economy.

However, one needs also to be clear as to the limits of the foreign direct investment process and should not place excessive expectations on such a process, particularly as regards regional economic development. The role of multinationals is not to develop less developed countries or 'grey' areas of developed ones but to make money. Consequently, in sourcing for supplies, as in other aspects of their operations, the paramount motive is efficiency leading to profitability. Similarly, if local managers, engineers, technicians, foremen and skilled labour can be found, or can be trained reasonably quickly, subsidiaries have a very good reason, on grounds of cost, to use them, since using such people from elsewhere is costlier and could also prove inefficient. Multinationals are not charity institutions, so, if domestic suppliers (regional or otherwise) can supply components, materials and parts at the quality and quantity required and at competitive prices, most probably they will be preferred, both on cost grounds and public relations grounds with the host authorities. Earlier work in this area has shown that, in most instances, it has been the inability of local suppliers to meet the exact specifications required by the subsidiaries that has led them to sourcing from outside the host country. Such basic economic questions are common to all subsidiaries, irrespective of nationality, and must be answered before one looks for second or even third order determinants, like culture or nationality of the subsidiary, to explain their differences in decision-making.

What FDI can provide, however, is a stimulus to certain sectors of the host economy and through its multiplier effects can help in the restructuring of those sectors. This restructuring can be achieved if the foreign direct investment manages to trigger off the energy and interest of domestic resources, so that through a process of contact and emulation such domestic resources can be utilized and the host economy can achieve a managerial and entrepreneurial competence. Indeed, the higher the complementarity of foreign direct investment with domestic investment, the higher the degree of success of the restructuring process of the host economy. If such resources happen to be directed to specific regions then it is only to be expected that some of the benefits of foreign direct investment referred to will be felt in that region, for example, the southern coastal areas of China and other South East Asia growth triangles have been greatly affected by inward foreign direct investment. However, trying to estimate such effects on regions will present probably insurmountable difficulties. The plethora and the kind of disaggregated data required, particularly as regards leakages, to estimate impact and other multipliers for specific regions, is such as to make a project of this nature very difficult, if not almost impossible, to achieve.

As regards the different entry modes of multinationals to different markets for all practical purposes we can distinguish, as the author does, between a greenfield investment and an acquisition or takeover of a domestic firm. This can result in the subsidiary either being owned exclusively by the parent company or taking the form of a joint venture with a local producer. Each of these entry modes has advantages and disadvantages and the actual mode which is chosen in each particular case requires the weighing up of such advantages and disadvantages. While we are told that Japanese multinationals have used acquisitions and joint ventures to a significantly higher degree when entering the US market than the European market, we are not offered any reasons for their preference. Yet it would be helpful to know so that we can assess better the significance of such entry modes as explanatory variables in the modelling exercise, particularly if they are to be proxied by dummy variables.

When it comes to measuring the regional impact of FDI, the author rightly sets out 'to consider its effect on key economic variables such as employment, technology, linkages and spillovers, competitiveness, entrepreneurial capacity and the balance of payments'. Leaving aside for the moment the appropriateness of the choice of the balance of payments in a regional context, the proposed model only deals with two of these variables: employment and linkages. Nothing is said of the rest. Why not? Are they not important? In fact one could argue that the effects of FDI on employment at best can only be modest, given the technological bias and the capital intensive nature of most foreign direct investment. For example, effects on output might be a more appropriate variable to consider, and one which can be more readily available, which the author does not consider.

Turning to some methodological points, generally, the kind of econometric model we build depends on the usage that will be made of it, whether for analytical, forecasting or policy purposes. Typically, the effects of changes in an exogenous variable, like foreign direct investment, on appropriately chosen endogenous variables, for example, output, over a given period of time can be measured by means of impact, interim (dynamic) and total multipliers. Such multipliers can be estimated, depending on the nature of the structural form of the model, either from the reduced form or the final form of the model. This will require a time-series dynamic econometric model, which must show not only how the current values of the endogenous variables are generated from knowledge of the predetermined variables and the stochastic terms, but could also show how the time paths of the exogenous and the stochastic terms determine the time path of the endogenous variables of interest (Theil 1971; Petrochilos 1989: 114). If one is not interested in estimating multiplier effects, but merely concerned with the significance of particular determinants on a specific dependent variable, one need only proceed with the estimation of the structural relationship(s). In all cases, however, the relationships must be specified correctly and must be identified. In the case of a one-equation model, again what is required is correct specification, so that important explanatory variables are not omitted. If dynamic effects are needed then the model must be formulated as an appropriate distributed lag.

It is not at all clear how this can be achieved by what the author proposes, although it could be argued that there may be a different interpretation to the terms 'direct', 'indirect' and 'dynamic impact upon the economy' and the way they can be measured. Nevertheless, the idea that 'the dynamic effects would need to be studied by means of a more qualitative approach such as structured interviews', rather than what was suggested earlier simply puts a completely different meaning to the word dynamic from that normally used in economics. More importantly, the proposed model (two equations, functions) to estimate employment is flawed on a number of grounds. To mention a few points: it is not made clear whether it is a one-equation model, or a simultaneous two-equations model, which will have implications about the appropriate estimating method to be used; on whether one is dealing with time series or cross-sectional data, most probably the latter in which case we cannot derive dynamic effects; in addition there is no evidence of any dynamic formulation, since no lags are present. There is little by way of convincing analysis on the variables entering the regression; on how such variables are measured; on the appropriateness of representing foreign direct investment by dummies of the type SUB, OWN, MOE instead of level variables, such as millions of pounds; on how one justifies the values given to the dummies by which certain variables will be represented; on why the structure of the labour markets – by which one may justifiably mean a competitive or monopsonistic or monopolistic regime, can be represented by the regional unemployment rate; on how the industrial sectors are to be represented; and, on what the a priori expectations are regarding the signs of the regression coefficients.

In short, one is left with a bitter taste of ad hockery and entitled even to ask whether such a model is really necessary in the first place, in the light also of the fact that the author has published very similar material elsewhere and still no quantification is offered. If one is interested in the employment effects of foreign investors in a particular region, this can easily be accomplished through official data or questionnaires, but one certainly does not need an econometric model, elaborate or otherwise for this purpose. That the performance of multinationals is affected by the mode of entry is only to be expected: output and employment are bound to be higher under greenfield than under any other type. However, nationality, culture and other aspects tend to be second or even third order determinants, as mentioned above, and one may have better pickings by concentrating attention to economic determinants, which are first order.

REFERENCES

Burgenmeier, B. and Mucchielli, J.L. (eds) (1991) *Multinationals and Europe*, London: Routledge.

Caves, R.E. (1996) *Multinational Enterprise and Economic Analysis*, 2nd edn, Cambridge: Cambridge University Press.

Dunning, J.H. (1993) *Multinational Enterprises and the Global Economy*, Reading MA: Addison Wesley.

Financial Times (1996) 'Multinationals spur surge in investment', 25 September.

Petrochilos, G.A. (1989) *Foreign Direct Investment and the Development Process: The Case of Greece*, Aldershot: Avebury.

Theil, H. (1971) *Principles of Econometrics*, Chichester: John Wiley.

UNCTAD (1996) *World Investment Report, Investment, Trade and International Policy Arrangements*, Geneva and New York: United Nations.

11

SHALLOW FOUNDATIONS

Labour and the selective regulation of free trade

Robert O'Brien

In recent decades the liberalization of trade and other international economic activity has been accompanied by an expansion of international regulation. Indeed, a sound regulatory framework is a necessary component of such liberalization. This regulation has taken place primarily in fields designed to facilitate competition between private firms. Such regulation is thought to accomplish a number of tasks. First, it increases efficiency as competition takes place in a larger market as a result of countries liberalizing their economies. Second, it provides a common set of rules creating a fair and stable decision-making environment for companies and investors. Third, the regulatory framework can serve to mediate conflict and depoliticize trade disputes as they are channelled through an international legal structure. However, the question of which fields to regulate and how regulation should be accomplished is not simply a technical or economic matter. It is also a political question and requires some consideration of political issues.

The existing strategy of regulation in areas meant to increase competition, but not in what might be called areas of 'social' regulation creates two problems. The first problem is that selective regulation is seen to benefit some social interests and harm others. For example, removing restrictions on the flow of investment may be seen to serve the interests of mobile capital and harm the interests of less mobile labour. This leads to the second problem – the conflict between groups trying to repoliticize the issue of international economic regulation and those seeking to continue the limitation of the regulatory package to technical issues.

The argument of this chapter is that international economic regulation should increasingly be thought of as an issue of political economy, rather than one of economic or technical questions. Failure to take account of wider political and social concerns leads to a four-stage process which produces less than satisfactory results. The process unfolds as follows:

1   Initially, proposals are advanced which aim to regulate in a narrow economic manner.

2   These proposals generate opposition by groups that feel their concerns have been ignored or worsened by such proposals. They attempt to politicize the issue and shift the regulatory agenda onto other fields.

3   A compromise is reached which favours the initial economic regulation, but makes minor concessions to other forms of regulation. Since the concessions are part of an ad hoc bargaining process rather than an integral aspect of the regulatory framework, the result can be peculiar in terms of implementation and effect.

4   Regulatory conflict leaves the framework with shallow support in national societies and subject to future amendment or even repudiations.

This chapter is an illustration of the four-staged process, with particular reference to labour issues. The first section examines the expanding nature of trade liberalization and the degree to which this is turning economies inside out. Activity that was originally considered to be the preserve of those inside a particular political community defined by state borders is now considered to be of concern to those outside the community. The second section considers the expansion of international regulation to facilitate this movement from inside to outside. The issue of subsidy regulation is put forward to demonstrate a key element of the regulatory framework – the variability of its powers to ensure compliance and enforce norms according to the particular institution and issue in question. The exclusion of particular forms of regulation is also highlighted. Section three concentrates on labour and its attempts to reregulate social issues as they also follow the logic of externalizing the internal. Following brief overviews of developments in North America (NAFTA) and the European Union (EU), the issue of labour standards at the World Trade Organization (WTO) will be examined.

The issue of labour standards at the WTO is crucial because it is one indicator of the degree to which international economic regulation will be flexible enough to accommodate broad social interests. The labour–WTO debate centres around whether labour issues will be handled in a forum which has a high chance of securing compliance through the eventual threat of enforcement and sanction. The alternative is for the more economic regulation to be backed by a high degree of compliance via the WTO while other forms of regulation languish in consultative institutions. The chapter concludes by arguing that this latter approach may undermine the political legitimacy of the WTO and prove to be a fatal weakness in the stability of the emerging system of international political economic regulation.

EXPANDING TRADE

The trade liberalization process can (and is) interpreted in numerous ways. Two of the most obvious are: as a constant knife-edge struggle between the forces of liberalization and those of protectionism (Bhagwati 1988), and as a slow but inexorable drive to the creation of a single worldwide economic unit (Dicken 1992). Although these appear as rival interpretations, they can be complementary if applied to different time frames. The knife-edge struggle is more appropriate when looking at specific moments of decision in which the fate of particular initiatives lies in the balance. The more teleological vision of ever-increasing liberalization is a more accurate representation of the whole post-1945 experience. Put another way, the liberalizing initiative is contingent upon particular events and political struggles that could edge it in other directions.

An overview of the history of the General Agreement on Tariffs and Trade (GATT) will demonstrate how these views reflect reality at different time periods. There is no doubt that there has been a struggle to liberalize trade in the postwar period. The early failure of the International Trade Organization, GATT Tokyo Round disputes about non-tariff barriers and the Uruguay Round collisions over agriculture, cultural industries and regulation of services stand as evidence of the particular battles fought over economic liberalization (Brown 1950; Winham 1986; Croome 1995). However, from the perspective of 1995, one can look back and trace a history of increasing liberalization punctuated with occasional pauses.

The pre-1970s experience of trade liberalization was one of continuing success at reducing the primary barrier to trade – tariffs. While some areas were avoided such as textiles and agriculture, the reduction of tariffs, especially between developed countries was continual and dramatic. Indeed, the decrease in tariffs and movement to what would formerly have been considered free trade was so great that focus moved to non-tariff barriers (NTBs) to trade. These NTBs can take many forms and may or may not have trade hindrance as their primary intention. They cover a large range of domestic economic regulation and can include items such as health and safety measures, use of subsidies to support domestic industries, discriminatory taxes, aid to cultural industries, discriminatory treatment favouring domestic firms, environmental regulations, fair trade legislation. NTBs remain an obstacle to pure free trade, but their very presence on the agenda signals the success of liberalization efforts in more traditional areas.

The conclusion of the Uruguay Round, although much delayed and fraught with conflict, signals another advance in the liberalization process. One of the most obvious accomplishments was the establishment of the World Trade Organization. After the failure of the International Trade Organization to make it past the US Congress in the early 1950s, the multilateral system had been forced to extend use of the temporary GATT to coordinate trade liberalization. Over forty years later it was finally agreed that trade needed a proper institution to facilitate further work. Another long-lasting problem was breached in the Uruguay Round – the liberalization of agriculture. The tariffication of agricultural protection represents a strategic victory for free traders, as these will eventually be reduced and eliminated.

More important than reform in the agricultural sector for the expansion of the notion of free trade was the inclusion of three new areas into multilateral negotiations: services, intellectual property rights (TRIPs) and trade related investment measures (TRIMs). By reaching an agreement to regulate in these fields, the very definition of what free trade should apply to was expanded from the exchange of manufactured goods and commodities to areas of the economy that were increasingly valuable to many states. These issue areas share two characteristics but have one important difference from the subject of later parts of this chapter – labour standards. The similarities to discussion about labour standards is that these issues were formerly considered to be areas of domestic jurisdiction and there tended to be a split between government representatives from Northern and Southern countries. Southern leaders were initially reluctant to put the subjects on the negotiating table. The primary difference with the issue of labour standards is that regulation in the areas of services, intellectual property and investment restrictions were sectors which would benefit Northern corporate interests. Indeed, the emergence of these issues reflects a shift in comparative advantage in Northern economies to emerging activities in the service and knowledge fields.

The issue of restrictions on investment as a trade issue brings our attention to the general link between what is usually called trade liberalization and investment. One of the dominant economic trends of the postwar years has been the growth of transnational corporations. As their share of economic activity has increased, so has their importance in influencing trade flows. Although it is extremely difficult to find precise figures, one estimate is that more than half of total trade (exports and imports) of both the USA and Japan is conducted within transnational corporations. The estimates for UK trade in manufactures is as high as four-fifths (Dicken 1992: 49). A result of this increasing importance of transnational investment to trade flows is the emergence of trade agreements which have more to do with attracting and keeping investment than breaking down barriers to the movement of goods. The Canada–US Free Trade Agreement (FTA) and the North American Free Trade Agreement (NAFTA) are good examples. While there is no doubt that the FTA was about liberalizing trade, it was primarily concerned with facilitating investment into the Canadian market. The Canadian government's primary objective was not to free trade, but to secure access to the US market so that investment would continue to take place in Canada. In a similar manner, the Mexican government valued NAFTA for the signals it would send to investors about the emergence of the Mexican economy as a safe home for funds to be located.

To summarize, one could describe the implications of the increasing liberalization of trade as turning national economies inside out. What was formerly considered to be inside the boundaries of a national political community now spills over into the international arena and what used to be other political communities' domestic economy. This externalizing of the economy has led to demands for, and efforts at, creating inter- or supra-national regulations to govern this activity. As such, discussions about trade regulation are increasingly about regulating domestic economies.

INTERNATIONALIZING REGULATION

One of the interesting aspects of deeper economic integration and the increasing movement to liberalizing or freeing trade has been the need for more extensive international regulation. As economic activity becomes inter-nationalized activities in one country have an increasingly important effect on others. The last decade has witnessed an explosion of attempts at international economic regulation. The conclusion of the Uruguay Round is an example of increased and deeper regulation on a multilateral basis. The NAFTA signals a move from bilateral ad hoc regulation to formalized continental economic regulation. To use President Reagan's phrase, it was an attempt to create an economic constitution for North America. The relaunch of European integration in the 1980s with the Single European Act and enforcement of competition policy signifies an extension of continental regulation. Even in the Asia–Pacific region, characterized by market led integration and open regionalism, the need for institutions to facilitate economic interdependence has led to the creation and elaboration of the Asia Pacific Economic Cooperation Forum (APEC).

Before proceeding to the next section it is necessary to clarify what is meant by international regulation and to identify the key variable of compliance. This chapter takes international regulation to mean the creation and agreement of rules guiding activity within and across state borders through institutions that sit above or outside individual states. While discussion in economics literature often uses the term regulation, the discipline of inter-national relations refers to the practice as governance. Indeed, an international relations literature continues to grow around the concept of governance without government (Rosenau and Czempiel 1992).

Broadly interpreted, regulation can take many forms in a variety of subject areas. For example, multilateral economic institutions such as the IMF can participate in regulating the economies of developing countries through the implementation of structural adjustment programmes. Private bond rating agencies can assist in the regulation of national and local budgets by their

pronouncements on the credit worthiness of particular states or munici-
palities (Sinclair 1994). Both of these examples may be considered loose or
indirect regulation in that advice is offered about how economic activity
should be structured, but the decision is left to the political authorities
involved as to whether or not they will accept that advice. Choice is
restricted, however, in that the economic cost of ignoring such advice may
be capital flight or diversion.

Existing international regulation is marked by a plethora of institutions
and actors such as the IMF, World Bank, European Union, NAFTA, APEC,
UN, bond rating agencies, financial markets and the GATT/World Trade
Organization. Their ability to secure compliance with regulations varies from
institution to institution and even across issue areas in the same institutions.
For example, the UN has been successful in securing Iraqi compliance to its
resolutions with regard to the territorial integrity of Kuwait, but has had less
success in its resolutions in Israeli-occupied territory on the West Bank or the
violent struggles in Bosnia. Compliance has a relationship to the ability to
enforce decisions, especially upon the most powerful state actors.

The issue of subsidy regulation is particularly useful for judging
compliance and enforcement because it infringes upon national regulation in
explicit terms in that it seeks to restrict the freedom of governments to spend
as they see fit. Thus, it is a hard case from which one can gauge the ability of
these regulatory agreements to ensure national compliance with international
regulation. It is helpful briefly to consider the issue of compliance and
enforcement of regulation in three arenas where these issues have recently
been highlighted – NAFTA, the EU and GATT/WTO.

To simplify a complicated tale, it appears that regulation and enforcement
in the subsidy area ranges from weak in North America to strong in the
European Union with the multilateral framework moving from a weak
GATT to a strong WTO (O'Brien 1997). Canada and the USA were unable
to agree to a common subsidy code, despite years of negotiation and the
prominence of the issue in bilateral relations. The sensitivity of the Canadian
public to a US-centric code and the unwillingness of the US Congress to
consent to a diminution of its trade enforcement powers forced a unique
compromise upon the negotiators. The Canadians were unwilling to agree to
a subsidy code that targeted cherished domestic policies such as regional
development, natural resource policies and protection of cultural industries.
The US Congress was loath to restrict its ability to countervail Canadian
producers who cheated in trade by drawing upon government assistance. The
result was that the Canada–United States Free Trade Agreement and the
North American Free Trade Agreement were restricted to the establishment
of binational and trinational panels tasked with ensuring that domestic legislation was applied fairly. There was no possibility of reaching common
standards or creating a mechanism that would police subsidy practices on a
continental basis.

Not surprisingly, given its more elaborate institutional structure, the EU has a much stronger enforcement mechanism for policing its subsidy regulatory arrangements. The European Commission is empowered to rule against national subsidy practices and order the abolition or repayment of illegal subsidies. In the push for a single market by 1992 a number of Competition Commissioners took the lead in revitalizing control over state aids and enforcing discipline upon member states. Although state aid decisions are often influenced by political considerations, the degree of success that they have achieved is remarkable. In addition to intervention in a number of high profile cases such as the British government's bargain sale of British Aerospace, there is some evidence that the Commission's policy is shifting state intervention strategies into narrow areas permitted by subsidy regulations. Preliminary evidence seems to suggest that EU governments have shifted state aid away from intervening on behalf of particular firms or industries to either horizontal or regional aid. Horizontal aids are those which are not specific to particular sectors, such as aid to assist in environmental protection, support of small and medium enterprises, or energy conservation. Comparisons of the periods 1986–8 and 1988–90 reveal that the percentage of manufacturing sector aid aimed at particular sectors has decreased from 26 to 20 per cent while the percentage for horizontal aid has risen from 40 to 42 per cent and the percentage of regional aid has risen from 34 to 38 per cent (European Commission 1992: 27).

If the North American case illustrates an unimpressive degree of compliance and enforcement of subsidy norms and the European Union an impressive case, the multilateral level seems to be in transition from weak to strong. The inability of GATT to restrict subsidy practices was a source of great frustration to industries and government in the USA and became a point of contention in both the Tokyo and Uruguay GATT rounds of negotiations. The Uruguay Round made significant strides in tightening up subsidy practices. Contracting parties were finally able to agree upon a definition of subsidy, the category of prohibited subsidies was expanded, the US specificity test was enshrined, and demands for notification strengthened. Equally important was the revision of dispute settlement procedure at the World Trade Organization which eliminated the ability of a state on the 'losing' end of a panel decision to block general acceptance of an investigative report.

Conflict over subsidy regulation at the WTO will continue as provisions in the areas of restricting subnational subsidies, the question of specificity and environmental exceptions will most likely be the subject of considerable dispute. Significantly, the legal basis of implementing decisions has been tightened up and it may be the case that even the most powerful states will accede to international subsidy regulation despite controversial cases. The jury will be out on the eventual success of this procedure until the USA is faced with a decision to accept or reject a controversial ruling in this domain.

It is clear that different disciplines and degrees of regulation of the subsidy issue exist in different regulatory arenas. It is also clear that the trend is towards increased international, if uneven, regulation in this sphere. For this study the interesting question is why such regulation is needed for the liberalization of economic relations. From a strictly liberal position there is no need to regulate subsidy practices as they are of little economic importance. Their effect is to give a gift from the government and tax payers of one country to the consumers of another. Governments should not take any retaliatory action against subsidized exports as 'no country can gain at the expense of another by subsidizing its exports or restricting its imports' (Stone 1988: 119). From a purely liberal economic perspective, instituting counter-vailing duties against subsidized imports is counterproductive as they only raise the cost of products to domestic consumers and producers (Rugman 1986: 372). They are as inefficient for the country levying them as subsidies are for the exporting country. In theory, countries need not concern them-selves greatly about other countries' subsidy practices. Yet, regulation in the subsidy area is deemed essential if liberalization is to continue. Why?

There are two explanations. The first has to do with the political economy of liberalization and the second has to do with the desire to create single markets. In the first instance, subsidy disputes are about the conflict generated by increasing competition. This conflict emerges from two sectors. The first is from workers displaced by competition who turn to trade laws as a form of protection in the absence of other adjustment mechanisms. The second impetus for conflict is the corporate strategy of firms seeking compet-itive advantage by tying competitors up in legal knots. The goal is to impose high costs (both in terms of money and time) upon commercial rivals. Regulation may be necessary to contain interstate conflict generated by firms and workers using the subsidy issue and accusations of unfair trade to bludgeon competitors. In the subsidy area, regulatory mechanisms have been designed to channel political conflict generated by increased economic interdependence.

The second argument in favour of subsidy regulation concerns eliminating distortions in the market caused by government intervention. This is particu-larly convincing in the case of highly integrated markets or where attempts are being made to create single markets. The justification for an intensified European competition policy was based on the argument that the move to a single market could be frustrated or distorted by national governments pursuing active state aid policies (European Commission 1989). For example, a single market in European airline transportation would be frustrated if British Airways operated as a private company, but Air France was propped up by government subsidies. This would harm the commercial success of the most efficient enterprise and skew the distribution of resources within the market. This logic is a more market oriented case for international subsidy regulation.

Moving on from the subsidy issue example, one can see the expansion of international regulation into many areas formerly considered the preserve of national states. State spending initiatives will be increasingly constrained by agreements regulating government procurement. Competition policy governing the behaviour of firms is set to take its place alongside subsidy policy. The expansion of trade regulation into services opens up the possibility of international regulation of financial services and professional standards. Intellectual property agreements indicate a move to international regulation of patents and royalties. The tariffication of agriculture foreshadows international regulation of agricultural policy. Although the specifics of arrangements in these fields have yet to be decided and the degrees of compliance and enforcement will undoubtedly vary, the movement to expanded international economic regulation appears clear enough.

As important as the advances in international regulation are, the absences of regulation are equally telling. The regulation/non-regulation divides rest upon a particular view of economic and political regulation. Regulation is sought in the strictly economic spheres and avoided in those that are 'political'. Economic regulation has to do with assisting in the free movement of capital, goods and services. Subjects outside this area are not 'economic' in that they may deal with social issues or be racked by political considerations. To take a slightly different view, those regulations which assist in freeing market forces and increasing competition between private enterprises are seen as being economic, while those that might pose restrictions upon market forces are viewed as political. For example, competition and subsidy policies will increase the competitiveness of markets by ensuring a level playing field for all firms and restricting the activity of government to particular narrow policy fields. In contrast, environmental or labour standards are seen to lessen competition by reducing differences upon which comparative advantages are based. They will interfere with the market's efficient allocation of resources based upon differences in factor endowments. Equally seriously, they will generate political conflict as some governments attempt to defend their sovereign rights from interference in such political matters.

The desirability of a firm distinction between economic and political or social regulation supported by economic liberals and the majority of trade negotiators is not universally shared. The movement of particular regulatory powers from state to international arenas accompanied by an insistence that others remain confined to domestic jurisdiction raises questions about the interests being served by such a segregation. Having struggled for decades to bind together a humane form of regulation encompassing 'economic' and 'social' regulation in the form of the welfare state, it is unlikely that privileging of economic regulation at the international level will be met with acquiescence. The next section of the chapter examines three examples of how this struggle over regulation in the labour field is being played out.

SOCIAL REGULATION RETURNS

In his attempt to explain the rise of fascism and the great transformation of the early twentieth century, Karl Polanyi (1957) points to a key double movement in the historical process. The first part of this movement was the post-World War I attempt to reimpose a liberal economic system (primarily in the form of the gold standard) upon a population which had been mobilized by the horrors of total war and were looking for new political and economic arrangements. The second part of the historical movement was the counter-initiative by sectors of civil society and the politicians who led them to regain control over the economic system through government intervention and planning. Polanyi interprets the rise of fascism, the US New Deal and communist five-year plans as different manifestations of the similar desire to reassert control over the liberal market economy.

One need not accept Polanyi's views of the socialist conclusion to the battle over control of the economy to recognize that the success in liberalizing economic activity has brought forth a response from elements of civil society seeking to reimpose regulation on the market economy. The ever-widening reach of international competition, the increase in jurisdiction of international economic and legal institutions, and the mobility of capital has led those groups most threatened and vulnerable to such activity to take steps to restrict their losses. Although lagging behind the initiatives of business, a number of groups are attempting to externalize national regulation in areas of most concern to themselves. This section will briefly examine the experiences of the EU and NAFTA before concentrating on the emerging conflict at the WTO.

The European Union

Economic liberalization in Western Europe has made steady progress since the early 1950s. It has been institutionalized through the European Coal and Steel Community (ECSC), the European Economic Community and more recently the European Union. Critical to progress in this most elaborate form of international regulation has been a commitment to wide-ranging regulation encompassing both 'economic' and 'social' elements.

The ECSC was the first postwar European integration effort which contained an element of supranationalism. Its purpose was to create a common market for coal and steel which would facilitate further European integration and contribute to peaceful relations between France and Germany. Although the goal was to liberalize economic activity and regulate on a transnational basis, provision was made for the welfare and support of workers in less competitive areas. Despite a desire to eliminate subsidies, special arrangements were implemented allowing state assistance to the weaker industries of Belgium and Italy because of the weak state of their coal industries (Diebold 1959: 194–222).

The founding of the European Economic Community was greatly facilitated by a major act of social regulation known as the Common Agricultural Policy (CAP). In 1958, 24 per cent of the French, 16 per cent of Germans and 33 per cent of Italians were engaged in agriculture (Nagle 1976: 22). Across the new Community, 20 per cent or approximately 15 million people were engaged in farming (Swann 1992: 222). The central political deal allowing for the general economic liberalization of the EEC was trading German desire for free access for its manufactured goods against the French desire for access and support for its agricultural goods. While the CAP has been the source of considerable dispute, it was the essential political deal providing social regulation which laid the foundation for extensive Western European liberalization under the EC umbrella.

Accompanying the drive to a single European market in the 1980s has been the effort to build and regulate a 'social' Europe through the establishment of a set of social rights and a greater voice for labour in European decision-making (Wise and Gibb 1993). On the labour front, an attempt was made in 1985 to bring together the major social partners of labour, business and government through a social dialogue. The Val Duchesse talks proved of little value as employers saw them primarily as a forum for discussion while the labour unions wanted the talks to influence Community policy. Although the plans for macro consultation have proved futile, some movement has occurred at the micro level with initiatives to encourage consultation and participation at the individual firm level through European Works Councils. With regard to social regulation, in December 1989 all EC states except for Great Britain adopted the Charter of Fundamental Social Rights of Workers.

The most recent struggle over European integration and regulation has been around the issue of monetary union. In the late autumn of 1995 French workers took to the streets in protest at the government's attempt to slash expenditure. The French government was under immense pressure to reduce its budget deficit to meet the economic convergence criteria set out by the Maastricht Treaty for monetary union. European integration demanded that a particular economic and monetary policy be followed regardless of a country's unemployment rate or domestic environment. International economic regulation was seen to be supplanting domestic decisions about social regulation. In the case of France the result was that politics moved into the streets as French social interests were channelled into extra-parliamentary politics. Some French commentary interpreted this struggle not simply as one over monetary union, but a backlash against liberalism and globalization in a liberal form (*Le Monde* 1996).

The European integration project has been more concerned with a wide range of regulation than other attempts at economic liberalization. This may account for its success in deepening and strengthening international regulation. However, even in this case the driving forces appear to favour liberal economic regulation. This has left an interesting situation where one country has been able to exclude itself from community social regulation. In addition, integration in the 1990s has become increasingly associated with deflation and unemployment. The drive for monetary union based on inflexible targets seems to be undermining the political support for further integration, regulation and even liberalization.

NAFTA

The trade agreements between Canada and the USA and then between these countries and Mexico were attempts at liberalizing economic relations and depoliticizing internal and transnational economic relations. The method for depoliticizing the issues was to move topics that were the source of debate in the political arena into overreaching legal forums. Depoliticization would be enhanced by committing future governments to similar economic policies and reducing the art of the possible in each national political economy.

The primary objective of the Canadian government was to depoliticize trade relations with its southern neighbour. The Canadians wanted trade policy taken away from Congressional politics either by gaining an exemption to their legal innovations or by the creation of a legal mechanism that would check politically motivated US administrative protectionism. Administrative protectionism refers to the obstacles thrown up to imports by the regular operation of US trade law. In Mexico the concern was with limiting the policy options of future administrations so that investors could be lured back into Mexico.

The FTA and NAFTA were successful in liberalizing economic activity on a continental basis, but unsuccessful in depoliticizing trade relations. The proposed continental regulatory framework's attempt to exclude issues such as labour standards, environmental controls and adjustment mechanisms generated an intense political response. Broad based social coalitions formed in Canada and the USA to campaign against the agreements. They brought together labour unions, environmentalist, women's and social activist groups. In Canada, the FTA was only decided after a general election, while US pressure resulted in the appending of labour and environmental accords to the NAFTA package. Although representing a wide spectrum of interests, the coalitions demanded attention to social issues in any agreement liberalizing continental economic activity.

In many ways the NAFTA debate can be seen as a turning point in the repoliticizing of trade relations (Rupert 1995). Labour unions and social activists argued that selectively regulating activities resulted in empowering some elements of society and restricting the freedom of others. A Mexican union activist characterized increased economic liberalization in the following terms: 'What it means is that companies have the freedom to have plants in Mexico without real unions . . . without protecting our health and safety or the environment. The workers have the freedom to work for almost nothing'

(Brecher and Costello 1991: 15). Economic regulation would ensure that goods, services and investment would flow more smoothly across the continent, but attempts to deal with social aspects of continental regulation were avoided.

Confining the agreement to economic regulation was increasingly less feasible as the USA drifted into an election year. Indeed, the electoral swing to the Democratic party forced creation of side accords on labour and the environment to make a gesture in the direction of social regulation. The side accords were limited to providing a monitoring service to encourage each country to live up to existing labour and environmental legislation. The labour side accord was particularly weak in that dispute settlement procedures were confined to areas of health and safety, child labour, minimum wage and technical labour standards (Levinson 1993; Robinson 1993: 37–46). Crucial issues such as the right to organize, the right to bargain collectively and the right to strike are reserved as guiding principles that the government are 'committed to promote' (*International Trade Reporter* 1993: 1555).

The result of the NAFTA debate was that labour and environmental issues were incorporated into the economic liberalization and regulation debate. Their method of incorporation was grudging in that they were relegated to side accords. The effectiveness of these accords remains to be tested. One of the key products of the intense political debate was that the social forces mobilized have moved on from the continental framework to the multilateral arena. Many of the US-based organizations turned their attention to the GATT Uruguay Round agreement following the passage of NAFTA. More recently, North American social movements have taken the lead in building an international coalition to confront liberal globalization. For example, in the wake of the passage of NAFTA and the GATT Uruguay Round agreement the International Forum on Globalization (IFG) was established in San Francisco in January 1994. The IFG brings together 40 organizations in 19 countries to confront global liberal restructuring. The Forum connects some of the NAFTA debate participants with other social movement groups such as the Third World Network based in Malaysia. Prominent members of the IFG's steering committee include representatives from a number of organizations deeply involved in the NAFTA struggle such as the Council of Canadians, Action Canada Network, Institute for Policy Studies, Public Citizen and the Institute for Agriculture and Trade Policy. The IFG held the first of several public teach-ins at Columbia University from 10–12 November 1995 in an attempt to focus attention on alternatives to liberal globalization.

World Trade Organization

The World Trade Organization has the potential to make great advances in international regulation. The advances would be in both breadth and in depth. The breadth concerns the new areas in which it will be acting – agriculture, services, intellectual property. The depth is provided by new decision-making rules reversing the old GATT unanimity rules which frustrated enforcement of norms. GATT panel reports used to require unanimous acceptance which implied the acceptance of the party displeased by the report. In the WTO, unanimous rejection is required to prevent the acceptance of a report's finding. Since the party benefiting from the panel report is unlikely to agree that it be rejected, there is a much greater likelihood that most reports will be accepted.

As the breadth and depth of the WTO's regulation increases and political progress is made in advancing the project of social regulation in North America and Western Europe, so too does the pressure to integrate social regulation into the WTO's mandate. This section of the chapter outlines the key issues surrounding the debate over labour standards and the WTO in the context of the earlier discussion about regulation selectivity.

The first broad point is to outline the forces in favour and against the linking of labour standards and trade relations (Woolcock 1995). On the pro side we have some governments in developed countries influenced by centre left parties and trade unions in developed and developing countries. The US government pressured by the Democratic Congress was forced to put the issue of labour standards and trade on the multilateral agenda. In France, the leadership of the Socialist French President Mitterrand was key in pushing the position in the European Union. The advocacy by the International Confederation of Free Trade Unions (ICFTU) of a WTO social clause draws upon the support of 127 million workers through 190 affiliates in most countries of the world. On the anti side we have business organizations, liberal economists, officials in trade organizations and governments of the centre right in the developed world and most governments in developing countries. Thus, while the Malaysian government is opposed to a social clause, so were the British. Following the Republican victory in the US Congress and the capture of the French presidency by a conservative, the US and French government's enthusiasm may also dissipate. The issue provides a good example of a class-based issue between workers and employers being fed through the state system.

A second point to note is that the tone of the debate is often cast in North/South terms. Governments representing Northern countries have tended to press for a social clause, while governments of many developing countries have resisted. Accusations can fly about Northern countries forcing their values on Southern countries through a new form of imperialism. Fears exist that Northern countries are seeking to create new barriers to trade which will frustrate the import of products from developing countries.

Worries about social regulation in Northern countries becoming a form of protectionism against Southern exports are not diminished when some activists openly champion their cause in books with counterproductive titles such as *The New Protectionism* (Lang and Hines 1992).

This discussion raises familiar questions for international relations scholars about the units of analysis under consideration. The international legal system is a state system and in such a context it is plausible to see a divide between many Southern and Northern countries. However, if one looks at the position of people working (as opposed to owning) industries in the developed and developing world, the North–South dimension disappears. This was graphically illustrated in the television coverage of the March 1995 Asia–European Union summit in Thailand. While Asian leaders inside the conference warned Europeans against imposing Western views of basic labour standards, Thai workers in the toy industry begged for just such a policy. Similarly, independent Malaysian trade unions push for a social clause at the WTO while their government vigorously opposes such action.

A third point is that proponents of international labour standards are advocating very modest measures which would seek to support basic human rights rather than homogenize wage rates through a global minimum wage. The ICFTU's proposal is for adoption of key conventions of the International Labour Organization which would provide for freedom of association, the right to collective bargaining, abolition of forced labour, prevention of discrimination in employment and a minimum age for employment (ICFTU 1996). Critics argue that a move to labour standards linked to trade sanctions would harm developing countries as it would undermine their comparative advantage and result in a new protectionism. The accusation is that the governments of developed countries and labour unions are simply seeking to protect their markets.

These accusations are difficult to support when the proposals on the table are examined. The ICFTU's suggestion is for a mechanism which would respond to complaints by initiating investigations and publishing reports with recommendations. If a country was found to be violating basic rights they would be given two years to begin to remedy the situation, at which time another report would be issued. If the country remedies the situation, no action would be taken. If the country was working to eliminate the problem, another report would be made after a waiting period of another year or two. Only in the case of a failure to act would some trade-related sanction take place, and this would only be after one more year's grace for the offending party to introduce reforms. The sanctions contemplated are limited and would be implemented in a gradual manner. In short, the mechanism being proposed stresses cooperation, consultation and turns to withdrawal of trade privileges or sanctions only at the end of a long road of negotiation.

An important element of the trade and labour standards debate is the significance that labour standards supporters and opponents put on the issue being incorporated into the remit of the World Trade Organization. The International Labour Organization already exists to encourage labour standards, but its role is largely confined to persuading states to adopt and enforce key conventions. Although the director of the ILO is seizing the existing opportunity to increase the role and profile of the ILO, its powers are clearly restricted (Hansenne 1996). The significance of the WTO is its presumed ability to ensure future compliance and perhaps enforcement of key norms in the trading system.

Sanctions are not the backbone of GATT or the WTO, but they do create a different environment than the ILO. Most states would seek to avoid the imposition of WTO sanctions, if at all possible. As a result, few trade disputes can actually be expected to go through the entire dispute settlement procedure as states agree to resolve the issue before it ever gets to the stage where sanctions are put in place. This creates a culture of compliance, without the need for enforcement. However, the ability to enforce is extremely helpful for encouraging compliance. It is this increased compliance that is at the centre of the issue of moving labour standards into the WTO in some form or another. Countries would be more likely to adhere to labour standards if the WTO is involved than if it is just the ILO.

Having labour standards at the heart of the trade organization would considerably raise the stakes for countries refusing to support basic rights. They would have to determine whether their acceptance as legitimate members of the trading system was more important than their reasons for suppressing such rights. For stronger countries the calculation would be whether their refusal to adhere to labour standards might jeopardise the functioning of the multilateral system. As in other areas of trade disputes, powerful states will be encouraged to abide by particular standards because the gains from continued open trading will exceed the possible costs of international compliance.

The Director-General of the World Trade Organization indicated that he did not want to see the issue of trade and labour standards addressed at the first WTO ministerial meeting in Singapore in December 1996. As manager of the process, Mr Ruggiero would like the historic meetings to revolve around a non-confrontational agenda. Labour issues are sure to generate conflict, especially between representatives of Northern and Southern country governments. This may indeed be the case, but similar concerns did not prevent consideration in the regulation of services and intellectual property rights. Mr Ruggiero's own statements about labour standards being used by an 'insidious neo-protectionsim' indicate that it is not just representatives of developing countries and business organizations who see a threat in labour standards (*Financial Times* 1995).

It may be the case that the waters can be calmed by keeping labour issues off the Singapore agenda, but the issue will not disappear. It is likely that the Singapore meeting will see a counter-gathering of social movements seeking to repoliticize the trade discussions. Labour standards, environmental protection and the WTO's movement into regulation of investment will be of intense concern to the international alliance of social movements. Their campaign to influence the WTO's agenda can be expected to intensify, just as their efforts to influence World Bank and International Monetary Fund policy have developed. In addition, key countries such as the USA and some members of the European Union seem to remain committed to pushing the trade and labour standards onto the WTO agenda for the future. The outlook for labour regulation and the WTO seems to be that it will not be addressed, but will not be abandoned by its proponents.

CONCLUSION

The struggle over international economic regulation continues on two fronts. The first is the deepening of regulation in areas of concern during the Uruguay Round negotiations. Here the difficulty will be in implementing agreements, extending disciplines and coaxing governments to abide by rules already agreed. Not surprisingly, the most difficult task will be the initial cases which go against the strongest economic powers such as the USA and the EU. In the end, will they consent to being bound by stringent international regulation?

The second area of conflict is over the scope and content of economic regulation. Is it to have a narrow definition and be confined to issues such as tariffs, competition policy and intellectual property? Alternatively, are we on the verge of acknowledging that economic regulation and economic institutions are also concerned with what some might term social regulation in areas such as labour standards and environmental protection? Is it possible that the regulatory package with which we are familiar at the state level may be recreated at the international level? Those in favour of international labour standards would urge movement in that direction.

The expanding reach of international regulation is a matter of some controversy. As part of a process of globalization we see some elements of authority moving away from state decision-makers into the international arena. The difficulty with regulating selectively on narrow economic issues is that it leaves such structures with shallow legitimacy in national societies. It is clear that such regulation increases competition, but it is less obvious what benefits this brings to large groups of society. Avoiding the argument about the benefits of such a system, it is possible to note that workers, communities and industries feeling the strain from global competition lack the enthusiasm of liberalization advocates.

Raising the issue of international labour standards in the presence of liberal economists is similar to waving a red flag in front of a bull. Such standards threaten the utopia of a perfectly competitive international market.

Whereas such analysts might agree that minimum national standards can be tolerated, their concern ends at the state's borders. While economic considerations about efficiency and the warnings against protectionism should be carefully weighed, economists should pause and consider the importance of legitimacy for international agreements. The web of international regulation being assembled requires legitimacy if it is to survive. The question becomes what form of regulation will convince actors to be bound by its decisions? What form will be seen as being legitimate?

This chapter has argued that recent regulation projects have initiated responses from wide sections of national and international society. These groups are pressing for an inclusive form of regulation. They seek to anchor international regulation in the shoals of civil society. A failure to do so will result in a regulatory framework with shallow and shaky foundations. Inclusion of minimum labour standards in the international regulatory basket would go some way to bolstering the legitimacy of the expanding powers of international regulatory agencies. A World Trade Organization which assisted in the protection of basic rights of association and collective bargaining while working for the abolition of forced labour, child labour and discrimination in employment would have a stronger claim that it was acting on behalf of all members of the global community. In times of difficulty, when its authority was challenged and its structure under pressure, especially from the larger powers, the WTO would find itself being supported by additional groups in domestic and international politics. It is in the long term political, as well as economic, interests of those pushing for increasing economic liberalization to accommodate forces concerned about minimum labour standards. A failure to do so will result in the selective economic regulation supporting free trade being increasingly seen as a mechanism for freeing capital and restricting all other social interests. The implications of this are increased political struggle around free trade and an increasing political vulnerability for those advocating further international economic regulation.

A political economy approach to international economic regulation would suggest that for such a system to flourish and survive it may require deep roots in domestic societies. These roots should go beyond the support of liberal economists, multinational corporations and 'consumers' to individuals and communities that share legitimate social concerns. An effort to expand the purview of international economic regulation from simply increasing competition might go some way to establish these roots. This chapter has suggested that one place to start could be with labour standards and the WTO.

ACKNOWLEDGEMENT

This research was facilitated by funds from the Economic and Social Research Council grant L120251027, 'Global Economic Institutions and Global Social Movements'. It is a two-year project which is part of the ESRC's ongoing Global Economic Institutions research initiative.

REFERENCES

Bhagwati, J. (1988) *Protectionism*, Cambridge MA.: MIT Press.

Brecher, J. and Costello, T. (1991) *Global Village vs. Global Pillage. A One-World Strategy for Labor*, Washington: International Labor Rights Education and Research Fund.

Brown, W. (1950) *The United States and the Restoration of World Trade*, Washington DC: Brookings Institution.

Croome, J. (1995) *Reshaping the World Trading System: A History of the Uruguay Round*, Geneva: World Trade Organization.

Dicken, P. (1992) *Global Shift*, London: Paul Chapman.

Diebold, W. (1959) *The Schuman Plan: A Study in Economic Cooperation 1950–1959*, New York: Council on Foreign Relations.

European Commission (1989) 'A bonfire of subsidies', *European Commission Press Release*, 10 March, IP(89)156.

—— (1992) *Third Survey on State Aids in the European Community in the Manufacturing and Certain Other Sectors*, Brussels: Commission of the European Communities.

Financial Times (1995) 7 July, 14 December.

Hansenne, M. (1996) 'Trade and labour standards: can common rules be agreed?', address by Director-General, ILO, to 464th Wilton Park Conference, Sussex, 6 March.

ICFTU (1996) *International Worker's Rights and Trade: The Need for Dialogue*, Brussels: ICFTU.

International Trade Reporter (1993) 'Annex 1 Labor Principles, North American Free Trade Agreement Side Accords on Labor and Import Surges', 15 September: 1555.

Lang, T. and Hines, C. (1992) *The New Protectionism: Protecting the Future Against Free Trade*, London: Earthscan.

Le Monde (1996) 'La Grande révolte française contre l'Europe liberale', *Le Monde Diplomatique* 502 (43) January.

Levinson, J. (1993) 'The labor side accord to the North American Free Trade Agreement', Washington: Economic Policy Institute.

Nagle, J. (1976) *Agricultural Trade Policies*, Lexington: Saxon House.

O'Brien, R. (1997). *Subsidy Regulation and State Transformation in North America, the European Union and the GATT*, London: Macmillan.

Polanyi, K. (1957) *The Great Transformation*, Boston: Beacon Hill.

Robinson, I. (1993) *North American Trade as if Democracy Mattered*, Ottawa: Canadian Centre for Policy Alternatives.

Rosenau, J. and Czempiel, E. (1992) *Governance Without Government: Order and Change in World Politics*, Cambridge: Cambridge University Press.

Rugman, R. (1986) 'U.S. protectionism and Canadian trade policy', *Journal of World Trade Law* 20 (4): 363–80.

Rupert, M. (1995) '(Re) Politicizing the global economy: liberal common sense and ideological struggle in the US NAFTA debate', *Review of International Political Economy* 2 (4): 658–92.

Sinclair, T. (1994) 'Passing judgement: credit rating processes as regulatory mechanisms of governance in the emerging world order', *Review of International Political Economy* 1 (1): 133–60.

Stone, C. (1988) 'International trade,' in I. Sawhill (ed.) *Challenge to Leadership*, Washington DC: Urban Institute Press.

Swann, D. (1992) *The Economics of the Common Market*, 7th edn, London: Penguin.

Winham, G. (1986) *International Trade and the Tokyo Round Negotiation*, Princeton: Princeton University Press.

Wise, M. and Gibb, M. (1993) *Single Market to Social Europe*, New York: Longman.

Woolcock, S. (1995) 'The trade and labour standards debate: overburdening or defending the multilateral system', Global Economic Institutions Working Paper Series no.4, London: Centre for Economic Policy Research.

12

COMMENTARY ON CHAPTER 11

George A. Petrochilos

Robert O'Brien is concerned with the selective regulation of free trade, particularly the fact that labour issues tend to be left originally outside such regulation. Subsequently, when forced through pressure onto the agenda, they receive less than satisfactory treatment, thus resulting in conflict and shallow support for such regulation in national societies. He starts by arguing that international economic regulation should be seen as an issue of political economy, rather than as an economic or technical question. As an example, he proceeds to consider how the question of subsidy impinges on international trade and compares its treatment in the contexts of the EU, NAFTA and the WTO. He concludes that in order for international economic regulation to acquire legitimacy in national societies, it must also include 'social' issues such as environmental questions and, more importantly, labour standards.

One can have sympathy with the main argument of the chapter, namely the need to consider international economic regulation as an issue of political economy. In fact, a great deal of such regulation is approached from a political economy perspective and indeed the discussions of the Uruguay Round, which finally turned GATT into the WTO, were no exception. However, therein lies an inherent weakness, since under 'political economy' one can try to push for the discussion/inclusion of whatever issues one wishes. Which ones are actually included will largely depend not only on value judgements but also on the political clout of the participants and the need for pragmatism to achieve certain minimum results. Attempts from some parties to include many more 'social' issues will tend to limit the chances of obtaining agreement, thus making international economic regulation more difficult to achieve in the first place and increasingly cumbersome to monitor, police and enforce subsequently.

Naturally the author feels strongly about the central theme, which sometimes clouds the discussion and explains some slanted argumentation. For example, the author is concerned that selective regulation of free trade is seen to benefit some social interests and harm others. Any policy measure – unless Pareto optimum – is likely to benefit some and harm others. There is nothing new in having inequities in economic activity or even gainers and losers. A whole area of welfare economics is concerned with this issue and the need for interpersonal comparisons and compensation. Even the example given, that removing restrictions on the flow of investment may seem to serve the interests of mobile capital and harm the interests of less mobile labour, is not very convincing without further qualifications. Flows of foreign direct investment (FDI) help less mobile labour in host countries and certainly do not harm it; this may also help labour in investing countries through tie-in arrangements. In any case one cannot pronounce on these matters without prior examination of such investment flows, particularly since FDI is of the nature of a non-zero sum game. Admittedly, however, very important distributional issues do arise, as they could under free trade, which seem to concern the author, but these are typically the preserve of national authorities rather than supranational ones. However, one wonders about the efficacy of a supranational body dealing with distributional issues worldwide and dispensing social justice.

The author is right in pointing out the emergence of trade agreements aiming at attracting and keeping FDI rather than removing barriers to trade. In the past a number of studies have demonstrated that one of the most potent determining factors of FDI flows has been tariff protection and, for example, the product cycle hypothesis is built around this idea. However, this is more a feature of bilateral rather than of multilateral trade negotiations/ agreements. Similarly, as regards the issue of subsidy, the author, adopting a 'political economy' perspective, rightly points to the need of regulation for good reasons. Subsidies represent 'negative tariffs', which when used in international trade take the form of dumping. Whether one treats this as price discrimination, that is, selling abroad cheaper than at home or selling at a price lower than average cost, it is considered as an unfair trading practice which is proscribed in most developed countries, whatever the views of libertarian (rather than liberal) economists may be. Nevertheless, there are cases where certain types of subsidies may be used by countries to support economic activities, such as direct payments, tax concessions, soft loans and government guarantees and equity participation. Such subsidies may be industry specific or generally available. Yet we observe a differential treatment of compliance and enforcement of subsidy regulation under the EU, NAFTA and GATT/ WTO. This has to do with the use or not of countervail to nullify the concessions made through the multilateral trade negotiations. In the EU member states cannot countervail the activities of others but they have to abide by much stricter competition rules and also face a strong regulatory mechanism of monitoring and enforcement. Under GATT/WTO rules there is greater subsidy freedom, but there is also the threat of country specific countervail. Under the GATT/WTO the objective is to agree on minimum standards of subsidies that cannot be used and what importing countries can do to offset their effects. Accordingly, under GATT/WTO rules 'legal' subsidies cannot be countervailed.

To help clarify the issues and the subsequent discussion, it is necessary to spell out that it is not surprising that different forms of economic integration have different implications about monitoring, policing and enforcement not only of economic issues such as subsidy regulation but also of social ones such as the environment and labour. We need to be clear that in considering what happens under the EU, NAFTA and WTO we do compare like with like. These are different institutions set up to achieve different objectives. The various forms of economic integration are in order of ascendance: free trade areas, customs unions, common markets and economic unions. The economic benefits under the first two forms are sought in the reallocation of resources according to comparative advantage, brought about by trade liberalization. Under the latter two forms, in addition to the static benefits of resource reallocation, one can add the dynamic benefits resulting from various structural changes due to the free movement of resources of all kinds. It is precisely because of these larger expected benefits that member countries accept a certain loss of national sovereignty in favour of a pooled sovereignty. Generally speaking, the stronger the degree of economic integration, the higher the expected gains and, correspondingly, the greater the loss of their national sovereignty. In addition, under common markets and economic unions the participants may find the need to regulate many other aspects of social life and not only the ones with a direct economic impact, since it could be argued that even the purely political ones, that is, foreign and defence policies, have an economic impact through, for example, military budgets. Therefore, it becomes evident that the higher the economic integration required, the deeper and stronger the regulation implied. This is why the EU, for example, requires a strong regulatory mechanism to ensure monitoring and enforcement. Linking this discussion with the chapter, it would mean that the two weakest forms of economic integration, that is, free trade areas like NAFTA and customs unions, tend to follow an 'economic' or 'technical' approach – although nothing prevents the participants from including other aspects, while the two strongest, that is, common markets and economic unions like the EU, take a 'political economy' approach.

The preceding discussion may have helped to show that the distinction between economic and political regulation is fraught with difficulties. What is economic and what is political is not always clear-cut and a great deal of grey area exists between the two. For example, environmental pollution (requiring 'political' regulation?), caused in order to confer comparative advantage to one party, imposes social costs not only to that party but also to others. Who pays for such costs? At the same time, if the polluters are large developing countries, for example, China and India, who is to say that they must eschew development and deny large sections of the population their first bowl of rice, so that Northerners can go on enjoying, undisturbed, their tenth or even hundredth bowl?

127

However, agreement on more international regulation, restricting national sovereignty, is not something easily achieved, as the author shows and as the experience of the EU demonstrates. Most if not all governments are loath to relinquish national power and turn it over to a supranational body which they cannot control. The history of GATT, established in 1947 with the aim to liberalize trade (rather than to achieve free trade, as implied by Chapter 11) before it was turned into the WTO almost half a century later, is a further testimony to the difficulties involved. Nevertheless, from modest beginnings in 1947, involving 23 mostly developed countries at the Geneva Round, GATT has managed to reduce the average tariff on manufactured products of the industrial countries to 4 per cent from a weighted average duty of 35 per cent before its creation. It also increased its membership to 128 countries as of early 1995. Perhaps the most interesting aspect of this development is the ever-growing participation of developing countries in the GATT/WTO. The original GATT (1947) concerned itself up to the mid-1980s with tariff reductions, agreement on antidumping and certain codes of conduct on specific non-tariff measures. The Uruguay Round (1986–94) considered and achieved additional reductions in tariffs, elaborated further the codes of conduct of the earlier Tokyo Round (1973–9) and agreed on bringing into GATT agriculture, clothing and textiles, creating the WTO and agreements on services (GATS) and intellectual property rights (TRIPs). Trade-related investment measures (TRIMs), for example, local content requirements and export performance of FDI were also agreed, but are limited in nature and subordinate to GATT.

As regards labour issues there are two relevant points: labour costs and labour standards. Despite the fact that there is a connection between the two, the author rightly concentrates on the latter because there is no question of regulating the former. Differential labour costs, in the form of wages, insurance and social security, reflect factor endowments, technological capabilities, labour productivity and institutional arrangements. Such differences in costs confer comparative advantage and explain the gains from international trade. However, labour standards such as human rights, the right of workers to organize in trade unions, prohibition of forced labour and abolition of child labour are areas where the WTO could play a role, as the author suggests. One can sympathize with some of the arguments of governments of certain developing countries, namely, that raising labour standards may amount to a tax on unskilled labour, which could result in unemployment and poverty, or that the choice a child has is not one between school or work but rather one between work or prostitution. A major problem in this context is also that in countries with weak or non-existent labour unions workers simply do not trust their own national authorities and look to supranational bodies to improve working conditions at home. The political correctness argument, used by Asian leaders, of Northerners trying to impose their own views on Southerners, should not deter efforts at bringing minimum labour standards under the ambit of WTO. Many Asian countries have reached a stage of development that is commensurate with if not higher than many Northern states. In addition, a great deal of international trade is accounted for by multinationals so regulating labour standards should be easier, since such firms may be sensitive to pressure groups in their home countries. In fact there is evidence that some firms are already reacting to this issue.

However, as the author suggests, at the insistence of France and the USA labour standards were introduced into the Uruguay Round, but no action was taken and political expediency prevailed. In fact political expediency, rather than principles or rules, seems to underlie much international activity. Two examples will suffice. The first is the passing of the Helms– Burton Act in the USA and its impact on world trade. The extra-territorial nature of this Act clearly makes it a very iniquitous law. The second is the conduct of Turkey which has signed a customs union treaty with the EU. The European Parliament, when approving the treaty, insisted that Turkey should improve its human rights record, introduce democratic institutions and resolve the Cyprus and Kurdish problems. Not only have matters worsened in almost all these areas, but in addition Turkey has been threatening with war a member of the EU, Greece, and is preparing for yet another invasion of northern Iraq. The European Parliament has been forced to suspend the economic aid due to Turkey as part of the customs union until that country provides a clear explanation on these subjects. Such unilateral behaviour is clearly inconsistent with multilateral arrangements, yet it is tolerated. At the same time it must be recognized that as things stand the GATT is a simple agreement; the staff of the WTO is around 450, compared to over 3,000 for OECD, over 2,000 for IMF and over 6,000 for the World Bank. Under present conditions the WTO cannot undertake monitoring and compliance procedures on new areas, although it could make a start by initiating research on minimum labour standards. In the meantime, to that effect, pressure should be stepped up on WTO by all those concerned.

REFERENCES

Hoekman, B. and Kostecki, M. (1995) *The Political Economy of the World Trading System: From GATT to WTO*, Oxford: Oxford University Press.
Petrochilos, G.A. (1991) 'The economic and social dimensions of the single European market: the issues', *British Review of Economic Issues* 13 (13).

13

RICHARD COBDEN AND THE DEMOCRATIC PEACE[1]

Martin Wolf

America, for fifty years at peace, with the exception of two
years of defensive war, is a spectacle of the beneficent effects of
that policy which may be comprised in the maxim – As little
intercourse as possible between the *Governments*, as much
connection as possible between the *nations* of the world. And
when England (without being a republic) shall be governed
upon the same principles of regard for the interests of the
people, and a like common sense view of the advantages of
its position, we shall adopt a similar motto for our policy; and
then we shall hear no more mention of that costly chimera, the
balance of power.

(Cobden 1969: 216)

The more any nation traffics abroad upon free and honest
principles, the less it will be in danger of wars.

(Cobden 1969: 222)

If . . . the consent of the citizens is required to decide whether
or not war is to be declared, it is very natural that they
will have great hesitation in embarking on so dangerous an
enterprise. . . . But under a constitution where the subject is
not a citizen, and which is therefore not republican, it is the
simplest thing in the world to go to war. For the head of state
is not a fellow citizen, but the owner of the state, and a war
will not force him to make the slightest sacrifice so far as
his banquets, hunts, pleasure palaces and court festivals are
concerned.

(Kant 1970: 100)

Richard Cobden, father of the Anti-Corn Law League, whose great triumph
was the repeal of 1846, was motivated by more than Britain's commercial
greatness. Unilateral free trade was, for him, part of a wider system of ideas
that linked free trade to prosperity and peace. He argued in two major
pamphlets published in the mid-1830s on 'England, Ireland and America'

and 'Russia' (Cobden 1969) that the defeat of protectionism would mark a revolutionary change not just in commercial policy, but in the foreign policy of his own country, and, he hoped, of the world. Free trade would, he hoped, bring peace.

These hopes were disappointed. But the peaceful international relations Cobden sought do, it appears, develop among democracies. The principal purpose of this chapter is to show that this is so, explain why this might be so and indicate what might follow for international relations today.

COBDEN'S VIEW OF INTERNATIONAL RELATIONS

Notwithstanding the failure of Cobden's hopes, his pamphlets were influential at the time and remain fascinating even today. Beautifully written and cogently argued, they challenge the prejudices of those who believe that intervention in the affairs of foreign nations is either desirable or efficacious. His biting attack on the almost universally held belief of his compatriots – that it was in the national interest of Britain to protect Turkey from Russia – seems, for example, entirely persuasive.

In this, Cobden was confronting the classical 'realism' of Lord Palmerston, Foreign Secretary and Prime Minister in the mid-nineteenth century, who famously remarked that 'we have no eternal allies and no permanent enemies'. But 'our interests are eternal, and those interests it is our duty to follow' (Briggs 1959: 352). Cobden agreed that Britain had permanent interests, but argued that Palmerston and those who thought like him had no idea what they were. In particular, they thought British prosperity depended on its power, on its navy and on its colonies. Cobden argued, against them, that Britain's power, its navy and its colonies depended on its prosperity.

Cobden's argument for non-interventionism in foreign affairs had four principal components.

1   The prosperity of a nation is determined by its internal development, combined with effective exploitation of opportunities to trade. This was one of the motivations for his successful agitation for free trade. It was also for this reason that he prophetically pointed to the USA as the principal threat to British supremacy: 'It is to the industry, the economy, and peaceful policy of America, and not to the growth of Russia, that our statesmen and politicians, of whatever creed, ought to direct their anxious study; for it is by these, and not by the efforts of barbarian force, that the power and greatness of England are in danger of being superseded; yes, by the successful rivalry of America, shall we, in all probability, be placed second in the rank of nations' (Cobden 1969: 78).

2   A nation's prosperity cannot be augmented by conquest or plunder, but only by efficient internal development. There was, therefore, no national interest in securing empire, or in holding the balance of Europe, a notion he dismissed as a chimera. These activities consumed resources in taxation and government debt that enfeebled the nation, making it less productive and efficient in the long run.

3   The correct policy to follow is the policy he commended for its beneficent effects on the USA: 'That policy will be based upon the *bona fide* principle (not Lord Palmerston's principle) of non-intervention in the political affairs of other nations; and from the moment this maxim becomes the load-star by which our government shall steer the vessel of the state – from that moment the good old ship Britannia will float triumphantly in smooth and deep water, and the rocks, shoals, and hurricanes of foreign war are escaped forever' (Cobden 1969: 254).

4   'If it be objected, that this selfish policy disregards the welfare and improvement of other countries . . . we answer that, so far as the objects we have in view are concerned, we join hands with nearly every one of our opponents' (Cobden 1969: 254). But he rejected the notion that people can be forced to improve: 'Our opponents would promote the good of their neighbours by dint of the cudgel: we propose to arrive at the same end by means of our own national example' (Cobden 1969: 255).

LIMITATIONS OF UNILATERAL LIBERALISM

Cobden's ideas on foreign relations have, in practice, been as widely ignored as his arguments for unilateral free trade. Andrew Moravcsik (1993) argues that they have both been rejected for similar reasons.

Domestic interests in favour of interventionist foreign policies are as potent as those in favour of protectionism. Similarly, the idea that power brings prosperity is as enduring as the belief that liberal trade is a favour done to foreigners at one's own country's expense. Again, people gain pleasure from the power of their state, just as they care about their collective ability to control, or at least influence, their country's economic structure.

In practice, the most effective solution to the resistance to unilateral free trade has been multilateral bargaining on the basis of reciprocity. At the price of criticism from purist free traders, Cobden himself started off this process with the Cobden–Chevalier Treaty of 1860, which committed France to trade liberalization and, through the most-favoured nation clause, spread liberal trade throughout Europe. The post-war General Agreement on Tariffs and Trade (GATT), based on non-discrimination (or the most-favoured nation clause), was no more than a modernized version of this nineteenth-century *système des traités*.

RICHARD COBDEN AND THE DEMOCRATIC PEACE

Similarly, the best way yet found to establish Cobden's ideas on peaceful international relations has been through a mixture of domestic political reform with international alliances. In making their own trade policies, most countries are influenced by the policies of others. Similarly, in their foreign policies, countries are influenced by the policies of others. It is unsurprising that the policy of unilateral non-interventionism did not endure, since it is less soundly based than the policy of unilateral free trade, for three reasons.

1   Even if prosperity is not advanced by an interventionist foreign policy, national independence and individual freedom are also legitimate objectives.
2   Unilateral freedom to import does not entail diminution of national prosperity, contrary to a common presumption. But a policy of absolute non-intervention might lead to invasion by a hostile power.
3   Not only did Cobden ignore the possibility of such injurious malevolence by a foreign country, he also understates the chances of effective benevolence by a great power on behalf of a weaker one.

LIBERALISM, REALISM AND THE NATIONAL INTEREST

A country's ability to pursue a policy of peaceful non-intervention depends partly on the goals pursued by others and partly on what its citizens think important. Here another body of liberal thought becomes relevant – the idea that democracies will so define their interests and so behave as to make peace with one another their natural state. For this it is necessary to go back to Immanuel Kant, greatest of German philosophers.

In the late eighteenth-century, Kant had predicted that republics would not make war upon one another. What, for Kant, was a republic? It was a state 'founded upon three principles: firstly, the principle of freedom for all members of a society (as men); secondly, the principle of the dependence of everyone upon a single common legislation (as subjects); and, thirdly, the principle of legal equality for everyone (as citizens)' (Kant 1970: 99–100). In sum, a republic enjoys representative institutions, institutional checks and balances, private individual rights and the rule of law.

These ideas descended to President Woodrow Wilson of the USA, whose fourteen points defined the US war aims in World War I. These 'sound almost as though Kant were guiding Wilson's writing hand', according to Professor Bruce Russett (1993: 4), principal author of a comprehensive analysis of 'the democratic peace' – the idea that democracies do not fight one another. The link between the German philosopher and the later US president is not surprising, since the ideas animating the founding fathers of the USA were those of the eighteenth-century enlightenment, among whose most influential thinkers was the German philosopher.

The ideas remain vital today. President Bill Clinton, for example, told the UN in September 1993:

> In a new era of peril and opportunity, our overriding purpose must be to expand and strengthen the world's community of market-based democracies. During the Cold War, we sought to contain a threat to survival of free institutions. Now we seek to enlarge the circle of nations that live under free institutions, for our dream is of a day when the opinions and energies of every person in the world will be given full expression in a world of thriving democracies that co-operate with each other and live in peace.
>
> (cited in Kissinger 1995: 805)

Kant had defined his ideas against those of an older tradition, classical realism, which in European history goes back to Cardinal de Richelieu, first minister of France between 1624 and 1642. For realism, read also *raison d'état* and *Realpolitik*.

According to Henry Kissinger, Secretary of State under President Richard Nixon and unlikely winner of the Nobel Peace Prize:

> *Raison d'état* asserted that the well-being of the state justified whatever means were employed to further it; the national interest supplanted the medieval notion of a universal morality. The balance of power replaced the nostalgia for universal monarchy with the consolation that each state, in pursuing its own selfish interests, would somehow contribute to the safety and progress of all the others.
>
> (Kissinger 1995: 58)

Kant himself identified this tradition with a belief 'that the true glory of a state consists in the constant increase of its power by any means whatsoever' (1970: 94). When Cobden assailed the doctrine of the balance of power, it was with the British version of this tradition that he was expressing his disagreement.

To the classical realist, states live in a Hobbesian state of nature where life is nasty, brutish, but – countries being virtually immortal – long. They acknowledge neither superior law nor morality, only their own national interest. They remain at peace only if the balance of forces make it in the interest of each to do so. How a state judges its national interest was also held to be unaffected either by its own political structure or by those of the states with which it interacted, perhaps because the major players were monarchies.

Realism has evolved from these seventeenth-century beginnings. The 'realist' Dr Kissinger argues, for example, that 'it is reasonable for the United States to try to buttress equilibrium with moral consensus. To be true to itself, America must try to forge the widest possible moral consensus around a global commitment to democracy' (Kissinger 1995: 834).

Yet he also insists that 'American leaders will have to articulate for their public a concept of the national interest and explain how that interest is served – in Europe and in Asia – by the maintenance of the balance of power. America will need partners to preserve equilibrium in several regions of the world, and these partners cannot always be chosen on the basis of moral considerations alone. A clear definition of the national interest needs to be an equally essential guide to American policy' (Kissinger 1995: 810–11).

The defect of the realist approach is that it is normally either empty or wrong. It is empty to the extent that it states that whatever goals a country pursues must be in its interests or that it ought to pursue its interests, whatever they are. Such propositions provide no guide either to determining what policies should be pursued or to predicting what policies will be pursued.

To the extent that realism is not empty, it has tended to be wrong for the same reason that mercantilism is wrong as a basis for trade policy. Both are based on incorrect or incomplete notions of national interest, the concept Kissinger states must be defined, but then fails to do so.

Traditionally, realists have tended to make two mistakes in analysing national interest. First, because they are obsessed with the idea of power, they have assumed that the national interests of states are in conflict, or zero sum. But in most cases national interests are complementary, or positive sum. Trade is an excellent example of such a positive-sum game. So, more importantly, is peace. Second, realists tend to analyse countries as if the interests they pursue are independent of their internal political structure. But a democracy will, quite properly, reflect broader interests than those of a predatory despot.

Thus how a country defines its interest and acts upon that definition will depend on the sort of state it is and the sorts of states it is dealing with, precisely as liberals, following Kant, have argued. In this fact appears to lie the world's best hope for peace.

DEMOCRATIC PEACE

In 1977, Sir Michael Howard, then Professor of the History of War at Oxford University, agreed that 'one of Kant's prescriptions for perpetual peace, that "the Civil Constitution . . . shall in every State be Republican" has been validated' (Howard 1977: 6–7). Peace among democracies is, in the words of another scholar, 'the closest thing we have to an empirical law in the study of international relations' (Levy 1989: 88).

Working with a number of collaborators, Professor Russett (1993) has provided probably the most systematic investigation of relevant evidence. In analysis of recent experience, he defines war as inter-state conflict, with at least 1,000 battle casualties, and democracy by the presence of wide franchises, regular and fair elections and a longevity of at least three years, rather than by civil rights or economic liberties. The data on conflict include all politically relevant pairs of states – meaning that they are either geographically close to one another or at least one of them is a major power – for every year between 1946 and 1986. During that period, democracies make up 13 per cent of all the relevant pairs.

The study concludes that: democracies are far less likely to use lethal violence towards other democracies than towards autocracies or than autocracies towards one another; no sovereign, stable democracy has waged war against another in the modern international system; and peace among democracies is not just the result of economic and geopolitical features of these states, but of the very fact of democracy. The difference in behaviour is huge. Over the past fifty years, pairs of democratic states have only been one-eighth as likely as other kinds of states to threaten to use force against one another and only one-tenth as likely to carry out such threats.

As might be expected, it turns out that democracy is not all that matters. The richer and more economically dynamic a pair of countries, the less likely they are to come into serious conflict with one another, just as Cobden would have expected. So does sharing membership of the same alliance. But the more stably democratic is any pair of countries the less likely they also are to clash, all other things being equal.

Perhaps the most intriguing result of this recent research is that democracies are not, in general, more peaceful than other states, merely with one another. This would probably have disappointed Cobden, just as the infrequency of unilateral trade liberalization would have disappointed him. But Kant would have been less disappointed – and less surprised.

This conclusion may need to be modified. Another group of authors (Rousseau et al. 1995) tentatively suggests that 'democracies are less likely to initiate crises with all other types of state, but once in a crisis democracies are only less likely to initiate violence against other democracies'. If true, this would suggest that democracies play the game of 'tit for tat' with non-democracies. They rarely initiate conflict, but retaliate when provoked.

The statistical analysis is careful and highly suggestive, but the experience is but a recent one. Democracies were rare until this century. But their number is growing, which will enrich the experience from which conclusions may be drawn. At present, what can be said with confidence is that Kant's hypothesis has not been refuted by experience.

An excellent indication of the desperate search of realist critics for some example of war between democracies is their citation of the declaration of war on Finland by Britain and its allies during World War II. But this episode was the expedient result of the desire to preserve the tactical alliance with Stalin, who had attacked Finland. Moreover, there were no combat casualties between Finland and the Western democracies.

EXPLANATIONS FOR THE DEMOCRATIC PEACE

The question is why democracies behave in the way they appear to do. Three broad categories of explanation can be advanced: ideas, institutions and interests. Under the first fall the norms that define what is legitimate for democracies; under the second come constraints upon executive action; and under the third fall the nature of the interests expressed within – and felt by – democratic polities.

'It is hard to trust a regime that has no faith in its own people.' These words – written in 1988 by Mr Andrei Kozyrev, subsequently Russia's Foreign Minister – exactly capture the distinction that democracies draw between their relations with other democracies and those with non-democracies. Since autocrats do not represent the interests of their citizens, their actions have little or no legitimacy for democracies. Thus in wars against autocracies, democracies almost always distinguish the people, with whom they have no quarrel, from the ruler, with whom they do.

For one democracy to tyrannize over another is, however, to violate fundamental democratic norms. This is why the line that divides the USA from Canada has, notwithstanding the gross imbalance in power between these two countries, remained peaceful. It is, more importantly, why Britain, chief protagonist of the balance of power, responded to the rise of the USA, not by allying with the world's emerging second power, Germany, but by seeking alliance with the USA itself, even at the price of abandoning its aspiration to global supremacy. Britain felt threatened by Germany, much less so by the USA. Contrary to the best realist principles, the great believer in the balance of power judged its potential adversaries not by their capacities, but by their intentions.

Relations between the UK and the USA provide potent support for the hypothesis that there is something special about relations between democracies. These two countries have been the world-girdling commercial powers of the last century and the present one, respectively. Yet the transfer from Britain to the USA was managed not merely without serious conflict between them, but to the relief of the declining power.

The American Civil War was certainly the last occasion on which Britain had any hope of averting this danger, if danger indeed it was. Some argued that it was both right and in Britain's interests to support the South in that struggle. Yet, largely for moral reasons, Britain stood aside, thereby allowing the North its victory and ensuring the emergence of a single, commercially dynamic USA, spanning an entire continent. In so doing, Britain proved that narrow pursuit of power is not the sole objective of a great nation.

Later in the nineteenth century dispute with the USA occurred over minor imperial claims in Latin America. These passed without open conflict, partly no doubt because war would have been foolish, but also because of a growing amity between the two Anglo-Saxon democracies. In explaining the subsequent alliance between the two countries, one historian has pointed out that Germany and the USA 'were rising imperial powers with growing navies. Both threatened British interests in various regions of the globe. Yet Britons, while they detested and feared Germany, almost universally admired the United States and felt minimal apprehension at her ambitions' (Rock 1989: 86–7). Out of this concord emerged the alliance that saved the world from barbarism.

The second line of explanation for the democratic peace notes that the checks and balances within democracies slow down the processes that lead towards war, as does the need for public debate if consensus is to be reached. With no fear of surprise attack, there is time for the democratic norms of negotiation and compromise to come into play. An important aspect of these is the permeation of domestic law by international legal processes and procedures. Indeed, international law functions best in democracies because it has a domestic rule of law through which to operate. Yet this is just one aspect of the fundamental feature of democracy – the plurality of interests represented and the need for peaceful means of resolving disputes.

The third line of explanation depends on the breadth of the interests that operate within democracies. There are always interests in favour of war. But, as was remarked by William Godwin at the very end of the eighteenth century (1976: 507), 'war and conquest . . . elevate the few at the expense of the rest; and consequently they may never be undertaken but where the many are the instruments of the few'. Despots, military castes and merchants seeking monopolies in foreign markets naturally fall into this bellicose category. In similar vein, Cobden (1969: 254) argued that 'having the interests of all orders of society to support our argument in favour of peace, we need not dread war. These, and not the piques of diplomatists, the whims of crowned heads, the intrigues of ambassadresses, or schoolboy rhetoric upon the balance of power, will henceforth determine the foreign policy of our government'.

Being intrinsically destructive, wars always damage the participants in aggregate. Wars must usually return less to each of the countries engaged than they cost. It may be far more fun to be king of a great country than a small one, but his ordinary subjects are not likely to be made any better off by his aggrandizement, even after the conquest is completed. If all domestic interests are represented in all the parties, they are unlikely to want war. This need not be so, however, if one were an aggressive despotism and the other a democracy most of whose citizens believe they would be worse off if they surrendered than if they fought.

One way to synthesize realism with liberalism would be to argue that 'liberals define national interest in such a way that co-operation with fellow liberal democracies is required' (Owen 1994: 122). They do so because they recognize that they have more to gain from peaceful relations than from conflict and trust the other democracy to see the relationship in the same way.

The operation of interests against war is made more effective by the internationalization of economies and the realization that a country can gain more from peaceful commerce than from conquest or Colbertism. The theories of Adam Smith and his successors not only explain why free trade is more fruitful than mercantilist rivalry, they have also slowly changed how countries perceive their interest, so making commercial conflict less likely. It is no surprise therefore that economic interdependence has, as Kant argued, proved yet another obstacle to war among democracies.

This is not to state that economic interests are, of themselves, sufficient to prevent war. When Norman Angell (1911) argued, famously, that a major conflict would be unprofitable, he was correct. But that did not mean it could not happen. Sometimes war would seem to be a moral necessity. At other times, rational calculation can be upset by the tribalism of human beings, by mistaken beliefs, by criminal values, by misunderstanding of the interests at stake or by exclusion of significant forces from the political process. But such unhappy outcomes are, at the least, discouraged by the habits of debate normal in a stable commercial democracy.

Massive miscalculations were, by contrast, almost doomed to happen in late nineteenth-century Europe, where the old military ruling classes used hyper-nationalism and bellicosity to justify – and so retain – power. The military castes made preparation for war their substitute for democracy. To justify their own existence, they tended naturally to exaggerate the benefits of war, preaching the advantages of territorial expansion over peaceful commerce. This happened in mild form in all European states, even Britain. In Wilhelminian Germany members of the military caste thwarted the rise of inclusive political institutions, creating, instead, a state army with themselves at the head. Ultimately, they made Europe a desert and justified it as *Realpolitik*.

Whenever it is possible to pass on the risk and cost of bellicosity to less powerful members of society, international conflict becomes more likely. Without a selective draft, the USA could probably not have started the Vietnam War. Similarly, the possession of independent sources of revenue allows rulers to engage in policies that suit their own purposes, though not those of their citizens. This is true of Saddam Hussein. Research suggests it was true of the kings of early modern Europe as well (Kiser *et al.* 1995: 109–38).

LIBERAL DEMOCRACY AND TODAY'S
FOREIGN RELATIONS

At least four conclusions can be drawn from this analysis of the democratic peace.

First, Cobden was right to condemn naive realism. It is not that self-interested behaviour is morally wrong – that is merely an arguable proposition. It is rather that the way states actually behave, what they see as their interests and how they seek to defend them depends on what they are. It is not true, for example, that the broadly defined interests of states are in conflict. Properly understood and articulated, they are more often in harmony, as Cobden believed. Equally, interests are more likely to be properly understood by representative democracies. Thus the USA did not seek an overseas empire because its citizens never thought the idea right or sensible.

Second, federalist Europeans may have reached the wrong conclusion from history. Understandably, many decided after World War II that the existence of independent sovereign states guaranteed endless conflict. The answer, they concluded, was to subordinate these nations within what would ultimately become a European federal state. But while an economically integrated and politically cooperative Europe is certainly desirable, a federal Europe may not be the answer: civil wars are, after all, always possible – the USA was forged by a particularly brutal one and China has a ghastly history of internal conflict. Past European wars are as likely to have been the result of the narrow range of interests represented in policy-making as of national independence per se. A federal Europe is therefore neither necessary nor sufficient to eliminate the fear of another big war on the continent.

Third, the democratic peace may now spread. Not only are the world's richest and most powerful states democracies, but by the early 1990s about half of all the states in the world had become, to a greater or lesser degree, democratic. Since the forces, both economic and political, that are driving countries towards the acceptance of representative political institutions are powerful, there is a chance that the number of democracies will grow. Whatever some apologists for 'Asian values' may claim, any objective observer of that region would recognize the growing demand for more representative and responsive government. The same is true of Latin America.

Finally, President Clinton was correct. The West is right to help promote democracy in the former Soviet Union and Central and Eastern Europe; to devote its efforts to creating and sustaining the international economic institutions that underpin a harmonious and prosperous global economic order; and to distinguish between the democracies that are, *pace* Palmerston, its friends and the non-democracies with which its relations must remain watchful and wary.

POSTSCRIPT

Ultimately, free trade did not last and the peace Cobden desired was not secured, even for his own country. Today's question is whether the spread of democratic governance and multilateral liberalization will succeed where nineteenth-century liberalism failed.

NOTE

1 An earlier version of this chapter appeared in the *Financial Times* on 28 December 1995.

REFERENCES

Angell, N. (1911) *The Great Illusion*, London: Heinemann.

Briggs, A. (1959) *The Age of Improvement 1783–1867*, London: Longman.

Cobden, R. (1969) 'England, Ireland and America', first published 1835 and 'Russia', first published 1836, in *The Political Writings of Richard Cobden in Two Volumes*, London: T. Fisher Unwin, 1903; New York: Kraus Reprint.

Godwin, W. (1976) *Enquiry concerning Political Justice and Its Influence on Modern Morals and Happiness*, first published 1798, Harmondsworth: Penguin.

Howard, M. (1977) *War and the Liberal Conscience*, The George Macaulay Trevelyan Lectures in the University of Cambridge, New Brunswick NJ: Rutgers University Press.

Kant, I. (1970) 'Perpetual peace: a philosophical sketch', first published 1795, in H. Reiss (ed.) *Kant's Political Writings*, trans. H. B. Nisbet, Cambridge: Cambridge University Press.

Kiser, E., Drass, K. A. and Brustein, W. (1995) 'Ruler autonomy and war in early modern Western Europe', *International Studies Quarterly* 39 (1): 109–38.

Kissinger, H. (1995) *Diplomacy*, London: Simon & Schuster.

Levy, J. S. (1989) 'Domestic politics and war,' in R. I. Rotberg and T. K. Rabb (eds) *The Origin and Prevention of Major Wars*, New York: Cambridge University Press.

Moravcsik, A. (1993) 'Liberalism and international relations theory', Working Paper 92–6, Harvard University: The Center for International Affairs.

Owen, J. M. (1994) 'How liberalism produces democratic peace', *International Security* 19 (2) Fall: 87–125.

Rock, S. R. (1989) *Why Peace Breaks Out: Great Power Rapprochement in Historical Perspective*, Chapel Hill: University of North Carolina Press.

Rousseau, D., Gelpi, C., Reiter, D. and Huth, P. K. (1995) 'Does it take two to tango? Assessing the dyadic nature of the democratic peace, 1918–88', unpublished.

Russett, Bruce, with Antholis, W., Ember, C. R., Ember, M. and Maoz, Z. (1993) *Grasping the Democratic Peace: Principles for a Post-Cold War World*, Princeton NJ: Princeton University Press.

14

COMMENTARY ON CHAPTER 13

Jacob Kol

In his chapter, Martin Wolf's main concern is how war can be avoided. In this perspective the chapter deals with two themes:

- democracy and peace;
- free trade and peace.

DEMOCRACY AND PEACE

Most of Wolf's chapter is on the theme of democracy and peace. With Cobden (1835, 1836), Wolf believes that democracies are less likely to start a war than countries ruled otherwise. This viewpoint is firmly based on empirical and theoretical evidence.[1] With Kant (1795), Martin Wolf underlines the significance of a democracy's constitution that is republican in nature. Under such a constitution people are regarded as citizens, whose consent is needed for waging war and getting killed. Under other constitutions and in situations without one, people are regarded as subjects. This implies for the head of state less need for consultation or none at all before starting a war.

The truth of this insight may be illustrated as follows. British soldiers still die for Queen and Country; American troops fight under the Constitution of the USA, that opens with the words: 'We the People'. There is a marked difference in concern for the life of their troops between American and British generals, even in the Gulf War of 1991.

NON-INTERVENTION

Cobden (1835, 1836) believed that intervention in the affairs of foreign nations is neither desirable nor efficacious. Intervention consumes resources and enfeebles the nation in the long run. Wolf, however, rightly points out that there are justifiable exceptions to this rule.[2] Indeed, Britain's two interventions on the continent of Europe against dictatorship – against Napoleon and against Hitler – can only be remembered gratefully and are entirely justified from a historical perspective and a moral point of view. Yet, also in economic terms these interventions can be justified. The Cobden–Chevalier Treaty of 1860 liberalized trade between Britain and France. This treaty sparked off a range of other free trade agreements among European countries in the 1860s. It led furthermore to deregulation with respect to foreign investment and to monetary cooperation (Duroselle 1990). Free trade among European countries including Britain would have been impossible under Napoleon I, but was implemented under Napoleon III. It soon collapsed, however, when the economic crisis began in 1873 and countries took refuge in protectionism.

Likewise, the Common Market of European countries and their membership of GATT would have been unthinkable under Hitler, but were accomplished after World War II. These examples indicate that intervention in foreign countries can also be justified on economic grounds.

DEMOCRACY, ECONOMIC GROWTH AND FREE TRADE

Cobden (1835, 1836) hoped that free trade would bring peace, but these hopes were disappointed (Wolf 1998). Indeed, the fate of the Cobden–Chevalier Treaty of 1860 and the free trade zone in Europe that it induced illustrate that forces of nationalism and protectionism may at times prove stronger, especially in case of an economic crisis.

Yet, there is a connection between free trade and peace. In their survey article Alesina and Perotti (1994) concluded from a sample of 113 countries that democracy and GDP per capita are highly and positively correlated. Furthermore, there is overwhelming evidence that the degree of trade liberalization is highly and positively correlated with economic growth (De Rosa 1991; IMF 1992; Kol 1995).

Admittedly, the causal relationships involved are difficult to disentangle.[3] Nonetheless, since democracy decreases the chances of outbreak of war, the intercorrelations reported above indicate that Cobden's hope that free trade will bring peace are not entirely misplaced. Only forces other than the tendency for liberalization may prove stronger.

THE WRONG CONCLUSION

The analysis in Wolf's chapter rightly points to the intercorrelations between:

- democracy (especially under a republican constitution);
- free trade and international economic interdependence;

- prosperity and economic growth;
- peace.

In his concluding remarks Wolf observes that after World War II the European federalists concluded that the continued existence of independent sovereign states would guarantee endless conflict and that supranational decision-making would be needed to prevent war and keep the peace. Wolf opposes this view: A federal Europe is neither necessary nor sufficient to eliminate the fear of another big war on the continent, because 'past European wars are as likely to have been the result of the narrow range of interests represented in policy-making as of national independence per se'.

This conclusion is right in its literal wording, but wrong in terms of its implications, namely that one should not aim for supranational decision-making in Europe, or anywhere else. It is not true, of course, that without a federal Europe the outbreak of war is a certainty or that with a federal Europe the absence of war is guaranteed (supporting the non-necessary and non-sufficiency elements in Wolf's conclusion). But it most certainly can be argued that supranational decision-making may be a powerful instrument in preventing war and keeping the peace. The following arguments apply.

First, leaving maintenance of free trade and peace entirely to independent nation states – even when they are republican democracies – is hazardous. Wolf observes already that resistance against unilateral free trade and non-interventionism can be strong and that multilateral bargaining and international alliances are required.[4]

Second, discussing the fragility of the international trading order to constrain nationalism, discrimination and protectionism, Wolf (1988) concludes: 'The problem remains that the economy is global but government is not.' When considering the international trading order as a public good, he observes: 'Theory suggests that provision of a public good will be inadequate, unless there is coercion.' Coercion, for instance, that is embodied in GATT constraints on export subsidies (Wolf 1987).

More in general, the Uruguay Round strengthened rules with respect to a number of trade policy instruments, such as safeguards, antidumping and subsidies. The Uruguay Round has further strengthened dispute settlement arrangements by various measures. These changes are now embodied in the World Trade Organization (WTO), successor to GATT. Apparently the 117 countries that signed the Uruguay Round Agreement are of the opinion that 'strong multilateral rules enhance the ability of governments to control domestic pressures for protection' (IMF 1994).

Third, it seems that Wolf regards the nation state as the embodiment of the optimal level of decision-making.[5] This is unlikely to be true as:

- nation states differ very much in size: Luxembourg versus the USA;

- nation states differ with respect to authorities left or given to provinces: Germany versus France.

Fourth, the present nation states have evolved in a process of unification of counties, duchies and independent cities. The history of most countries is full of war among such cities and counties.[6]

Even the relatively democratic cities in ancient Greece were at war with each other almost continuously. Peace among cities, countries and the like was not realized because these territories became democratic but because – willingly or unwillingly – the execution of military force decision-making authority was transferred to the national level.

Fifth, supranational decision-making is a unique feature of the European Union; it is not provided for explicitly in NAFTA or other regional agreements. It was introduced by the founders of the European Community for Coal and Steel, who believed that prevention of war would be served by withdrawing coal and steel – the two main commodities in the war machinery at the time – from the national authorities and placing them under the supranational High Authority. Likewise, even if all nation states became democracies with a republican constitution, they might still go to war in the future over a shortage of water or other essential resources.

Supranational decision-making is needed when important effects of decisions transgress the boundaries of nation states. The supranational level might involve a continent (or units such as the EU) or the world at large. Important issues in this respect might be the preservation of the environment, utilization of resources, including the oceans, and the prevention of war (Tinbergen 1991a, 1991b). A transfer of authority from the national to the continental or world level should be subject, of course, to democratic control.

NOTES

1 See Chapter 13, pp. 135–9.
2 See Chapter 13, pp. 133–5.
3 Liberalization of trade, for instance, in order to be effective in promoting economic growth, has to be complemented and partly preceded by sound policies for the domestic economy (IMF 1992).
4 See Chapter 13, pp. 132–3.
5 This was certainly the view of the Conservative Government of the UK; its policy on Europe had a major inconsistency. Brussels was feared for its centralism while no authority was transferred to Scotland and Wales.
6 The history of the Middle Ages records frequent wars among Holland, Utrecht, Guelders and other provinces, in what is now the Netherlands, as well as civil wars within these provinces and wars between individual cities and castles. In 1579 these wars had ended when the Republic of the United Provinces was formed by the Union of Utrecht. Similar records apply to most present-day nation states.

REFERENCES

Alesina, A. and Perotti, R. (1994) 'The political economy of growth: a critical survey of the recent literature', *The World Bank Economic Review* 8: 351–71.

Cobden, R. (1835) 'England, Ireland and America', in *The Political Writings of Richard Cobden*, London: T. Fisher Unwin, 1903.

——— (1836) 'Russia', in *The Political Writings of Richard Cobden*, London: T. Fisher Unwin, 1903.

De Rosa, D. (1991) 'Protection in Sub-Saharan Africa hinders exports', *Finance & Development* September: 42–5.

Duroselle, J.B. (1990) *Europe: A History of its People*, London: Viking.

IMF (1992) *Issues and Developments in International Trade Policy*, Washington DC: IMF.

——— (1994) *International Trade Policies: The Uruguay Round and Beyond*, vols I and II, Washington DC: IMF.

Kant, E. (1795) 'Perpetual peace: a philosophical sketch', in H. Reiss (ed.) *Kant's Political Writings*, trans. by H.B. Nisbet, Cambridge: Cambridge University Press, 1970.

Kol, J. (1995) 'Extent and evaluation of protection in developing countries', *Open Economies Review* 6: 81–104.

Tinbergen, J. (1991a) 'The velocity of integration', *De Economist* 139: 1–11.

——— (1991b) 'The optimal economic and security order', in T.K. Kaul and J.K. Sengupta (eds) *Essays in Honor of Karl A. Fox*, Amsterdam: North-Holland.

Wolf, M. (1987) 'Why trade liberalization is a good idea', in J. Michael Finger and Andrzej Olechowski (eds) *The Uruguay Round: A Handbook on the Multilateral Trade Negotiations*, Washington DC: World Bank.

——— (1988) 'An unholy alliance: the European Community and developing countries in the international trading system', in L.B.M. Mennes and J. Kol (eds) *European Trade Policies and the Developing World*, London: Croom Helm.

——— (1998) 'Richard Cobden and the democratic peace', Chapter 13, this volume.

15

THE CORN LAWS AND THE CAP

Christopher Bliss

Who gained and who lost from the Corn Laws, and by how much? The debates from 1815 to 1846 always posed the issues in these distributional terms, and this essay will do the same. Certainly Cobden and the Anti-Corn-Law League made it absolutely clear who gained and who lost. The landlords gained from the high rents, and these 'social parasites', so the vulgar pamphlets had it, were the 'great oppressors of the country . . . enriching themselves at the expense of the other classes of the community' (Blaug, 1958, pp. 202 and 203). The urban working man suffered from the 'bread tax,' and free trade was hailed as a remedy for all of common labor's social ills. Manufacturers suffered since they had to pay higher nominal wages, their export trade was repressed, and their profits were choked off.

(Williamson 1990: 130)

INTRODUCTION

Just 150 years ago, the anniversary which we now commemorate, the Corn Laws were repealed. A certain irony attaches to the celebration, because today we have 'Corn Laws' back with us, now Western Europe-wide, thanks to the Common Agricultural Policy of the European Union (henceforth CAP and EU respectively). This chapter takes advantage of that irony to compare and contrast the effects of agricultural protection on manufacturing 'competitiveness', as they existed in the first half of the nineteenth century, and as they exist now at the end of the twentieth century. What those effects may be, and what economists perceive them to be, are of course not necessarily the same. A tendency for agricultural protection to depress manufacturing exports, which would be one interpretation of a competitiveness effect, has not for the most part received the leading emphasis from economic writers. Thus David Ricardo, whose ideas are discussed more fully below, placed more emphasis on the effect on manufacturing profits than on the level of exports, although such an effect is implicit in his model. Similarly, Howarth (1992), in an essay pitched strongly against the CAP, lays stress on costs to consumers and taxpayers, while making no mention of adverse consequences on European manufacturing exports. In the nineteenth century the Anti-Corn Law League did claim explicitly that the 'bread tax' inhibited exports. However, particularly in Manchester, industrial prosperity and export success were virtually synonymous.

CORN LAWS: HISTORY AND THEORY

The Corn Laws will always merit interest because they crystallized early theoretical attempts to analyse the consequences of protection, and because they functioned as a powerful political totem. Their precise effect is complicated to assess, mainly because by anti-protecting manufacturing the Corn Laws may have produced a beneficial improvement in Britain's terms of trade. Ricardo thought otherwise but Torrens disagreed with him and the latter may well have been right. In any case, some contemporary arguments which maintained that the Corn Laws had no great effect on the domestic price of food were seriously misleading. Sometimes surprisingly similar arguments were employed at the time of Britain's entry to the then European Common Market, and with an equal lack of validity. For example, the claim that the availability of food on the world market is absent or about to dry up unites the debates of the two periods, as does an emphasis on national food security.

Britain, especially at the opening of the century, was close to self-sufficient in food. This was more the result of protection itself than the product of high transport costs, even to inland destinations.[1] Obviously the rapidly growing population made it harder to maintain self-sufficiency. However there was rapid technical progress in agriculture associated with capital accumulation. Indeed the landlords argued that agricultural protection should be maintained to recompense them for the expensive capital accumulation which they had undertaken. Such an argument presupposes, wholly reasonably, that the capital cannot costlessly take itself off to the manufacturing sector. On the modelling of this specific factor aspect of capital, see below.

Towards the end of the twentieth century Britain is again close to self-sufficiency in what one might call raw food, although the high value added element in modern foodstuffs turns the balance into a deficit for food products. Again that outcome is to an important extent the result of the agricultural protection, in this case provided by the CAP.

RICARDO

David Ricardo wrote much about the Corn Laws and developed his opposition to them more extensively than any other classical economist. It would be an oversimplification, however, to suppose that Ricardo wished to see the Corn Laws swept away as quickly as possible. He favoured the gradual reduction of duties. One reason why he preferred gradualism is to be found in his theory of rent. According to Ricardo the effect of agricultural protection is to raise the rents of agricultural land and to lower the profits of industry. As rents exhibit a tendency to sluggishness, because contracts are only renewed periodically, an immediate unexpected abolition of duties would produce extremely disruptive effects which Ricardo wished to avoid.

That point retains its relevance until today. The architects of the CAP chose to ignore Ricardo when they supposed that raising agricultural prices would help cultivators. David Ricardo could have told them it helps landowners and offers little to those whose contribution to agricultural production is the labour of their hands.[2] However an instantaneous abandonment of the CAP tomorrow would lead to a crash in European land prices, with echo shocks through banking systems, which the governments involved would take some pains to avoid.

Two kinds of arguments can be mounted against protection, called for the sake of simplicity static and dynamic. The static argument claims that protection moves the average market price upwards and away from its long-run optimal value. The dynamic argument argues that protection, by isolating the domestic market from the world market, is destabilizing. When protection takes the form of a constant import quota, this last conclusion is clear. It would not be clear with a constant tariff which, for the case of a small country, causes the domestic price to be the world price plus a tariff mark-up. Then fluctuations in domestic production simply affect the level of trade. When a large country stabilizes the domestic price, as with the CAP for many products, there is a stabilization of domestic prices, and criticism should concern itself with the static case.

Ricardo mixes discussion of static and dynamic points:[3]

> This fall [in agricultural prices] has been increased by the operation of the present Corn Laws, which have the effect of driving capital to the cultivation of poor lands, and of making the price of corn in average years in this country greatly exceed the price in other countries. The price in such circumstances must be high, but in proportion as it is raised, so it is liable to a greater fall; for in abundant seasons, the whole increased quantity gluts our own market.

It is not obvious why the whole increased quantity gluts the domestic market, as all, or at least a considerable portion, would attract the export subsidy. What is true is that protection may move a country from a system in which it nearly always imports corn, so that the domestic price is the world price plus transport costs, to a system which jumps between two states. In one state there are imports, and the domestic price is the world price plus the tariff. In the other state domestic production exceeds domestic demand – far more probable when protection has produced near self-sufficiency – and the domestic price is the world price plus the export subsidy. With the export subsidy lower than the tariff, there is more price instability than that already present in the world price.

Perhaps this is what Ricardo means in the passage quoted above. If so, it could have been much more clearly expressed.

Leaving aside issues of stability and transition, Ricardo's position with regard to the long-run effects of agricultural protection is plain. He writes to McCulloch:[4]

> My opinion is this – if we were allowed to get corn as we could get it, by importation, profits would be considerably higher than they now are; but this is very considerably lower here than abroad.

Ricardo's most extensively developed discussion of the effects of the Corn Laws and similar issues is to be found in *Protection of Agriculture and the Rate of Profit*.[5] In line with the above quotation, he centres his interest on the effect of protection on capital – on its allocation and on its return.

> Instead of giving any security to the British capitalist, that wages shall not be un-naturally raised in this country . . . corn is to be rendered habitually and considerably dearer in this country, than in others.
>
> (ibid.: 246)

The consequence is that capital is pulled into agriculture. Ricardo lays stress on the point that marginal land is brought into cultivation, but plainly this interpretation is not required. A constant land area could be more intensively cultivated, or both extensive and intensive margins could be widened. One reason why Ricardo liked to emphasize marginal land is it is for such land that his famous 'Corn Theory of Profit' applies. The rate of profit on marginal land is determined as a pure number:

$$r = \frac{C - w}{c} \qquad (1)$$

where r is the pure corn rate of profit; w is the corn wage rate; and C and c are respectively the output of corn per acre, and the input of seed corn per acre.

Allowing there to be zero-rent marginal land only encourages the illusion that the rate of profit is determined somewhere, and simply and separably from the rest of the economic system. The zero rent assumption means that the rent of land is not part of costs and hence excluded from the numerator of (1). But this is achieved only at the cost of leaving unspecified where that marginal land may be found. Even so, for Ricardo held back from maintaining the wage to be determined as a constant cost of maintenance of labour supply, the wage rate appears as an unknown. This led Ricardo to argue that wage costs are the leading determinant of the rate of profit. While the conclusion is certainly correct, it should not be supposed that it follows simply as arithmetic from (1).

David Ricardo is sometimes depicted as the advocate of the capitalist's interest against that of the landlord. While it is impossible to prove what may or may not have been the motivation within his heart, he is quite sophisticated enough to employ as ammunition against agricultural protection the argument that protection is inefficient. To use modern terminology, even as a means of helping landlords, protection carries an excess burden. In a letter to Trower, supporting McCulloch against his correspondent, he explains the point with great clarity:[6]

> 'The extra rents to the landlord are not the measure of the whole loss sustained by the public in consequence of the Corn Laws', says McCulloch and to this doctrine you demur. I apprehend that he means to say that the loss to the country is a real one. It must not be supposed that because the landlord gets a high price, which is paid by the consumer, the whole inconvenience to the country is an improper and unjustifiable transfer of property – it is much more than this, the landlord does not gain what the consumer loses – there is real diminution of production, and the real loss is to be measured by such diminution of production, without any regard to price or value.

Defenders and perpetuators of the CAP, take note.

SECTORS AND AGGREGATION

In reality an economy embraces many different sectors consisting of numerous different economic activities. When they are aggregated to form grand sectors, such as agriculture, manufacturing or services, the view is taken, often implicitly, that the economic activities so aggregated share enough important qualities in common to give sense to the exercise. That there are many possible pitfalls in proceeding this way is well known. For instance for early nineteenth-century Britain there are no systematic records for the products of small-scale local manufacture of such items as carts, leather goods and cooking utensils. In effect manufacturing means the output of the new large-scale factories producing cotton or porcelain.

One could argue that the grand categories exist only in economists' minds, but that would not be correct. They also exist in policy-makers' minds and influence, for example, the choice of tariff policies. Therefore a model which pretends that the economy has only very few sectors is not to be dismissed out of hand. Williamson, see the quotation given below, argues for a three-sector specification: agricultural products, manufactures and non-tradables. For a small open economy if factor prices are fixed by the processes producing tradables, it may be possible to set the non-tradable sector aside and concentrate on tradables alone.[7]

With two tradable sectors, agriculture and manufacturing, how many factors have to be taken into account? No model can engage with the contemporary debates concerning the Corn Laws which does not include at least capital, labour and land. For the present argument it is not necessary to compute incomes of domestic factors, which calculation needs to take into account tariff revenue and its disposition. The open economy specification effectively isolates domestic production from domestic demand. Hence changes in domestic production and factor prices consequent upon a removal of protection depend only on the alteration in relative producer prices induced.

Land will be treated as homogeneous, so there will be no extensive margin. This makes things usefully simpler. There is no difficulty in having land vary in quality and to obtain an extensive margin, as in Ricardo. However, as argued above, Ricardo's view according to which the extensive margin is of crucial theoretical significance is entirely mistaken. To facilitate comparison with the Stolper–Samuelson model, assume that the national capital supply is given. Ricardo certainly saw the international mobility of capital to be significant, although it would be wrong to attribute to him an assumption of perfect capital mobility.

Because the Corn Laws increased the demand for unskilled labour used intensively in the production of food, thus producing a rise in wages, but also raised the price of grain, there is an apparent ambiguity as to what their effect was on the real wage of the industrial labourers who paid the Anti-Corn Law League's 'bread tax'. Williamson (1990: 131) asserts the existence of such an ambiguity without explaining why the Stolper and Samuelson (1941–2), henceforth S–S, conclusion, according to which protection of a labour intensive industry raises the real wages of labour in terms of any final product does not dispose of that ambiguity. In fact Williamson, with the historian's eye for detail, has in mind a more complicated model than that used by S–S. He mentions capital market segmentation. His distinction between unskilled labour and common labour points to the segmented labour market assumption which his general equilibrium model embodies.

The issue of labour market segmentation is controversial. Harley[8] does not regard it as significant:

> Removal of tariffs affected both the prices of goods and the incomes of labourers, capitalists and landlords. Landlords were located, of course, in agriculture and their incomes would fall. But workers were located everywhere: in the very agriculture made worse off by the fall of protection, in manufacturing made better off, and what is most important in the vast sector of goods and (especially) services that did not cross Britain's borders on their way from producer to consumer. Workers were not committed to one vulnerable sector.

With the help of a number of heroic assumptions we have arrived at two tradables sectors and three factors; too many factors, according to factor price equalization theory, to determine factor prices independently of demand. However the special, but not unreasonable, assumption according to which land is employed to a significant extent only in agriculture can make the problem easier to crack, as will be shown below.

CAPITAL INTENSITY

Meanwhile an important question has to be considered. Obviously the assumption that land is used only in agriculture makes agriculture land intensive. But what about capital and labour? Ignoring land, which is the capital intensive sector, meaning using capital intensively relative to labour; agriculture or manufacturing?

Eli Heckscher based his famous discussion of the division of labour in nineteenth-century trade across the Atlantic on the assumption that the land abundant New World would export food to a labour abundant Old World which would export manufactures. Later economists wanted to get capital into the model, because it was too important to leave out. So they dumped land, and now the textbooks featured capital intensive manufacturing and labour intensive agriculture. By the 1970s US agriculture had become more capital intensive than US manufacturing. Agriculture involves huge invisible capital inputs. Lengthy waiting for inputs to yield a return, which no factory owner would contemplate, are unavoidable. Obviously tractors are capital: but so are horses, and they can involve higher capital costs. A tractor stays in the barn through the winter snows while a horse has to be fed.

Table 15.1 shows factor shares for agriculture and manufacturing (Crafts 1985: 83 ff.). The ground given for there being no entry for land in the case of manufacturing is the unavailability of data. That would fit with the present assumption that the entry would be negligible were it available. Notice that when land is ignored labour shares equally with capital in the

Table 15.1 Factor shares by sector

	Agriculture %	Manufacturing %
Capital	20	50
Labour	40	50
Land	40	–

output of manufacturing, while in agriculture labour takes twice what capital takes. Manufacturing is capital intensive.

STOLPER–SAMULESON EXTENDED

A simple model makes it possible to capture some of Ricardo's ideas, extend them and compare them with modern trade models of the Stolper–Samuelson variety.[9] There are two sectors producing tradables, agriculture and manufacturing. It is necessary, however, to take into account three factors: labour, land and capital. That could introduce large complications relative to the standard 2×2 trade model. A simple and appropriate assumption avoids this outcome. Land is only used to a negligible extent in manufacturing. Therefore in the simple model it is employed only in agriculture. That is close enough to the truth to serve very well and it greatly simplifies the analysis. Assuming the labour market not to be segmented, can we apply the simple model to show the effect of agricultural protection on the real food wage of labour. Then the model can arbitrate between Cobden and Bright and the Anti-Corn Law League on the one hand, and Ricardo on the other. The Anti-Corn Law League claimed that agricultural protection produced a bread tax, that is a fall in the food wage of workers. Ricardo on this interpretation held that it taxed profits.

Figure 15.1 illustrates the effect of a fall in agricultural protection on the assumption that manufacturing is capital intensive relative to agriculture.

For given output prices, and for a land rental consistent with equilibrium at those prices, the figure shows various combinations of the factor prices R and W, measured in terms of agricultural output, which are consistent with cost price equality for agriculture and manufacturing respectively. Ignore the broken curves at this stage. The curve AA' shows factor price combinations consistent with cost price equality for agriculture; the curve MM' shows factor price combinations consistent with cost price equality for manufacturing. Equilibrium factor prices are given – uniquely in this case – by the intersection of the two curves at B.[10] This is standard Stolper–Samuelson analysis.

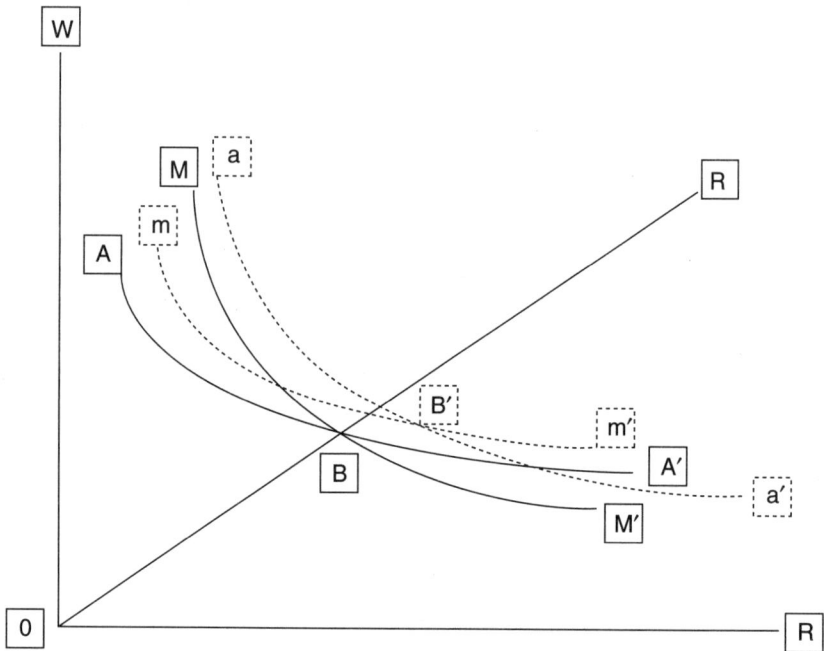

Figure 15.1 Equilibrium in the generalized Stolper–Samuelson model

Now let a cut in agricultural protection raise the relative price of manufactures. This allows manufacturing to sustain higher factor prices as is
shown in the figure by an upward shift of the curve MM′ to the dotted curve
mm′. The price change will cause agricultural production to fall. Then to
absorb the fixed supply of land, land rents will have to fall. When they do,
agriculture will be able to sustain higher factor prices as is shown in Figure
15.1, by an upward shift of the curve AA′ to the dotted curve aa′. The two
curves aa′ and mm′ intersect at B′. The effect of a cut in agricultural protection on the food wage rate is ambiguous. In the Figure B′ is higher than
B, so that a cut in agricultural protection raises the food wage rate. However
it is plainly possible to draw the figure in such a way that the food wage
rate falls with a cut in agricultural protection. As the MM′ curve shifting
upwards causes the food wage rate to fall (simple Stolper–Samuelson), there
will be a fall in the food wage rate in the figure if the effect caused by lower
land rents is negligible, so that the AA′ curve barely shifts. We may note the
unambiguous conclusion that the rental of capital is always increased by a
cut in agricultural protection. The ambiguity which has been noted does not
affect Ricardo's conclusion that protection is bad for the capitalist.

To determine exactly what happens the model has to be calibrated. This is
done in the Appendix, where it emerges that for a Cobb–Douglas specification using the numbers taken from Crafts (1985), the outcome is as depicted

in Figure 15.1. Cutting agricultural protection raises the food wage rate of all labour, including for an economy with mobile labour, manufacturing labour.

SOME CURIOSA

The alert reader may notice that the argument organized around Figure 15.1 is a little loose. It is based on two assumptions which it did not even bother to state:

- The relative output price change consequent upon the removal of agricultural protection will cause a decline in agricultural output; hence a fall in the demand for land; hence a fall in land rents.
- The relative factor price change for labour and capital will not by itself affect the demand for land, and in particular will not induce such a large increase in the demand for land that more will be demanded despite the fall in agricultural output.

Neither assumption is guaranteed to be correct. Thus if labour and capital are used in fixed proportions in both agriculture and manufacturing, a small change in output prices will not affect outputs. This is the same as saying that output changes in the Heckscher–Ohlin–Samuelson model depend upon factor substitutions. With fixed proportions there would be no decline in agricultural output with the removal of agricultural protection, and therefore no decline in the demand for land. In order to make this case work, without supposing a chance equality of factor supplies and factor demands with no flexibility on either side, one would have to suppose land to be substitutable so that its rent would fall to get it fully employed. Then the fall in the price of food would lower the marginal product of land, which would be reflected in an equivalent fall in the rent of land.

Leaving aside fixed proportions, the force of the second assumption can be shown by imagining capital and land to be perfect substitutes so that only their sum matters. Then the fixed supply of land automatically allocated to agriculture becomes simply part of its capital supply. As a fall in agricultural protection raises the real price of capital, it will do the same to the rent of land. This case looks unrealistic too. Capital in agriculture substitutes for labour more than it substitutes for land. The evidence is that agricultural protection does raise land rents. This was seen in Britain after the Corn Laws were abolished,[11] when land rents fell, and again after the CAP had restored protection, when land rents rose.

THE SHORT RUN AND SPECIFIC FACTORS

It is interesting to find the possibility of theoretical support for Cobden and Bright from an extended S–S model. Yet such an argument is historically anomalous. Cobden and Bright wrote one hundred years in advance of the publication of the simple S–S model. To attribute to them a gut comprehension of an extended S–S model, a model which has to be calibrated and solved with the aid of a computer, is extremely farfetched.

All versions of the S–S model depict a long-run outcome in which factors have relocated to equalize marginal products across sectors. To see the Anti-Corn Law League as representing the interest of 'labour' in this sense may be to miss the point. For one thing, Cobden and Bright were manufacturers, not industrial labourers, so that their argument from the interest of their labour, let alone all labour, must be slightly suspect. Even leaving that point aside, suppose that one could go back in time and convince Cobden and Bright that a cut in agricultural protection would eventually cause capital to leave agriculture, and that the consequent decline in agricultural employment would produce such an influx of workers into manufacturing as to depress wages. They might well be unimpressed. That process could take quite a time to work, and in the meantime manufacturing workers would benefit from the rise in the price of their product relative to food, and who knows what the world may look like after some considerable time. In other words, if we can contemplate applying the S–S model to the Corn Law debate, why not apply the specific factors model?

For a review of the literature on the specific factors model, and an excellent exposition, see Jones and Neary (1984: 21–7). The model is designed to depict the impact of a change in prices, such as the abolition of the Corn Laws would produce. During the medium-term period, one factor, the relatively mobile factor, has moved between the sectors so as to equalize marginal products. The other factor, whichever it may be, is frozen in the quantities for each sector appropriate to long-run equilibrium prior to the price change. On the usual interpretation, labour is the relatively mobile factor.

Taking into account capital immobility, consider what happens in the sector whose relative price has risen. Measure prices, including factor prices, in terms of the other good. That sector will lose mobile labour, raising the marginal product of the labour that remains, and lowering the marginal product of capital in that sector. The other sector will gain labour, as the model assumes full employment. The marginal product of labour will rise in both sectors in terms of the good whose price has not risen, but will fall in terms of the other good, because more labour has been added to a fixed capital supply. Note the contrast with the Stolper–Samuelson model, where factor price movements are in the same direction for all goods.

Can one apply this model to the Corn Laws to decide the issue of the bread tax? Suppose that labour is the mobile factor, as in the usual specific factors model, and that a sudden imposition of Corn Law protection raises the relative price of labour intensive food. Then sudden agricultural protection would lower the food wage of labour in both sectors. One could say that this effect would be produced by the failure of temporarily immobile capital to move into agriculture following the price rise.

The behaviour of the specific factors model is history dependent, because it is governed by where the short-run immobile capital is located. To replicate the debate in which the Manchester free traders took part we should consider a case in which agricultural protection has been in place for some time, so that capital has been pulled into agriculture, just as Ricardo claimed. Then the protection is removed, as the free traders advocated. The food wage of labour is higher in the short run, before any capital has relocated itself, than it will be in the long run. There is more capital in agriculture and less in manufacturing than will be the case in the long run, and this holds the food wage higher than the Stolper–Samuelson model would predict.

Cobden and Bright had no formal model, but may be interpreted as emphasizing immediate effects, which makes a specific factors model appropriate for representing their views. Certainly the specific factors model is good for an Anti-Corn Law League interpretation of labour's interest.

THE COMMON AGRICULTURAL POLICY

It is tempting to analyse the CAP as simply the Corn Laws replicated in the twentieth century. There is something in that analogy but care has to be exercised in pushing the comparison too far. Realistically for modern economies, it is appropriate to assume capital mobility for small countries. Then the policy could be seen as raising food prices relative to manufacturing prices, and lowering the food wage relative to the food rent of land. This has happened in modern EU Europe. The contemporary arguments concerned with the Corn Laws were, implicitly at least, about poverty and income distribution. For a bread tax surely fell on the poor, if not the poorest; and landlords and capitalists were likely to be rich. As food is particularly important for the budgets of the poor, it is reasonable to suppose that the CAP has a regressive and poverty increasing effect.

This is the opposite to the intentions of the original designers of the CAP, who saw themselves as pushing income distribution in favour of poor farmers. The error involved is easily described. These thinkers overlooked the fluidity of factor ownership, and the mobility of the factors themselves. Arguably the Corn Law abolitionists made a similar mistake. They neglected to consider that the decline in domestic agriculture, which they were advocating in effect, would generate an increased supply pressure on the market for manufacturing labour. However, we have seen that, while this might have made their case invalid, for the long run at least, it did not necessarily do so.

In theory the CAP should have raised real wages and helped to retain labour in agriculture. Why it did not do so cannot be truly explained by any static model. Technology was changing very rapidly during this period, and in ways unfavourable to the demand for labour in agriculture. That feature itself unites the two periods. Large price-reducing changes in world agriculture (and particularly in food transportation) came hard upon the heels of Corn Law abolition. These proved in the end to be more important than the tariff reduction itself.

CONCLUSIONS

Discussion of the Corn Laws by economic historians has neglected one of the most famous results of trade theory – the Stolper–Samuelson theorem. At first sight it looks as though this lacuna might be very serious. If the simple S–S model could be applied to the problem, the conclusion would be that agricultural protection should increase the real wage of labour; that the bread tax would be negative; that with regard to the long run at least, the Anti-Corn Law League pleaded a fallacious case.

The generalized three-factor S–S model shows these issues in an entirely different light. With land in the model, a cut in agricultural protection produces a fall in the rental of land. Because that happens there is no necessity for the other factor used intensively in agriculture – labour – to become cheaper. Indeed it may become more expensive. That is what happens in the calibrated model of the Appendix, which uses Cobb–Douglas production functions and numbers consistent with historical values.

To attempt to throw light on historical views using modern economic analysis is inevitably to run the risk of producing absurd and anomalous arguments. It is not plausible to imagine that the Anti-Corn Law propagandists instinctively understood an economic argument involving subtle and indirect effects. It is more reasonable to suppose that they took a more superficial view of the issues, and that a short-run or specific factors model might capture their ideas better than a long-run S–S approach. Be that as it may, the Anti-Corn Law League's instincts were not necessarily wrong, not even for the long run. Quite possibly, 150 years after the abolition of the Corn Laws, it remains correct to regard these laws as a 'bread tax'.

Finally, the tempting analogy between the Corn Laws and the CAP is not to be taken too far or too seriously. Agriculture in modern European economies accounts for a low share of national product in comparison with the mid-nineteenth century. Further, the cut in real wages, which is certainly an effect of the CAP, has qualitatively different consequences in a modern economy with a social security system which makes possible non-transitory unemployment without family support.

To illustrate this last point, consider what high food prices do to the incentive to seek work when the alternative is to claim unemployment benefit. It depends on how the benefit level is chosen. If the political process selects the benefit level with reference to an acceptable minimum standard of living, then high food prices implicitly push up the money value of unemployment benefit, but not necessarily to the same extent as the market wage rate. In that case the CAP might cause unemployment in a manner which would not seem plausible for the Corn Laws.

NOTES

1 See Hobsbawm (1968: Chapter 5).
2 For the original designers of the CAP this point would have seemed relatively unimportant because on mainland Europe cultivators were typically small-scale farmers who owned the land they cultivated. Long-term trends, sometimes attributed to the CAP, but to a greater extent the result of technical change and rising incomes, have raised farm sizes and increased the relevance of the distinction between rents and cultivator labour income.
3 Ricardo (1951–) *Protection of Agriculture*, Volume IV, Pamphlets 1815–23.
4 Ricardo (1951–) Volume VIII, 422, pp. 357–8.
5 In Ricardo (1951–) Volume IV, Pamphlets 1815–23.
6 Ricardo (1951–) Volume IX, Letters 1821–3, p. 499.
7 That would depend on it being possible to postpone the consideration of demand until after prices are known, i.e. on a non-substitution theorem type of result which obviously depends on constant returns to scale.
8 Harley, K. (1994) 'Foreign trade, comparative advantage and performance', in R. Floud and D. N. McCloskey (eds) *An Economic History of Modern Britain Since 1770*, Cambridge: Cambridge University Press, p. 315.
9 See Stolper and Samuleson (1941–2) and any textbook of international economics.
10 Uniqueness is guaranteed when AA is everywhere flatter than MM, as will be the case with the strong factor intensity assumption.
11 Other changes, apart from a fall in the level of tariffs, followed the abolition of the Corn Laws. Free on board agricultural prices trended downwards during the second half of the nineteenth century. The effect of this on British land rents was the same as the direct effect of tariff abolition.

REFERENCES

Blaug, M. (1958) *Ricardian Economics*, New Haven: Yale University Press.
Corry, B.A. (1987) 'Robert Torrens', in J. Eatwell, M. Milgate and P. Newman (eds) *New Palgrave Dictionary of Economic Thought*, London: Macmillan.
Crafts, N.F.R. (1985) *British Economic Growth during the Industrial Revolution*, Oxford: Clarendon Press.
Fairley, S. (1965) 'The nineteenth century Corn Law reconsidered', *Economic History Review*, 2nd ser. 18 (3): 562–75.

—— (1969) 'The Corn Laws and British wheat production 1829–76', *Economic History Review*, 2nd ser. 22 (1): 88–116.

Floud, R. and McCloskey, D.N. (eds) (1994) *An Economic History of Modern Britain Since 1770*, 2nd edn, vol. 1: 1700–1860, Cambridge: Cambridge University Press.

Foreman-Peck, J. (1983) *A History of the World Economy*, London: Harvester Wheatsheaf Books.

Hicks, J.R. (1939) 'The foundations of welfare economics', *Economic Journal* 48.

Hilton, B. (1987) 'The Corn Laws', in J. Eatwell, M. Milgate and P. Newman (eds) *New Palgrave Dictionary of Economic Thought*, London: Macmillan.

Hobsbawm, E.J. (1968) *Industry and Empire: An Economic History of Britain since 1750*, London: Weidenfeld and Nicholson.

Howarth, R. (1992) 'The common agricultural policy', in P. Minford (ed.) *The Cost of Europe*, Manchester: Manchester University Press.

Jones, R.W. and Neary, J.P. (1984) 'Positive theory of international trade', in R.W. Jones and P.B. Kenen (eds) *Handbook of International Economics*, vol. I, Amsterdam: North-Holland.

Kaldor, N. (1939) 'Welfare propositions in economics', *Economic Journal* 49.

Kindleberger, C.P. (1975) 'The rise of free trade in Western Europe 1820–1875', *Journal of Economic History* 35 (1) March: 20–55.

McCloskey, D.N. (1980) 'Magnanimous Albion: free trade and British national income, 1841–1881', *Explorations in Economic History* 17 (3): 303–20.

Ricardo, David (1951–) *The Works and Correspondence of David Ricardo*, ed. P. Sraffa, with the collaboration of M.H. Dobb, London: Royal Economic Society. Volume IV Pamphlets 1815–23; Volume IX Letters 1821–3.

Robbins, L.C. (1935) *The Nature and Significance of Economic Science*, 2nd edn, London: Macmillan.

Stolper, W.F. and Samuelson, P.A. (1941–2) 'Protection and real wages', *Review of Economic Studies* IX: 58–73.

Williamson, J.G. (1990) 'The impact of the Corn Laws just prior to repeal', *Explorations in Economic History* 27: 123–56.

APPENDIX

The appendix calibrates the generalized S–S model using values derived from Crafts (1985). The model assumes Cobb–Douglas functions and is:

$$y_a = \left[k_a^{\alpha} \cdot \ell_a^{1-\alpha} \right]^{\beta} \cdot N_0^{1-\beta} \tag{2}$$

$$y_m = k_m^{\gamma} \cdot \ell_m^{1-\gamma} \tag{3}$$

Table 15.2 implies $\alpha = \tfrac{1}{3}$; $\beta = 0.6$; $\gamma = 0.5$. These values satisfy the requirement that manufacturing be capital intensive which requires $\gamma - \alpha > 0$. Cost–price equality gives:

$$r^{0.2} \cdot w^{0.4} \cdot q^{0.4} = 1 \tag{4}$$

$$r^{0.5} \cdot w^{0.5} = p \tag{5}$$

where r, w, and q are the factor prices of respectively capital, labour and land, all in terms of agricultural output; and p is the price of manufactures in terms of agricultural output.

Outputs in a diversified equilibrium are determined by:

$$y_a \cdot \frac{\alpha \beta}{r} + y_m \cdot \frac{\gamma}{r} = K_0 \tag{6}$$

$$y_a \cdot \frac{(1-\alpha)\beta}{w} + y_m \cdot \frac{1-\gamma}{w} = L_0 \tag{7}$$

$$y_a \cdot \frac{1-\beta}{q} = N_0 \tag{8}$$

These equations may be rewritten as:

$$0.2 \cdot y_a + 0.5 \cdot y_m = r \cdot K_0 \tag{9}$$

$$0.4 \cdot y_a + 0.5 \cdot y_m = w \cdot L_0 \tag{10}$$

$$0.4 \cdot y_a = q \cdot N_0 \tag{11}$$

From (9) and (10):

$$y_a = 5 \cdot \left[w \cdot L_0 - r \cdot K_0 \right] \tag{12}$$

$$y_m = 2 \cdot \left[2 \cdot r \cdot K_0 - w \cdot L_0 \right] \tag{13}$$

From (4) and (5):

$$w = \frac{1}{p^2 \cdot q^2} \tag{14}$$

$$r = p^4 \cdot q^2 \tag{15}$$

Now (14–15) together give:

$$2.5 \cdot q \cdot N_0 = 5 \cdot \left[\frac{1}{p^2 \cdot q^2} \cdot L_0 - p^4 \cdot q^2 \cdot K_0 \right] \tag{16}$$

$$y_m = 2 \cdot \left[2 \cdot p^4 \cdot q^2 \cdot K_0 - \frac{1}{p^2 \cdot q^2} \cdot L_0 \right] \tag{17}$$

From (17):

$$2 \cdot p^4 \cdot K_0 \cdot q^4 + N_0 \cdot q^3 - \frac{2 L_0}{p^2} = 0 \tag{18}$$

Call the left-hand side of (18) $h(q)$. Then:

$$h(0) < 0 \tag{19}$$

$$\frac{dh(q)}{dq} = 8 \cdot p^4 \cdot K_0 \cdot q^3 + 3 \cdot N_0 \cdot q^2 \tag{20}$$

Note that (18) cannot take the value zero, which it must do at a turning point, for a positive value of q. Therefore (18) has a unique positive root. Note that the solution of (18) depends only on the ratios of factor supplies:

$$2 \cdot p^4 \cdot \frac{K_0}{N_0} \cdot q^4 + q^3 - \frac{L_0}{N_0} \cdot \frac{2}{p^2} = 0 \tag{21}$$

Table 15.2 shows solutions to the model, via solutions to the quartic equation (21). For a wide range of values of $\frac{L_0}{N_0}$, shown in the top row, the second row shows values for $\frac{K_0}{N_0}$ for which the model solution gives the output of agriculture close to one-half the output of manufacturing, for the

Table 15.2 Model solutions

$\dfrac{L}{N}$	0.2	0.4	0.6	0.8	1.0	1.2	1.4	1.6	1.8	2.0
$\dfrac{K}{N}$	5.8	4.6	4.0	3.6	3.3	3.1	3.0	2.8	2.7	2.6
w	.166	.268	.352	.428	.500	.565	.621	.686	.741	.796
	.186	.301	.395	.480	.560	.633	.696	.769	.831	.893
$\dfrac{y_a}{y_m}$	.646	.666	.669	.675	.683	.684	.671	.688	.686	.688
	.478	.492	.493	.497	.503	.504	.495	.506	.505	.506

higher value of p. Then the two lower rows show solution values for the food wages rate and for the ratio of agricultural output to manufacturing output. For each case two values are given; on top the value for $p = 1$, below the value for $p = 1.1$.

The solutions shown exhibit two notable features:

- A 10 per cent increase in p invariably increases w. This is already contrary to the simple S–S model. As with the simple S–S model, however, a 10 per cent increase in p leads to a more than 10 per cent increase in w, so that labour gains even if it only consumes manufactures. This is magnification, but in the wrong direction: a fall in protection for the labour intensive industry helps labour in terms of any good.
- The last feature is entirely due to the presence of the third factor, land. Another feature of Table 15.2 is also accounted for by the intervention of land. As the labour/land ratio rises (moving from left to right in the table), the capital/labour ratio has to fall to keep the share of agricultural output roughly constant. This again is contrary to the simple S–S model, where the labour/capital ratio has to stay constant to keep output shares constant.

    A rise in the labour/land ratio tends to augment agricultural production because it represents an increase in the factor used abundantly in agriculture. A rise in the labour/land ratio tends to augment manufacturing production because it lowers the marginal opportunity cost of labour in agriculture making it available more cheaply to manufacturing. What we see in Table 15.2 is the second effect predominating.

16

COMMENTARY ON CHAPTER 15

Hylke Vandenbussche

If a prize were to have been awarded for the most original and relevant idea to the conference's title, in my view Christopher Bliss should have got it. The issue he addresses in his chapter is: What are the effects of agricultural protection on manufacturing competitiveness? This question was raised in the nineteenth century at the time of the Corn Laws and is still relevant today in the context of the European Union's Common Agricultural Policy (CAP). The first question that springs to mind when one reads about a comparison between the Corn Laws and the CAP is: have we learned nothing from history? Does history repeat itself or are we comparing two different things? The chapter by Bliss seems to suggest that the nineteenth century does not differ too much from the present for the comparison to be appropriate.

In what follows, however, I would like to raise a number of issues that, despite the appealing logic of the comparison, intuitively cast doubt on its adequacy. According to Bliss, Ricardo's analysis is still useful today when we analyse CAP. David Ricardo was a proponent of abolishing the Corn Laws because, in his view, agricultural protection will depress manufacturing profits. Wages, in Ricardo's model of perfect competition and one factor of production, are subsistence wages and constitute the most important determinant in manufacturing profits. However, I find it intuitively difficult to believe that:

1 Today's profits in the manufacturing sector are solely determined by wages.
2 The price of agricultural products is the prime determinant in wages today.

First, I will comment on why I have difficulty in accepting the idea that profits in the manufacturing sector are mainly determined by wages. Manufacturing sectors where wages are relatively high can still be very competitive, namely in those areas where the labour cost in relation to total production costs is relatively low. This is the case in the more capital intensive industries where, according to the theory of comparative advantage, a trade bloc like the EU should have some advantage over its neighbours such as the Central European countries. If wages are the sole determinant of profits nowadays, then I fail to see why all manufacturing producers do not go to Central Europe and set up their plants there. According to several recent studies, delocalization of firms is far less than expected. Hence, there must be other factors apart from wages to explain company profits, if we believe that these are what firms are trying to maximize.

A second aspect where life in the nineteenth century differs from the present is that in my view wages are no longer solely determined by the price of European agricultural products. What I believe has changed in relation to a century ago is that the world is no longer about wheat and corn, but increasingly about differentiated products with a lot of substitutes for each one. Although I am not suggesting that when the price of European potatoes goes up people will massively switch to eating rice. In general, however, substitution is a lot easier nowadays than it was a century ago. I therefore find it difficult to see why CAP should be the sole determinant of European wages in manufacturing today. To that extent I seriously doubt that this is the main reason underlying the perceived or real reduction in Europe's competitiveness. Personally I feel that other factors such as the political clout of the trade unions in the industry and the level of social security payments will affect wages just as significantly. In order to illustrate this, let us consider a country such as Belgium. When it is ranked according to gross wages over productivity it comes out very badly, but in terms of net wages (net of taxes and social security payments) over productivity it is quite competitive.

Although I doubt the magnitude of the effect of CAP on wage levels, this does not mean I approve of it. I can see at least two good reasons why CAP should be abolished. The purpose of CAP is twofold: providing income for European farmers and securing European self-sufficiency. Although I have some sympathy for the former, the tools used to achieve that objective are too distortive. CAP is maintained through subsidization of prices which is far more distortive than, say, subsidization of farmers' income. It also creates the wrong incentives. We only have to think about butter mountains and milk lakes to know that this is true. With subsidization of prices no gradual adjustment is possible. Either the government subsidizes prices until they reach world levels or it does not, whereas with income subsidization, a gradual approach is possible. Gradualism was also very much favoured by Ricardo.

The national defence argument I find difficult to swallow. Trade, as it was pointed out in other papers presented at the conference, is the best way to ensure peace. The more integrated markets are, the more interdependent they become, which reduces the risk of wars in a military sense.

I admit that my comments on the chapter by Bliss are very intuitive. I fully recognize that intuition, vital to the economist as it may be, can often be misleading. Only analytical work can affirm one's intuition or prove it wrong. I sincerely hope to come across more studies that address this issue in an analytical or a numerical manner. The chapter by Bliss is one of the few serious attempts in that direction.

17

ANTIDUMPING ACTIONS IN HIGH TECHNOLOGY INDUSTRIES

The case of semiconductors

Harald Gruber

INTRODUCTION

The semiconductor industry is the supplier of key technologies and products in modern society. The invention of the semiconductor device known as the transistor in 1947 at the Bell Laboratories in the USA ushered in what many have called the second industrial revolution. Since the first large-scale industrial applications of semiconductors, these products have fundamentally changed the world. As a result of the striving for miniaturization, cost reduction and increasing performance, semiconductors have found direct application in almost everything produced and have spurred the development of other important industries, such as computers, telecommunications and consumer electronics. It is therefore not surprising that semiconductors are sometimes referred to as the key raw material for our information society or as the oil of the next century. There is, of course, also a political–strategic dimension, as it has become clear that military supremacy is crucially dependent on access to key semiconductor technology. The impressions of the high-tech features of the recent Gulf War are still alive in our memories to remind us of how effectively technological supremacy can be used.

This study illustrates, by means of the semiconductor industry, the problem of identifying the appropriate trade policies in oligopolistic industries, in particular with respect to antidumping actions. Because of the pervasiveness of 'learning by doing' effects in semiconductor production, temporary below cost pricing can be a non-predatory business strategy. Traditional methods of assessing dumping are therefore not appropriate to detect it. They are also likely to find dumping when below cost pricing is not necessarily part of a strategy deliberately to drive local competitors out of the market. As a result, antidumping investigators should model the cost curve to assess dumping properly and take account of product specific differences.

Antidumping actions can be seen as a GATT/WTO-conform device for providing protection to this allegedly strategic industry. But even in this case the selection of the appropriate policies requires deep knowledge of the industries involved. These issues are analysed in the special context of the antidumping actions undertaken by the European Commission.

The study is arranged as follows. The second section provides a brief guide to the key propositions of strategic trade theory and assesses their relevance. The third section argues that antidumping duties have been used to protect the semiconductor industry. The fourth section discusses the consequences of this policy.

GENERAL ASPECTS OF STRATEGIC TRADE POLICY

This section provides a brief guide to the main propositions of strategic trade policy. The frequent recourse to antidumping actions for the promotion of so-called strategic industries should be seen in the wider context of the academic debate on trade policy. Mainstream orientations in trade policy have undergone significant changes during the last decade. Traditionally free trade minded countries, such as the USA, have shown increasing interest in pursuing an 'activist' role to influence trade flows. This interest has been spurred on the one hand by the success stories of Japan and other newly industrializing countries which had assigned an active role to the state in trade policy, and on the other by the perception of relative economic decline by the industrialized countries, especially the USA (e.g. Prestowitz 1988; Tyson 1992; Krugman 1994).

A sort of legitimacy for the change of tack concerning free trade has also come from the academic side with new trade models which question if not the benefits at least the rationales for unfettered free trade (Helpman and Krugman 1989). In oligopolistic industries, trade policy induces the shifting of oligopoly rents. Countries therefore have incentives to manipulate trade. From this a crucial question emerges: if trade should be manipulated, can theory tell us what are the right instruments? Precise answers are of prime importance for the effectiveness of policy. Unfortunately, theory can give only limited guidance.

The theory

The theoretical basis of strategic trade theory goes back to the 1970s and is associated with the stone-rolling work of economists such as Krugman, Dixit, Helpman, Brander and Spencer (Krugman 1986). The approach is based on a change of paradigm, mainly the shift from the perfect competition framework to that of imperfect competition, or oligopoly.

With perfect competition models, international trade is driven by the fact that countries differ either in their factor endowments or in their technology. Gains from trade essentially originate from specialization, according to comparative advantage. The implication for trade policy is that, apart from some special cases, government intervention is in general not welfare improving because intervention distorts the functioning of perfectly competitive markets. A country should export the goods in which it has a comparative advantage in production and import the goods in which it has a comparative disadvantage. As a result, trade should be most intensive between countries which differ in their factor endowments and the goods imported should differ from the goods exported.

This approach has been challenged by the empirical observation that the largest part of trade occurs among industrialized countries and the goods traded are very similar (Grubel and Lloyd 1975). This induced a revision of the basic assumptions underlying models of perfect competition. For instance, departures from traditional assumptions on cost, by allowing for economies of scale, produce outcomes that are different from perfect competition results. The focus in trade theory has shifted toward the integration of imperfectly competitive markets into the trade framework. The departure from the assumption of perfectly competitive markets therefore needed a blending of trade theory with the theory of industrial organization. As a result, trade theory also became afflicted by the difficult problems of endemic multiplicity of equilibrium outcomes, which have been summarized in the industrial organization literature by the statement 'with oligopoly anything can happen' (Sutton 1991). Problems become most strikingly evident once the effects of different trade policies are analysed. For example, Spencer and Brander (1983) have shown that in a duopoly with Cournot competition subsidizing exports would be welfare improving. On the other hand, Eaton and Grossman (1986) have demonstrated the opposite with Bertrand competition; to increase welfare the government should rather levy a tax on domestic exports. Precise predictions of outcomes depend crucially on the characteristics of markets and firm behaviour. Moreover, apparently small changes of basic characteristics of the industry may entail radical changes in policies.

The complexity of strategic trade models increases when cost is determined through learning by doing. This is a field that theory still needs fully to explore. The most common proposition is that protection gives leeway to domestic firms for learning, improving thereby international competitiveness along the lines of the infant industry protection arguments (Dasgupta and Stiglitz 1988). Given, however, the importance of timing in the dynamic setting, the optimal policies depend very much on a series of industry specific parameters and also intertemporal issues such as time consistency. Leahy and Neary (1994) have shown that when the policy-makers cannot precommit themselves to future policies and learning is sufficiently rapid, then it may be optimal to tax exports. This because a firm has an incentive to take actions in the present that will increase the subsidy it receives in the future. To counteract this socially wasteful strategic behaviour, the government has to tax rather than subsidize the exports.

Policy implications

The effects of trade policy in the context of perfect competition have been analysed extensively and there is widespread agreement on them. The main tenet is that trade policy in most of the cases does not improve welfare and therefore should be avoided except in very particular circumstances. In trade models with imperfectly competitive markets the opposite holds. The question is rather what are the most appropriate tools for trade policy. As seen above, policy conclusions are extremely sensitive to the behavioural assumptions in the model and very few robust results can be obtained. Moreover, the conclusions of welfare improving trade policy hinge on the assumption that foreign countries do not retaliate. If there is retaliation, both are worse off, thereby producing the well-known 'prisoner's dilemma' situation. One may therefore conclude that, after all, unrestricted free trade is the most sensible policy.

Even though this may be accepted in general, pragmatists raise the question of how to deal with countries that are adopting an activist trade policy, which are often perceived as 'unfair traders'. Is there a middle way between 'turning the other cheek' and the threat of 'tit-for-tat' retaliation? One way would be to resort to multilaterally accepted conflict settlement institutions, in particular the GATT. This approach is often despised because of alleged lack of normative clout or slow procedure. There are, however, few alternatives on which mutual agreement could be found.

Trade policy has become an especially contentious issue during the last years especially with reference to high technology industries. Because these industries generate apparently strong technological spillovers which are not internalized by firms, there appears to be large scope for government intervention (Krugman 1986; Tyson 1992). However, the policies of the different countries are likely to enter into conflict with each other. Examples are the dispute between the USA and Japan on semiconductors or the argument between USA and several European countries on aircraft construction such as the Airbus programme. As a matter of fact, under certain circumstances trade policy can also be very successful. Several studies on the Japanese success in the semiconductor industry attribute this to a large extent to strategic trade policy. These have consisted of mainly protectionist practices, such as tariff and non-tariff barriers as well as restrictions on foreign direct investment (Okimoto et al. 1984).

Dumping

The issue of dumping is controversial, both theoretically and empirically. The question is in many respects similar to the problem that industrial economists have encountered with predatory pricing; they find it difficult to distinguish between predatory pricing and 'tough' price competition (Roberts 1987). With dumping, it may be hard to separate it from normal competition. From a theoretical point of view, the definition of dumping is difficult as it may mean different things according to the situation. From a practical point of view, evidence of dumping is very hard to quantify and there are very few empirical studies describing these situations.

Dumping is said to occur if a foreign producer sells its output in an export market:

- either at a price below what it charges on the domestic market or in third countries (price discrimination);
- or at a price that does not permit recovery of all production costs (below cost sales).

Dumping is considered by most countries as an unfair trade practice, despite the theoretical possibility that everyone in a country receiving the dumped goods could be made better off than before dumping. The consumer interest is generally neglected in favour of domestic producers. GATT rules permit antidumping duties, provided that dumping causes injury to domestic producers. Concerning the question of injury, there are two aspects. First, injury must be caused by an increase in the volume of imports. Second, those imports must be causally linked to a change in the price which therefore hurts domestic producers.

Article VI of the GATT authorizes the imposition of antidumping duties on dumped exports in the case that dumping hurts the domestic industry of the products concerned, and that there is an economic interest in protecting the domestic industry. The maximum amount of the antidumping duty that is admitted is the 'margin of dumping'; that is, the difference between the price at which the good is sold on the home market of the exporter and the price of the good when exported. If the price of the good on the home market is not available, a price is constructed. This takes account of the exporter's production cost, including selling cost and profit. Alternatively, the highest available export price for the like good to a third country may be used.

Both of the above definitions of dumping can be reconciled with circumstances where the intent of the foreign firm is not to harm the importing country, but dumping turns out to be the result of a profit-maximizing price strategy. For instance, this can be the case in the well-known example of markets with different demand elasticity, in international oligopolies (Brander 1981), or the result of business cycles (Ethier 1982). Dumping can be of either a temporary or permanent nature. A particular form of dumping can be induced by the learning curve (Gruenspecht 1988). Here non-myopic firms choose a pricing strategy not based on current cost, but on long run cost. This entails below current cost pricing for the early stages. However, judged by the long-term criterion, dumping does not occur. Unless location of production matters, dumping could be socially beneficial because learning is quicker (Cabral and Riordan 1994).

Both the USA and EU have GATT-conform antidumping legislation where dumping is assessed in a basically static framework, that is, prices are compared to current cost (Dick 1991). The way in which the EU anti-dumping authorities[1] construct the price biases antidumping investigations against exporters (Hindley 1988; Messerlin 1989). Of all the trading nations, the EU uses antidumping investigations the most (Finger 1992). The sector that is most heavily affected by EU antidumping actions is the electronics industry. This sector accounts for 86 per cent of the total value of imported goods in 1991 affected by antidumping measures. Moreover, antidumping actions are almost exclusively targeted to imports from Japan and South Korea, which represent 83 per cent and 6 per cent respectively of the total value of imported goods in 1991 affected by antidumping measures (European Parliament 1993).

Antidumping actions also play a strategic role in signalling political determination to protect the industry. They indicate a government's intention to take tough stances on trade policy concerning a particular industry. This may result in softening the exporter's aggressiveness on pricing. The threat of an antidumping investigation induces exporters to proceed in two directions. The first is the negotiation of export restraint agreements as a means of reducing the volume of imports, either through quantitative restrictions on imports or the establishment of price floors and/or ceilings. The second is to transfer production facilities to the country taking the action, in order to circumvent duties.

Empirical investigation of past antidumping decisions by Tharakan and Waelbroeck (1994) has shown that the functioning of the US and EU antidumping systems is remarkably similar. In both cases the presence of political influence could be established. However, there is the difference that the injury decisions are more susceptible to political interference in the EU than in the USA.

TRADE POLICY FOR THE SEMICONDUCTOR INDUSTRY

Trade in semiconductors has been and still is a recurrent subject in international trade disputes. Tariffs are low, with the USA and Japan having a zero tariff rate since 1985, but trade in semiconductors is exposed to a great deal of political interference. All countries have industry support schemes of varying size and success. However, trade disputes are traditionally ignited by the question of dumping. Trade policy in semiconductors therefore often consists of antidumping actions, especially in the case of the EU. Moreover it is also questioned whether the actual results are expected and/or desirable. Particularly in the case of the EU, minimum price agreements for semiconductors are bound to increase the domestic price of semiconductors, thereby hurting the user industry and slowing down the spread of innovative electronic equipment. Moreover, this policy does not seem to be noticeably successful in reducing import penetration by foreign producers.

Dumping in semiconductors

Antidumping actions and market access are recurrent issues of trade negotiations, especially with countries which have built up a strong semiconductor industry at a later stage than the USA. In particular, exports from Japan, and now more frequently from South Korea, are a recurrent target of antidumping investigations from the USA and the EU (Tyson 1992).

The semiconductors subject to antidumping investigation are usually commodity chips such as Dynamic Random Access Memories (DRAMs) and Erasable Programmable Read Only Memories (EPROMs). These memory chips are semiconductors designed for the storage and retrieval of information in binary form. They represent about 30 per cent of the semiconductor market.[2]

In the case of semiconductors, exporters accused of dumping normally charge the same prices on the domestic market that they do on the export market. To prove dumping, antidumping authorities have to show that this price is below cost, and they therefore have to construct a price. Constructing prices gives the antidumping investigators considerable discretion in establishing the case for dumping as well as the size of the dumping margin. Antidumping authorities typically adopt a current cost approach, whereby the 'normal value' must cover current cost plus a 'reasonable' profit margin. Because of the learning curve, assessing dumping by means of a constructed price based on current average cost is not meaningful for semiconductors.[3] It may be a perfectly rational and competitive pricing strategy for firms in certain circumstances to price below current cost with the view that increasing sales helps to drive cost down. This is not a recent strategy which has been adopted only by Japanese firms. Already in the early 1970s Texas Instruments had a reputation for its 'forward pricing' strategy for semiconductors (Hazewindus and Tooker 1982). Therefore it does not come as a surprise that during certain periods chip makers almost bankrupt themselves in selling early generations of memory chips.

To justify antidumping duties, alleged dumping must cause injury and affect economic interest. On the question of injury, there are two conditions.

First, injury must be caused by an increase in the volume of imports. Second, those imports must be causally linked to a change in the price which therefore hurts domestic producers. In a context such as the semiconductor industry where rapid price declines are endemic, this injury test may not have much significance.

Since more or less all industrialized countries consider the semiconductor industry as 'strategic', they attach a particular economic interest to avoiding injury to this industry by dumping or other unfair trade practices. Thus economic interest is expressed very clearly.

Trade policy in the EU

On several occasions during antidumping proceedings the Commission has expressed the strategic role that it assigns to the semiconductor industry, in particular as key component supplier for the computer, telecommunication and automotive industries.[4] Indigenous production of semiconductors is considered to be important in order to have permanent alternative supply sources and to alleviate the risk of foreign dependence. This risk is perceived as particularly sensitive in relation to Japanese suppliers which are generally vertically integrated into the downstream user industries.

The EU's present trade policy for semiconductors can be summarized as follows. There is a common external tariff of 14 per cent for semiconductors. In the EU semiconductors carry a higher tariff rate than downstream products such as computers and telecommunication equipment, on which tariff rates from 4.5 to 7.5 per cent are applied. Moreover, by acknowledging the strategic importance of the semiconductor industry, the EU has made repeated use of antidumping actions.

During the last years there have been several antidumping investigations with respect to semiconductors originating in the Far East, in particular on EPROMs and DRAMs. Antidumping actions on semiconductors are typically initiated by a complaint from the European Electronic Components Association (EECA), the industry association, on behalf of some of its members. Antidumping investigations on semiconductors usually end up with positive findings; that is, with price undertaking entailing minimum export prices and the imposition of definitive antidumping duties for non-participant companies. This seems to confirm the results of more general studies on the implications of antidumping actions in the EU. It has been argued that EU antidumping methodology is strongly biased against exporters to its market (Hindley 1988). More detailed analysis has shown that the current EU regulations, even if consistent with GATT rules, have a strong protectionist drift (Messerlin 1989; Vandenbussche 1995). This produmping bias is exacerbated by not taking into account explicitly the learning effects which are pervasive in semiconductors. The sequel discusses in detail the antidumping actions for DRAMs and EPROMs as promoted by the European Commission.

Antidumping action in DRAMs

The antidumping investigation against DRAMs originating in Japan[5] was initiated in 1987 and concluded with the imposition of antidumping duties and minimum price undertakings in 1990. The procedure was quite lengthy and motivated by the complex features of DRAM production. The period of investigation for alleged dumping was twelve months, from April 1986 to March 1987.

The dumping complaint was filed by EECA 'on behalf of practically all actual or potential producers of DRAMs', made up of the following firms: the UK subsidiary of Motorola, SGS, Thomson (since 1988 SGS-Thomson) and Siemens. The definition that these firms represent the 'Community industry of DRAMs' has been disputed, as none of them was actually producing DRAMs at the time of alleged dumping. These firms claimed to have had the intention to set up DRAM production, but adverse price movements induced them to decide otherwise. Only Siemens entered into DRAM production, but later in 1988. On the other hand, five of the eight Japanese firms accused of dumping (which included the Japanese subsidiary of Texas Instruments) had actual DRAM assembly plants in Europe. However, these firms were importing DRAMs on wafers (i.e. at this stage the most important production steps are already carried out) and were themselves under investigation. As a result assembly plants were excluded from the definition of 'Community industry'. IBM's DRAM plant in Germany was also excluded from this definition because it was producing only for the company's internal consumption. As a result, the complaining companies were actually only 'potential' producers.

According to the Commission's calculations, DRAMs were sold below cost on the Japanese market. Conditions for applying domestic prices under orderly conditions of trade did not apply and therefore domestic prices could not be used to calculate dumping margins. Thus normal values based on cost data supplied by Japanese DRAM producers were used to assess the dumping margin. Normal values for DRAMs have been based on quarterly cost data, including R&D cost imputable to the relevant period. On top of this a 'reasonable profit rate' was added. This profit rate was decided by the Commission.

The dumping margin is expressed as the difference between the normal value and the export price. The Commission requested that the price should be set in order to recover all costs within twelve months. This method of allocating cost does not allow for forward pricing strategies, especially if learning takes longer than one year. In this way dumping margins of 8.5 per cent to 206.2 per cent emerged, according to the firms and types of DRAMs.

The Commission argued that injury was found to occur as a result of dumping by Japanese firms. The injury had in particular taken the form of material retardation of the establishment of a competitive industry. Factors contributing to the injury were the increasing market share by Japanese firms and the low prices. This had apparently discouraged the complaining companies from establishing DRAM production. In 1983 Japanese firms were still the second suppliers to the Community market behind the USA. In 1984 Japan moved into first position. Since US firms were moving out of DRAM production on a worldwide scale, the Japanese market share in the Community increased from 70 per cent in 1985 to 85 per cent in 1986. However, it has to be stated that at that time EU production of DRAMs was virtually non-existent. Prices were also declining during the same period on a worldwide scale. As a result, the behaviour of Japanese market shares and prices replicated in the Community followed a trend that was set on a global scale.

All the Japanese firms accused of dumping have accepted price undertakings. The minimum prices of DRAMs are based on the weighted average cost of production, with the weighting done on the basis of each Japanese producer's sales volume to the EU. On top of this, a 9.5 per cent profit margin is added. On other importers from Japan antidumping duties of 60 per cent apply.

The decision to impose these residual antidumping duties seems peculiar since all exporters have accepted price undertakings. Moreover, it may appear unfair to prospective exporters since they face an antidumping duty even if they would sell above the minimum price. The Commission's motivation is of a pre-emptive nature. Residual antidumping duties are deemed necessary to avoid the situation where firms did not produce/export the goods during the investigation period or those that did not make themselves known at that time are put at a competitive advantage vis-à-vis such exporters which accepted undertakings.

In 1991 a similar antidumping action was initiated on DRAMs originating in South Korea.[6] The South Korean companies accused of dumping were Samsung, Goldstar and Hyundai. The period of alleged antidumping refers to the whole year of 1990. The investigation was remarkably rapid and antidumping duties were imposed in 1992. The complaint was brought forward by the industry association EECA on behalf of the UK subsidiary of Motorola and Siemens. However, only Siemens was producing DRAMs in 1991. Although the UK subsidiary of Nippon Electronic Company (NEC) was also producing DRAMs in the EU at that time, this firm did not complain.

The Commission applied normal values to determine dumping margins. The motive adopted was that the domestic sales of exporters were too small for most of DRAM products to be representative for comparisons. The dumping margins were calculated in the range of 18.1 per cent and 122.4 per cent. Although South Korea had only a small share of the EU market, the rapid growth of imports was considered as evidence for causing injury. In 1986 the market share of Korean firms in the EU was 6 per cent, then 15 per cent in 1988 and 25 per cent in 1990. All three firms agreed to price undertakings and a residual antidumping duty of 10.1 per cent was decided.

Antidumping in EPROMs

In parallel with the antidumping action in DRAMs, the Commission has also taken action on EPROMs originating in Japan.[7] The period of alleged dumping under investigation was twelve months from April 1986 to March 1987, the same as for DRAMs. However, this investigation has taken much longer. It has started earlier, in 1986, and finished later, in 1991. The length of investigation has been motivated by 'the complexity of the EPROM industry, combined with the internationalisation of manufacturing processes'. There was also less urgency for antidumping actions against Japanese firms because they did not have such a dominant position in EPROMs as they did in DRAMs.

The complaint was lodged by the industry association EECA 'allegedly on behalf of all actual or potential Community producers of EPROMs'. The Community complainants were SGS and Thomson, subsequently merged into SGS-Thomson. SGS-Thomson is actually the only EPROM producer in Europe. Three out of the five Japanese firms accused of dumping (which included the Japanese subsidiary of Texas Instruments) had assembly operations in the EU. However, again as in the case of DRAMs, these were not included in the definition of 'Community industry' because the investigation was also extended to imported wafers.

For each Japanese firm the domestic prices were compared with the weighted average cost of production. It was found that for most of the products prices did not cover costs. It was therefore concluded that the domestic price for EPROMs is not representative for sales made in the 'orderly course of trade'. As a result, normal values were calculated. It was established that normal prices should recover cost within one year. Here, as in the case of DRAMs, this does not allow for forward pricing strategies, and in particular when the time to move down the learning curve takes longer than one year. It has been shown (Gruber 1994) that for EPROMs learning takes typically longer than for DRAMs. As a result, it is much more likely that firms are found to price below cost, especially when they adopt an aggressive pricing strategy. Moreover, it was decided to calculate normal values on an annual basis, whereas for DRAMs they were calculated on a quarterly basis. Given the strong learning effects, especially at the early stages of production of a new generation, this method is likely to overestimate cost, especially for new generations. Failure to model the learning curve is likely to bias the outcome of the investigation towards positive findings of dumping.

Dumping margins in the order of 35 per cent to 106 per cent were calculated by the Commission. Price undertakings were accepted in 1991 by the companies accused of dumping and the reference price level was to be assessed on a quarterly basis. The residual antidumping margin was set at 94 per cent, which was considered very high. This has been motivated by the fact that there exists a 'grey market' for EPROMs in Japan which has much lower prices than the those officially quoted by firms. Thus protection was mainly aimed against those products. The Commission gives also a detailed description of how this antidumping margin has been calculated. The Japanese weighted domestic sales prices were compared with the costs of production of Community producers. A profit margin of 25 per cent was added to these costs. This 'reasonable profit margin' was obtained from a specific study on necessary profit levels for the Community DRAM industry which, according to the Commission, is broadly similar to the EPROM industry. Dumping margins established for all but one Japanese exporter were lower than the margins required to remove injury. It was decided that by taking into account the exporter with the highest dumping margin, a duty of 94 per cent would be sufficient to eliminate the injury caused to the Community EPROM industry.

The identified injury factors as a result of dumping were mainly in the volume and market share of EPROMs of Japanese origin, as well as the evolution of prices. Even though there was an increase in sales over the period of alleged dumping, the market has grown even faster, thereby reducing the market share of Japanese firms. Concerning prices, it was realized that 'in the EC and world markets prices decreased significantly prior and during the period under investigation'. Price movements adverse to producers were therefore not a fact that is unique to the EU market.

CRITICAL ASSESSMENT OF ANTIDUMPING

The failure to model the learning curve for semiconductor production makes findings of below cost pricing very likely. Below cost pricing may however be part of a non-predatory and profit maximizing price strategy. If anti-dumping action is a trade policy to provide protection, the question arises as to whether this is an efficient means.

Gruber (1996) has shown that the market response to antidumping may be quite different as factors related to industrial structure enter into play. The fact that European producers do much better in EPROMs than DRAMs should be attributed to structural factors rather than antidumping action.

Trade policy based on the imposition of antidumping duties and price undertakings such as floor prices may have two kinds of effects. If the floor price is set too low, in the sense that it is lower than the cost of production of domestic producers, then it is actually not a device for protection. If the floor price is set high enough to ensure sufficient profit margins to domestic producers and is also higher than the world price, then it provides effective protection. Floor prices have similar effects to tariffs, with the major differ-ence that the 'duty' is collected by the exporter. The welfare implications are particularly negative, even though domestic semiconductor producers may gain. The price raising effect of antidumping action based on EU legislation has also been emphasized by Hindley (1988). However, raising the price of important intermediate products such as semiconductors hurts downstream industries using semiconductors. Moreover, the home country also forgoes the tariff revenues. The really big winners appear to be the foreign exporters.

However, antidumping duties are unlikely to redress the rather dismal performance of the European semiconductor industry. The reasons why Europe is doing badly are extensively studied and related to a series of structural handicaps. These range from low R&D expenditure, lack of qualified personnel, small and protected home markets as well as domestic market oriented companies (Malerba 1985). Even though European producers received considerable subsidies, they were used to cover up inefficiencies rather than to improve competitiveness. Europe therefore appears to lack sufficiently trained managers (Hobday 1989). In addition to the structural weakness of European semiconductor companies, the EU is not very attractive for foreign direct investment, mainly because of high factor cost and other structural rigidities. For instance, EECA (1992) has shown that the EU has a total unit cost disadvantage of 9.1 per cent against the USA and of 13.8 per cent against Japan. Moreover, R&D support used to be granted at national level with a high degree of duplication and dispersion of efforts (Malerba 1985).

One may conclude from this that if the semiconductor industry needs support in the EU, this should be placed on a much broader base involving the whole environment in which the industry is operating. Comparative advantage can be created in this industry to a certain extent. But the question is what is the cost of promoting this industry. Since the root of the problem is not competition from foreign suppliers, but is rather home based, antidumping action does not appear to be the appropriate tool for handling the issue. There are problems with the way in which the policy is set up at present: if protection is ineffective (because floor prices are too low) then it is pointless; if protection is effective, it tends to hurt users, slows down the diffusion of semiconductors and benefits foreign suppliers of semiconductors.

CONCLUSIONS

The semiconductor industry is considered by all major industrialized countries to be strategic and therefore worthy of public support. Trade policy is one of the most popular tools for providing this support. The ways in which import protection is provided may also be disguised by GATT-conform measures, such as antidumping actions. Traditional methods of establishing dumping are inappropriate for semiconductors. Because of the strong learning effects, below current cost pricing is a legitimate and profit maximizing business strategy. Current antidumping rules are likely to find evidence for dumping, even when firms are not adopting a dumping strategy. Thus dumping regulation is heavily biased against foreign exporters in the case of semiconductors. If the aim of antidumping action is to establish whether dumping occurs and to restore fair competition, then antidumping margins should be modelled according to the learning curve.

Insistence on antidumping actions under present rules could therefore be seen as an apparently GATT/WTO-consistent trade policy tool to protect domestic producers. Minimum prices and antidumping duties have been adopted as a result of antidumping investigation for both DRAMs and EPROMs. However, the results have been different in the two markets. Floor prices have not helped to improve the position of EU producers in DRAMs. For EPROMs, European producers have improved their position, but it is not clear whether this can be imputed to antidumping action.

Suppose that at present antidumping actions were a way of protecting the semiconductor industry: the question is then whether this is efficient. It is argued that antidumping actions in the semiconductor industry make the EU a high-cost location for the semiconductor user industries, slowing down the diffusion of innovative products and production processes. This would add to the structural handicaps that Europe has in the semiconductor and electronics industry, putting it at a competitive disadvantage vis-à-vis the USA and Japan. On balance, the kind of protection granted to the semiconductor industry has not helped significantly to slow down import penetration, nor has it increased the ability to export.

NOTES

The views expressed are those of the author and need not necessarily reflect those of the EIB.

1 EU antidumping actions are based on the European Council Regulation no. 2423 of 1988.
2 Memory chips are classified into generations according to their storage capacity in terms of binary information units (bits). Technical progress is characterized by increasing memory capacity per chip and also by a rise in the speed of operation. For details of the economics of the semiconductor business, see Gruber (1994).
3 Gruber (1994) has estimated that the typical learning curve for semiconductors is of the 78 per cent type, i.e. doubling cumulative output reduces average production cost by 22 per cent.
4 See, for instance, the Communication on the industry, issued by the Commission SEC(91) 565, 3 April 1991.
5 See *Official Journal of the European Communities* L193, 25 July 1990 and references therein.
6 See *Official Journal of the European Communities* L66, 18 March 1993 and references therein.
7 See *Official Journal of the European Communities* L61, 12 March 1991 and references therein.

REFERENCES

Baldwin, R. (1990) 'The US–Japan semiconductor agreement', CEPR Discussion Paper No. 387.

Brander, J. (1981) 'Intra-industry trade in identical commodities', *Journal of International Economics* 1: 1–14.

Cabral, L.M.B. and Riordan, M.H. (1994) 'The learning curve, market dominance, and predatory pricing', *Econometrica* 62: 1115–40.

Dasgupta, P. and Stiglitz, J. (1988) 'Learning by doing, market structure and industrial and trade policies', *Oxford Economic Papers* 40: 246–68.

Dick, A.R. (1991) 'Learning by doing and dumping in the semiconductor industry', *Journal of Law & Economics* 34: 133–59.

Dosi, G. (1984) *Technical Change and Industrial Transformation: The Theory and an Application to the Semiconductor Industry*, London: Macmillan.

Eaton, J. and Grossman, G.M. (1986) 'Optimal trade and industrial policy under oligopoly', *Quarterly Journal of Economics* 101: 383–406.

EECA (European Electronic Component Manufacturer Association) (1992) *The Costs of Manufacturing Semiconductors. A Comparison of Costs in: Europe, USA, Japan, South East Asia*, Brussels: EECA.

Ethier, W.J. (1982) 'Dumping', *Journal of Political Economy* 90: 487–506.

European Parliament (1993) *The Economic Impact of Dumping in the Community's Anti-dumping Policy*, Economic Series Working Papers E-1, European Parliament: Strasbourg.

Finger, J.F. (ed.) (1992) *Antidumping*, Ann Arbor: University of Michigan Press.

Grubel, H.G. and Lloyd, P.G. (1975) *Intra-Industry Trade: The Theory and Measurement of International Trade in Differentiated Products*, London: Macmillan.

Gruber, H. (1994) *Learning and Strategic Product Innovation: Theory and Evidence for the Semiconductor Industry*, Amsterdam: North-Holland.

Gruber, H. (1996) 'Trade policy and learning by doing: the case of semiconductors', *Research Policy* 25: 723–39.

Gruenspecht, H. (1988) 'Dumping and dynamic competition', *Journal of International Economics* 25: 225–34.

Hazewindus, N. and Tooker, J. (1982) *The US Microelectronics Industry*, New York: Pergamon Press.

Helpman, E. and Krugman, P.R. (1989) *Trade Policy and Market Structure*, Cambridge MA: MIT Press.

Hindley, B. (1988) 'Dumping in the Far East trade of the European Community', *The World Economy* 11: 445–63.

Hobday, M. (1989) 'The European semiconductor industry: resurgence and rationalisation', *Journal of Common Market Studies* 28: 155–86.

Krugman, P. (ed.) (1986) *Strategic Trade Policy and the New International Economics*, Cambridge MA: MIT Press.

Krugman, P. (1994) *The Age of Diminished Expectations*, Cambridge MA: MIT Press.

Leahy, D. and Neary, J.P. (1994) 'Time consistency, learning by doing and infant-industry protection: the linear case', *Economic and Social Review* 26: 59–68.

Malerba, F. (1985) *Semiconductor Business. The Economics of Rapid Growth and Decline*, Madison: University of Wisconsin Press.

Messerlin, P. (1989) 'The EC Antidumping Regulations: a first economic appraisal, 1980–85', *Weltwirtschaftliches Archiv* 125: 563–87.

Okimoto, D.R, Sugano, T. and Weinstein, F. (eds) (1984) *Competitive Edge. The Semiconductor Industry in the US and in Japan*, Stanford: Stanford University Press.

Prestowitz, C.V. (1988) *Trading Places. How We Are Giving Our Future to Japan and How to Reclaim It*, New York: Basic Books.

Roberts, J. (1987) 'Battles for market share', in T.F. Bewley (ed.) *Advances in Economic Theory*, Cambridge: Cambridge University Press.

Spencer, B.J. and Brander, J.A. (1983) 'International R&D rivalry and industrial strategy', *Review of Economic Studies* 50: 707–22.

Sutton, J. (1991) *Sunk Cost and Market Structure*, Cambridge MA: MIT Press.

Tharakan, P.M.K. and Waelbroeck, J. (1994) 'Antidumping and countervailing duty decisions in the E.C. and in the U.S. An experiment in comparative political economy', *European Economic Review* 38: 171–93.

Tyson, L. (1992) *Who's Bashing Whom? Trade Conflict in High Technology Industries*, Washington: Institute for International Economics.

Vandenbussche, H. (1995) 'How can Japanese and Central European exporters to the European Union avoid antidumping duties?', *World Competition* 18: 55–73

18

COMMENTARY ON CHAPTER 17

Hylke Vandenbussche

The contribution of Chapter 17 clearly lies in the great effort taken by Harald Gruber to give a detailed description of the semiconductor industry in Europe. Studies such as his are a necessary prerequisite for modelling the industry and the effects of trade policy measures like antidumping. My main comment on this chapter is that in my view Gruber is trying to address two different issues which he does not always disentangle clearly. The first issue raised is whether antidumping measures are the appropriate tool to assess fairness in the exporting country's behaviour. In this respect, Gruber is very clear. He rightly points out that antidumping action is inappropriate to assess an exporter's pricing behaviour in an industry with learning economies because the dumping legislation looks at prices and costs in a static framework, while industries with learning economies ought to be assessed in a dynamic cost framework. Therefore the European Union to some extent accuses the innocent. The main crux of the chapter is devoted to developing this argument.

Second, Gruber raises the question of whether antidumping protection can be an effective tool of infant industry protection for the European semiconductor industry. On the second issue, which is only marginally addressed, the analysis is more ambiguous in the sense that the available evidence on the European DRAM production does not show signs of a boost in European production or market share. However, for the European EPROM industry, European antidumping protection appears to have been quite successful. In my view, the issue of whether antidumping protection can be used effectively as a successful means of infant industry protection is the more interesting for three reasons. The first is an entirely selfish one. For some time now I have been working on the economic implications of the antidumping legislation. One of the results I arrived at from a theoretical angle in a partial equilibrium framework is that, under imperfect competition, antidumping duties can be net welfare enhancing for the importing country; a result which is strongly reinforced in the presence of learning economies in the domestic industry country (see Vandenbussche and Pauwels 1996).

The second reason is that an analysis of the appropriateness of antidumping policy in industries with learning economies is not entirely new. Andrew Dick (1991) did an analysis along similar lines on the use of US antidumping action against semiconductors from Japan and broadly arrived at the same conclusions as Gruber. Third, and most important, this type of analysis takes off from the view that the purpose of antidumping policy is to prevent predatory pricing by foreigners. The main argument, developed in Gruber's chapter, is that the reason why Japanese and Korean importers of semiconductors in the EU qualify as alleged predators is that European antidumping law cannot discriminate well between predatory and other types of dumping. However, the majority of antidumping specialists are convinced that the laws are not in the first instance an attempt to deter or prevent predation. Predation can only occur in concentrated industries with high entry barriers. If the EU was trying to prevent predation, surely its analysis would in the first instance involve an examination of market structure. But when one studies the legislation carefully this is not what happens. Protectionist measures can be imposed when there is dumping causing injury to a domestic industry. These are necessary and sufficient conditions for protection and they simply involve price comparisons. This leads me and others to conclude that predation is not the heart of the matter. Therefore alternative explanations for the use of antidumping measures ought to be explored. However, this line of thought is not pursued in much depth by Gruber.

In search for alternative explanations for antidumping action it is useful to distinguish between two opposing assumptions on how governments work. Either one assumes a rational, welfare maximizing government or one assumes a government consisting of politicians which merely operates along lobbying pressures. If one believes that government is trying to maximize the sum of consumer surplus, domestic profits and duty revenue, two possible explanations for antidumping measures come to mind. One is the strategic trade policy argument for protection: is it possible to use antidumping measures to shift rent from foreign producers to the domestic country. From a theoretical point of view the answer is yes (Veugelers and Vandenbussche 1996). A second explanation is the infant industry protection argument. Is it possible that temporary protection of an industry with learning economies can actually increase welfare (see Leahy and Neary 1995).

Once the assumption of a welfare maximizing government is dropped, one is left with the political economy of protection as a possible explanation. This interpretation of antidumping actions has seen some empirical validation in papers by Finger *et al.* (1982) and Tharakan and Waelbroeck (1994). Here the hypothesis is put forward that politicians are not so much interested in maximizing national welfare but care mostly about their own personal welfare. The demand for protection coming from European producers is usually well organized, well informed and therefore more politically efficient than those who oppose protection such as consumers. Therefore, domestic producers are usually in a better position to exercise pressure on government to get alleviation from competitive pressures.

The question that would interest me is what are the explanations underlying antidumping action in the European semiconductor industry. In that respect I was lucky in being a discussant for Gruber's chapter, which is very useful in my attempt to try to answer that question.

REFERENCES

Dick, A. (1991) 'Learning by doing and dumping in the semiconductor industry', *Journal of Law and Economics* 34.

Finger, J.M., Hall, K. and Nelson, D. (1982) 'The political economy of administered protection', *American Economic Review* 72, part 2.

Hoekman, B. and Leidy, M. (1992) 'Cascading contingent protection', *European Economic Review* 36: 883–92.

Leahy, D. and Neary, P. (1995) 'Learning by doing, precommitment and infant-industry protection', discussion paper, Centre for Economic Performance, London School of Economics: 43.

Tharakan, M. and Waelbroeck, J. (1994) 'Antidumping and countervailing duty decisions in the EC and in the US: an experiment in comparative political economy', *European Economic Review* 38 (1): 171–93.

Vandenbussche, H. (1996) 'Is European antidumping protection against Central Europe too high?', *Weltwirtschaftliches Archiv* 132, March.

Vandenbussche, H. and Pauwels, W. (1996) 'Infant-industry antidumping protection and learning economies', mimeo, University of Antwerp, UFSIA.

Veugelers, R. and Vandenbussche, H. (1996) 'European antidumping policy and the profitability of national and international collusion', CEPR discussion paper 1469, London.

19

SUBSIDIES, EXCHANGE RATES AND JOB PROTECTION IN THE BRITISH STEEL INDUSTRY, 1967–85

Anthony Cockerill

INTRODUCTION

Repeal of the Corn Laws was 'undoubtedly the greatest of the victories of free trade' (Hill 1985), benefiting the manufacturing industries through the scope for increased output, exports and employment. Cotton manufacturing was the principal – but not the only – sector to benefit, the iron and later the steel trades did too, as the demand for metal goods and machinery increased.

Trade protection and employment issues have been – and still are – at the heart of policy towards the modern steel industry in the European Union (EU). Coal and steel were the first two sectors to be opened to free(er) trade in Europe after World War II, through the formation in 1951 of the European Coal and Steel Community (ECSC).

This chapter examines the impact on employment in the British steel industry between 1967 and 1985 of two factors affecting trade: subsidies (a form of protection) and exchange rate movements. The analysis has both current and historical relevance: in the first instance to the achievement of a single European market, and in the second to comparative advantage and the growth of industrial trade following repeal of the Corn Laws.

The chapter estimates the amounts of subsidy given to the British steel industry between 1967, when the greater part of the sector was nationalized, and 1985 when government aid had almost come to an end. It then analyses the respective contributions of subsidies and exchange rate movements in affecting the international cost competitiveness of the industry and, thus, in influencing the level of employment from the time of Britain's accession to the European Communities in 1973 until 1984. The chapter shows that the industry received more than £7 billion in public funds during the period,

188

only a small part of which was remunerated or repaid. These funds supported, *inter alia*, output, employment, capital expenditure and the costs of rationalization.

In the second section of the chapter, the development and financing of the industry are reviewed briefly. The third section gives calculations of the subsidy element in the funds supplied. The fourth section analyses trends in the competitiveness of the industry to identify periods of high relative employment costs per tonne of steel produced. Estimates are then made in the fifth section of the amount of job protection by comparing actual employment in the British industry with the levels that would have been necessary to match unit labour costs in an 'efficient' industry, using the steel industry of the Federal Republic of Germany (West Germany) as the comparator. The sixth section relates the subsidies to the estimates of the numbers of jobs protected, to indicate the average cost of each job saved. Some implications of the results of the analysis are considered in the final section.

THE DEVELOPMENT OF THE INDUSTRY

The study is concerned with most of the long period of public ownership of the British steel industry which lasted from the formation of the British Steel Corporation (BSC) in 1967 through the fusion of the thirteen largest inte-grated[1] steel companies to its privatization in 1988. At its formation BSC accounted for three-quarters of the annual production of crude steel and more than half of the output of finished steel in the UK. The balance of output came from a number of small independent producers, engaged mainly in the manufacture of special steels or in rerolling and finishing crude steel.

In the first six years after nationalization, annual crude steel output in Britain varied between 21.5 and 26.1 million tonnes, but then a period of decline began, output falling below 12 million tonnes in 1982 before recovering to 14 million tonnes in 1985.[2] The fall in output resulted from the combined effect of a decline in the major steel-using industries (in particular motor vehicles, shipbuilding, construction and engineering) and a deterioration in the balance of steel trade as import penetration increased. Employment in the industry fell from more than 250,000 in 1967 to less than 70,000 in 1984.[3] By March 1985, BSC's accumulated loss was more than £1.1 billion (British Steel Corporation 1986).

External finance was supplied to the industry for three main reasons:

1   Capacity expansion and modernization. At the time of nationalization, domestic and foreign demand for steel was expected to grow strongly in the future, as real incomes and industrial output rose in the developed countries. On the basis of this, BSC needed to expand capacity in order to meet the growth in demand. Moreover, technical change, in the form of

basic oxygen steelmaking and continuous casting,[4] was making existing production processes obsolete and extending the economies of scale,[5] obliging firms to close small, high-cost mills and to invest in large-scale works. BSC's profitability prospects were not sufficient for plans to be made to finance the necessary expenditures from internal cash flows, so support from public funds was necessary – indeed, this was a main reason given to justify nationalization (Ministry of Power 1965). Capital expenditure increased sharply between 1968 and 1971 as the first stage of reorganization and expansion took place. A much larger plan for expansion and modernization was announced in 1973 (Department of Trade and Industry 1973), to be spread over ten years, that would have raised annual crude steel capacity from 24 million tonnes to between 33 and 35 million tonnes. The annual rate of capital expenditure more than doubled between 1973 and 1976, after which falling demand and increasing financial losses caused the plan to be abandoned.

2 Deficit financing and job protection. The fall in UK steel production after 1973 was the result of reductions in consumption and net exports. Domestic consumption fell as the effect on incomes and prices of the first oil shock was felt and as the composition of total economic output shifted away from steel-intensive goods. The import content of steel consumption rose from one-tenth in 1973 to one-quarter in 1978 because of intense price competition from foreign producers and, in some instances, the inability of the British industry to supply (Cockerill 1974). Export volume was affected by the world recession and a lack of price competitiveness on the part of British manufacturers. After making operating profits in the two financial years from 1973–4, BSC incurred losses in subsequent years until 1985–6. The fall in demand and output came when BSC was introducing new capacity in line with its development plan, and was intending to close many small mills. The government was concerned about the impact of these measures on regional and national employment, and BSC's expansion plans were cut back and plant closures were halted in an effort to maintain employment until the industry's prospects became clearer. More than £3 billion of external finance was required to support investment and cover losses between 1974–5 and 1978–9 (see Table 19.1).

3 Rationalization. The government announced in 1978 that BSC's future capital expenditure was to be restricted to essential modernization and the completion of current projects. The need for rationalization was recognized, and BSC was permitted to negotiate plant closures at its discretion (Department of Industry 1978). At the same time, the European Commission was endeavouring to put measures in place to stabilize the steel market within the Community. By 1980 these had been developed into a comprehensive system that linked output quotas and minimum prices to agreements on capacity reduction and the

Table 19.1 Supply of long-term finance to British Steel Corporation, financial years 1967–8 to 1985–6

	(1)	(2)	(3)	(4)	(5)	(6)
	Increase/(decrease) in long-term finance				Total finance supplied	
Financial years	Loans from Secretary of State £m	Foreign and other loans £m	Public Dividend Capital £m	Together £m	At current prices £m	At 1980 prices[a] £m
1967–8	309	—	700[b]	1009	1009	4406
1968–9	(27)	2	—	(25)	984	4152
1969–70[c]	40	—	—	40	1024	4180
1970–71	32	27	—	59	1083	4102
1971–2	156	(23)	—	133	1216	4150
1972–3	142	4	—	146	1362	4217
1973–4	(3)	45	—	42	1404	4035
1974–5	(78)	215	45	182	1586	3897
1975–6	131	229	345	705	2291	4423
1976–7	161	236	490	887	3178	5359
1977–8	216	103	444	763	3941	5917
1978–9	(161)	(48)	850	641	4582	6134
1979–80	(209)	(52)	905	644	5226	6206
1980–81	(50)	(97)	1233	1086	6312	6312
1981–2	—	10	806	816	7128	6462
1982–3	—	(185)	743	558	7686	6514
1983–4	—	(9)	396	387	8073	6474
1984–5	—	(183)	667	484	8557	6552
1985–6	—	(62)	556	494	9051	6554

Notes: a Gross domestic product deflator, calendar years
        b Commencing capital
        c Six months

Sources: British Steel Corporation (various years) Annual Reports and Accounts, London: BSC; unpublished information; Central Statistical Office, UK National Accounts 1986, London: HMSO, 1986 (for GDP deflator)

amount and application of national subsidies. BSC's capacity was cut sharply after 1979 and more than 100,000 jobs were lost in the period to 1985. External finance during this time was needed to cover capital expenditure, operating losses and restructuring and redundancy costs.

THE AMOUNT OF SUBSIDY

Estimates are made in this section of the annual subsidy, expressed in total and per tonne of crude steel produced, provided to the British steel industry between 1967 and 1985. The subsidies are calculated on the basis of the assistance given to BSC as very little specific aid was given to the independent producers.[6] Subsidies affect the relative prices of the factors, goods or services to which they relate (Prest 1976: 65). They may be general or specific in nature. General subsidies are available to all enterprises, subject to certain qualifying rules, while specific subsidies are restricted to a given enterprise or sector. This analysis is concerned only with specific subsidies.

Assistance has been given to UK nationalized industries in several ways, including operating grants, deficit payments, reduced rate-of-return targets, and subscriptions of unremunerated capital (National Economic Development Office 1976; Wilson 1979; Cockerill 1980). The latter is the main form in which subsidies were given to the steel industry. In theory, the effect of this kind of subsidy is to permit an enterprise to operate at a rate of return that is below the risk-adjusted opportunity cost of capital. The level of subsidy may then be expressed in terms of the difference between the actual profit earned (or loss incurred) before interest and tax, and that required to satisfy the opportunity cost of capital.

In this inquiry, the opportunity cost of capital is proxied by the gross redemption yields on long-dated (twenty-year) British government securities. The provision of external finance to BSC can be considered to have had an impact on government borrowing at the margin, the cost of which is reflected by the return on long-term government bonds (gilts).[7] It may be objected that this overstates the competitive rate of return in the private sector, as enterprises can reduce dividends in times of poor trade and may have raised long-term debt in the past at fixed rates that are below current interest rates. But this is in essence a short-term consideration. In due course, competitive enterprises will have to earn a sufficient return to compensate their shareholders and will have to refinance their capital debt at the market rate.

An alternative proxy is the average rate of interest charged each year on BSC's outstanding long-term capital, but the drawbacks are the same: the funds which comprise the total have been supplied at different times in the past and carry different interest rates, so the average does not reflect the current opportunity cost of capital. Rather than being too high as a comparator, the long-term return on gilts may be, in fact, too low. Investment in gilts

192

is virtually risk free: as nationalized undertakings are trading enterprises, the opportunity rate of return should, in theory, be raised to take account of the market and other risks they face.

The amount of annual subsidy paid to BSC (and, hence, to the steel industry as a whole) is calculated by subtracting interest and dividends paid each year from the return that would have been payable had the cumulative total of external finance supplied since 1967 been remunerated at the opportunity cost of capital. The subsidies are thus calculated in relation to the funds supplied and not to the balance sheet value of the assets to which, in part, they were applied: this avoids the need to adjust for the replacement cost of capital, or for write-offs.

Wilson (1979: 263–4) has suggested that the rate of return used to calculate nationalized industries' subsidies may be chosen from the rate that covers financial charges (interest and depreciation); the rate set as a target by the Secretary of State; and the rate of return in the private sector. These are deficient as proxies for the opportunity cost of long-term funds, however, because the first takes no account of equity capital. The second does not recognize that target rates of return for nationalized industries have been reduced to allow for externalities. The third does not adjust for the presence of monopoly profits in the private sector.

Another approach to the measurement of subsidies is to calculate the amount of external finance supplied that would not have been available without government assistance (see Federal Trade Commission 1977). But there are difficulties in determining the amount of such funds and their composition as between debt and equity that a private sector enterprise would have received, and the amounts of capital that would have been written off or lost in any capital reconstruction or bankruptcy. In the estimates given here, the amounts of BSC's debt and equity written off in capital reconstructions are included in the total external funds outstanding each year. It is possible to argue that these amounts should be excluded in calculating subsidies because they represent the losses that would have fallen upon the shareholders of a private sector enterprise (see House of Commons 1983: 111). But nationalized industries' statutes have no provision for bankruptcy and the authorities have discretion about the amount and timing of any capital reconstruction.

Table 19.1 analyses the long-term capital funds supplied to BSC to the end of 1985. Finance was provided in the following forms:

- Interest-bearing debt from the National Loans Fund (NLF), authorized by the Secretary of State of the Sponsoring Department, with the approval of the Treasury. These were loans, usually for between 15 and 18 years, carrying a fixed rate of interest, set at the time the loan was taken up.
- Other interest bearing debt, mostly raised abroad and of shorter duration than NLF debt. Decisions to raise foreign debt were governed by

nominal interest rate differentials and official exchange rate policy. The Treasury provided a partial guarantee against adverse exchange rate movements during the period of the loan.

- Public Dividend Capital (PDC). These funds were non-repayable, but ranked for dividends at a rate equivalent to that on comparable NLF debt, taking one year with another, unless the Secretary of State agreed in any year that the obligation to pay dividends should be waived. From March 1978, funds of this kind were supplied to BSC as 'New Capital' under Section 18 (1) of the Iron and Steel Act 1982, and represented almost all long-term financing from that date.

Table 19.1 shows that, until 1974–5, the funds supplied to BSC in addition to its commencing capital of £1,009 million were all interest bearing, amounting in total to £704 million at current prices, or about half its total capital. In the next four years, as capital expenditures rose with the implementation of the development plan and as operating losses increased, more than £2.5 million of external finance was supplied, about half of which was interest-free PDC. Thereafter, as operating losses, capital expenditure and rationalization costs were financed, virtually all new funds were interest free. Over the whole period about £7.9 billion was supplied, excluding commencing capital.

Table 19.2 sets out the calculation of the annual subsidies paid to BSC between 1967 and 1985. In column 1 the cumulative external finance analysed in Table 19.1 is re-expressed on a calendar year basis. Column 2 shows the opportunity cost of capital, which is used to calculate the imputed return on funds given in column 3. Column 4 lists the amounts of interest and dividends actually paid each year. The annual relief to the profit and loss account (column 5) is then the difference between columns 3 and 4. Column 6 gives the annual crude steel output of the British industry. The annual subsidies per tonne at current and 1980 prices are shown in column 7. The subsidy did not exceed £3.50 a tonne (at current prices) until 1974, after which time it rose sharply as operating losses and rationalization costs increased, almost reaching £66 a tonne in 1982. The total subsidy over the period was £7.5 billion at current prices (£8.8 billion at 1980 prices), or £19.47 a tonne (£23.07 a tonne at 1980 prices). It is striking that the total calculated subsidy at current prices is close to the total of external finance supplied net of commencing capital.

LABOUR COST COMPETITIVENESS

Having estimated the amounts of subsidy given to the UK steel industry, this chapter now turns to an analysis of the extent of job protection, and the respective contributions to this of subsidies and exchange rate movements. The first stage is an analysis of the labour cost competitiveness of the British

Table 19.2 British Steel Corporation: theoretical calculation of interest and dividend relief, total and per tonne of crude steel produced, 1968–85 (calendar year basis)

Year	(1) Total finance supplied £m	(2) Opportunity cost of capital %	(3) Imputed return £m	(4) Interest[a] and dividends paid £m	(5a) Relief to profit and loss account Current prices £m	(5b) Relief to profit and loss account 1980 prices £m	(6) Crude steel production '000 tonnes	(7a) Relief per tonne of crude steel Current prices £m	(7b) Relief per tonne of crude steel 1980 prices £m
1967[b]	1009.0	6.80	34.3	6.0	28.3	123.6	12139	2.33	10.18
1968	1002.7	7.55	75.7	23.5	52.2	220.3	26276	1.99	8.40
1969	1004.0	9.05	90.9	22.8	68.1	278.0	26845	2.54	10.37
1970	1068.3	9.25	98.8	24.6	74.2	281.1	28329	2.62	9.92
1971	1182.8	8.90	105.3	30.8	74.5	254.3	24146	3.09	10.55
1972	1325.6	8.97	118.9	35.9	83.0	257.0	25283	3.28	10.15
1973	1393.6	10.78	150.2	58.4	91.8	263.8	26649	3.44	9.89
1974	1540.6	14.77	227.5	65.6	161.9	397.8	22379	7.23	17.76
1975	2114.9	14.39	304.3	81.6	222.7	429.9	19780	11.26	21.74
1976	2956.4	14.43	426.6	125.4	301.2	507.9	22396	13.45	22.68
1977	3750.4	12.73	477.4	169.9	307.5	461.7	20474	15.02	22.55
1978	4421.9	12.47	551.4	187.9	363.5	486.6	20302	17.90	23.96
1979	5065.2	12.99	658.0	169.9	488.1	579.7	21472	22.73	26.99
1980	6040.7	13.79	833.0	145.0	688.0	688.0	11278	61.00	61.00
1981	6924.2	14.74	1020.6	86.5	934.1	846.9	15321	60.97	55.28
1982	7546.7	12.88	972.0	66.0	906.0	767.8	13740	65.94	55.88
1983	7976.5	10.80	861.5	50.8	810.7	650.1	14980	54.12	43.40
1984	8436.3	10.69	901.8	31.0	870.8	666.8	15214	57.24	43.83
1985	8927.8	10.62	948.1	21.5	926.6	671.0	15766	58.77	42.56
Totals	n/a	n/a	8856.3	1403.1	7453.2	8832.3	382769	19.47[c]	23.07[c]

Notes: a On long-term debt

b Six months

c Annual average

Sources: Columns 1 and 4: Table 19.1, pro-rated to a calendar year basis. Column 2: Central Statistical Office, Financial Statistics, London: HMSO, 1973, 1974 (April issues), 1979, 1981, 1986 (December issues), 1987 (September issue). Column 6: Eurostat, 1984, Iron and Steel 1952–1982, and Eurostat, 1987, Iron and Steel Yearbook 1986, Luxembourg: Statistical Office of the European Communities

industry. For the purposes of the study, job protection is defined as occurring when British labour cost per tonne of steel produced is greater than an international competitiveness comparator, measured in a common currency (£). Under these conditions, given output and hourly labour costs, employment in the UK industry would have to be reduced and productivity increased for unit labour costs to match the international comparator, which is taken as a level of unit labour cost in the West German steel industry. Over the period of the analysis, West Germany was the most efficient of the EC steelmakers, in terms of labour productivity (Aylen 1982). Although productivity rates were higher in Japan and the USA, the West German industry may be regarded as having been on, or close to, the European steel industry's production frontier.

It is important to note that the equivalence of unit labour cost is neither a necessary nor sufficient condition for international competitiveness. An industry in one country may have a higher unit labour cost in a common currency than the same industry in another and yet remain competitive because, for example: other production costs are lower; transport and distribution costs protect the home market; the characteristic product has a higher added value, or lower profit margins are accepted. Data on these aspects are not available in sufficient detail to allow a comparison to be made of total costs in the British and West German industries but, in any case, labour cost may in general be regarded as a reliable indicator of international competitiveness (Ward 1985).

Unit labour cost expressed in a common currency is a function of: man hours per tonne (the inverse of productivity); hourly labour costs; and the exchange rate. Low relative productivity can be compensated by low hourly costs and a depreciation of the exchange rate to give unit labour cost equivalence. Figure 19.1 shows comparisons of productivity and levels and movements in hourly and unit labour costs in the two countries between 1973 and 1984.

Figure 19.1a demonstrates that productivity (as indicated by man hours per tonne) in the British industry was lower than in West Germany throughout, but improved sharply after 1980. Over the whole period, however, the rates of increase of hourly labour costs (Figure 19.1b) and labour cost per tonne measured in local currencies (Figure 19.1c) in Britain were much greater than in West Germany. The number of man hours required to produce a tonne of crude steel was more than four-fifths as high again in Britain as in West Germany in 1973.

Between then and 1978 there was no discernible trend in productivity in either country; short-run movements in output against fairly constant employment levels caused man hours per tonne to fluctuate. Output and prices became more stable after 1978, and productivity began to improve in both countries, although there was a dislocation in Britain in the strike year of 1980. By 1985, man hours per tonne in Britain were only 20 per cent higher than in West Germany.

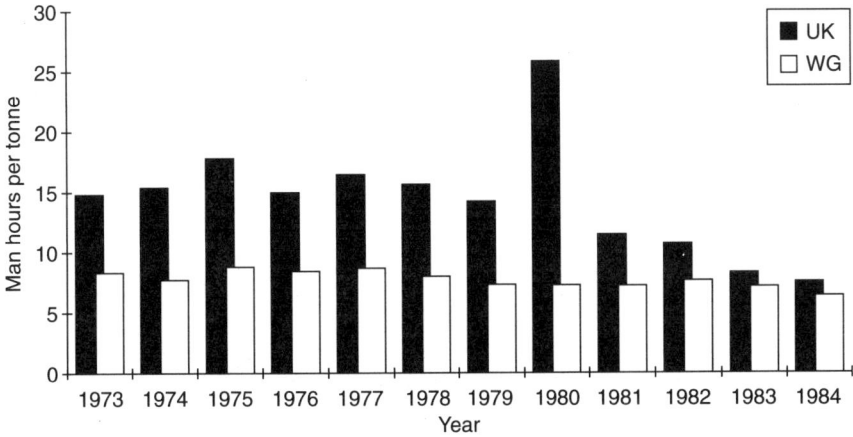

Figure 19.1a Productivity (man hours) per tonne of crude steel, UK and West
Germany, 1973–84
Source: Statistical appendix, cols 5, 12

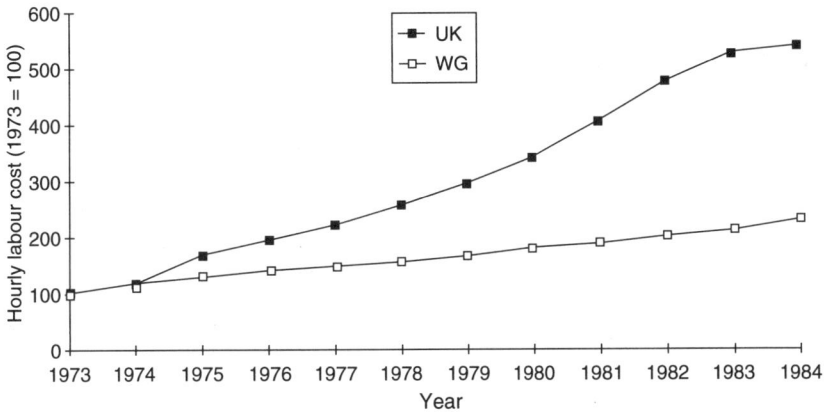

Figure 19.1b Hourly labour costs, UK and West Germany, 1973–84
Source: Statistical appendix, cols 6b, 13b

In contrast, hourly labour costs, which include employers' administration
costs and social security contributions, increased through the period at more
than twice the rate in Britain than in West Germany.[8] The effect of this,
when combined with the productivity movements, was to cause British cost
competitiveness in terms of local currencies to decline until 1982, after
which there was an improvement as labour cost per tonne began to fall more
quickly than in West Germany.

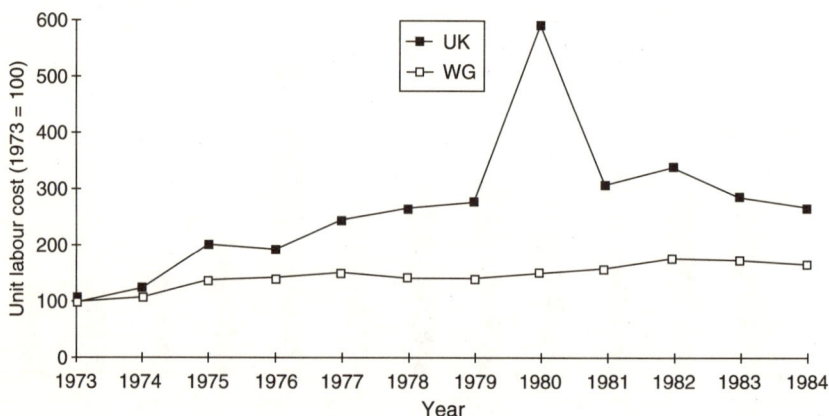

Figure 19.1c Unit labour cost, local currencies UK and West Germany, 1973–84
Source: Statistical appendix, cols 7b, 14b

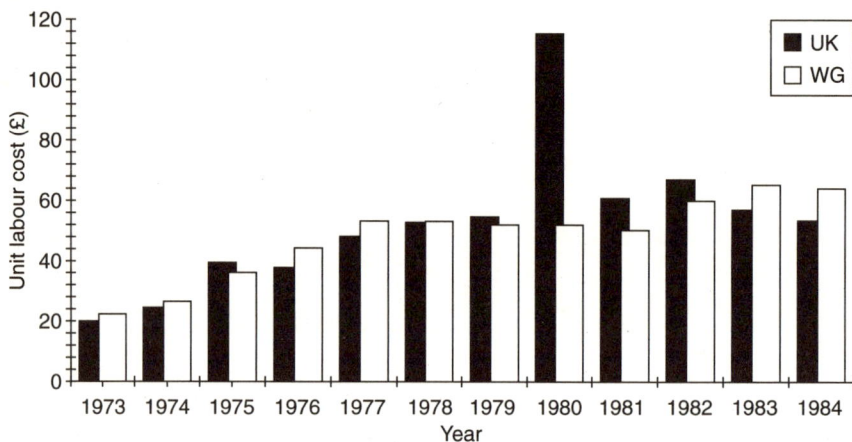

Figure 19.1d Unit labour cost (£), common currency (f), UK and West Germany, 1973–84
Source: Statistical appendix, cols 7a, 16b

Figure 19.1d compares unit labour cost in the two countries in terms of a common currency and shows that depreciation in the £:DM exchange rate played a vital part in maintaining the cost competitiveness of the British industry by offsetting the relative increase in labour cost per tonne in local currency terms. As a result, over the whole period, Britain's relative cost position improved. In 1973, British labour cost per tonne was roughly 90 per cent of that in West Germany; by the end of the period it was just less than 84 per cent. The exchange rate fell progressively between 1973 and 1978, from DM6.52 to DM3.85. British unit labour cost was not fully compensated by this fall between 1973 and 1975 and again from 1976 to 1978; in 1975 British costs rose above those in West Germany. Sterling strengthened against the DM between 1978 and 1981, before depreciating again to DM3.79 in 1984. British unit labour cost was above that in West Germany in each year from 1979 to 1982, after which the combination of the falling exchange rate and the reduction in unit labour cost gave the British industry its greatest cost advantage of the entire period. It is clear, therefore, that employment in the British steel industry was above that necessary to achieve cost equivalence with West Germany for less than half the period studied; in 1975, and between 1979 and 1982. Competitiveness in other years was maintained in large part by exchange rate depreciation.

JOB PROTECTION

This section of the chapter estimates the number of jobs protected in the British steel industry by subsidies and exchange rate movements. Subsidies can maintain employment by compensating for unit costs that are higher than those of competitors, or by allowing prices to be charged that are lower than is necessary to cover full costs, including the opportunity cost of capital. Exchange rate movements may offset, partially or wholly, productivity growth that is lower, or hourly labour costs that are higher, than those of competitors.

The general approach used is to estimate the difference between the actual employment levels in each year in the British industry and those that would be necessary to achieve international competitiveness, given assumptions about output, hourly wage rates, productivity and exchange rates. The estimates are made on the basis of the following heroic assumptions:

1 Competitiveness for the British steel industry is defined as achieving unit labour cost equivalence with West Germany in terms of a common currency. Given the actual hourly costs of employment in each country and a constant exchange rate, if unit labour costs are higher in Britain than in West Germany in terms of a common currency, employment must be reduced and productivity improved to obtain unit labour cost competitiveness. If British costs are lower, however, no employment reduction is implied and it is possible, in theory, for jobs to be increased without losing cost competitiveness. Unit labour cost is used as a proxy for total unit costs in indicating competitiveness (see section above). This imparts a bias to the estimates of the number of jobs protected to the extent that the absolute and relative values of the items that together make up total unit costs vary between the two countries.

2 No adjustment is made to actual annual steel output to allow for the lower unit costs that competitiveness would require. Because steel is an

undifferentiated product, steelmakers are usually price takers. In Europe, it has been German manufacturers that typically have led prices. Subsidies maintained firms' market shares at the prevailing price. Hence, reducing costs would allow subsidies to be cut back, leaving price and output unchanged.

3   Only first-round effects are considered, so no adjustments are made to British average hourly earnings to reflect the improvements in productivity required for competitiveness.

Given these conventions, it is possible to calculate the level of employment in each year in the 'competitive' industry in the following way:

- To match West German labour costs (ULC_d) at hourly labour cost levels in Britain (w), producers will need to achieve a productivity level expressed in man hours per tonne (MHT) given by:

$$\frac{ULC_d}{w} = MHT.$$

- The total number of employees (L_t) required for this level of productivity, given average annual hours worked per employee (h) and the annual output of crude steel (Q), will then be given by:

$$\frac{MHT \cdot Q}{h} = L_t.$$

- The number of jobs saved (S) each year will be the difference between actual (L_a) and theoretical employment (L_t) at the efficient rate of operation, or:

$$L_a - L_t = S; \quad S \geq O.$$

The non-negativity constraint is necessary to take account of years in which actual unit labour costs in Britain were below those in West Germany. Theoretically, in these circumstances employment in the British industry could be *increased*, to raise unit costs to equivalence with those in West Germany; i.e. $L_a < L_t$, and S becomes negative. This condition is not relevant to estimates of jobs saved, however, and S is assumed equal to zero in these years.

- The estimates of L_t are very sensitive to the DM:£ exchange rate, as the level of employment in Britain that is necessary for unit cost equivalence is determined in the model by unit labour costs (ULC_d) in the West German industry.

L_t is therefore evaluated in terms of three exchange rate assumptions: current rates (L_t^{cur}); the constant (1973) rate (L_t^{con}); and the purchasing power standard rate (L_t^{pps}), using Eurostat data.[9] The estimates of jobs saved under each assumption may then be compared to show the relative significance of subsidies and exchange rate movements in protecting employment.

Full details of the calculations are given in the Statistical Appendix. The first three columns of Table 19.3 show estimates of the numbers of annual jobs protected under each of the exchange rate assumptions. Column 1 shows the variations in employment from the actual levels in each year that would have been necessary to achieve cost equivalence, calculated at current exchange rates. The negative values indicate the increases in numbers employed that would have raised British unit costs to equivalence with West Germany in those years in which Britain had a cost advantage. Positive values occur in years in which UK unit costs were greater than those in West Germany, and indicate the reductions in the actual levels of employment that would have been required to attain cost equivalence. Movements in the exchange rate maintained in broad terms Britain's cost competitiveness over the period. The analysis indicates that jobs were protected in 1975, and again between 1979 and 1982, when the sustained rise in sterling reduced Britain's competitiveness.

Columns 2 and 3 indicate the amounts of annual job protection that would have been necessary had the exchange rate either not moved from the 1973 parity or had adjusted to maintain the purchasing power standard. In column 2, the employment variations are shown for cost equivalence with West Germany if the bilateral exchange rate had remained throughout at its 1973 level. Britain had a cost advantage over West Germany at the beginning of the period but poorer productivity and higher hourly cost increases subsequently eroded competitiveness (see Figure 19.1). The assumption of a fixed exchange rate allows no compensation for this, with the result that unit labour costs in Britain, as calculated, were higher than in West Germany in every year after 1973, indicating that reductions in employment would have been necessary for cost equivalence. The data in the column show that the British industry's competitive disadvantage in the absence of exchange rate compensation was particularly great between 1977 and 1980.

The choice of the 1973 exchange rate is somewhat arbitrary, however, even though in that year the British industry was broadly competitive with West Germany in terms of unit labour costs. The estimates in column 3 are obtained by basing the calculations on purchasing power standard (PPS) exchange rates. Movements through time in the PPS indicate broad trends in the relative competitiveness of the tradeable sectors of the countries concerned. Subject to qualifications about cross-national differences in the composition of the outputs of the tradeable sectors, and their importance

Table 19.3 Estimates of numbers of jobs protected in the British steel industry, 1973–84, and decomposition into subsidy and exchange rate effects

	(1)	(2)	(3)	(4)	(5a)	(5b)
		Jobs protected ('000)			*Exchange rate effect*	
Year	At current exchange rates	At 1973 exchange rate	At PPS exchange rate	Subsidy effect[a]	1973 rate[b]	PPS[c]
1973	-20.1	-20.1	67.7	0	0	67.7
1974	-14.8	0.4	69.2	0	0.4	69.2
1975	17.6	46.4	80.2	17.6	28.8	62.6
1976	-29.7	34.3	55.9	0	34.3	55.9
1977	-21.0	55.2	63.2	0	55.2	63.2
1978	-2.3	68.3	68.7	0	68.3	68.7
1979	8.7	70.8	61.8	8.7	62.1	53.1
1980	73.6	94.7	84.8	73.6	21.1	11.2
1981	17.0	41.1	22.1	17.0	24.1	5.1
1982	8.4	34.2	15.7	8.4	25.8	7.3
1983	-9.6	21.7	2.8	0	21.7	2.8
1984	-12.2	19.0	-0.1	0	19.0	0
		Totals of annual jobs protected		125.3	360.8	466.8

Notes: a Column 1, with negative values set to zero (see text)
 b Column 2 *minus* column 1 (negative values set to zero)
 c Column 3 *minus* column 1 (negative values set to zero)

Source: Statistical Appendix, Table 19.A3

relative to gross domestic product, PPS exchange rates may be taken as indicating 'equilibrium' exchange rates. If the British steel industry's competitiveness relative to West Germany moved in line with the relative competitiveness of the two countries' tradeable sectors, adjustments in the PPS exchange rate would maintain cost equivalence, subject to assumptions about comparability of product mix and the absence of trade barriers. Improvement or deterioration in the British cost position would indicate that the competitiveness of the steel industry was changing relative to that of the tradeable sector as a whole.

The analysis shows that the 1973 exchange rate of £1 = DM6.52 under-valued sterling significantly in relation to the PPS rate of £1 = DM10.96.[10] In PPS terms, Britain had an initial cost disadvantage of £6.67 a tonne. The PPS exchange rate declined progressively during the period against the DM and converged with the current rate, as the relative competitiveness of Britain's tradeable sector fell. The initial undervaluation of the sterling exchange rate in relation to the PPS and the deterioration in the relative competitiveness of the British steel industry over much of the period cause the amount of labour protection attributable to current exchange rate move-ments in relation to the PPS to be substantial in each year until 1980, after which the improvement in the British industry's operating performance and the convergence of the PPS and the current exchange rate reduce sharply the amount of job protection associated with exchange rate movements.

It may be concluded from this analysis that exchange rate movements have played an important role in maintaining the cost competitiveness of the British steel industry and, therefore, in compensating for its low labour productivity and relatively high rate of hourly labour cost growth. It is possible to allocate the total number of jobs protected each year between the effects of subsidy and the exchange rate; this is done in the last two columns of Table 19.3 The subsidy effect (S^{sub}) is shown in column 4, and is defined as the numbers of jobs that would need to be cut each year to achieve cost equivalence at the current exchange rate (subject to the non-negativity constraint). Subsidies are estimated to have protected a total of 125,300 annual jobs in 1975 and between 1979 and 1982.

The exchange rate effect (S^{er}) refers to estimates of the annual numbers of jobs protected as a consequence of movements in the current exchange rate, and can be defined as the difference between the job reductions necessary for cost equivalence at 1973 or PPS exchange rates and those necessary at current exchange rates, each subject to a non-negativity constraint:

$$S^{er} = [L_a - L_t^{con/pps}] - S^{sub}; \qquad L_a - L_t^{con/pps} \geq 0$$
$$S^{sub} \geq 0$$

The estimates given in column 5 show that movements in the current exchange rate in relation to its 1973 level protected a total of 360,800 annual

203

jobs, while movements in the rate relative to the purchasing power standard saved 466,800 annual jobs.

SUBSIDIES AND JOB PROTECTION

The analysis of the previous section has shown that the British steel industry was competitive internationally in terms of its labour costs per tonne of crude steel during most of the period between 1973 and 1984. 'Surplus' employment can be identified only in a few years. It follows that the greater part of the substantial subsidies that were provided was not used directly to compensate for high relative unit labour costs, but to support the cash flow and continued operation and investment of BSC. The subsidies had five main applications. First, a considerable part of the external finance supplied to BSC was used for fixed capital formation, in particular during the capacity expansion and modernization period. The effect of subsidies and of capital write-downs was to provide BSC with up-to-date and efficient equipment at a very low cost to the enterprise. Second, some non-labour costs were probably higher from time to time in Britain than in other major competitor countries. This applies particularly to energy costs. Third, BSC incurred substantial redundancy and closure costs during its adjustment to lower output, capacity and employment after 1979. Fourth, governments imposed non-commercial obligations on BSC that reduced its revenues and increased its costs. The most notable of these were the holding back of price increases until 1975, the requirement to keep redundant capacity in operation between 1974 and 1978, and the obligation to purchase coking coal from the British coal industry at prices above the world level (Cockerill 1980). A final point is that UK steel prices were probably held below market levels from time to time to make import penetration more difficult and to maintain output and employment in the domestic industry.

While financial assistance to the steel industry has not been used in the main to subsidize labour costs, it is clear that the effect has been to maintain steel output and employment. By any commercial criteria, BSC would have filed for bankruptcy in the mid-1970s. It is legitimate, therefore, to relate the annual subsidies at constant prices to the estimates of jobs saved in order to indicate in approximate terms the costs of job protection. This is done in Table 19.4, column 3 which shows that the annual cost per job saved, in those years in which employment protection occurred, was between £24,400 and £91,400 if the abnormal result for the strike year of 1980 is excluded. As the subsidies supported BSC as a going concern, the total of the annual subsidies over the whole period can also be related to the total of the annual jobs saved. This indicates a cost per job of £53,800.

These estimates are approximate and in gross terms. In particular, they do not allow for the benefits to the public purse of increased tax receipts and

Table 19.4 Estimates of cost of annual jobs protected, at 1980 prices, 1973–84

Year	(1) Subsidy £m	(2) Jobs protected '000	(3) Cost of annual jobs protected £ '000
1973	263.8	0	—
1974	397.8	0	—
1975	429.9	17.6	24.4
1976	507.9	0	—
1977	461.7	0	—
1978	486.6	0	—
1979	579.7	8.7	66.6
1980	688.0	73.6	9.3
1981	846.9	17.0	49.8
1982	767.8	8.4	91.4
1983	650.1	0	—
1984	666.8	0	—
Totals	6747.0	125.3	53.8[a]

Note: a Column 1/Column 2
Sources: Column 1: Table 19.2, column 5b. Column 2: Table 19.3, column 4

lower welfare expenditures that the protection of employment conferred. It is, apparent, nonetheless, that the costs of supporting steel production and employment at times of low productivity and rising employment costs were high.

CONCLUSION

The study has shown that, over the period of the analysis, both subsidies and exchange rate movements protected jobs in the British industry, with the exchange rate having greater effect. Subsidies can help offset the social costs of an industry's adjustment to international competitiveness, but there is a risk that they will be used to inhibit adjustment in order to protect jobs in the short run.

In a similar way, exchange rate movements can provide flexibility while adaptation takes place; but they can also enable output and employment to be higher for longer in inefficient producers than would be the case with fixed exchange rates or a single currency. The implication of these conclusions is clear for the debate about European economic and monetary union. They would be recognized and vigorously debated also by Bright, Cobden, Disraeli and Peel.

ACKNOWLEDGEMENTS

The research on which this chapter is based extends work undertaken for the Trade Policy and Economic Adjustment Program of the Institute for International Economics, Washington DC, and has been supported financially by the Economic and Social Research Council (Grant R/000/23/1181). I am grateful to Dr Pikay Richardson for research assistance and for helpful comments and advice to Gary Hufbauer, Howard Rosen, Jonathan Aylen and Ted Denham, and to staff seminars at Cardiff Business School, Loughborough University, Manchester Business School and the Universities of Central Lancashire and North Staffordshire. The usual disclaimer applies.

NOTES

1 Integrated steel companies combine iron-making with the melting, casting, rolling and finishing of steel.
2 See Iron and Steel Statistics Bureau (1985: Table 34).
3 See Iron and Steel Statistics Bureau (1985).
4 Basic oxygen steelmaking involves blowing oxygen through molten iron in a vessel lined with alkaline (basic) refractories. The oxygen speeds the conversion process and removes nitrogen and other impurities. Continuous casting involves the extrusion of molten steel into long narrow channels, along which it solidifies and is withdrawn as long lengths of metal of rectangular cross-section.
5 See Cockerill (1974).
6 A scheme to provide £22 million to special steelmakers for re-adaptation costs was announced by the government in 1980 and later increased to £35 million. In addition, a further £16 million was offered towards the costs of two large-scale restructuring schemes, making a total of about £51 million. This aid was made available under Section 8 of the 1982 Industrial Development Act.
7 See Prest (1976).
8 Between 1973 and 1984, hourly labour costs grew at compound annual rates of 16.5 per cent in Britain and 7.7 per cent in West Germany.
9 The purchasing power standard (PPS) is the bilateral exchange rate, or multilateral set of exchange rates, that renders the price of a given basket of commodities the same in each country in terms of a common currency. The Eurostat PPS exchange rates are derived by calculating price ratios between the member states for an agreed list of products. These are then applied to GDP in national currencies and the parities scaled such that the value of the GDP of the Community in 1975 in PPS is the same as in European Currency Units (ECU). See Eurostat (1987).
10 See Statistical Appendix.

REFERENCES

Aylen, J. (1982) 'Plant size and efficiency in the steel industry: an international comparison', *National Institute Economic Review* 100, May: 65–76.

British Steel Corporation (1986) *Report and Accounts 1985–86*, London: BSC.

Cockerill, A. (1974) *The Steel Industry: International Comparisons of Industrial Structure and Performance* (in collaboration with Aubrey Silberston), University of Cambridge, Department of Applied Economics Occasional Paper 42, Cambridge: Cambridge University Press.

—— (1980) 'Steel and the state in Great Britain', *Annals of Public and Co-operative Economy* 51 (4) October–December: 439–57.

Department of Trade and Industry (1973) *British Steel Corporation: Ten-Year Development Plan*, Cmnd 5226, London: HMSO.

—— (1978) *British Steel Corporation: The Road to Viability*, Cmnd 7149, London: HMSO.

Eurostat (1987) *National Accounts ESA 1960–1985*, Luxembourg: Statistical Office of the European Communities.

Federal Trade Commission (1977) *The United States Steel Industry and its International Rivals: Trends and Factors Determining International Competitiveness*, Staff Report, Bureau of Economics, Washington DC: Government Printing Office.

Hill, C.P. (1985) *British Economic and Social History, 1700–1982*, 5th edn, London: Edward Arnold.

House of Commons (1983) *The British Steel Corporation's Prospects*, Second Report from the Industry and Trade Committee, HC212 (1982–3), London: HMSO.

Iron and Steel Statistics Bureau (1985) *Annual Statistics for the United Kingdom 1985*, Croydon: ISSB.

Ministry of Power (1965) *Steel Nationalisation*, Cmnd 2651, London: HMSO.

National Economic Development Office (1976) *A Study of UK Nationalised Industries*, London: HMSO.

Prest, A.R. (1976) 'The economic rationale of subsidies to industry', in A. Whiting (ed.) *The Economics of Industrial Subsidies*, London: HMSO.

Ward, M. (1985) *Purchasing Power Parities and Real Expenditures in the OECD*, Paris: Organisation for Economic Cooperation and Development.

Wilson, L.S. (1979) 'The incidence of subsidies to the nationalised fuel industries 1970–75', *Scottish Journal of Political Economy* 26 (3) November: 261–73 .

STATISTICAL APPENDIX

Table 19.A1 Productivity, hourly labour costs and labour costs per tonne of crude steel, Britain 1973–85

Calendar years	(1) Employment, all employees ('000)	(2) Average annual hours worked per employee	(3) Total man hours worked (millions of hours)	(4) Crude steel production ('000 tonnes)	(5) Man hours per tonne (hours)	(6a) Hourly labour costs (£)	(6b) Index (1973 = 100)	(7a) Unit labour costs (£ per tonne)	(7b) Index (1973 = 100)
1973	197.1	2004	394.99	26,649	14.82	1.31	100	19.41	100
1974	191.6	1801	345.07	22,379	15.42	1.53	117	23.59	122
1975	191.1	1844	352.39	19,780	17.81	2.18	166	38.83	200
1976	179.4	1866	334.76	22,396	14.95	2.52	192	37.67	194
1977	180.0	1877	337.86	20,474	16.50	2.88	220	47.52	245
1978	170.0	1863	316.71	20,302	15.60	3.34	255	52.10	268
1979	162.0	1883	305.05	21,472	14.21	3.84	293	54.57	281
1980	133.4	2194	292.68	11,278	25.95	4.44	339	115.22	594
1981	96.0	1824	175.10	15,321	11.43	5.28	403	60.35	311
1982	81.9	1801	147.50	13,740	10.74	6.21	474	66.70	344
1983	67.3	1836	123.56	14,980	8.25	6.87	524	56.68	292
1984	62.3	1841	114.69	15,214	7.54	7.05	538	53.16	274

Table 19.A2 Productivity, hourly labour costs and labour costs per tonne of crude steel, West Germany, 1973–85

Calendar years	(8) Employment, all employees ('000)	(9) Average annual hours worked per employee (hours)	(10) Total man hours worked (millions of hours)	(11) Crude steel production ('000 tonnes)
1973	227.5	1,792	407.68	49,521
1974	230.6	1,776	409.55	53,232
1975	226.8	1,558	353.35	40,415
1976	220.3	1,624	357.77	42,415
1977	214.2	1,570	336.29	38,985
1978	205.1	1,590	326.11	41,253
1979	203.9	1,640	334.40	46,040
1980	201.0	1,583	318.18	43,838
1981	192.0	1,561	299.71	41,610
1982	181.3	1,504	272.68	35,880
1983	168.9	1,499	253.18	35,729
1984	156.5	1,585	248.05	39,389

Table 19.A2 (continued)

Calendar years	(12) Man hours per tonne (hours)	(13a) Hourly labour costs DM	(13b) Index (1973 = 100)	(14a) Unit labour costs DM per tonne	(14b) Index (1973 = 100)	(15a) Exchange rates Current DM:£1	(15b) Purchasing power standard DM:£1
1973	8.23	16.96	100	139.58	100	6.5226	10.9596
1974	7.69	19.99	118	153.72	110	6.0485	10.1985
1975	8.74	21.96	129	191.93	138	5.4451	8.5135
1976	8.43	23.58	139	198.78	142	4.5295	7.6638
1977	8.63	24.92	147	215.06	154	4.0513	6.9742
1978	7.91	25.70	152	203.29	146	3.8500	6.5458
1979	7.26	27.62	163	200.52	144	3.8844	5.9381
1980	7.26	30.01	177	217.87	156	4.2176	5.1852
1981	7.20	31.32	185	225.50	162	4.5450	4.8544
1982	7.60	33.35	197	253.46	182	4.2394	4.7012
1983	7.09	35.32	208	250.42	179	3.8679	4.6091
1984	6.30	38.24	225	240.91	173	3.7894	4.5263

Table 19.A2 (continued)

Calendar years	(16a) 1973 exchange rates (£/tonne)	Unit labour costs (in £ per tonne) at: (16b) Current exchange rates (£/tonne)	(16c) PPS (£/tonne)
1973	21.39	21.39	12.74
1974	23.55	25.41	15.07
1975	29.41	35.25	22.54
1976	30.46	43.89	25.94
1977	32.95	53.08	30.84
1978	31.15	52.80	31.06
1979	30.72	51.62	33.77
1980	33.38	51.66	42.02
1981	34.55	49.61	46.45
1982	38.83	59.79	53.91
1983	38.37	64.74	54.33
1984	36.91	63.57	53.22

Table 19.A3 Estimates of the numbers of jobs protected in the British steel industry under three exchange rate assumptions, 1973–84

Calendar years	(17a) West German unit labour costs at: 1973 exchange rates (£/tonne)	(17b) Current exchange rates (£/tonne)	(17c) PPS (£/tonne)	(18) UK hourly labour costs: (£)
1973	21.39	21.39	12.74	1.31
1974	23.55	25.41	15.07	1.54
1975	29.41	35.25	22.54	2.18
1976	30.46	43.89	25.94	2.52
1977	32.95	53.08	30.84	2.88
1978	31.15	52.80	31.06	3.34
1979	30.72	51.62	33.77	3.84
1980	33.38	51.66	42.02	4.44
1981	34.55	49.61	46.45	5.28
1982	38.83	59.79	53.91	6.21
1983	38.37	64.74	54.33	6.87
1984	36.91	63.57	53.22	7.05

Table 19.A3 (continued)

Calendar years	(19a) Man hours per tonne to match West German unit labour costs at: 1973 exchange rates	(19b) Current exchange rates	(19c) PPS	(20a) Theoretical employment: 1973 exchange rates	(20b) Current exchange rates	(20c) PPS
1973	16.33	16.33	9.73	217,155	217,155	129,389
1974	15.39	16.61	9.85	191,234	206,394	122,395
1975	13.49	16.17	10.34	144,703	173,450	110,914
1976	12.09	17.42	10.29	145,106	209,077	123,501
1977	11.44	18.43	10.71	124,786	201,031	116,823
1978	9.33	15.81	9.30	101,673	172,289	101,347
1979	8.00	13.44	8.79	91,225	153,257	100,233
1980	7.52	11.64	9.46	38,656	59,834	48,628
1981	6.54	9.40	8.80	54,934	78,957	73,917
1982	6.25	9.63	8.68	47,682	73,468	66,221
1983	5.59	9.42	7.91	45,609	76,858	64,538
1984	5.24	9.02	7.55	43,303	73,541	62,393

Table 19.A3 (continued)

	(21a)	(21b) Jobs 'saved'	(21c)
Calendar years	1973 exchange rates	Current exchange rates	PPS
1973	−20.1	−20.1	67.7
1974	0.4	−14.8	69.2
1975	46.4	17.6	80.2
1976	34.3	−29.7	55.9
1977	55.2	−21.0	63.2
1978	68.3	−2.3	68.7
1979	70.8	8.7	61.8
1980	94.7	73.6	84.8
1981	41.1	17.0	22.1
1982	34.2	8.4	15.7
1983	21.7	−9.6	2.8
1984	19.0	−12.2	−0.1

Sources and derivations:

Column

(1) Eurostat (1983) *Iron and Steel Yearbook 1982*, Table 2.1; Eurostat (1985) *Employment and Unemployment 1985*, Table VII/1; Eurostat (1987) *Employment and Unemployment 1987*, Table III/9, Luxembourg: Statistical Office of the European Communities.
Data for all employees are not available for 1973. The figure given is pro-rated on the basis of the number of manual workers.

(2) Eurostat (1983) *Iron and Steel 1952–82*, Tables 2.1, 2.2; Eurostat (1987), *Employment and Unemployment 1987*, Table VI/9, Luxembourg: Statistical Office of the European Communities.
Data for 1973–80 are pro-rated on basis of average annual hours worked per manual worker.

(3) Column 1 × column 2.

(4) Eurostat (1984) *Iron and Steel 1952–1982*, Table 3.3; Eurostat (1987) *Iron and Steel Yearbook 1986*, Table 3.14, Luxembourg: Statistical Office of the European Communities.

(5) Column 3/column 4.
(6) Eurostat (1978) *Quarterly Iron and Steel Bulletin*, p. 3; Eurostat (1987) *Iron and Steel Yearbook 1986*, Table 8.18, Luxembourg: Statistical Office of the European Communities.

   Data for 1973–7 are pro-rated on the basis of costs for manual workers.
(7) Column 5 × column 6.
(8) Eurostat (1974) *Emploi et Chomage*, Table 1; Eurostat (1983) *Iron and Steel Yearbook 1982*, Table 2.1; Eurostat (1987) *Employment and Unemployment 1987*, Table III/9, Luxembourg: Statistical Office of the European Communities.

   Data for all employees are not available for 1973. The figure is pro-rated on the basis of the number of manual workers.
(9) Eurostat (1987) *Employment and Unemployment 1987*, Table VI/9, Luxembourg: Statistical Office of the European Communities.

   Data for 1973–9 are pro-rated on the basis of average annual hours worked by manual workers.
(10) Column 8 × column 9.
(11) Eurostat (1987) *Iron and Steel Yearbook 1986*, Table 3.14. Luxembourg: Statistical Office of the European Communities.
(12) Column 10 × column 11.
(13) As for column 6.
(14) Column 12 × column 13.
(15) Calculated for Eurostat (1987) *National Accounts ESA 1960–1985*, Luxembourg: Statistical Office of the European Communities.
(16) Column 14/column 15.
(17) Column 16.
(18) Column 6.
(19) Column 17/column 18.
(20) (Column 19/column 2) × column 4.
(21) Column 1 − column 20.

20

COMMENTARY ON CHAPTER 19

Lynden Moore

In the manufacturng process the steel industry is located between the coal industry upstream supplying it with fuel, and the motor vehicle and shipbuilding industries – at one time motor vehicles alone used to take up one-tenth of the output of the steel industry. The British government has intervened in all of these industries.

I therefore admire the way that Anthony Cockerill, while being aware of this, has nonetheless been willing to focus entirely on the steel industry to calculate the government's subsidization, the opportunity cost of doing so and the benefits in terms of jobs protected. He finds that most of the job protection was due to a decline in the exchange rate. But if we concentrate on the subsidy by dividing the subsidy bill by the jobs protected due to it the average subsidy per job appears to be £53,800.

The problem I find with his approach is that the extra funds, £7 billion from 1973 to 1984, have been used to invest in new equipment, that is, to move to a different kind of technique, more fuel efficient, less labour intensive, producing more coated steel. Indeed this is the type of reconstruction that the EC allowed. So although the subsidization appeared to be maintaining employment, it had the reverse effect. However a great deal of strike breaking was required to put into effect the reduction in the labour force to 17 per cent of the previous level.

Recently the UK has been one of the lowest cost producers, chiefly because much of its debt was written off. But the European Coal and Steel Community (ECSC) is anxious not to allow any expansion of the UK industry because of the difficulty it has had in persuading the Italian and Spanish governments not to subsidize their industries and because of the vast quantity of low-grade steel than can be produced in Eastern Europe. The European steel market is a long way from being a competitive one.

21

EAST–WEST TRADE IN TRANSITION

The case of Austria

Jarko Fidrmuc, Christian Helmenstein and Peter Huber

INTRODUCTION

A cross-country inspection of aggregate trade data reveals a spectacular growth of trade flows between the Central and East European (CEE) countries and Austria. Overall trade with the Czech Republic, Slovakia, Hungary and Poland grew at an average annual rate of 19.3 per cent between 1989 and 1994. While in 1989 a mere 9.7 per cent of Austria's exports flew to the CEE countries, up to 1994 their share rose to 13.4 per cent.

This chapter analyses trade flows between Austria and Central and Eastern Europe. Using SITC two-digit and three-digit data for Austrian trade flows with Albania, Bulgaria, (former) Czechoslovakia, Hungary, Poland and Romania, we investigate the relationship between aggregate trade expansion and changes in the commodity structure. We demonstrate that substantial regional differentiation, large variations across commodities, and a rapid expansion of intra-industry trade have accompanied overall trade growth. Simultaneously, membership in the European Economic Area and, since 1995, in the European Union (EU) has exposed the Austrian economy to an increasing degree of competition. As a consequence, some sectors benefited from the lifting of the iron curtain while others suffered. Our findings suggest that Austrian East–West trade is becoming increasingly similar to intra-EU trade. This result refutes often voiced concerns that the East European economies might be captured in low-wage/low technology equilibria (Rodrick 1993). Conversely, West European economies should encounter production losses pertaining only to individual commodities rather than to entire industries. If this development continues, it should contribute to overcome politico-economic reservations to EU Eastern enlargement.

The opening of Eastern Europe initiated substantial changes in the foreign trade orientation of the reform countries. Prior to the economic reforms, the trade of the East European economies concentrated on the Comecon zone. Following the first reform steps, the EU and the EFTA countries became the most important trade partners of all East European countries. EU exports to Eastern Europe are now four times as high as in 1988.[1] Imports from that region doubled between 1989 and 1994. Tables 21.1a and 21.1b show that this reorientation has been most pronounced for the Central European countries (Czech Republic, Hungary, Poland, Slovakia, CEE4).

Given these developments, previous studies (Collins and Rodrick 1991; Baldwin 1993) concentrated on the growth potential and regional reorientation of CEE trade, employing highly aggregate trade data, or on the implications of trade liberalization in particular commodities. According to these estimates, trade with the CEE economies is expected to grow faster than trade among West European countries. On the basis of a gravity model approach, Holzmann et al. (1994) conclude that the increasing competition from trade may result in significant losses of employment in Western Europe due to restructuring. For Austria these losses are estimated to amount to 5 to 6 per cent of total employment until 2002. Winters (1995) shows that for the steel industry the benefits from liberalizing imports to the EU exceed the costs.

Recently, structural changes in the dynamics of trade flows have been in the focus of research. Dimelis and Gatsios (1995) as well as Martin and Gual (1995) analysed structural changes in the trade patterns between the CEE countries and Greece and Spain, respectively. A stylized fact revealed by these studies is that increases in intra-industry trade have been the foremost reaction to trade liberalization with CEE countries. However, both Spain and Greece are special cases in many respects: Greek trade flows show a dominant affinity towards Bulgaria, Macedonia and Albania. Spain, in turn, is relatively distant from the CEE countries. The trade with CEE countries has mainly played an indirect role for Spain due to increased competition on third markets. Austrian trade relationships with CEE countries, by contrast, concentrate on the Visegrad countries which account for the largest share of East–West trade. Although Austria entered the Union as late as 1995, it applied almost the same liberalization policy towards Eastern Europe. Already in December 1991, the EU Association Agreements (the so-called Europe Agreements) were signed with Hungary, former Czechoslovakia and Poland. Due to similar EFTA agreements with Central and Eastern Europe, the liberalization of Austrian trade with Eastern Europe occurred simultaneously. As a consequence, Austria's joining of the EU in January 1995 did not significantly influence the legal framework of Austrian trade with Eastern Europe.

Austria has the highest ratio of exports to Eastern Europe within the EU (12.5 per cent of total exports).[2] On the import side, 7.6 per cent of Austrian imports originate in Eastern Europe. Therefore Austria reached the second highest trade surplus of all EU countries with Eastern Europe, accompanied

Table 21.1a Shares of the CEE countries in total EU imports

	East Europe		CEE4		SEE		Former USSR		Baltic states	CIS
	1988	1994	1988	1994	1988	1994	1988	1994	1994	1994
Belgium–Lux.	1.81	1.93	0.37	0.61	0.09	0.11	1.35	1.21	0.03	1.17
Denmark	2.08	4.13	1.34	2.31	0.07	0.10	0.67	1.72	0.52	1.20
Germany	3.62	7.42	1.67	4.31	0.39	0.43	1.56	2.68	0.17	2.51
Greece	4.87	4.45	1.90	0.72	0.86	1.59	2.11	2.14	0.01	2.12
Finland	14.46	12.48	1.88	2.09	0.14	0.09	12.45	10.29	1.18	9.12
France	2.36	2.39	0.51	0.74	0.30	0.21	1.56	1.44	0.05	1.39
Ireland	1.03	0.61	0.65	0.43	0.05	0.02	0.33	0.15	0.05	0.11
Italy	3.85	5.98	0.91	1.75	0.67	0.74	2.26	3.50	0.05	3.45
Netherlands	1.89	2.63	0.58	1.14	0.17	0.19	1.14	1.30	0.35	0.95
Austria	5.87	7.56	3.69	5.32	0.27	0.33	1.91	1.91	0.03	1.89
Portugal	0.53	1.24	0.17	0.23	0.10	0.05	0.26	0.96	0.07	0.89
Sweden	2.94	4.32	1.20	1.51	0.14	0.45	1.60	2.37	0.93	1.45
Spain	2.43	2.11	0.34	0.62	0.26	0.15	1.83	1.33	0.05	1.28
UK	1.34	1.82	0.54	0.76	0.12	0.15	0.68	0.91	0.30	0.62
EU15	2.88	4.23	0.97	1.92	0.29	0.32	1.62	2.00	0.19	1.81

Note: SEE: Bulgaria, Romania; Baltic countries: Estonia, Latvia, Lithuania; CIS: Commonwealth of Independent States. Current prices in US$.
Source: International Monetary Fund, Institute for Advanced Studies

Table 21.1b Shares of the CEE countries in total EU exports

	East Europe		CEE4		SEE		Former USSR		Baltic states	CIS
	1988	1994	1988	1994	1988	1994	1988	1994	1994	1994
Belgium–Lux.	1.08	2.13	0.39	1.18	0.12	0.13	0.57	0.82	0.07	0.75
Denmark	1.45	4.10	0.82	2.28	0.08	0.16	0.55	1.66	0.39	1.27
Germany	3.46	7.40	1.42	4.51	0.38	0.45	1.66	2.43	0.23	2.20
Greece	3.76	9.65	0.94	1.30	1.20	5.72	1.62	2.63	0.04	2.59
Finland	16.08	12.01	0.93	3.24	0.16	0.21	15.00	8.56	2.99	5.58
France	1.78	2.14	0.46	1.22	0.16	0.20	1.16	0.71	0.04	0.67
Ireland	0.42	1.11	0.23	0.48	0.06	0.03	0.13	0.61	0.02	0.58
Italy	2.60	5.07	0.74	2.96	0.21	0.63	1.64	1.49	0.07	1.42
Netherlands	1.18	3.20	0.59	1.71	0.12	0.23	0.46	1.27	0.14	1.13
Austria	7.62	12.54	3.98	10.15	0.76	0.55	2.88	1.84	0.06	1.78
Portugal	0.85	0.72	0.14	0.23	0.10	0.06	0.61	0.42	0.04	0.38
Sweden	1.66	3.70	0.97	1.95	0.13	0.28	0.56	1.47	0.62	0.84
Spain	1.07	1.67	0.31	1.06	0.09	0.10	0.66	0.50	0.04	0.46
UK	1.32	1.99	0.53	1.11	0.16	0.16	0.62	0.72	0.05	0.67
EU15	2.53	4.50	0.90	2.62	0.23	0.34	1.40	1.53	0.19	1.34

Note: SEE: Bulgaria, Romania; Baltic countries: Estonia, Latvia, Lithuania; CIS: Commonwealth of Independent States; CIS: Commonwealth of Independent States. Current prices in US$.
Source: International Monetary Fund, Institute for Advanced Studies

by a high degree of openness to East European exports. (Only Finland has a higher share of imports from Eastern Europe.) From the point of view of recent developments, Finnish trade with Eastern Europe stagnated and trade with the former USSR even declined since 1989. Germany, Italy, France, Austria and the UK account for three-quarters of the Union's trade with Eastern Europe. Hence the Austrian regional trade structure is similar to the average trade structure of the EU, and our results bear some potential for generalization.

The chapter is organized as follows. In the next section we document the extent of trade growth and the changes in the product structure in Austrian trade with CEE countries and elaborate the differences between the CEE countries. In the third section we address the issue of how these changes affect the cooperation between Austria and the CEE countries. We draw upon various indicators that may allow forecasts about the future trade structure of the CEE countries with Austria. We also examine to what extent the growth in trade between the CEE countries and Austria is due to the reintegration of the CEE countries into the world economy. The fourth section concludes the chapter.

GROWTH AND STRUCTURAL CHANGES OF AUSTRIAN TRADE WITH EASTERN EUROPE

We employ annual trade data at the SITC two-digit and three-digit levels[3] for the period between 1988 and 1994. An analysis of the data has to take into account that the starting conditions in Central and Eastern Europe varied widely across countries. Each of the four Visegrad countries (Czech Republic, Hungary, Poland, Slovakia) and Slovenia, which are featured by a comparatively advanced stage of reforms, recently acquired a rank among the twenty most important Austrian trading partners. Exports to Hungary and Poland witnessed a large increase of over 20 per cent each already in 1989 due to the early start of reforms, while exports to Czechoslovakia started to expand no earlier than during 1990. Since then a continuous growth of exports was registered only for former Czechoslovakia and Hungary. Polish exports, by contrast, have been oscillating between significant increases and substantial falls. Traditionally, trade with Bulgaria, Romania and Albania is much less important for Austria in terms of both imports and exports. Their aggregate share in total Austrian trade reaches less than 1 per cent.[4]

Despite the dramatic growth of Austrian trade with the CEE countries, we observe strong regional differences (see Tables 21.1a and 21.1b). The regional variation is significant even within close regional groups. For example, Austrian exports to the South East European countries show quite hetero-geneous dynamics: while exports to Albania and Bulgaria have decreased by about 30 to 40 per cent, exports to Romania experienced an increase of 154 per cent over the period from 1989 to 1993. During the same period exports to the Visegrad countries increased between about 70 per cent for Poland and almost 230 per cent for former Czechoslovakia.

Only incomplete data are available for Austrian trade with the Baltic states, Slovenia, Croatia, the Czech Republic and Slovakia, and the CIS. Table 21.2a displays available data for both individual countries as well as the respective (former) country aggregates such that it is possible to infer at least some tentative results about the regional variation of exports. Total exports to the area of the former Soviet Union (including the Baltic republics) decreased during the entire time period from 1989 to 1993. Judging by the 1994 data, exports to and imports from the former USSR revived, though from a low level. Table 21.2a demonstrates that the largest growth of exports was experienced in the Central and East European countries with a relatively smaller output decline during the transitional recession.

The import side of Austrian trade relationships is characterized by similar regional differences (see Table 21.2b). But this differentiation takes place at markedly lower growth rates while it exhibits a more stable trend. The dissolution of the Comecon and the subsequent reduction in trade among the CEE countries themselves is one of the driving forces behind the growing intensity of Austrian trade relationships with the CEE countries. Part of the exports which previously went to other Comecon countries were rerouted to Western countries.

An essential feature of Austria's trade with Central and Eastern Europe is the significant changes in the structure of trade. We correlate both the export and import structure of consecutive years to the export and import structure of 1988 by calculating Pearson's correlation coefficient for two-digit and three-digit trade data. For purposes of comparison we choose the Austrian–Italian trade structure on the a priori expectation that in this case there should not have occurred extraordinarily large structural changes during the period under consideration.[5] (See Table 21.3.)

Commonly, statistical tools other than the correlation coefficient are used for trade data analyses. Since structural changes in exports and imports usually involve long periods of time, if applied for a five-year period this indicator may not be sufficiently powerful to measure the ongoing structural change. To illustrate, for Italian exports in 1994 compared to 1988 we find a correlation coefficient of 0.98 which indicates a large degree of structural equivalence. In the case of East–West trade, however, the results of our correlation analysis reveal that the comparatively short transition period was sufficiently long to trigger off large adjustments.

Compared to the Austrian–Italian case, the correlation coefficients for trade flows between Austria and the CEE countries are much lower with a minimum of 0.04 for Albania and a maximum of 0.84 for the former CSFR. Note that the degree of structural change has its analogy in the total trade volume. In general, countries with slower export growth such as Albania and

Table 21.2a Annual growth rates of Austrian exports to the transition countries

	1989	1990	1991	1992	1993	1994	Share	Total change (%)
Former CSFR	6.83	72.51	6.04	50.74	11.74	15.84	3.49	281.27
Czech Republic						18.08	2.62	
Slovakia						9.62	0.88	
Poland	40.74	−16.51	70.89	−5.55	−8.84	−6.74	1.17	61.23
Hungary	27.13	20.75	38.66	7.09	6.37	21.05	3.91	193.54
Albania	22.64	2.39	−27.59	−45.97	33.02	−8.42	0.01	−40.15
Bulgaria	−15.25	−32.31	0.09	−0.58	−1.90	−2.30	0.26	−45.28
Romania	0.24	98.65	4.41	12.67	8.20	15.14	0.29	191.87
F. Yugoslavia	18.16	34.95	−23.00	−2.54	11.63	28.65	2.61	71.84
Slovenia					20.69	17.40	1.56	
Croatia					47.9	47.69	0.82	
Former USSR	4.09	−12.18	−7.35	−13.76	−5.14	20.37	1.80	−16.61
Russia					−9.58	20.12	1.46	
Estonia					0.89	185.04	0.02	
Latvia					83.00	71.41	0.02	
Lithuania					−2.43	66.82	0.02	
EE and f. USSR	14.05	14.73	8.42	7.26	4.87	17.21	13.55	87.04
Total exports	12.03	8.56	2.78	1.78	−4.18	9.57	100.00	33.58

Table 21.2b Annual growth rates of Austrian imports from the transition countries

	1989	1990	1991	1992	1993	1994	Share	Total change (%)
Former CSFR	11.34	-4.86	16.06	48.96	10.80	25.69	2.45	155.03
Czech Republic						23.76	1.80	
Slovakia						31.29	0.66	
Poland	2.67	15.18	12.82	-11.37	-6.62	9.81	0.82	21.24
Hungary	23.11	11.44	31.41	4.17	-9.47	18.53	2.04	101.51
Albania	-52.58	61.26	-48.65	-68.59	-38.91	61.64	0.00	-87.82
Bulgaria	35.99	14.27	9.55	13.76	-16.20	21.71	0.11	97.50
Romania	6.74	-37.53	35.23	29.87	-13.20	57.56	0.21	60.16
F. Yugoslavia	28.19	7.15	-9.16	-12.12	-4.03	17.05	0.92	23.17
Slovenia					12.65	20.30	0.65	
Croatia					47.27	9.08	0.24	
Former USSR	-1.28	20.18	-4.79	-11.30	1.28	35.08	1.88	37.07
Russia					2.33	32.84	1.62	
Estonia					24.34	74.10	0.01	
Latvia					37.40	-18.86	0.01	
Lithuania					48.45	24.29	0.01	
EE and f. USSR	11.36	9.07	9.23	4.62	-1.41	23.67	8.43	69.23
Total exports	14.01	8.07	6.41	0.34	-4.89	11.42	100.00	39.42

Source: Institute for Advanced Studies, Austrian trade statistics

Bulgaria were simultaneously featured by larger structural adjustment needs.[6] Countries with less need for structural change, by contrast, tend to have larger increases in total exports. This result points to the crucial role played by the starting conditions in explaining the trade patterns with Central and Eastern Europe and the close interaction of growth and structural change in this field. Austria has been able substantially to expand its exports to countries whose import structure was closest to the one which would have resulted under 'free market' conditions while in countries which faced the need for comprehensive structural adjustment import growth was much lower.

The analysis of SITC three-digit data indicates that the reward offered for further disaggregation is small since the most important structural changes are already observable on the two-digit level. Yet with further disaggregation, besides an increased sensitivity to measurement errors and rounding errors, the results are biased due to a non-trading effect. With an increasing level of disaggregation for an ever larger number of SITC classes, no trading activity is registered during the periods under consideration. The correlation coefficients hence tend to overstate the degree of structural permanence in the trade flows which helps to explain the relatively high correlation coefficients for imports from Poland on the SITC three-digit level. For this reason, our subsequent analysis mainly draws upon SITC two-digit data.

THE ROLE OF INTRA-INDUSTRY TRADE IN AUSTRIAN TRADE WITH EASTERN EUROPE

The preceding section revealed that Austrian trade with Central and Eastern Europe has undergone substantial changes not only in the volume of trade but also in its structure. In this part we investigate the impact of these changes on the structure of trade between Austria and the CEE countries in further detail.

Neven (1995) points to the role of trade growth due to intra-industry trade expansion versus inter-industry trade growth. As far as factors are more mobile within industries than across industries, an increase of intra-industry trade, which requires restructuring within industries, should be less costly in welfare terms than an increase in inter-industry trade. However, taking into consideration that small groups are easier to organize than large ones, a politico-economic perspective may suggest that intra-industry trade growth, by affecting smaller groups of manufacturers, may lead to stronger political pressure towards protectionism than inter-industry trade growth.

Indices of revealed comparative advantage (RCA) are widely used for the analysis of industrial trade. These indices measure the commodity-specific degree of comparative advantage by one country compared to other countries. A formula commonly[7] used is:

Table 21.3 Structural change in Austrian trade with CEE countries

Exports

	Two-digit SITC commodity groups							Three-digit SITC	
	Italy	F. CSFR	Hungary	Poland	Romania	Bulgaria	Albania	Hungary	Poland
1988	1.00	1.00	1.00	1.00	1.00	1.00	1.00	1.00	1.00
1989	1.00[a]	0.99[a]	0.97[a]	0.91[a]	0.98[a]	0.93[a]	1.00[a]	0.91[a]	0.77[a]
1990	0.99[a]	0.90[a]	0.88[a]	0.60[a]	0.76[a]	0.88[a]	0.72[a]	0.82[a]	0.41[a]
1991	0.98[a]	0.90[a]	0.77[a]	0.50[a]	0.39[a]	0.50[a]	0.75[a]	0.70[a]	0.31[a]
1992	0.98[a]	0.84[a]	0.74[a]	0.49[a]	0.19	0.48[a]	0.62[a]	0.69[a]	0.28[a]
1993	0.98[a]	0.82[a]	0.75[a]	0.60[a]	0.34[a]	0.34[a]	0.04	0.67[a]	0.34[a]
1994	0.98[a]	0.75[a]	0.73[a]	0.55[a]	0.34[a]	0.50[a]	0.06	0.64[a]	0.30[a]

Imports

	Two-digit SITC commodity groups							Three-digit SITC	
	Italy	F. CSFR	Hungary	Poland	Romania	Bulgaria	Albania	Hungary	Poland
1988	1.00	1.00	1.00	1.00	1.00	1.00	1.00	1.00	1.00
1989	0.99[a]	0.98[a]	0.99[a]	0.99[a]	0.88[a]	0.93[a]	0.42[a]	0.98[a]	0.99[a]
1990	0.99[a]	0.94[a]	0.91[a]	0.99[a]	0.83[a]	0.97[a]	0.48[a]	0.92[a]	0.99[a]
1991	0.99[a]	0.83[a]	0.79[a]	0.98[a]	0.88[a]	0.93[a]	0.68[a]	0.87[a]	0.98[a]
1992	0.99[a]	0.65[a]	0.66[a]	0.98[a]	0.73[a]	0.86[a]	0.18	0.73[a]	0.98[a]
1993	0.98[a]	0.79[a]	0.58[a]	0.95[a]	0.62[a]	0.71[a]	-0.03	0.63[a]	0.96[a]
1994	0.97[a]	0.76[a]	0.54[a]	0.82[a]	0.57[a]	0.49[a]	0.17	0.61[a]	0.83[a]

Source: Institute for Advanced Studies
Note: Pearson's correlation coefficients for exports and imports (two-digit and three-digit SITC commodity groups), current year to 1988.
[a] Significant at the 1% significance level.

$$RCA_{it} = \frac{X_{it} - M_{it}}{X_{it} + M_{it}} \qquad (1)$$

where RCA_{it} is the index of revealed comparative advantage in sector i at time t, X_{it} are Austrian exports to Eastern Europe of sector i at time t, and M_{it} are Austrian imports from Eastern Europe at time t in goods category i.[8]

There are two kinds of patterns in the RCA index which may provide information related to the future Austrian trade structure. A constant value of the revealed comparative advantage index in a certain category over the whole time period suggests that the respective goods category as a whole was not affected by structural changes in trade. On an aggregate level the need for industrial adjustment may therefore be below the average. On the contrary, a trend in the RCA index may indicate major restructuring requirements across the particular industry. Jumps and oscillations of the RCA, however, are difficult to interpret and provide no reliable information concerning the future development of trade. They may be results of short-term factors (import restrictions), or statistical artifacts.

Austria has a strong and stable RCA in the SITC categories 5, 6, 7, and 8 with the CEE countries except for Slovenia. Similarly, in the SITC categories 2, 3, and 4 Austria seems to have a comparative disadvantage but trade in the SITC categories 3 and 4 is too thin to allow reliable conclusions. The SITC categories 0 and 1 are those with the strongest dynamics: Austria's comparative disadvantage has changed towards a slight comparative advantage.

The RCA indices in Austrian trade with Italy are much more stable than in Austrian trade with the CEE countries. Austria's specialization in its trade with Italy is similar to the specialization of the CEE countries in their EU-oriented trade.

Ballance *et al.* (1987) find a high degree of inconsistency among alternative RCA indices as a cardinal measure for the commodity-specific degree of comparative advantage. Thus, the results of empirical studies may be highly sensitive to the particular index chosen. Moreover, the pattern of comparative advantage is sensitive to the disaggregation level. At high levels of aggregation the index is based on composite goods which represent a whole industry or sector rather than specific commodities. In light of the increasing importance of intra-industry trade relationships, a country may face a comparative disadvantage for a composite good and yet have a comparative advantage for a particular niche within this composite good (Vollrath 1991).

Since data at the one-digit SITC level are too highly aggregated to identify an industry, the results obtained above may be misleading when the changes in revealed comparative advantages are considered. This is illustrated by the fact that the revealed comparative advantage is not uniformly retained at the

SITC two-digit level. For a more reliable analysis of the data we therefore define four different groups:

- industries with stable comparative advantage;
- industries with stable comparative disadvantage;
- industries with a continuously falling RCA;
- industries with a continuously rising RCA.

According to the results of our cross-country analysis, Austria is losing its RCA in more than one country in five SITC two-digit categories (52, 66, 72, 74, 84) but fails to provide a clear picture for other than these five categories. We expect the manufacturers of these goods to face the need of major restructuring. SITC categories with rising RCA, by contrast, differ across countries. This observation reflects an increasing degree of specialization between Austria and Central and Eastern Europe.

These findings indicate an increase in intra-industry trade. While the inter-industry trade turns out to be unfavourable to Central and Eastern Europe in the long run due to the expected specialization on low-wage products, product differentiation coupled with the active search for product niches on the side of the CEE countries may help develop new comparative advantages.

To address the intra-industrial trade issue, we use the Grubel–Lloyd index (Grubel and Lloyd 1971) of intra-industry trade which is defined as

$$B_{it} = 1 - \frac{|X_{it} - M_{it}|}{X_{it} + M_{it}} \tag{2}$$

where B_{it} is the share of intra-industry trade in category i at time t and X_{it} and M_{it} are exports and imports in the same categories at time t. Note that the Grubel–Lloyd index is just $1-|RCA_{it}|$. We conduct the analysis at the two-digit SITC level.[9] For the sake of a clear presentation of the results, however, we only report averages at the SITC one-digit level in Table 21.4. That is, the measure given in this table is:

$$B_{jt} = \frac{1}{n_j} \sum_{i=1}^{n_j} B_{it} \tag{3}$$

with n_j as the number of SITC two-digit groups in a SITC one-digit category.

Table 21.4 displays the intra-industry trade indicator B_{jt} for selected countries. In general, the indicator is low when compared with international standards. In 1994, intra-industry trade with CEE countries was small in comparison with Italy, although the share of intra-industry trade in Austrian trade with Italy declined between 1988 and 1994. Breuss (1983) calculates the same indicator for some West European countries. All countries in his sample have higher shares of intra-industry trade with Austria already in 1981 than the CEE countries in 1993. This result underlines the fact that the cooperation between the EU and the CEE countries on the branch level is considerably less developed than within the EU. In addition, Table 21.4 hints at future changes in the trade structure. Across all CEE countries, intra-industry trade has risen since 1989, and we expect this tendency to persist during the next years.

We proceed with an investigation as to what extent the creation of trade has been due to an increased specialization in Central and Eastern Europe. To tackle this issue we decompose the overall trade growth into the components of intra-industry trade growth and of inter-industry trade growth. Re-arranging the definitional equation of intra-industry trade, from equation (2) we have

$$B_{it}\left(X_{it}+M_{it}\right)+\left|X_{it}-M_{it}\right|=X_{it}+M_{it}\,. \tag{4}$$

Subtracting the trade volume at time (t-1) and using Δ as difference operator, we obtain:

$$\Delta\left(B_{it}\left(X_{it}+M_{it}\right)\right)+\Delta\left|X_{it}-M_{it}\right|=\Delta\left(X_{it}+M_{it}\right)\,. \tag{5}$$

Dividing by $(X_{it}+M_{it})$ gives:

$$\frac{\Delta\left(B_{it}\left(X_{it}+M_{it}\right)\right)}{X_{it}+M_{it}}+\frac{\Delta\left|X_{it}-M_{it}\right|}{X_{it}+M_{it}}=\frac{\Delta\left(X_{it}+M_{it}\right)}{X_{it}+M_{it}}\,. \tag{6}$$

On the right-hand side of equation (6) we have the growth rate of trade while the left side is composed of two components. The first component measures the contribution of intra-industry trade to total trade growth, and the second represents the contribution of inter-industry trade to overall trade growth.

Table 21.5 shows the results of this decomposition at the SITC two-digit level, aggregated to the SITC one-digit level for the sake of a condensed presentation. A large variation of this indicator over time and across countries becomes obvious. In the groups with the highest growth of trade, that is the SITC groups 1, 6, 7 and 8, intra-industry trade has contributed between about one-quarter up to more than one-half of total trade growth. Conversely, in the groups where trade has been decreasing, intra-industry trade as a rule has proven to be less affected than inter-industry trade. These findings

Table 21.4 Intra-industry trade by commodity type and country

F. CSFR	SITC0	SITC1	SITC2	SITC3	SITC4	SITC5	SITC6	SITC7	SITC8	Total
1988	32.24	37.20	27.00	3.75	13.86	39.19	36.86	32.67	47.76	30.06
1989	25.28	65.42	23.73	3.49	7.02	40.88	38.82	37.86	48.92	32.38
1990	22.30	68.63	32.57	33.42	11.38	38.91	47.30	42.08	42.98	37.73
1991	43.64	35.04	38.02	16.32	43.15	40.64	55.46	39.58	53.70	40.62
1992	45.92	10.54	39.07	24.07	11.88	42.12	65.80	28.55	59.76	36.41
1993	51.25	31.48	54.23	22.68	42.01	39.22	73.42	32.70	58.77	45.08
1994	49.80	15.35	49.39	45.56	19.01	51.23	70.98	48.32	56.75	45.16

Hungary	SITC0	SITC1	SITC2	SITC3	SITC4	SITC5	SITC6	SITC7	SITC8	Total
1988	33.99	51.70	51.32	3.44	50.30	45.32	52.50	24.80	54.42	40.87
1989	37.34	33.61	36.72	8.53	27.35	45.97	49.99	30.40	63.96	37.10
1990	47.69	28.63	41.88	6.52	51.57	39.18	53.56	40.25	57.11	40.71
1991	49.16	51.24	41.85	7.62	27.90	38.88	55.39	52.22	54.71	42.11
1992	43.04	27.77	46.47	9.91	47.39	42.38	56.18	47.41	55.76	41.81
1993	45.04	5.24	47.68	11.84	51.32	41.89	53.85	37.74	52.32	38.55
1994	50.38	2.95	43.98	14.62	63.46	51.95	52.08	39.80	56.75	41.78

Poland	SITC0	SITC1	SITC2	SITC3	SITC4	SITC5	SITC6	SITC7	SITC8	Total
1988	14.71	23.12	7.20	4.82	0.00	38.53	42.91	42.63	35.81	23.30
1989	5.47	12.80	17.74	14.58	4.78	40.79	51.64	30.19	47.99	25.11
1990	22.66	4.39	28.04	23.71	4.83	34.92	59.30	35.86	45.26	28.77
1991	37.21	0.09	21.20	33.30	8.12	43.47	55.71	19.72	50.63	29.94
1992	27.04	0.94	13.08	33.17	0.00	46.46	58.19	27.79	36.65	27.04

Table 21.4 (continued)

Poland	SITC0	SITC1	SITC2	SITC3	SITC4	SITC5	SITC6	SITC7	SITC8	Total
1993	18.28	5.73	21.78	24.00	30.30	41.21	53.91	35.73	33.24	29.35
1994	33.37	7.46	17.97	16.49	0.22	29.52	57.99	42.13	21.41	25.17

Slovenia	SITC0	SITC1	SITC2	SITC3	SITC4	SITC5	SITC6	SITC7	SITC8	Total
1992	31.94	8.07	29.78	16.88	10.41	33.52	61.43	25.54	50.89	29.83
1993	33.22	5.26	31.92	11.08	6.09	39.88	60.05	30.02	51.15	29.85
1994	26.70	5.19	25.85	10.98	3.49	38.82	63.53	23.33	48.22	27.35

Italy	SITC0	SITC1	SITC2	SITC3	SITC4	SITC5	SITC6	SITC7	SITC8	Total
1988	41.80	53.47	33.68	38.07	7.64	70.84	56.85	57.68	49.00	45.45
1989	38.79	45.11	31.03	8.47	2.52	68.56	57.45	57.97	47.21	39.68
1990	35.60	50.25	35.68	29.87	16.77	67.72	56.17	54.43	44.66	43.46
1991	40.92	57.51	29.32	20.91	8.79	69.13	57.42	55.80	47.47	43.03
1992	43.18	68.28	28.69	6.17	29.47	71.50	57.94	58.16	46.87	45.58
1993	30.22	73.71	28.70	5.48	23.93	71.48	58.69	58.12	41.33	43.52
1994	33.62	67.08	31.31	34.04	41.80	62.99	57.03	54.78	36.85	46.61

Source: Institute for Advanced Studies

Table 21.5 Growth of inter-industry and intra-industry trade

CSFR	SITC0	SITC1	SITC2	SITC3	SITC4	SITC5	SITC6	SITC7	SITC8
Intra	120.43	90.39	55.09	78.65	4.81	64.63	425.32	126.81	319.37
Inter	86.14	640.80	11.12	2.21	-6.58	38.03	125.82	103.24	227.56
Total	206.57	731.19	66.22	80.87	-1.77	102.66	551.14	230.04	546.92

Hungary	SITC0	SITC1	SITC2	SITC3	SITC4	SITC5	SITC6	SITC7	SITC8
Intra	66.22	-40.10	-14.83	17.61	-15.75	26.22	63.20	147.85	291.32
Inter	32.68	333.26	-2.20	26.35	-29.81	11.49	58.96	185.94	217.92
Total	98.90	293.16	-17.03	43.96	-45.56	37.70	122.17	333.78	509.24

Poland	SITC0	SITC1	SITC2	SITC3	SITC4	SITC5	SITC6	SITC7	SITC8
Intra	6.11	-4.86	10.89	45.15	0.10	-4.39	59.64	44.14	60.83
Inter	-43.72	149.62	-10.21	157.90	-54.91	20.04	17.20	61.81	290.55
Total	-37.62	144.76	0.68	203.06	-54.81	15.65	76.84	105.95	351.39

Romania	SITC0	SITC1	SITC2	SITC3	SITC4	SITC5	SITC6	SITC7	SITC8
Intra	45.51	1.34	63.07	145.03	-1.82	11.65	35.22	189.46	54.64
Inter	41.05	4352.78	149.54	-10.76	-92.45	-7.29	35.85	245.21	130.19
Total	86.56	4354.12	212.61	134.27	-94.27	4.37	71.07	434.67	184.83

Note: 'Inter' refers to the growth rate of inter-industry trade between 1988 and 1994; 'intra' to the growth rate of intra-industry trade; and 'total' to the overall growth of trade during the respective time period.
Source: Institute for Advanced Studies

suggest that the growth of trade between Central and Eastern Europe and Austria has to a large extent been due to increases in intra-industry trade.

CONCLUSIONS

The opening of Eastern Europe was the precondition for rapid changes in the regional structure of intra-European foreign trade. While the share of the CEE countries in total EU exports and imports nearly doubled between 1988 and 1994, trade expansion with the Visegrad countries was particularly large. While the share of the CEE countries in overall EU trade is still moderate on average (below 5 per cent), trade with Eastern Europe accounts for approximately 10 per cent of total trade and more in the neighbouring regions.

Austria has the highest share of exports to Eastern Europe within the EU. Together with the four largest EU economies, Austria ranks among the leading EU exporters to and importers from Eastern Europe in volume terms. Germany, Italy, France, Austria and the UK account for three-quarters of the Union's trade with Eastern Europe. While Austria shows a high exposure to Central and East European exports, Austrian exports to the CEE countries are still higher than the imports from this region. Our findings for Austria may be interpreted as to how the liberalization of trade will impinge on the future trade structure of other EU members.

By using disaggregated trade data, we demonstrate that structural changes in trade with the CEE countries have been a crucial feature of recent trade growth. Structural changes emerge from a reshaping of trade flows across Europe that is characterized by the creation of competitive edges in specific product niches. This development is reflected by the dynamic growth of intra-industry trade. When compared with the EU countries, however, the shares of intra-industry trade are still small. For this reason, we expect East–West trade to be likely to witness an ongoing expansion of intra-industry trade in the coming years.

From the point of view of the CEE economies, concerns that the East European economies might be captured in low-wage/low-technology equilibria appear to be overstated. Although the adjustment needs in response to the opening of Eastern Europe are high in both Eastern and Western Europe, growing shares of intra-industrial trade in overall trade suggest that many CEE firms have been able to develop products and product lines with a higher value added, thereby reaping some benefits from specialization. Regarding Western Europe, the considerable contribution that the growth of intra-industry trade has made to overall trade growth indicates less significant production losses than suggested by early estimates. The effects of these transitional trade dynamics on employment, however, remain to be studied.

ACKNOWLEDGEMENTS

We have benefited from comments by Magdolna Sass and Andreas Wörgötter. The research by Jarko Fidrmuc and Peter Huber was financially supported by the Austrian Ministry of Science.

NOTES

1 We used trade data in current prices in US$ provided by the IMF Direction of Trade Database.

2 Data according to the IMF Direction of Trade Database differ slightly from Austrian trade data that will be used in the following sections. According to national data, the share of exports to Eastern Europe is even higher (13.6 per cent).

3 The data set is provided by the Austrian Statistical Office and reports all Austrian imports and exports according to their regional structure as of SITC Rev. 3.

4 The extremely low volume of trade between Albania and Austria raises concerns about the usefulness of these data since single export contracts may lead to considerable fluctuations even on the two-digit level. The interpretation of our results for the Austrian–Albanian trade flows is therefore subject to a caveat.

5 The choice of Italy as a 'control country' is motivated by the fact that Italy is Austria's second largest single trading partner which, in contrast to most other important trading partners, has like the CEE countries undergone a series of devaluations in the period from 1988 to 1994. Therefore we expect that the trade structure with Italy is also subject to change as far as exchange rate fluctuations are concerned.

6 Using Kendall's tau statistic as a non-parametric measure of association for ordinal variables, we also conducted a rank correlation analysis. The rank correlation between export growth and structural change is estimated to be 0.66 which is significant at the 10 per cent level.

7 Balassa (1989: 46) also introduced the following frequently used index of revealed comparative advantage (R) which is defined as $R_{t,k} = (X_{t,kij}/X_{t,kj})/(X_{t,ij}/X_{t,j})$, where $X_{t,kij}$ are exports of product k by country i to country j, $X_{t,kj}$ are world exports of product k to country j, $X_{t,ij}$ are total exports of country i to country j, and $X_{t,j}$ are world exports to country j. We did not use this index in order to ensure better comparability with other country studies on East–West trade (see, for example, Martin and Gual 1995; Collins and Rodrick 1991). Moreover, estimates of world trade flows are available only with considerable delays.

8 We also checked for trade imbalances in Fidrmuc et al. (1995) but the results do not differ significantly.

9 We use the term 'intra-industry' trade in a broad sense, that is, trade within the same SITC two-digit group.

REFERENCES

Balassa, B. (1989) 'Trade liberalization and "revealed comparative advantage"', in *Comparative Advantage, Trade Policy and Economic Development*, London: Harvester Wheatsheaf, p. 46.

Baldwin, R.E. (1993) 'The potential for trade between EFTA and Central and Eastern Europe', Occasional Paper No. 44, Geneva: EFTA.

Ballance, R.H., Forstner, H. and Murray, T. (1987) 'Consistency tests of alternative measures of comparative advantage', *Review of Economics and Statistics* 69: 157–61.

Breuss, F. (1983) *Österreichs Außenwirtschaft 1945–1982*, Vienna: Signum Verlag.

Collins, S.M. and Rodrick, D. (1991) 'Eastern Europe and the Soviet Union in the world economy', *Institute for International Economics* 32, Washington DC: IIE.

Dimelis, S. and Gatsios, K. (1995) 'Trade with Central and Eastern Europe: the case of Greece', in R. Faini and R. Portes (eds) *European Union Trade with Eastern Europe, Adjustment and Opportunities*, London: CEPR, pp. 123–66.

Fidrmuc J., Helmenstein, C. and Huber, P. (1995) 'Investigating disaggregate East–West trade data: the reshaping of the international division of labor', *East European Series* 23, Vienna: Institute for Advanced Studies.

Grubel, H. and Lloyd, P. (1971) 'The empirical measurement of intra-industry trade', *Economic Record* 47: 494–517.

Holzmann, R., Thimann, C. and Petz, A. (1994) 'Pressure to adjust: consequences for the OECD countries from reforms in Eastern Europe', *Empirica* 21: 141–96.

Martin, C. and Gual, J. (1995) 'Trade and foreign direct investment with Central and Eastern Europe: its impact on Spain', in R. Faini and R. Portes (eds) *European Union Trade with Eastern Europe, Adjustment and Opportunities* London: CEPR, pp. 167–200.

Neven, D. (1995) 'Trade liberalisation with Eastern nations. Some distribution issues', *European Economic Review* 39 (3/4): 622–32.

Rodrick, D. (1993) 'Do low-income countries have a high-wage option?', NBER Working Paper 4451.

Vollrath, T.L. (1991) 'A theoretical evaluation of alternative trade intensity measures of revealed comparative advantage', *Weltwirtschaftliches Archiv* 127: 265–79.

Winters, L.A. (1995) 'Liberalizing European steel trade', *European Economic Review* 39 (3/4): 611–21.

22

COMMENTARY ON CHAPTER 21

Magdolna Sass

The chapter by Jarko Fidrmuc, Christian Helmenstein and Peter Huber analyses one of the most interesting questions from the point of view of the present and future of the transforming economies in Eastern and Central Europe, namely, the pattern of their 'insertion' into the international economy in the first years of transformation. Their analysis is based on the case of Austria which, besides Germany, has the closest and most intensive trade links with the countries in question. The chapter thoroughly examines the different characteristics of the process of changing trade patterns and presents an overall picture, with rather optimistic conclusions based on the developments of the first five years after the beginning of the reform process. The methodological problems of this type of statistical analysis, which are burdened with additional difficulties when transforming economies are analysed, are mentioned by the authors, so I do not want to add other elements to this list of problems.

What I would like to concentrate upon is one of the main points of the conclusion of the chapter: that 'concerns that the East European economies might be captured in a low-wage/low-technology equilibria appear to be overstated'. I think that this statement does not follow from the previous statistical analysis. In the period of transition foreign trade, and especially export performance of the transition economies, does not fully reflect the changes in the competitiveness of their products. To put it another way, the high growth of exports to the markets of developed countries is not necessarily connected with the improvement of the competitiveness of the export sector of the countries in question. Other indicators and deeper research are necessary to arrive at this conclusion.

The reason for this can be found in the special characteristics of transition. These countries inherited a capital base and a company and sector structure which needs massive reorganization. The successful reorientation of foreign trade of the transforming economies to the markets of the developed countries for certain export products may cover only short-term 'export successes'. These will disappear in the long run due to two factors. First, the struggle of the company to survive, especially in the first years of transition, will cause an increase in its exports to the developed countries that is not sustainable in the long run (e.g. it is unprofitable, covers only the variable costs or is 'forced' export). Second, the effect of other factors, which in the short run cause export growth, will not be present in the longer run.

I would like to mention some of the factors that can affect actual export performance of the countries in question and which are also present in their trade with Austria. First, the outward processing trade (DPT) was responsible for most of the growth of trade in textiles and some consumer goods (especially clothing and shoes) between the EU and certain transforming economies. The same is true for Austria (see, for example, Stankovsky 1995). However, before Austria joined the EU, the rules of origin regulations hindered the re-export of those products, which were processed in Eastern Europe. Thus the contribution of outward processing to the improvement in the competitiveness of Austrian products remained limited. This has been changed by Austria's accession to the EU and can thus result in an even bigger growth in the outward processing trade between Austria and the transforming economies.

For Hungary, outward processing, with some annual fluctuations, gives about one-fourth of total exports to the developed countries. The ratio may be similar for other Visegrad countries (Poland, the Czech Republic and Slovakia) and even higher for Romania and Bulgaria. Outward processing is footloose and moves on quickly when labour costs increase. This is especially true for those sectors which dominate the outward processing trade of the Visegrad countries, namely textiles and clothing. In other more skill-intensive sectors, the outward processing can grow into a closer, more 'equal' and prosperous form of inter-company relationship, for example, supplier or direct investment. These 'deeper' forms of cooperation can help restructuring and thus create a basis for competitive export in the longer run. However, at present the OPT, especially in textiles and clothing, is enough only for the survival of the Eastern company and does not induce and help restructuring.

Second, entrepôt trade gives quite a high and persistent share of the trade of the countries in transition. Among others, Austria is one the biggest mediators. This traffic is in reality trade between the former CMEA countries. However, because of payment problems, they are realized through foreign (mainly Austrian, Swiss, Dutch, German) mediation. For Hungary, approximately 5 to 10 per cent of export to the developed countries is 'going back' to former CMEA countries, mainly in the form of agricultural products and machinery.

Third, we cannot neglect the effect of the exchange rate policies on the export (and foreign trade) performance of the analysed countries. Undervalued real exchange rates help uncompetitive exports to survive. For example, both Poland and Czechoslovakia started the reform process with a substantial devaluation of their currencies. This promoted exports during the following years. (See, for example, Halpern and Wyplosz 1995, about the exchange rate policies and their evaluation in the economies in question.) Real appreciation of the currencies in the region makes part of this export uncompetitive. This effect shows up at different times in different countries, depending on exchange rate developments.

The above factors have a short- to medium-term distorting effect on the export performance of the countries in question. This can result in significant short- to medium-term growth in their export to the developed countries, without any improvement in their competitiveness.

To refer to the other side of the problem, in the circumstances of massive restructuring and investment needs, of low savings and investment ratios, and more or less missing (active) industrial policies, foreign direct investments can play an important role in shaping future export performance of the countries in transition. The effect of FDI on foreign trade structure takes effect only slowly. Among the transforming economies, Hungary has attracted the most foreign direct investments. By now, around 50 per cent of total Hungarian export (about 60 per cent of manufacturing export) is undertaken by companies with foreign participation (1995). These are partly former state-owned companies, bought and restructured by foreigners and partly foreign greenfield investments. (The share of the companies with foreign participation in the total capital base is only around one-third, which underlines their higher propensity to export.) The restructuring effect of foreign direct investments can be the reason behind the relatively good performance of Hungary in that analysis, which shows the changes in competitiveness of export of transforming economies (*Economic Bulletin for Europe* 1995).

Summarizing the above argument, I think that the successful (in volume terms) reorientation of foreign trade of the transition economies to the developed markets cannot be a ground for drawing any conclusion about a longer run pattern of their participation in international trade. In the longer run, supply side aspects, namely the need for a massive restructuring, are determining. This can be 'deviated' in the shorter run by other factors. These factors influence significantly the present trade pattern between the developed countries and transforming economies.

REFERENCES

Economic Bulletin for Europe (1995), vol. 47, New York and Geneva: Economic Commission for Europe, United Nations, 46–8.

Halpern, L. and Wyplosz, Ch. (1995) 'Equilibrium real exchange rates in transition', CEPR Discussion Paper Series no. 1145.

Stankovsky, J. (1995) 'Passiver Veredelungsverkehr als Instrument der Handelspolitik und als Unternehmensstrategie', *Monatsberichte/ÖIW* 68 (9): 568–79.

23

FREE TRADE MOVEMENT IN ASIA PACIFIC

APEC's Osaka Action Agenda and its implications for multilateral trade liberalization

Ippei Yamazawa

FREE TRADE MOVEMENT IN ASIA PACIFIC

In commemoration of the 150th anniversary of the repeal of the Corn Laws, let me start with its impact on a then small island country in the Far East. Japan opened its doors to trade with Europe and the USA in 1858, when the momentum for free trade mounted after the repeal of the Corn Laws. This reached its peak with the Cobden–Chevalier Treaty between Great Britain and France in 1860, when this newcomer concluded a trade agreement with the major Western trading nations. Under the terms of the treaty, Japanese import and export duties were limited to uniform rates as low as 5 per cent (*ad valorem* equivalent) on all commodities and Japan could not change these tariffs autonomously. These low tariffs continued until Japan acquired its tariff autonomy in 1899. Since non-tariff barriers had not yet been invented, Japan was under de facto free trade. Views are divided as to whether this initial condition of free trade thereafter did good or harm to Japanese industrialization (Yamazawa 1990: 141–6).

Japanese tariffs were raised steadily after Japan acquired tariff autonomy but rice was free from duty. Rice was imported from Hawaii and the Philippines only in bad crop years, which was a visible gain from foreign trade because the Japanese had suffered from famine in the bad crop years under the national isolation regime (1639–1858). Nobody dared to impose tariffs on daily necessities. Rice duty of 15 per cent was introduced as a part of emergency surcharges on land taxes and excise taxes on all possible sources to finance the Russo-Japanese War (1904–5). Rice duty remained even after the emergency surcharges were abolished and was incorporated into the national tariff schedule in 1906.

Under the general tariff revision in 1911 (when the treaty with major Western nations expired), a raising of tariffs was attempted for many commodities including rice. The rise in rice duty provoked a public controversy between landowners and industrialists over agricultural protection. Professor Tokuzo Fukuda of Tokyo College of Commerce (which later became Hitotsubashi University) argued for the repeal of the rice duty for the sake of industrialists, while Professor Sakuzo Yoshino of Tokyo Imperial University insisted on its continuance for the sake of landowners. Apparently both had in their minds the Corn Laws debate sixty years earlier.

Contrary to the British case, the Japanese Corn Laws debate was concluded at the Diet with a specific duty of one yen per 60 kilograms (its *ad valorem* equivalent was 23 per cent of the average import price of rice in 1910–12). However, then came an unexpected denouement. Rice imported from newly colonized Taiwan (since 1895) and Korea (since 1911) was free from duty, increased rapidly and drove imports from outside the empire down to 5 per cent of total imports by 1933. The rice duty did not work and the rice price was kept low (except during the inflation immediately after World War I). Some agricultural economists deplored the fact that Japanese rice farming was depressed for thirty years thereafter.

After World War II, having lost all its colonies, Japan resorted to self-sufficiency in rice in the name of food security. While import dependence on other agricultural products increased substantially, the import ban on rice continued. However, only since the late 1980s has its domestic price soared to seven times the world market price. The price differential was as low as 1.5 in 1960. As the disparity between farm and non-farm income increased throughout the rapid growth, the government continued to give all possible subsidies to rice farming in order to narrow this increasing gap. The distorted price differential was artificially maintained under the notorious Food Control System in order to appeal to the political voice of the farm lobby.

Today the Asia Pacific economies have exceeded all others in the economic growth race, while trade liberalization has been delayed until recently. Almost all East Asian economies developed close links with each other through active trade and investment. However, unlike in Europe, trade expanded not because trade barriers were eliminated but because of active business spurred by profit opportunities resulting from diversity within the region. High tariffs and non-tariff barriers still remain, especially in developing economies. These economies had not fully participated in multilateral trade negotiation until the Uruguay Round. However, they have learned over the past decades that foreign trade and investment are indispensable for modernization and economic development and have unilaterally liberalized trade and investment regulations (GATT 1993). They realize that they have to continue their open economic policy stance in order to attract foreign investment and maintain their high growth. Now free trade is pursued by Asia Pacific governments to follow the market-driven integration in the context of the Asia Pacific Economic Cooperation (APEC).

APEC is an emerging regional group of eighteen member economies in the Asia Pacific region: eleven Asians consisting of six ASEAN members plus China, Hong Kong, Japan, South Korea and Chinese Taipei; three Oceanians, Australia, New Zealand and Papua New Guinea; plus the USA, Canada, Mexico and Chile. APEC started in 1989 as an annual ministerial meeting but since 1993 the leaders' meeting has been setting its basic direction. In Seattle in November 1993, the APEC leaders envisioned APEC as a 'community of Asia Pacific economies', a flexible forum for promoting economic growth in the region. In Bogor in November 1994, the leaders declared their political commitment to an ambitious goal that developed members should achieve free and open trade in the region by 2010, with the rest of the members achieving the same by 2020, and facilitation and development cooperation should also be promoted (APEC 1995a).

The APEC Osaka meeting in November 1995 successfully concluded with the Economic Leaders' Declaration for Osaka Action Agenda regarding how to implement the Bogor Declaration. In preparation for the meeting in Subic in the Philippines in November 1996, APEC member governments drew up detailed concrete programmes to be implemented in January 1997. APEC has now become a major regional integration, second to the European Union in terms of members, including major economies, its comprehensive action programmes for trade liberalization, facilitation, and economic and technical cooperation. APEC is a process involving a regional integration group on a consensus basis. It has already extended beyond an annual series of leaders' and ministers' meetings, but has established a broad support base consisting of senior officials meetings, three standing committees, ten working groups and two non-governmental advisory groups as well as a small secretariat.[1]

Reflecting the preference of its Asian members, APEC has started with a loose informal structure of regional integration, which has tended to limit information to non-members, causing insufficient understanding of its aims and programmes. This chapter aims to fill this information gap by reporting on the recent movement toward free trade in Asia Pacific.

STRENGTHENING COOPERATION FROM DIVERSITY

A prerequisite to understanding APEC correctly is to recognize the salient features of the Asia Pacific economies. These economies, especially the developing economies in East and South East Asia, have continued to have the highest growth rate in the world for the past two decades and still retain high growth potential. With Japan's low growth performance during recent years, the Japanese hesitate to claim that their country is a part of this dynamic Asia. However, Japanese firms contribute to the dynamic growth of neighbouring Asia through adjusting their production to the appreciated yen rates and transfer of their capital and technology to those economies.

The main feature of Asia Pacific economies is the vast diversity among members. They are located over a huge area around the Pacific and differ in all respects more widely than any other region in the world.

First, they differ in natural resource endowment and in size of geographical area.

Second, they differ greatly in their stages of development. Some have already matured while others have developed over the past two decades or so and still possess high growth potential.

Third, they are divided into several groups of religious and cultural heritage and value judgement. The differences could have caused a 'clash of civilizations' (Huntington 1993).

Fourth, they were divided into market and socialist economies in the Cold War era. Although socialist economies are being transformed into market economies, it will take them a few decades to complete this transformation.

Fifth, there exist three subgroup free trade areas (FTAs) within the region: North American Free Trade Agreement (NAFTA); ASEAN Free Trade Area (AFTA); and Australia–New Zealand Closer Economic Relations Agreement (ANZCER).

Finally, the region has never attempted any regionwide formal integration. Thus the 'market-driven integration' of Asia Pacific is often referred to, vis-à-vis 'institutional integration based on treaty' in the European Union and NAFTA.

The diversity of the Asian Pacific has two aspects, positive and negative. On the positive side, Asia Pacific economies have taken advantage of their diversity and the resulting economic complementarity. A wide wage disparity and different resource endowments have generated high economic complementarity within the region, which in turn has stimulated active trade and investment and enabled many developing members to achieve the high growth that is called the 'East Asian miracle'. Developed economies have been able to maintain their growth through export of resources products, technology products and high value added services and to invest in manufacturing activities in developing economies. Thus Asia Pacific economies have achieved a strong inter-dependence and rapid development of the region. Intra-APEC trade increased from 56 per cent in 1980 to 66 per cent in 1990, which is also compared to an increase of the same ratio from 53 per cent to 63 per cent within the EC12. This continued high growth in Asia Pacific has been attracting the attention of firms all over the world. The main motivation in promoting APEC is to sustain this high growth in the region, which is shared by all members.

On the negative side this diversity causes insufficient understanding of each other and more time is taken to form a regionwide consensus and to take joint actions among members. This has made it difficult to create a formal structure. However, some may argue that the flexibility within the informal structure of APEC has turned out to be a clever device for promoting integration among divergent members. The European Union still suffers from divided views on this issue.

Nevertheless APEC's market-driven integration is now affected by persistent imbalances and frequent trade disputes between members. Bottlenecks in infrastructure in developing economy members impede further realization of their high growth potential. Asia Pacific economies need to strengthen their cooperation in order to mitigate these impediments to further growth of the region.

OSAKA ACTION AGENDA ON LIBERALIZATION AND FACILITATION

The Osaka Action Agenda consists of two parts: Part I for trade liberalization and facilitation; Part II for economic and technical cooperation. Only Part I will be focused upon in this chapter (APEC 1995b, c).

The Action Agenda for Liberalization and Facilitation started with eight general principles:

- comprehensiveness;
- WTO-consistency;
- comparability;
- non-discrimination;
- transparency;
- standstill;
- simultaneous start/continuous process/differentiated timetables;
- flexibility and cooperation.

The Agenda contains extensive coverage of fifteen areas:

- tariffs;
- non-tariff measures;
- services;
- investment;
- standard and conformance;
- customs procedures;
- intellectual property rights;
- competition policy;
- government procurement;
- deregulation;
- rules of origin; ·

- dispute mediation;
- mobility of business people;
- implementation of the Uruguay Round outcomes;
- information gathering and analysis.

The Action Agenda suggests a menu of actions by individual member governments and concerted actions by all members in individual areas.

The Agenda's unique modality, the way to implement liberalization and facilitation programmes, is the 'concerted unilateral liberalization' – individual member governments announce unilaterally their own liberalization and facilitation programmes and implement them in accordance with their domestic rules. However, individual APEC members keep close watch on each other's liberalization programmes and their implementation. They feel obliged to submit liberalization programmes that are as extensive as their neighbours'. They are encouraged to implement what they have committed themselves to. 'Peer pressure' is relied upon by APEC to urge all members to join the liberalization. This is the essence of concerted unilateral liberalization.

This modality may be regarded as unasserted in comparison with the Western approach of negotiating; under GATT and the WTO a liberalization agreement which is legally binding means that the signatories will be punished and sanctioned if they fail to implement their commitments. At this initial stage such a legalistic approach cannot be accepted by Asian members. However, this should not be understood as reluctance on their part to commit to liberalization. Asian members have so far implemented trade and invest-ment liberalization unilaterally and realize that their recent high growth has been based on their open economic policy. Continued efforts to liberalize trade and investment are indispensable for further growth, reflected in their leaders' commitment to the Bogor Declaration. The new modality is based on this past experience and calls for unilateral liberalization in a concerted manner within the Osaka Action Agenda.

This is a practical way to promote liberalization without losing the momentum which was enhanced by the Bogor Declaration. It would take several more years before APEC could be changed into a negotiating body like the GATT and WTO. Japanese leadership should be credited for this pragmatic action agenda which has been well accepted by many members. However, Japan's initiative is vital to the success of this modality. If Japan proposes a substantial liberalization programme, other members will follow with matching scenarios.

As regards the time schedule, leaders and ministers agreed on the follow-ing procedure. Individual member governments should:

- submit their individual action plans of liberalization and facilitation by the 1996 ministerial meeting in Manila;

- start implementing these action plans in January 1997.

Furthermore, leaders delivered part of their liberalization and facilitation programmes in concrete form as 'initial actions' at the Osaka meeting so that they could retain credibility for their commitment.

REMAINING IMPEDIMENTS TO TRADE AND INVESTMENT

Member economies are now preparing their own voluntary liberalization programmes along the lines of the Osaka Action Agenda toward the ministerial meeting in Subic in November 1996. Some have already been announced in Osaka as Initial Actions attached to the Leaders' Statement (APEC 1995d). They included the advanced implementation of the tariff reduction committed in the Uruguay Round negotiation, as well as privatization of government enterprises and deregulation of foreign investment. It is never easy to compare the liberalization effects of initial actions submitted by individual members, but there are both large and small packages. Meanwhile the Osaka Initial Actions on the whole turned out to be extensive enough to convince us that we had launched this stage of action.

However, we should prepare to face another difficult challenge hereafter. As individual member governments implement their domestic legislatures in accordance with unilateral liberalization programmes, they may face serious resistance by vested interest groups. Strong political leadership will be needed to break through such resistance.

How many impediments still remain to trade and investment in Asia and the Pacific? APEC commissioned two studies from PECC's Trade Policy Forum to conduct the first regionwide survey of these impediments (APEC/ PECC 1995a, b). They cover tariffs and non-tariff barriers on commodity trade, regulations of services trades, foreign investment and intellectual property rights. The level and structure of impediments to trade and investment differ greatly between APEC member economies, reflecting their different resource endowment and stages of industrial development.[2] However, a common pattern of impediments in Asia Pacific has been observed:

1   Tariff levels differ greatly between members. Developed economy members have around 5 per cent on many lines. Developing economy members have tariffs of 10 to 20 per cent, while a few developing economy members have over 30 per cent tariffs on many items. In both developed and developing economy members, higher tariffs still remain on textiles, leather goods, wood products (15–20 per cent in developed economy members and 25–60 per cent in developing economy members).

2   NTBs are imposed on agriculture, labour intensive manufactures, steel

and automobiles in many member countries. Adding the NTB elements, tariff equivalent rates (excess of domestic prices over import prices) reach very high levels, especially in agriculture.

3   Services trade amounts to one-third of the commodity trade of APEC. However, many service trade sectors are regulated and some are completely closed. Variation in remaining regulations is observed between members. Three to seven service trade sectors are still fully regulated in developed economy members, while more than half the service trade sectors are fully regulated in developing economy members.

4   FDIs are still restricted in market access and national treatment and are subject to fiscal incentives (subsidies and tax exemption) and performance requirements (local content requirements, export requirements, and foreign exchange balancing conditions).

5   Most members have made changes to existing domestic legal structures to put in place substantive intellectual property protections. Despite these initiatives there still remains a substantial variance and many developing members have some distance to travel to meet their Trade Related Intellectual Property (TRIP) obligations under the WTO.

The remaining impediments suggest that we should anticipate strong resistance to liberalization and deregulation by vested interest groups in those sectors. Generally speaking, two broad types of arguments are observed. One is the argument for infant industry protection by developing members. They are in the process of catching up with industrialization and may claim infant industry protection for new technology industries and high value added services.[3] However, the effectiveness of such a policy was eroded in the current state of industrial competition. First, it is no longer possible to nurture competitive industries within a single country market of average size. They invite FDIs to get technology and managerial skills for new industries but need foreign competition in order to encourage their competitive development.

Second, machinery production, like electronics and automobiles, relies on the exact and competitive supply of a great number of parts and materials located across borders. Tariffs and NTBs on parts and materials imports will even impede the competitive development of machinery industries. Third, no country can produce every product but needs to specialize in a few lines of industrial and service production and to rely on the import of others. It is hardly possible to protect these particular lines without undermining the competitiveness of others.

Neither the protection of one industry nor the protection of one country is feasible in a world of globalized industries and integrated markets. The best strategy for developing countries in their catching up process is to expose their infant industries to foreign competition in order to encourage competitive development. APEC should guide its members to quit conventional protection of infant industry, thus avoiding the resultant unnecessary conflicts.

Another argument concerns the protection of industries such as agriculture and labour intensive manufactures. This now emanates from the developed members but will be soon shared by developing members as they achieve high income levels. These industries cause another type of adjustment difficulty. APEC senior officials discussed whether agriculture can be excluded from the liberalization agenda until just before the Osaka meeting. The exclusion was then supported by only four members, Japan, Korea, Chinese Taipei and China, but agricultural protection can be extended to the ASEAN countries and Mexico in the near future as their economies develop further and income disparity widens between agriculture and other industries. Agricultural protection can be easily politicized so that rational economic solutions are often prevented. Increased budgetary burdens at home and international commitment to liberalization with WTO and APEC can be the only break-through.

Labour intensive industries such as textiles and footwear share the same difficulties as agriculture, although with less protection and political distortion. Currently only developed countries complain of increasing imports from sources of lower income, but APEC developing members currently exporting those products also impose high tariffs on imports of such products. The developing members will soon be importers of those products as their income levels increase and will restrict imports from lower income countries.

It is important for all of us not to exclude these industries from our liberalization agenda. For the moment we should watch closely the implementation of agricultural liberalization and the fading away of Multifibre Arrangements as committed at the Uruguay Round. It will be a major task of APEC to help the WTO to complete its Uruguay Round liberalization and to launch the next stage of liberalization of these difficult areas.

CONSISTENCY WITH MULTILATERAL LIBERALIZATION

Regional integration has often been criticized in the past as inconsistent with multilateral liberalization. But it has recently become widely acknowledged that regional integration and multilateral liberalization can be consistent and actually are in many respects. The OECD report (OECD 1995) surveyed existing regional integration such as the EC, EFTA and NAFTA and came to an interesting conclusion. Some aspects of regional integration, such as preferential tariff reductions and strict rules of origin, can by nature discriminate against non-members and indeed be contradictory to multi-lateral liberalization. However, these regional integration groups have also implemented measures such as harmonization of rules and standards, investment principles, services trade policy, intellectual property rights, and environmental protection and industrial cooperation. These measures do not discriminate against others but serve as a laboratory, a halfway station in the effort to move from national standards to a multilateral standard.

This new concept of regional integration is consistent with the 'open regionalism' often mentioned concerning APEC. 'Open regionalism' or 'open regional cooperation' implies the promotion of regional cooperation in a way which is consistent with multilateral rules. This catchphrase has become an important asset of APEC. It conveys a positive image of 'good regional integration' vis-à-vis 'Fortress Europe', often mentioned about the European Community several years ago. APEC's open regional cooperation does not fit a free trade area (FTA) in the textbook definition. A new term, 'open economic association' (OEA), has been proposed to characterize it by Western Pacific economists (Yamazawa 1992, 1996; Elek 1994; AJRC 1995). An OEA is:

- open in that its structure and policies do not lead to discrimination against trade and investment with the rest of the world;
- economic in its primary policy focus;
- a voluntary association in that its members do not cede sovereignty to any supranational regional institution.

Recognizing the increasingly sophisticated nature of international economic transactions, the scope of an OEA goes well beyond traditional FTAs. The tempo of trade liberalization may be less rapid, but liberalization is applied both to members and non-members on an MFN basis, and the gradual liberalization of trade in goods and services supplemented by facilitation to dismantle all impediments to all international economic transactions, as well as those to development cooperation. This balanced programme reflects the vast differences among members in stages of development, current levels of impediments to trade and investment, and preparedness for reform.

Because of their long-term interdependence on trade and investment links beyond the region, Asia Pacific economies have shown great interest in global trade liberalization and have participated actively in the Uruguay Round negotiations. The Osaka Action Agenda confirmed 'consistency with multilateral liberalization' as one of its general principles and suggested accelerated implementation of the liberalization commitments of the Uruguay Round.[4] Like other GATT/WTO commitment, it is likely to be ruled by the Most Favored Nations (MFN) treatment of GATT Article 1. Many APEC members will extend their APEC liberalization to members and non-members alike on an MFN basis. The implementation of these liberalization packages will be monitored and reviewed jointly for continued attention of all members and mutual encouragement.

APEC members have not yet agreed upon whether to apply the MFN treatment to non-APEC members. A majority of APEC members is supportive to non-discrimination to non-members, while a minority view objects on the grounds that it will allow the EU free-rider benefits and insists that the APEC liberalization should be applied to the EU only if it implements matching liberalization on the MFN basis. This reciprocal application of the APEC liberalization departs from the OEA model, but is still referred to as 'open regionalism',[5] which causes ambiguity of the term and invites criticism. This difference in philosophy has not yet been dissolved.[6]

However, it is unlikely that this difference will lead immediately to discrimination against non-members under the APEC liberalization programmes. The facilitation part of the programme as well as investment liberalization will not discriminate against non-members. Indeed, there will be some sensitive areas where unilateral liberalization is difficult to achieve. These, however, will be left for multilateral negotiation at a later stage.

Multilateral liberalization is the best course but we cannot be optimistic about its speedy progress. All cautious observers realize that multilateral liberalization will not move forward unless certain key players work together. The APEC group as well as the EC are supposed to be its prime movers.

APEC–EU JOINT INITIATIVE NEEDED

APEC governments should talk to the European Union (EU) and others, to encourage them to join in a similar accelerated implementation of the Uruguay Round outcome. At a later stage, they should invite the EU to initiate, jointly, a new round of global liberalization within the WTO.

The interaction between APEC and the EU will be critical to this process. Unlike the EU, APEC will not aim to establish a formal supranational body but will remain a more flexible OEA for the next quarter century. However, because its members include major economic powers and fast growing newly industrialized economies (NIEs), APEC will be likely to interact closely with EU members to build the WTO. The new WTO regime will certainly be affected by which liberalization programme APEC chooses to adopt. Some suggest that APEC should urge the EU with discriminatory liberalization unless it accepts similar liberalization. But such a tit-for-tat approach may drive the EU inwards and split the world economy into two groups. It will be imperative for APEC, with its slogan of open regionalism, to encourage the EU to maintain an outward-looking stance, and to promote mutual participation in each other's development. APEC and the EU share the same adjustment difficulty in agriculture and textiles and they will need a wider stage for coordination and negotiation of these difficult sectors than their own regional groups.

There seem to be a few signs of movement toward this direction. One is that the APEC trade ministers' meeting is scheduled for July 1996 in advance of the WTO ministerial meeting in Singapore in December of the same year. If APEC and the EU take a joint initiative in launching the new WTO round of multilateral liberalization, the free-rider issue will be dissolved and the momentum for multilateral liberalization will increase.

Another sign is the discussion at the first Asia–Europe Summit Meeting (ASEM) in Bangkok in March 1996. Asian leaders (from ten Asian members of APEC) urged their counterpart European leaders (from fifteen EU members) to match the accelerated implementation of the Uruguay Round liberalization by APEC (ASEM 1996). A high-ranking EU official responded positively that this would be seriously considered, but attention would be given to how much liberalization came out of the Subic APEC in November. We will have a better prospect of APEC–EU collaboration toward the end of this year.[7]

The Corn Law debate has never finished in Europe but has been extended to Asia Pacific. Protection of rice farming is now spreading to developing economies in East Asia. Another repeal of the Corn Laws will be a major task of WTO for the next two decades or so.

NOTES

Ippei Yamazawa is Professor of Economics, Hitotsubashi University, Tokyo, Japan and was honorary senior research fellow, Japan Centre, University of Birmingham (1995–6). He represented Japan in the APEC Eminent Persons Group from 1993 to 1995.

1 One of the two advisory groups, the Eminent Persons Group, contributed to this ambitious vision of APEC through their reports (APEC/EPG 1993, 1994, 1995).
2 The two reports avoid commenting on the protection of individual members in the main text for diplomatic reasons and give individual member information only in the appendices. However, it is necessary to examine the level of protection of individual member economies in detail, taking into consideration their respective situations. This is a big task for Asia Pacific economists.
3 One developing member increased tariffs on petroleum products and introduced a programme that nurtured its national car.
4 APEC/EPG (1995) proposed '50 per cent acceleration' of the Uruguay Round liberalization.
5 They contend that this is also consistent with GATT. Article 23 admits free trade areas, a departure from its basic principle of most favoured nations treatment in Article 1, as a transitory step for not more than ten years towards global liberalization.
6 Yamazawa (1994) examines this difference. APEC/EPG (1994) admits the application of the APEC liberalization both on an MFN basis or reciprocal basis.
7 *The Japan Economic Journal*, 3 March 1996 and *The Financial Times*, 4 March 1996.
8 In 1996 APEC leaders adopted the Manila Action Plan for APEC in which all APEC members submitted their individual action plans (IAPs) to be implemented from 1997 onward. A quick assessment of the IAPs was attempted by Yamazawa (1997a, b).

REFERENCES

AJRC (Australia–Japan Research Center) (1995) *Implementing the APEC Bogor Declaration*, Canberra: AJRC.

APEC (1995a) *Selected APEC Documents: 1989–1994*, Osaka: APEC, January.

APEC (1995b) *APEC Economic Leaders' Declaration for Action*, Osaka: APEC, November.

APEC (1995c) *The Osaka Action Agenda: Implementation of the Bogor Declaration*, Osaka: APEC, November.

APEC (1995d) *The Osaka Initial Actions*, Osaka: APEC, November.

APEC Eminent Persons Group (EPG) (1994) *Achieving the APEC Vision: Free and Open Trade in the Asia Pacific*, Singapore: APEC Secretariat.

—— (1995) *Implementing the APEC vision: The Third Report of the Eminent Persons Group*, Singapore: APEC Secretariat.

APEC/EPG (1993) *A Vision for APEC: Towards an Asia Pacific Economic Community*, Singapore: APEC.

APEC/PECC (1995a) *Survey of Impediments to Trade and Investment in the APEC Region*, Osaka: APEC.

APEC/PECC (1995b) *Milestones in APEC Liberalization: A Map of Market Opening Measures by APEC Economies*, Osaka: APEC.

ASEM (1996) 'Chairman's statement', Asia–Europe Meeting, Bangkok, 2 March.

Elek, A. (1994) 'Trade policy options for the Asia Pacific region in the 1990s: the potential of open regionalism', in R. Garnaut and P. Drysdale (eds) *Asia Pacific Regionalism: Readings in International Economic Relations*, New York: Harper Educational.

GATT (General Agreement on Tariffs and Trade) (1993) *International Trade and the Trading Systems: Report by the Director General for 1992–1993*, Geneva: GATT.

Huntington, S.P. (1993) 'The clash of civilizations?', *Foreign Affairs* 72 (3) Summer.

OECD (1995) *Regional Integration Agreements and the Multilateral Trading System: Are They Compatible?*, TD/TC (93)15, Paris: OECD.

Yamazawa, I. (1990) *Economic Development and International Trade: The Japanese Model*, Honolulu: East–West Center.

—— (1992) 'On Pacific economic integration', *The Economic Journal* 102 (415): 1519–29.

—— (1994) 'Asia Pacific economic community: new paradigm and challenges', *Journal of Asian Economics* 5 (3) Fall.

—— (1996) 'APEC's new development and its implications for non-member developing countries', *The Developing Economies* 34 (2) June.

—— (1997a) 'APEC's Trade Liberalization and the WTO', *The Australian Economic Review* 30 (1): 98–102.

—— (1997b) *APEC's ½ Progress toward the Bogor Target: A Quantitative Assessment of Individual Action Plans*, Japan National Committee for Pacific Economic Cooperation (JANCPEC) Tokyo, September 1997.

24

COMMENTARY ON CHAPTER 23

Gary Cook

Ippei Yamazawa's chapter gives an interesting insight into the operation and aspirations of the Asia Pacific Economic Cooperation (APEC) forum, with particular emphasis on its Osaka Action Agenda (as well as the history of Japan's own 'Corn Laws' debates in respect of rice). Yamazawa speaks with authority having represented Japan at APEC's Eminent Persons Group. One particular aspect of the operation and the evolution of the forum which seemed puzzling to the predominantly Anglo-Saxon audience he addressed at the conference was the de-emphasis of formal negotiation and legally binding agreements. There was a clear gap between Yamazawa's confidence that the principle of concerted unilateral liberalization was strong enough to sustain the progress made to date and the belief of many in his audience. What compounds this disbelief is the very diverse nature of the countries involved and the vested interests in favour of protection, both points clearly acknowledged by Yamazawa. Those who doubt whether its ambitious aims can be achieved can do no more than act on his injunction to the sceptical audience to 'just wait and see'. One important point Yamazawa did make was the view that trade is vital to modernization. This does identify a strong motivating factor for liberalization.

Yamazawa provides some interesting areas of comparison and contrast between APEC and the EU and also addresses some pertinent remarks to the future relationship between them. As he emphasizes, APEC is second in scope as a regional trade area to the EU and has committees active in quite a broad range of areas. Although these are on nothing like the same scale as the EU, the EU does have a head-start of more than thirty years. He also recognizes that both groups of countries have vested interests supporting protectionism in similar areas, notably agriculture and textiles (and in so saying he picks up a leitmotif from the original Corn Laws debate), services and intellectual property rights, although the latter two are not compared explicitly. He suggests that they may have a common interest in furthering liberalization in respect of these areas through the WTO, yet he acknowledges that there may be obstacles to cooperation between the two. The two regions also have comparable proportions of intra-regional trade and rates of growth of intra-regional trade.

Despite the areas of comparability, there are marked differences such as the greater heterogeneity of the countries in APEC, the much more rapid growth rates of some member countries compared to EU rates. There is evidently much further to go on harmonization of tariff rates. Yamazawa also argues that APEC is more open than Fortress Europe in that the dominant approach is for countries to liberalize unilaterally and to extend that liberalization on a most favoured nation basis to members and non-members of APEC alike. Indeed, herein lie the seeds of mistrust within APEC for the EU, which is seen as being likely to try and free ride on APEC liberalization. While Yamazawa argues that some basis for reciprocation with the EU should be found, he counsels against over-optimism that this will be a speedy process. Finally, he comes close to suggesting that formal structures within Europe may be associated with the level of disagreements among EU member states, whereas the less formal APEC may avoid clashes on overt points of principle.

Yamazawa provides a fascinating glimpse into the nature and thinking of APEC and this raises questions which space probably precluded being treated. While he asserts that there will not be secession of sovereignty along the lines of the EU, one can only wonder what if any formal institutional structures will emerge – but perhaps I am simply guilty of trying to view the future through Anglo-Saxon eyes. He suggests that, within South East Asia at least, Japan has played an important lead role. One wonders what points of comparison and contrast there might be with the role of Germany within the EU. Moreover, what is the nature of relations between Japan and the USA within APEC? The chapter is curiously silent on the role of the American participants. It would be interesting to know how the USA with its more legalistic approach to doing business accommodates itself to the less formal modus operandi described by Yamazawa. There is no mention of any widening of APEC, let alone any debate between widening versus deepening such as has been seen within the EU. While this may not be at the top of the agenda now, if APEC is going to be as successful as Yamazawa suggests, then it seems inevitable that a queue will form for membership. For the answers to many of these questions, we will all have to just wait and see.

25

KNOWLEDGE, TRADE AND GROWTH

Alvin Birdi

INTRODUCTION

Ricardo's ardent opposition to the Corn Laws was due to his firm conviction that the rate of profit would inevitably fall if his thesis on diminishing returns to agricultural investment which he had outlined in his *Essay on the Influence of a Low Price of Corn* (Ricardo 1815) was correct. A free trade in corn, on the other hand, was a sure method by which to arrest decreases in the rate of profitability since it held in check the inevitable rises in the price of corn that would impact on the wage rate and thus on general profits. In the absence of a free trade in corn the prognosis was that accumulation would eventually cease, culminating in stagnation.

The notion of free trade has retained a remarkable attraction among most economists since Ricardo. In the dominant tradition of economic theory, the Heckscher–Ohlin theory has demonstrated the superiority of free trade over managed trade within the framework of general competitive equilibrium. Nevertheless, until relatively recently, the economist's faith in free trade has been buttressed by a theoretical tradition which has largely neglected the importance of technical change and progress. Newer approaches (for example, Grossman and Helpman 1991), have attempted to rectify this neglect by introducing the production of knowledge into dynamic models of trade. It has been typical of this approach to model knowledge creation as either the purposeful activity of a number of researchers who are engaged in the production of new ideas or as the unintended consequence of some productive activity.

A major shortcoming that remains, however, is to incorporate many of the ideas which stem from a detailed study of knowledge, its organization, production and use, into trade analysis. Knowledge is multi-faceted. There are types of knowledge, just as there are types and varieties of capital goods. The production of these types of knowledge is as varied as there are varieties. For example, academic science is produced under conditions and incentives which are distinct from those that prevail in the production of blueprints for the development of new varieties of final good.

This chapter begins by discussing some aspects of knowledge which are relevant to dynamic models of trade and presents a simple extension of a model of Grossman and Helpman (1991) which breaks knowledge into two categories, basic and applied, and demonstrates how such a distinction may provide significantly different results from a model in which such a distinction is absent.

DIMENSIONS OF KNOWLEDGE

At the outset, it is worthwhile pointing to the distinction between the economics of science and the economics of scientific knowledge which is employed by Wade Hands (1994). The former is the study of the behaviour of people engaged in the production of knowledge, that is, the incentive structures under which they work and the ends that they achieve. It takes as given that knowledge is useful and the focus is on the allocations and trade patterns that result. The latter engages in an epistemological discourse concerning the nature of knowledge, how it comes to be constructed and what passes for knowledge. In truth, the two forms of enquiry are not so separate since the categories used within the economics of science must presuppose some epistemological categories even if the acceptance of such categories is not expressly stated. It is in this that modern trade theories which use knowledge have their shortcomings. The historical development of such theories has been one of seeking to explain the continued growth of economies by some mechanism which is explained within the theory itself. Mathematically, a way to achieve this is to employ a productive factor which is able to stem diminishing returns to the group of accumulable factors or to innovative activity. It is to fulfil this role that knowledge capital has been usefully employed. The implicit foundation for such a belief is that knowledge construction may be characterized as an activity which is the outcome of competitive forces and the results of which may be aggregated to form the knowledge stock in the economy. On a purely philosophical level this raises the question of reflexivity which has been discussed in the literature on the philosophy of economics (see, for example, Wade Hands 1994). Leaving aside such problems, the type of conclusion which one may wish to draw from such models is that knowledge creation is useful to explaining the continuing growth process. However, this conclusion is pre-empted by the requirement that any factor which will fill the mathematical role of stalling diminishing returns will create sustained growth. In other words, the pertinent question to ask is whether knowledge adequately fills this role. In other words, are knowledge and knowledge creation adequately represented by the categories used in such models?

At first glance the answer may appear to be affirmative. There seems to be no a priori reason why one should assume a limit to the growth of knowledge and casual empiricism would seem to attest to this. However, to use knowledge in this way circumvents a more interesting problem which is how knowledge creation contributes to economic welfare. An approach to this problem would necessarily begin at the level of the philosophy of knowledge and then bring the categories discovered from that study to the field of economics. In this way economists may better understand how countries differ in their abilities to produce and use knowledge and how this in turn will affect their trading relations and growth rates.

An appropriate distinction, to illustrate the above points, is Ryle's (1949) between knowing how and knowing that. The former is the ability to use knowledge to attain certain ends while the latter is the knowledge of certain phenomena which may or may not be turned to useful ends. One does not imply the other. A detailed economic discussion of these concepts is in Loasby (1996). From such a viewpoint, the concept of knowledge as applied in modern theories of trade would appear too simplistic. At the very least, there would need to be at least one intermediate step between the production of knowledge and its transformation into an economically useful process since the latter requires a different type of knowledge than the former. One way in which this example may manifest itself in actual economies is the initial discovery of some scientific phenomena followed by the development of some useful products which are based on that initial knowledge. But even here one can discern a more complicated sequence of events. Knowledge may be created in its most abstract form. This may be termed basic knowledge. This then leads to further knowledge which may suggest how the initial knowledge can be put to economic use. This knowledge may be thought of as applied knowledge. The actual implementation of the ideas into realizing the results will require the ability to put the applied knowledge into effect. This may require some specific know-how which comes through learning-by-doing, for example. The successful implementation of ideas is thereby seen as considerably more complex than the aggregative approaches would suggest.

Reality is undoubtedly more complex than the linear model of progress outlined in the above paragraph suggests. Recently, attention has focused to more complex inter-relationships between basic research activities and applied research activities (see OECD 1992; Nelson 1993). For example, the discovery of the transistor made possible the developments in microelectronics that have transformed production in the last few decades but it was the product innovations on the original transistors that made possible the further research that led to the microelectronics revolution. Metcalfe (1995), for example, refers to a 'symbiotic' as opposed to a 'sequential' relationship between various stages of innovation. In addition, much of what may be termed basic research is in practice the result of collaborative association between government and the end-users of that research (private firms) or indeed is simply privately funded. For example, in Japan much of what may be considered basic research occurs in private firms (see Odagiri and Goto 1993). This blurs to some extent the distinction between basic and applied research in that the resulting knowledge may be specific to the needs of an industry rather than being a public good which is appropriable nationally or even internationally.

In what follows, an extension to the model of Grossman and Helpman (1991: ch. 8) which employs a distinction between basic and applied research is outlined. Basic research is modelled as purposive activity located in the government sector and financed through taxation. It is used as a necessary input in applied knowledge which is modelled as a competitive activity as in Grossman and Helpman (1991). They demonstrate a stark hysteresis result which is that a country which begins ahead in the technology race will stay ahead and eventually dominate the high technology industry. My analysis will seek to understand the difference that is made by including publicly financed basic research into the innovation sector.

It will be clear that such an extension does not address many of the issues discussed above and which have been analysed in the 'new economics of science' (see Dasgupta and David 1994). However, the dependence of trade patterns on the structure of the knowledge sectors suggests that a full understanding of the relationship between knowledge creation and trade performance, and indeed on the desirability or not of free trade, will require a greater attention to the nature and the creation of knowledge.

BASIC AND APPLIED RESEARCH

Dosi (1988) lists five major stylized facts concerning contemporary innovation of which the second is 'the increasing reliance of major new technological opportunities on advances in scientific knowledge' (222). It is therefore of some importance whether a country engages in basic research. The UK government, for example, had by 1987 drastically reduced its expenditure on basic research to a proportion of GDP below that of France, Germany and the USA (see Walker 1993). If basic research is globally appropriable, then there are likely to be worldwide consequences of such a reduction in support for basic research. If basic research is locally appropriable, then a country's lack of support for such research could lead to serious consequences for its competitiveness in certain industries. It is assumed that basic knowledge is locally appropriable.

There is some evidence (Link 1981; Griliches 1986; Levin 1988, Jaffe 1989) which suggests that the returns to basic research may be significant. Together with the fact that basic R&D expenditures appear to be falling in industrialized countries, these may lend some support to the view that spending in this area is suboptimal.

One area in which such a model may have practical significance is in the explanation of the remarkable growth success of the South East Asian countries known as the 'tigers'. Undoubtedly many factors contributed to the export and growth success of these countries and some of these are discussed in the country specific studies found in Nelson (1993). In Taiwan in particular there appears to have been a considerable effort by the government to enhance the country's basic research and since the late 1950s the government has been very active in this area. The National Science Council (formerly the National Council for Long-term Development of Science) was founded to carry out basic scientific research. The establishment of this Council was only one of a concerted set of policies designed to enhance the basic knowledge capital in the country. Hou and Gee (1993) report that in 1986, three-fifths of R&D expenditure in Taiwan was public although only about one-tenth of this expenditure went to basic research. The government has since continued to remain active in this area.

INNOVATION AND PRODUCTION STRUCTURE

We suppose that applied research is produced using basic knowledge, K, and applied knowledge, N. To capture the notion that basic research is an essential input into applied research, we use a Cobb–Douglas specification as is done in Bailén (1994) so that in country i

$$\dot{N}_i = H_{N,i} K_i^{1-v} N_i^v \quad 0 < v < 1 \tag{1}$$

where $H_{N,i}$ is the labour devoted to applied research by country i and v is a parameter indicating the importance of basic in applied research. The country (A or B) is indicated by the subscript i. At the extreme, $v = 1$, basic knowledge ceases to be necessary (or indeed useful) to applied knowledge production and the features of the model become similar to those in Grossman and Helpman (1991: ch. 8).

Basic knowledge is produced using labour and previous basic knowledge so that:

$$\dot{K}_i = \frac{H_{K,i}}{a_i} K_i \tag{2}$$

where $a_i > 0$ is a productivity parameter and $H_{K,i}$ is labour devoted to this activity in country i. This knowledge is a non-congestible public good which is funded by government out of lump-sum taxation, τ_i, where:

$$\tau_i = w H_k = a_i w \frac{\dot{K}_i}{K_i}. \tag{3}$$

258

In the above, w is the wage rate of labour. The wage is not country specific since we will only consider cases in which factor price equalization results and there is a common worldwide wage rate.

We suppose that there are two goods produced, an homogeneous agricultural good and a differentiated high-technology good. The agricultural good, Y, is produced according to a linear production function:

$$y = H_{\gamma,i} \tag{4}$$

with H_γ denoting employment in this sector. This sector is characterized by perfect competition. The differentiated good, of which there are $N(s)$ varieties available at time s, is produced according to:

$$x(n) = \frac{H_{x,i}}{N_i(s)} \tag{5}$$

where H_x is employment in this sector as a whole. Each variety is produced by a single monopolistically competitive producer which enjoys infinitely lived patent rights over its own variety.

We consider a world consisting of two equally sized countries with the extreme assumption of no knowledge spillovers of either basic or applied knowledge. As noted above we shall also simplify the analysis by restricting ourselves to dynamic trajectories in which worldwide wages are equal. To justify this we shall need to assume that $H_{Y,i} > 0$ for $i = A, B$ at all times. This will require that each economy is large enough to ensure that the traditional good is always produced by both countries.

Note from (1) that N is taken to be a measure of applied knowledge as well as the number of goods in existence which is in fact a common device in the literature following Romer (1990) and Grossman and Helpman (1991).

DEMAND

The demand specification is the same as in Grossman and Helpman (1993). A representative agent in country i maximizes utility, U, given by:

$$U = \int_{t_0}^{\infty} e^{-p(t-t_0)} \log u \, dt \tag{6}$$

where the instantaneous utility function u is given by:

$$u = \left[\int_0^{N_A + N_B} x(n)^\alpha \, dn \right]^{\frac{\sigma}{\alpha}} y^{1-\sigma} . \tag{7}$$

Standard results give the instantaneous demands produced by maximizing (7) subject to a dynamic expenditure constraint as:

$$X_i(n) = \sigma(1 - \tau_i) E_i P_X(n)^{-\varepsilon} \left[\int_0^{N_A + N_B} P_X(n')^{1-\varepsilon} dn' \right]^{-1}$$

(8)

$$Y_i = (1 - \sigma) \frac{(1 - \tau_i) E_i}{P_Y}$$

(9)

where $\omega \in [0, N_A + N_B]$, P denotes the price of the subscripted good and E_i is aggregate expenditure in country i. Aggregate (world) demand for the two goods is therefore obtained by summing the above demands across countries. The dynamic optimization will ensure that

$$\frac{\dot{E_i}}{E_i} = r(t) - \rho$$

(10)

where $r(t)$ is the interest rate and ρ is the internationally identical time preference parameter. Normalization is chosen so that aggregate (world) spending $E = E_A + E_B$ is always unity. This implies that $\dot{E} = \dot{E_A} + \dot{E_B} = 0$ which in view of (10) implies that:

$$r(t) = \rho, \quad \text{for all } t.$$

(11)

EQUILIBRIUM

Perfect competition in the agricultural industry leads to marginal cost pricing:

$$p_Y = w.$$

(12)

Imperfect competition in the differentiated goods industry will lead to mark up pricing. Standard results give the equilibrium price charged for a variety n as:

$$p_x(n) = \frac{\epsilon}{\epsilon - 1} w$$

(13)

where ϵ is the elasticity of demand between any two varieties. The form of the utility function ensures that this elasticity is:

$$\epsilon = \frac{1}{1 - \alpha}$$

which is greater than unity implying imperfect substitutability between varieties. It is this which leads greater variety to show up as greater consumer utility.

The demand structure implies that a constant fraction, σ, of world post-tax expenditure is spent on the differentiated good and the remainder is spent on the traditional good. Using this fact and the pricing equation (13) we can calculate that a firm in country i which sells a variety n at time s will attain instantaneous profits equal to:

$$\pi(n,s) = \frac{(1-\alpha)\sigma E_\tau s_{X,i}}{N_i} \tag{14}$$

where $E_\tau = (1 - \tau_A - \tau_B)$ is aggregate post-tax expenditure and $s_{X,i}$ is the share of the differentiated goods industry owned by country i defined as:

$$s_{X,i} = \frac{N_i X_i p_i}{\sum_j N_j X_j p_j} \quad i,j \in [A,B].$$

Using the demands in (8) and (9) and the fact that wages (and therefore prices) are equal in the two countries, this share may be written as:

$$s_{X,i} = \frac{N_i}{\sum_j N_j}. \tag{15}$$

In the applied research sector, inventors of blueprints sell patent rights to firms in the differentiated goods industry. Free entry in this sector implies that pricing is at marginal cost. The price of a blueprint must equal the expected discounted stream of profits available to a firm that commercializes the blueprint at time t, namely:

$$\Pi_i(n,t) = \int_t^\infty e^{-\int_t^s r(m)\,dm} \pi_i(n,s)\,ds. \tag{16}$$

The unit cost of research is from (1) given by:

$$C_{N,i} = \frac{w}{N_i^v K_i^{1-v}}. \tag{17}$$

Using (11), (14), (16) and (17) we have that:

$$\int_t^\infty e^{-\rho(s-t)} \frac{(1-\alpha)\sigma E_\tau s_{X,i}}{N_i} \, ds = \frac{w}{N_i^v K_i^{1-v}} \tag{18}$$

which is a free entry condition and holds for any country which engages in applied research. Differentiating (16) gives the Fisher equation which rules out arbitrage. This is:

$$\frac{\pi_i + \dot{\Pi}_i}{\Pi_i} = r. \tag{19}$$

Turning to the allocation of the fixed labour stocks in each country we can derive the labour demands for each of the four sectors. In each country, the demand for labour into the agricultural sector is:

$$H_{Y,i} = \frac{(1-\sigma)E_\tau s_{Y,i}}{w} \tag{20}$$

where $s_{Y,i} = Y_i/\Sigma_j Y_j$ is the share of the Y industry in country i. From our assumption of equal wages, $s_{Y,i} > 0$ for both countries. The demand for labour into the differentiated goods industry is:

$$H_{X,i} = \frac{\sigma E_\tau \alpha s_{X,i}}{w}. \tag{21}$$

In the innovation sectors, the demand for labour may be calculated from equations (1) and (2) to be:

$$H_{K,i} = \frac{\tau_i}{w} \tag{22}$$

$$H_{N,i} = \frac{\dot{N}_i}{N_i}\left(\frac{N_i}{K_i}\right)^{(1-v)} = \gamma_{N,i}\Omega_i^{(1-v)} \tag{23}$$

where we define:

$$\Omega_i = \left(\frac{N_i}{K_i}\right)$$

to be the instantaneous level of variety to basic knowledge in country i and $\gamma_{N,i}$ to be the growth rate of variety in country i. If we let the labour stock of each country be denoted by $\bar{L}$, labour market equilibrium implies for each i:

$$(1-\sigma)E_{\tau}\frac{S_{Y,i}}{w} + \sigma E_{\tau}\alpha\frac{S_{X,i}}{w} + \frac{\tau_i}{w} + \gamma_{N,i}\Omega_i^{(1-v)} = \bar{L}. \tag{24}$$

BALANCED GROWTH

As noted above, we shall concentrate on an equilibrium where factor prices are equal. In equilibrium, as in Grossman and Helpman (1993), only one country will engage in applied research. This is so because of the assumption of a perfect capital market which will fund applied research only where its return is highest. If wages are equal across countries then the profits to be had from commercialization of applied research will be the same. Hence the value of firms will be the same in either country. Thus capital will flow to that country which has a lower cost of applied research as represented by (17) which is that country which has a higher quantity $N^v K^{1-v}$. We will assume that country A begins with a lower cost of research and so only in A is $H_N > 0$.

In A, in balanced growth, we impose the condition that the growth rate of the level of variety and the growth rate of basic research are identical, that is:

$$\frac{\dot{K}}{K} = \frac{\dot{N}}{N} = \gamma. \tag{25}$$

If these rates of growth differ then $(\dot{N}/N)$ will either converge to 0 or to infinity. This has the implication that in the long run the growth of basic knowledge must be sufficiently high to sustain a positive growth rate of variety. In B, $(\dot{N}/N)$ is equal to 0 but $(\dot{K}/K) > 0$.

Identical Countries

Assume initially that the governments of both countries tax at the same level (so that $\tau_A = \tau_B = \tau$) and that basic research productivities are identical ($a_A = a_B$). In this case, under our supposition that:

$$N_A^v K_A^{1-v}(0) > N_B^v(0) K_B^{1-v}(0) \tag{26}$$

we must have:

$$N_A^v(s)K_A^{1-v}(s) > N_B^v(s)K_B^{1-v}(s) \quad \forall s \in [t, \infty)$$

since $(\dot{N}_B/N_B) = 0$ and the growth rates of K_A and K_B are equal. Hence, if tax rates and basic research productivities are equal in the two countries, the country which initially engages in applied research will always be the only country that engages in applied research. Due to the assumption of local appropriability of research output, this would imply that the share of this country in differentiated goods will rise to unity. The country that begins behind will stay behind.

Imposing $s_{X,A} = 1$ on the labour market condition for country A and $s_{X,B} = 0$ on the labour market condition for B, summing and noting that $s_{Y,A} + s_{Y,B} = 1$ and $\gamma_{N,B} = 0$ we have:

$$2\bar{L} = \frac{(1-\sigma)E_\tau}{w} + \frac{\sigma E_\tau \alpha}{w} + \frac{2\tau}{w} + \gamma_{N,A}\,\Omega_A^{(1-v)}. \tag{27}$$

From (18) which applies to country A, setting $s_{X,A} = 1$ and performing the integration gives on rearrangement:

$$\frac{(1-\alpha)E_\tau \sigma}{(\rho + \gamma_{N,A})w} = \Omega_A^{(1-v)}. \tag{28}$$

Substituting this into (27) gives:

$$2\bar{L} = \frac{(1-\sigma)E_\tau}{w} + \frac{\sigma E_\tau \alpha}{w} + \frac{2\tau}{w} + \frac{\gamma_{N,A}\,\sigma(1-\alpha)E\tau}{(\rho + \gamma_{N,A})w}. \tag{29}$$

The last equation, together with the labour market constraint for country B, and the equation for the long run rate of innovation growth which from (2) and the balanced growth condition (25) is:

$$\gamma_{N,A} = \frac{\tau}{2w\alpha} \tag{30}$$

characterize the equilibrium. From the solution to this system, it can be shown that w^*, the equilibrium wage, solves a quadratic equation with real roots.

Until now, our model confirms the results of Grossman and Helpman (1993) in a setting where basic research is government financed and is produced using labour in a separate sector from applied research. The country which has the initial advantage in research will be the country which eventually dominates the high-technology goods industry.

Differing productivities

If we allow the basic research productivities to differ between countries then the balanced growth equilibrium is not necessarily characterized by a share approaching unity in the differentiated goods sector for the country which begins with a cost advantage in applied research. Notice first that different productivities mean that the growth rate of basic knowledge must differ as between the two countries even in a balanced growth equilibrium. This is permissible because it is consistent with the assumption that no inter-sectoral factor shifts are taking place. Provided that country A continues to enjoy a lower cost of applied research forever, the equilibrium of the last subsection is consistent with different basic research productivities.

This being said, it remains to be seen under what conditions a lagging country may catch up with the leading country. To derive a sufficient condition for catch-up we need to establish that country B, which begins with higher costs of applied research, eventually lowers its costs sufficiently that they coincide at some time with those of country A. In other words, we will require that $C_A(s) = C_B(s)$ for some s despite $C_A(0) < C_B(0)$. A sufficient condition for catch up is that:

$$\frac{\dot{C}_A}{C_A} - \frac{\dot{C}_B}{C_B} > \in \quad \in > 0. \tag{31}$$

For a proof, see the Appendix to this chapter.

Before turning to a transitional analysis, let us conjecture the existence of a transitional path in which the world has arrived at a situation where the share of the X industry belonging to country A is very nearly unity because it began with lower applied research costs than country B. Since we assume that A's share in this industry is approaching unity it must be that at this moment, $C_A < C_B$. Since we are close to $s_{X,A} = 1$, the world is characterized approximately by the equations derived in the previous section. Since we are close to a possible balanced growth equilibrium, the growth rates of K_A and N_A must be very nearly equal at:

$$\frac{\dot{N}_A}{N_A} = \frac{\dot{K}_A}{K_A} = \frac{\tau_A}{wa_A},$$

and the wage rate must be nearly constant. Using this and condition (31) we can derive the following condition which is sufficient to ensure that A's widening lead is not sustainable:

$$\frac{(1-v)}{a_B} - \frac{1}{a_A} > \epsilon \quad \epsilon > 0 \cdot \tag{32}$$

For any given a_A and a_B condition (32) is more likely to hold the more important is basic knowledge capital in applied research (the lower is v). The conclusion is that an advantage in basic research production may lead a country to dominate in high-technology products even where its productivity in applied research production is identical with other countries and when it begins behind in the technology race. The extent to which this is likely depends crucially on the extent to which basic research is important in applied research. If $v = 0$, for example, then this condition will be satisfied for very small differences between productivities such that $a_A > a_B$. However, a parameter such as v is not datum to an economy. The linkages between basic research and its use in applied research are at least partly the result of policies and collaborative efforts between research institutions. Recent discussions concerning 'end-users' and the applicability of research indicate the extent to which this is now recognized.

It may be objected that a laggard country in a perfect foresight equilibrium would choose not to continue to fund basic research because it contributes nothing to the welfare of the citizens of that country in the model specified above. However, if such a country eventually catches up then world welfare will be higher on the eventual balanced growth path since there will be a higher growth rate of variety on account of the fact that the initially lagging country is more productive in its basic research. A complete welfare analysis would however not only need to consider what happens during the transition to equilibrium but also the possible loss in welfare arising from expenditure of the lagging country on basic research over that period when it is catching up. Over this period, the expenditure on basic research is having no effect on consumption or growth but simply being used to build up a future stock of knowledge that will reverse trade patterns. It is true however that the optimal tax for a laggard country which can never catch up is $\tau = 0$ which is the tax that will maximize consumption possibilities for the country. This simple extension may be incorporated into the model without difficulty but we retain our specification for simplicity and because our interest is in the dynamics of catch-up and not on welfare issues.

TRANSITIONAL ANALYSIS

We continue to suppose that country A begins ahead in the precise sense that:

$$N_A^v(0)K_A^{1-v}(0) > N_B^v(0)K_B^{1-v}(0) \cdot$$

Since A engages in applied research, the free entry condition (18) must hold for this country. By making use of this condition and the no arbitrage condition (19) the following differential equation for the evolution of wages can be derived:

$$\dot{w} = \left(\rho + \frac{2\bar{L}v}{\Omega_A^{(1-v)}}\right)w + (1-v)\frac{\tau_A}{a_A} - \frac{(1-\sigma)E_\tau}{\Omega_A^{(1-v)}} - \frac{\sigma E_\tau \alpha v}{\Omega_A^{(1-v)}} - \frac{\tau_A v}{\Omega_A^{(1-v)}}$$
$$- \frac{(1-\alpha)\sigma(1-\tau_A-\tau_B)s_{X,A}}{\Omega_A^{(1-v)}}. \tag{33}$$

By differentiating the definition of Ω_A the following differential equation for its evolution may be derived:

$$\dot{\Omega}_A = \Omega_A^v\left(\frac{2\bar{L}w - (1-\sigma)E_\tau v - \sigma E_\tau \alpha - (\tau_A+\tau_B)}{w}\right) - \frac{\tau_A\Omega}{wa_A}. \tag{34}$$

The share of country A in the differentiated goods industry is governed by an equation which can be derived by differentiating (15). This gives:

$$\dot{s}_{X,A} = s_{X,A}\left(1-s_{X,A}\right)\gamma_{N,A} \tag{35}$$

where:

$$\gamma_{N,A} = \frac{2\bar{L}}{\Omega_A^{(1-v)}} - \frac{(1-\sigma)E_\tau}{w\Omega_A^{(1-v)}} - \frac{\sigma E_\tau \alpha}{w\Omega_A^{(1-v)}} - \frac{\tau_A+\tau_B}{w\Omega_A^{(1-v)}} \tag{36}$$

is derived from the labour market constraints of the two countries which have been summed to eradicate $s_{Y,A}$ and $s_{Y,B}$. Together with the following equation which determines the growth rate of basic knowledge in country B:

$$\gamma_{K,B} = \frac{\tau_B}{wa_B},$$

equations (33), (34) and (35) define the dynamic system that governs the variables of the model. We consider three cases, $v = 1$, $v = 0$ and $0 < v < 1$.

Case 1: v = 1

In this case, basic knowledge ceases to be important in the production of applied knowledge. The model becomes very similar to that of Grossman and Helpman (1991: ch. 8) except that taxation is used to produce useless basic knowledge. In so far as the main results of hysteresis are concerned however, there is no difference between this model and that of Grossman and Helpman (1991). In particular, a country which begins with lower applied research costs will be the one which engages in applied research and eventually dominates the industry. The country which finds its share of industry X rising to unity will be that country with an initial value advantage in costs. The equilibrium is therefore dependent on the initial value.

This result will of course continue to hold regardless of the values of the tax and productivity parameters since the basic research sector has no effect on the profitability of applied research.

Case 2: v = 0

In this case, only basic knowledge is used in the production of applied knowledge. This is tantamount to assuming that past applied research has no effect on future applied research. In this case, the country which finds that its share of the X industry rises to unity in the long run need not be the country which begins with lower costs. It depends on which country is more productive in basic research and on the relative resources devoted to the basic research sector. In other words, the equilibrium is independent of history.

Proposition 1 *Suppose that*

$$K_A(0) > K_B(0).$$

If the transition to balanced growth is characterized by equal wages at every point in time and if

$$\frac{\tau_B}{a_B} - \frac{\tau_A}{a_A} > \epsilon \quad \epsilon > 0, \tag{37}$$

then applied research must eventually switch into country B.

To establish this claim we argue as follows. At time 0, country A must be the only country engaged in applied research since its costs are lowest and capital markets are perfect. It must therefore see its share of the differentiated goods industry expand. If country B does not lower its costs to below those of country A then the world will eventually begin to resemble the balanced growth equilibrium characterized by equations (29) and (30) with

τ replaced by $(\tau_A + \tau_B)$. Since the wage rate is approaching a constant, condition (37) is sufficient to ensure that $C_B - C_A$ grows at a rate that is bounded away from zero. Thus, A's lead is not sustainable. Notice that condition (37) may be satisfied for any difference in basic research productivities such that $a_B < a_A$ if tax levels are identical or indeed any difference in tax levels such that $\tau_B > \tau_A$ if productivities are equal.

Case 3: $0 < v < 1$

The most complex case is that in which both basic and applied research are essential to applied research production. This case shares, however, the features of case 2 in that A's lead will be non-sustainable if B's basic research grows faster than A's around the time when $s_{X,A}$ is approaching unity.

Proposition 2 *Suppose that*

$$N_A^v(0)K_A^{1-v}(0) > N_B^v(0)K_B^{1-v}(0).$$

If the transition to balanced growth is characterized by equal wages at every point in time and if

$$\frac{(1-v)\tau_B}{a_B} - \frac{\tau_A}{a_A} > \epsilon \quad \epsilon > 0, \tag{38}$$

then applied research must eventually switch into country B.

Establishing this claim follows the same logic as used in case 2. The main difference with case 2 is that the condition for overtaking involves v. Cases 1 and 2 are in fact special cases of case 3 with respectively $v = 0$ and $v = 1$. Notice that if $v = 1$ then the required condition cannot be satisfied. It is however merely a sufficient condition so that the fact that it cannot be satisfied does not imply in itself that catch-up cannot occur.

Notice that if a taxation policy is used to establish catch-up, it need only be a temporary policy. After a while, the accumulated basic and applied research capital in the initially lagging country will be sufficient to sustain applied research in this country even with identical tax rates. The difference from the temporary subsidization policy discussed in Grossman and Helpman (1991) is that in their scenario applied research shifts to the lagging country immediately so that there is no further increase in the share of country A in the differentiated goods sector. By contrast, in this model, there is the possibility that country A continues to strengthen its lead for some time before succumbing to the higher taxation levels or the improved productivity in country B's basic research sector. It is in this sense that investment in basic research may be thought of as a long-term investment. It is unlikely that basic research will have immediate effects on output and growth. However, over time countries that concentrate on developing the infrastructure and linkages between basic science and applied researchers may be the countries which come to dominate in the crucial high-technology sectors of the future.

A further insight into this trade pattern reversal may be had by noting that B begins to undertake applied research when:

$$N_A^v(s)K_A^{1-v}(s) < N_B^v(s)K_B^{1-v}(s).$$

This may be rewritten as:

$$s_{X,A} < \frac{\left(K_B / K_A\right)^\theta}{1+\left(K_B / K_A\right)^\theta}$$

where $\theta = (1 - v)/v$. Both sides of this inequality are bounded above by unity. What therefore causes the trade pattern to reverse is that the basic knowledge stock in country B is so large that it offsets any advantage that the leading country has by virtue of its lead in the differentiated goods sector.

The picture which emerges here is of a world in which countries forge ahead only to see their dominance dissipated if they fall behind in basic research or fail to devote sufficient resources to it. A number of caveats need to be added. There is no doubt an overstatement of the importance of any particular country's efforts on basic research on their long run performance in this model. In reality, basic research output is likely to be disseminated and at least partly globally appropriable. This would tend to limit the advantages of any one country concentrating resources on this activity and would also lead to possible suboptimal allocations of resources on basic research due to its public good nature. Furthermore no welfare analysis has been undertaken in this chapter. This has been justified due to concentrating on the dynamics of convergence and catch-up but it needs to be recalled that in a trading world consumer benefits are unaffected by the source of the production. Whether country A or country B comes to dominate the high-technology sector is neither here nor there from a purely economic point of view.

The model presented here is intended to be suggestive of the types of results which might follow from treating knowledge in a more complex manner than has been customary in models of trade. There is clearly a marked difference between the ideas summarized in the early sections of this chapter and the relative simplicity of the knowledge specification in the formal model. Further attention devoted to the categorization and use of knowledge in models of trade will be necessary if we are fully to appreciate how the theorizing which justified the repeal of the Corn Laws may need to be modified for modern societies in which innovation plays an increasingly important role.

APPENDIX

Suppose:

(i) $C_B(0) > C_A(0)$

(ii) $\dfrac{\dot{C}_A}{C_A} - \dfrac{\dot{C}_B}{C_B} > \epsilon,$ with $\epsilon > 0.$

Then there exists an s such that $C_A(s) = C_B(s)$ with $s \in (0, \infty)$.

Proof
Since $\dot{C}_i/C_i = d \log C_i/dt$, condition (ii) implies that $d \log C_A/dt - d \log C_B/dt > \epsilon$. Therefore $\log C_B(s) = \log C_A(s)$ by the time $(1/\epsilon)(\log C_B(0) - \log C_A(0))$ at the latest. The result follows from the monotonicity of $\log ()$.

ACKNOWLEDGEMENT

I would like to thank Paul Madden for his comments. Any opinions or errors remain my own.

REFERENCES

Bailén, J. M. (1994) 'Basic research, product innovation and growth', presented at the 'First International Conference on Economic Theory', Universidad Carlos III de Madrid, June.

Dasgupta, P. and David, P. (1994) 'A new economics of science', *Research Policy* 23 (5): 487–521.

Dosi, G. (1988) 'The nature of the innovative process', in G. Dosi, C. Freeman, R. Nelson, G. Silverberg and L. Soete (eds) *Technical Change and Economic Theory*, London: Pinter.

Griliches, Z. (1986) 'Productivity, R and D and basic research at the firm level in the 1970s', *American Economic Review* 76: 141–54.

Grossman, G. M. and Helpman E. (1991) *Innovation and Growth in the Global Economy*, Cambridge MA: MIT Press.

—— (1993) 'Hysteresis in the trade pattern', in W. J. Ethier, E. Helpman and J. P. Neary (eds) *Theory, Policy and Dynamics in International Trade*, Cambridge MA: MIT Press.

Hou, C. and Gee, S. (1993) 'National systems supporting technical advance in industry: the case of Taiwan', in R. R. Nelson (ed.) *National Innovation Systems*, Oxford: Oxford University Press.

Jaffe, A. (1989) 'Real effects of academic research', *American Economic Review* 89: 957–70.

Levin, R. C. (1988) 'Appropriability, R and D spending and technological performance', *American Economic Review Papers and Proceedings* 78: 424–8.

Link, A. (1981) 'Basic research and productivity increase in manufacturing: some additional evidence', *American Economic Review* 71: 1111–12.

Loasby, B. J. (1996) 'On the definition and organisation of capabilities', mimeo, University of Stirling Economics Department Discussion Paper 96/6.

Metcalfe, J. S. (1995) 'The economic foundations of technology policy: equilibrium and evolutionary perspectives', in P. Stoneman (ed.) *Handbook of the Economics of Innovation and Technical Change*, Oxford: Blackwell.

Nelson, R. R. (ed.) (1993) *National Innovation Systems*, Oxford: Oxford University Press.

Odagiri, H. and Goto, A. (1993) 'The Japanese system of innovation: past, present and future', in R. R. Nelson (ed.) *National Innovation Systems*, Oxford: Oxford University Press.

OECD (1992) *Technology and the Economy: The Key Relationships*, Paris: OECD.

Ricardo, D. (1815, 1951–73) *An Essay on the influence of a Low Price of Corn on the Profits of Stock*, Cambridge: Cambridge University Press. Sraffa edition published in Volume 4 of *The Works and Correspondence of David Ricardo* for the Royal Economic Society.

Romer, P. (1990) 'Endogenous technical change', *Journal of Political Economy* 98, S71–S102.

Ryle, G. (1949) *The Concept of Mind*, London: Hutchinson.

Wade Hands, D. (1994) 'The sociology of scientific knowledge', in R. E. Backhouse (ed.) *New Directions in Economic Methodology*, London: Routledge.

Walker, W. (1993) 'National innovation systems: Britain', in R. R. Nelson (ed.) *National Innovation Systems*, Oxford: Oxford University Press.

26

COMMENTARY ON CHAPTER 25

Gary Cook

Alvin Birdi provides an interesting and careful extension on ideas set out in Grossman and Helpman (1991) regarding the nature of specialization in high technology under general equilibrium with free trade. What is particularly welcome is that Birdi produces a model in which the hysteresis result of Grossman and Helpman, which states that once a country has a lead in high technology it will retain it, is shown to be a special case. The framework which Birdi uses is a basic 2×2 model with two sectors, a competitive agricultural sector and a monopolistically competitive high technology sector, and two equally sized countries and an assumption of factor price equalization. What is important in his model is that knowledge is categorized as being basic and applied and basic knowledge is a factor which enters the production function for applied knowledge with an exponent which can vary between 0, which is Grossman and Helpman's case where basic knowledge is unimportant to the development of applied knowledge (an heroic assumption), and 1.

As Birdi argues, basic knowledge is in fact of fundamental importance to the progress of applied knowledge. Birdi is commendably careful to point out that the distinction between basic and applied knowledge is in practice fuzzy, even if the two must be separated for formal analysis. He demonstrates that whenever basic research is important to applied research, and the strength of that importance depends on the exponent on basic knowledge in the growth equation for applied knowledge, then a country which has superior productivity can always overtake a firm which has a lead, even if it is no more productive in applied research. He also suggests that government policy can aid the process by committing more resources to basic research, which in the model is a public good funded by a lump-sum tax, and also by fostering collaboration between basic and applied research sectors.

The chapter is a welcome step in the right direction of understanding the relationship between R&D, trade and international specialization in R&D. Due to reasons of tractability of the model and the requirement of brevity some simplifying assumptions were made which one would like to see relaxed and some questions left untouched which one would like to see explored. In Birdi's model, at least as reported in this volume, the growth of basic knowledge is a function of the stock of basic knowledge and the amount of labour devoted to it, whereas as he correctly suggests in his discussion of scientific knowledge, applied research is likely to feed back into basic research and it would be interesting to see how this would affect the results. Second, the importance of basic to applied research is assumed to be the same in both countries, whereas the informal discussion suggests that this can be influenced by institutional arrangements as well as government initiatives to foster collaboration. Ideally one would like more intuition about how these processes work. Third, the model has the result that one country ends up dominating in the high-tech sector. This seems to sit ill with the facts of international competition in high tech sectors which seem to be characterized more by competition between oligopolists of differing national origin. This is hardly a criticism of Birdi, since modelling such competition would be a formidable undertaking.

Finally, a natural extension to make the model more realistic would be to grapple with the very obvious and important fact that the fruits of both basic and applied research are appropriable and usually at less cost than the original costs of generation, rather than assuming there are no knowledge spillovers. One suspects that this has something to do with catch-up in practice. It also provides a route into considering international technology transfer and the means by which, for example, the Asian tigers have managed to harness technological innovations of other countries.

RAW MATERIALS IN THE HISTORY OF ECONOMIC POLICY

Or why List (the protectionist) and Cobden (the free trader) both agreed on free trade in corn

Erik S. Reinert

It's the eternal paradox – the poor live in nations which are
rich from Nature's bounties.
(José Cecilio del Valle, economist and vice president of the
short-lived Central American Republic, about 1830)[1]

The higher the civilization of a people, the less does it depend
on the nature of the country.
(Wilhelm Roscher, German economist and inspirer of Marx
and Schumpeter, founder of the New Historical School of
economics in Germany, about 1860)[2]

The commemoration of the repeal of the Corn Laws in 1846 presents an opportunity to look at the place of raw materials in what is virtually a non-existent field of academic enquiry: the history of economic policy. The history of economic thought has, to a large extent, become a study of the genealogy of neoclassical economics, which leaves out the history of an alternative tradition of economic policy which was not based on classical or neoclassical thought.[3] In this alternative economic tradition – which I call production-centred economics (as opposed to the barter-centred classical and neoclassical tradition) – raw material production alone cannot, in the absence of manufacturing, lead to national wealth. A genealogy of the alternative production-centred economic tradition over the last 500 years is shown in Figure 27.1.

The main debate on economic policy in the nineteenth century was between barter-centred English classical theory on the one hand, and production-centred economic theory, represented by Germany and the USA, on the other. Later, into this century, the same line of reasoning is found in Canada[4] and Australia.[5] These later developments, however, will not be discussed here. The aim of this chapter is to show that the repeal of the Corn Laws was a policy measure where both classical barter-based economics in England – represented by Richard Cobden – and production-based economics – represented by Friedrich List – fully agreed that free trade in corn was to the benefit of England. Free trade in corn being agreed upon both by the free traders and the protectionists at the time, I shall argue that the repeal of the Corn Laws should not be seen as a victory of the principle of free trade, but rather as the final demise of English feudal privileges.

The debate around the Corn Laws calls the attention to one important stylized fact in the history of economic policy: All presently industrialized countries have, in the early stages of industrialization – from fifteenth-century England to twentieth-century Japan and Korea – been through a period where economic policy was heavily discriminatory against raw material production, and/or heavily favouring manufacturing. The particular mix of anti-raw materialism and pro-manufacturing policies varied, depending on the special circumstances of each nation.

Throughout the chapter I shall attempt to show why this discrimination against raw materials was a necessary stage to go through – why production-based economics was right in seeing the exclusive specialization in the production of raw materials as 'bad trade'. I shall argue that the understanding of this point is a necessary step in order to comprehend an important aspect of the problem of world poverty and of sustainable economic development.

PRODUCTION-CENTRED VS. BARTER-CENTRED ECONOMIC THEORY

In the fundamentally barter-centred classical and neoclassical economic tradition there is, of course, no difference between raw materials and manufactured goods. I shall argue that there exists a very long alternative line of economic theory – which I shall refer to as production-centred (as opposed to barter-centred) – where an economy based on raw materials, in the absence of a manufacturing base, almost by necessity will be poor. I shall argue that all presently industrialized nations – the UK, USA, Germany and Japan – went through an important stage of production-centred economics, where the output of raw materials was seen as an inferior economic activity. Only after having completed the process of industrialization did the economic policy of these nations come more in line with the classical or neoclassical paradigm.

Neoclassical economics sees physiocracy (from *physio* = nature, *-cracy* = rule) as the starting point of its family tree. At the root of neoclassical economics there lies a preference for raw materials – for agriculture – over manufactured goods; not only in the name physiocracy, but also since, as Adam Smith pointed out, agriculture corresponds more closely to the 'natural' state of perfect competition. Raw materials behave 'more naturally' than manufactured goods. Neoclassical economics has also taken diminishing returns from Ricardo's corn economy to characterize its production functions, and, indeed most surprisingly, applies this constraint to a society of industrial mass production, which in reality is characterized by the opposite effect – by important increasing returns to scale. Here the problems created by general equilibrium analysis forced Alfred Marshall, although most reluctantly, to throw out of his model the increasing returns that he himself had observed as being perhaps the main characteristic of industrial society.[6] This is an early example of economic theory developing along what Paul Krugman has called 'the perceived line of least mathematical resistance'.[7]

The nature of neoclassical economists' tools and the quest for equilibrium forced them to stick to physiocracy – to the economic behaviour of the products of nature, not industry – as the basis for their science. As a consequence of this, the economic theory of the whole historical period whose main characteristic was industrial mass production – the 'Fordist techno-economic paradigm' – was accompanied by an economic theory deeply entrenched in the assumptions of pre-mass production: the absence of any scale effects (in trade theory) and diminishing returns in the production functions.

In the alternative production-based economic tradition, there is a 'curse of the resources' underlying the theory. Specialization in raw materials – without a parallel manufacturing base – causes poverty for a nation. In this chapter we shall argue that this argument belongs to a very old school in economic theory, which goes back to the Renaissance, a school that heavily influenced economic policy for centuries, but which all but died out with World War II. This alternative tradition differentiates itself by being oriented around production and knowledge ('mind') – in contrast with the classical and neoclassical traditions which are centred around barter (supply and demand) and matter (goods). A family tree of production-based economics is provided in Figure 27.1

The 1846 repeal of the Corn Laws was a case where both these schools agreed – both pre-Smithian production-centred economics and barter-centred classical economics viewed free trade in corn as being beneficial to England. Free import of corn was also seen as being beneficial in the pre-Ricardian *ancien régime* trade, under the set of policies we shall refer to as King's Taxonomy.[8]

We shall therefore argue that the repeal of the Corn Laws should not be seen as a victory of free trade, but merely as a final demise of the power of the British landed aristocracy.

This is the reason why Friedrich List – the famous protectionist – and Richard Cobden – the famous free trader – were fully in agreement on the

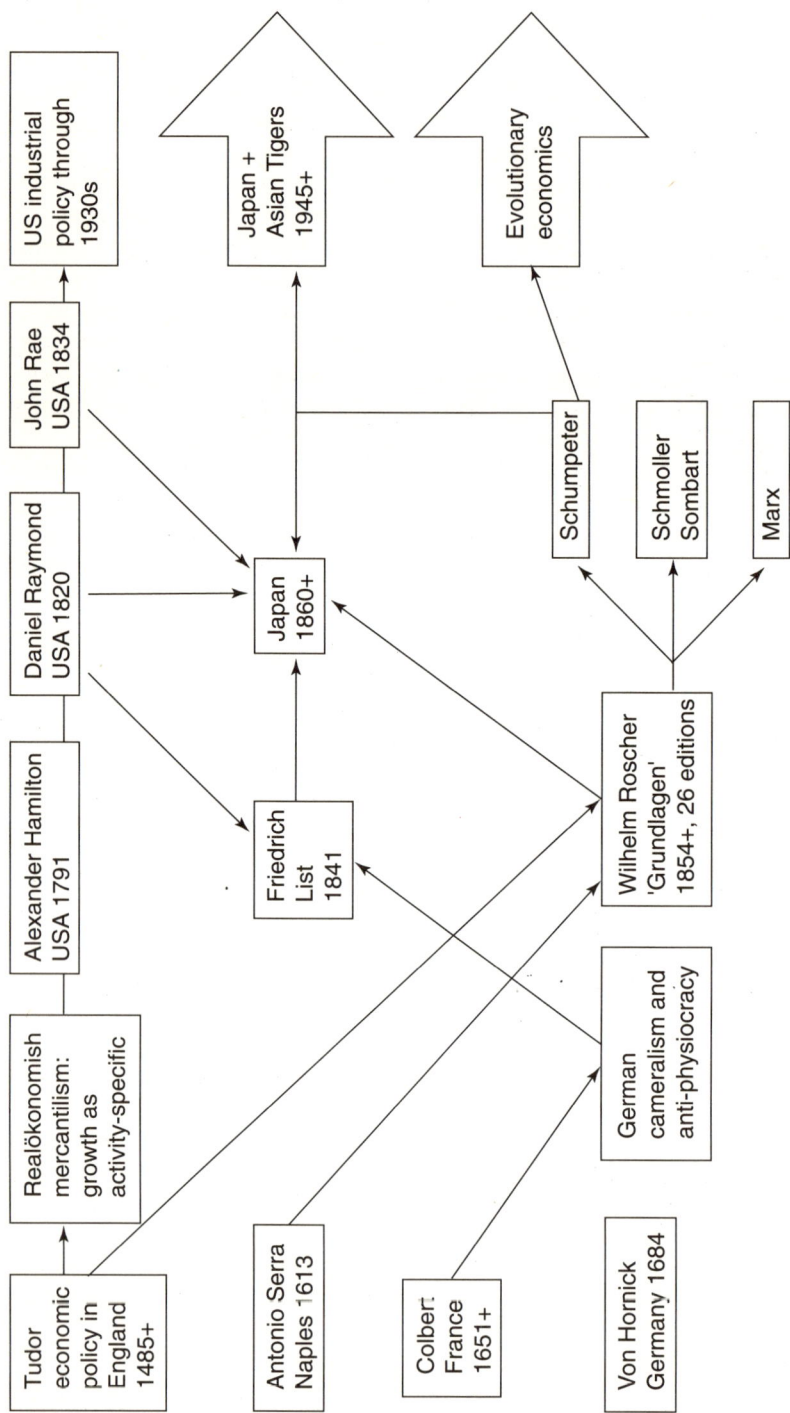

Figure 27.1 The knowledge- and production-based canon of economic theory

case of the Corn Laws. By 1846 Friedrich List had in fact been suggesting for more than twenty years that, in their own interest, the English move towards free trade in corn.

The core argument of 400 years of production-centred economics can be reduced to the statement that the circumstances of production of goods and services are the fundamental determinants of national economic wealth. These circumstances are determined by dynamic increasing returns – what Schumpeter called historical increasing returns – by diminishing returns, by the slope of the learning curve, and by the different levels of capital and skill which can profitably be absorbed by different economic activities at any point in time. The varying degrees of imperfect competition, and of barriers to entry which result from these factors, cause national differences in wage levels.

By essentially studying barter Adam Smith and his neoclassical descendants miss the influence of the circumstances of production national wage levels – which constitutes around 70 per cent of GNP in a modern nation. The alternative theoretical tradition – which was very strong both in the USA and Germany in the nineteenth century – argues that this influence is so powerful that, when trade takes place between nations of very different skill levels, free trade is frequently a decidedly suboptimal option. We have argued elsewhere that the take-off stages into industrialization of all presently industrialized countries – in a sequence started by England around 1485 – have been based on these production-centred and not barter-centred economic theories,[9] and that barter-based classical and neoclassical economics have replaced the production-based theories only when a competitive manufacturing base had been achieved. This pattern holds true both for England (pre-Smith), for the USA, Germany and Japan.

On 'good' and 'bad' trade

Historically the economic policies recommended in production-based economics follow two alternative lines of argument. The first concerns the risks and perils of a resource-based economy – being specialized in economic activities not requiring high labour skills and subject to diminishing returns. These two effects may combine into a lock-in effect trapping a nation in poverty (the 'Bolivia syndrome'), which technical change will not solve. Exporting natural resources constituted 'bad trade' in the orthodoxy of English economic policy until long after Adam Smith and David Ricardo. The most clear statement of this orthodoxy is contained in three volumes published by Charles King in 1721.[10] In King's Taxonomy exporting raw materials was 'bad trade'. We later find this same line of argument in nineteenth-century Germany, Japan and the USA and in twentieth-century Australia and Canada. The 'curses' of economies based on natural resources[11] are five:

- diminishing returns;
- low skills/low wages;
- perfect competition;
- price volatility;
- lack of ability to create national synergies/linkages.

The latter point is emphasized by Gerschenkron: 'the hope that industry in a very backward country can unfold from its agricultural activities is hardly realistic';[12] and by Hirschman: 'agriculture certainly stands convicted on the count of its lack of direct stimulus to the setting up of new activities through linkage effects: the superiority of manufacturing in this respect is crushing'.[13]

The second line of arguement concerns the benefits of concentrating a nation's economic activities in mechanizable, skill-absorbing activities, subject to increasing returns – a cluster of characteristics which for a long time could be efficiently shorthanded as manufacturing. Exporting goods from these activities qualified as 'good trade' in King's Taxonomy – the English orthodoxy which built its national strength. The Canadian and Australian arguments later added to this by showing that the presence of a national manufacturing base upgraded skills in the resource-based activity and prevented these from going into diminishing returns – making raw material exports from a manufacturing country a viable strategy. In a previous paper we have argued that what today is called competitiveness reflects the pursuit of dynamic imperfect competition which in previous centuries was sought under the names of 'good trade' or 'national productive powers'.[14]

In this chapter we shall concentrate on the first part of the argument and try to explain the risks and perils of resource-based economies, why 'bad trade' was more than a primitive pre-Smithian superstition. This will also explain why protectionist Friedrich List so clearly saw the benefits accruing to England from the repeal of the Corn Laws.

On the differing capacity of economic activities to absorb skills and capital

In order fully to comprehend the argument underlying the philosophy of 'good' and 'bad' trade, it is important to understand how economic activities differ as potential carriers of economic growth. At any point in time different economic activities can profitably absorb very different quantities of human knowledge and capital, they present different windows of opportunity. You cannot upgrade the level of skill and salary of a person picking lettuce to that of a computer engineer by educating the lettuce picker, because the absorption capacity of human skills for the two professions are different. The absorption capacity for capital and skill of lettuce picking will only change at the point in time when lettuce picking is mechanized. Upgrading the economic situation of the lettuce picker can only take place by his changing his job. That this fact applies to a nation as well as to an individual was the core argument of US economist Daniel Raymond in 1820.[15] Raymond laid the foundation for 'the American system of manufactures' and heavily influenced Friedrich List.

As long as there is a demand for goods produced with both high and low skills, economic growth – left to the market – will be very uneven and strongly history dependent. That vicious and virtuous economic circles originate in this fact was already indicated by Antonio Serra in 1613,[16] and also underlies nineteenth-century opposition to English classical theory both from Germany and the USA, and later from Japan. Only by producing a theory of economic barter – leaving out the production aspects – neoclassical trade theory proves that the wage earners in a nation making a living picking lettuce will be equally as rich as the wage earners in a nation of computer engineers.[17] If production is introduced, the theory would by valid only if one introduces the counter-factual assumption that all economic activities have the same capacity to profitably absorb skills and capital (i.e. that a barber shop profitably can be made as capital intensive as a nuclear power plant, and that picking lettuce profitably can be made as skill intensive as developing new computers). A fundamental difference between barter-based and production-based economics is therefore that in the latter the process of economic development is activity specific – it can only take place in certain economic activities at any point in time. Historically we tend to name historical periods according to the activities where economic development took place – in the stone age industry in the stone age, in the bronze age industry in the bronze age, and – in the machine age – in the economic activities which were being mechanized at any point in time.

To nineteenth-century Americans this point was brought home by looking at the cotton growing industry. The observable fact that cotton picking was only profitable with slave labour made any English hint that the USA would be better off producing cotton and leaving manufacturing industry to the English not very convincing outside the circle of slave-owners.[18] The US Civil War was therefore also a war between barter-centred English free trade theory, supported by the South, and production-centred economic theory, supported by the North.

In both Germany and in the USA there was a general feeling that England had achieved her wealth by going into skill- and scale-intensive manufacturing. By attempting to export a barter-centred economic theory which excluded these factors England was attempting to 'draw up the ladder' behind itself, in order to achieve a world monopoly in manufacturing. As we shall see, the writings of Richard Cobden all but confirm this.

THE 'RAW' AND THE 'COOKED' –
THE DIFFERENT PHILOSOPHICAL
UNDERPINNINGS OF BARTER-CENTRED
AND PRODUCTION-CENTRED ECONOMICS

In 1964 Claude Lévi-Strauss – a famous French anthropologist – published a book called *The Raw and the Cooked*, carrying the subtitle *Introduction to a science of mythology*.[19] Lévi-Strauss suggests that 'the cooked' among 'primitive' peoples symbolizes the realm of the human, whereas 'the raw' symbolizes nature. The myths, drawn chiefly from the Amazon Indians, but also from countries like France, can be interpreted as 'cooking' being what differentiates man from beast. The domination of fire can be seen as the watershed between the ape and man. The main distinctions between man and beast in primitive societies were associated with the use of fire: man cooked his food, and he 'cooked' his pottery. 'Unlike the deer, the Tarahumara (tribe) does not eat grass, but interposes between the grass and his animal hunger a complicated cultural cycle involving the care and use of domestic animals . . . Nor like the coyote does the Tarahumara avail himself of meat torn from a scarcely dead animal and eaten raw. The Tarahumara interposes between his meat and hunger a cultural system of cooking.'[20]

Primitive tribes seem to have had a need to emphasize what differentiates man from other animals. Man interposes his knowledge and social organization between himself and nature – and 'cooking' is an early and powerful image of what characterizes this knowledge. Primitive myths therefore often tell stories on the origin of fire, the origin of cultivated plants or the origin of pottery – the watersheds that made *Homo erectus* into *Homo sapiens*. The distinction between the raw and the cooked turns into the distinction between nature and culture. Lévi-Strauss supports this view with many examples from all over the world. To this very day, 'to sleep in the raw' is a colloquial English expression meaning 'to sleep naked'. In eighteenth-century France, *danser à cru* would mean 'to dance barefoot', and *monter à cru* would mean 'to ride bareback'.

In the nineteenth century there was a strong conflict between English economic thought – representing barter and matter – on the one hand, and German and US thought – representing production and mind – on the other. As a philosophical basis of this economic debate, we find – as in the myths of the Amazon indians – that the participants feel they have to define what differentiates man from beast: man the trader or man the producer and innovator. The replies to this question seem to distinguish the barter-centred from the production-centred economic theory (see Figure 27.2).

The different answers to this question from Adam Smith and Abraham Lincoln typified two kinds of trade policies: protectionism in Germany and the USA until a necessary skill level in production has been reached that enables the nation to compete fairly with England versus free trade under any

The reply from barter-centred economics

The division of labour arises from a propensity in human nature to . . . truck, barter and exchange one thing for another . . . It is common to all men, and to be found in no other race of animals, which seem to know neither this nor any other species of contracts . . . Nobody ever saw a dog make a fair and deliberate exchange of one bone for another with another dog.

(Adam Smith (1776) *Wealth of Nations*, Chicago: University of Chicago Press, 1976, p. 17)

The reply from production-centred economics

. . . Beavers build houses; but they build them in nowise differently, or better, now than they did five thousand years ago . . . Man is not the only animal who labours; but he is the only one who *improves* his workmanship. These improvements he effects by *Discoveries* and *Inventions*.

(Abraham Lincoln, Speech of the 1860 presidential campaign)

Unlike the deer, the Tarahumara (a tribe) does not eat grass, but interposes between the grass and his animal hunger a complicated cultural cycle involving the care and use of domestic animals . . . Nor like the coyote does the Tarahumara avail himself of meat torn from a scarcely dead animal and eaten raw. The Tarahumara interposes between his meat and hunger a cultural system of cooking.

(M. Zingg (1942) 'The genuine and spurious values in Tarahumara culture', in *American Anthropologist* 44 (1): 82. Quoted in Lévi-Strauss, op. cit.: 336)

Man's ability to harness and use to his advantage the forces of nature.

(E. Peshine Smith, US economist, 1814–82)

Man's ability to use tools.

(Karl Marx, German economist, 1818–83)

Man's rational will and ideas.

(Christian Wolff, German philosopher and economist, 1679–1754)

Figure 27.2 What differentiates man's economic activity from that of beasts?

circumstances – regardless of skill level – in English theory. No doubt Adam Smith also saw the general tendency of things to improve but, we would argue, this was not at all at the core of his system. At the core of his system was the division of labour, which he saw as resulting from a propensity to barter (from matter), not from a propensity to discover and invent (from the mind). We shall see below that this counterpoint between matter and mind was the essence of an important economic controversy in England in 1622–3. We would argue that today's mainstream economics carries the inherent weakness of an excessive focus on barter and matter – not on production and mind – from its founding father Adam Smith.

However, in the case of the repeal of the Corn Laws, both barter-centred and production-centred theories agreed. Friedrich List, who comes down in economic history as the incarnation of protectionism, fully agreed with free trader Richard Cobden that the repeal of the Corn Laws was in the interest of England. This seemingly curious agreement between protectionists and free traders indicates that the pre-twentieth-century protectionist debate was very much along the lines of 'matter' vs. 'mind' – 'raw' vs. 'cooked'. The German and American economists insisted that free trade in 'raw' goods – Friedrich List's *Urprodukte* – was something completely different from free trade in 'cooked' goods: goods where the human mind had added its skills. The industrial battle between nations is, in essence, the continual upgrading and adding of human skills to raw materials. Venetian glass blowers added value to sand, silicone chip producers add even more value per unit of sand. The nations which specialize in providing the 'raw' sand will inevitably lag behind in skills and, consequently, in the value of their manpower. As a result they will, as Marx put it, 'increasingly have to give up more hours of labour in exchange for less hours of labour'.

In the next part of the chapter, we shall see that in the long tradition of production-based economics, wealth was seen as being created by adding knowledge and social organization to the raw produce of nature, much as in the myths of Lévi-Strauss. Adding knowledge to nature was not only a better paid economic activity, this 'cooking' of raw materials was seen as being the very essence of man, the activity which separated man from beast. Man added 'mind' to raw materials, which without his interference was only 'matter'. Any economic theory that did not take man's mind into consideration was, in the German tradition, *Entgeistet* – void of spirit.

ECONOMIC THEORY: FROM 'PHYSICS ENVY' TO 'BIOLOGY ENVY' AND FROM 'MATTER' TO 'MIND'

Economic theory has, since its inception, carried with it an underlying counterpoint of 'raw' vs. 'cooked' – a counterpoint between the raw produce of nature and the products where Man had added his 'mind' to the products of nature. In today's economic theory we find this tension reflected in the movement of economic theory from 'physics envy' towards 'biology envy', and in the increasing importance of innovations – the creativity of man's mind – added to the physical matter of the products being exchanged.

This way of thinking originates with the Renaissance, when man redefined his relationship with creation as we shall briefly discuss below. The distinction between 'raw products of nature' (what List 300 years later characteristically calls *Urprodukte* – giving them a connotation of something primitive and prehistoric as in *Urmensch*, prehistoric man) and the products which have had value added by human creativity shows up in the earliest non-scholastic economic literature, in Italy in the 1580s and in England in mercantilist tracts of the 1620s. This is clearly an issue in the prolonged nineteenth-century conflict between English economic theory, especially trade theory, on the one hand, and German and US economic theory on the other. We shall argue that this was the reason why Richard Cobden, the champion of free trade, and Friedrich List, the protectionist, agreed that protecting raw materials was not a good economic policy.

The Renaissance was essentially a period where man became conscious of the legitimacy of being creative. Mediaeval man was the caretaker in the world that God had created; creation was definitely complete and trying to understand it or to tinker with it was decidedly off-limits to man. To Aristotle, mining was one such violation of the creation. Oxford philosopher Roger Bacon was imprisoned for his experiments in 1271, standing accused of making 'suspect innovations'. Starting with the influx of neo-Platonist ideas from the Byzantine empire to the Academy of Florence in the early fifteenth century, man came to see himself in a different light. The new argument went like this: man was created in the image of God. What characterizes God above anything else had to be his enormous creativity. But – if man was created in the image of God – then man should also be creative.

Out of this line of reasoning man's duty to invent and to create new knowledge is born. But this duty was a pleasurable one. The argument seems to have gone like this: it is man's duty to people the earth, therefore God made the duty of procreating a joyous one. Similarly, because it was man's duty to create, to invent and to discover was also a joyous duty. In England, Francis Bacon – statesman under Elizabeth I – was the carrier of these ideas and wrote 'An Essay on Innovations' around 1605. In Germany the philosophers Leibniz and Wolff later represented the same philosophical tradition. 'Some people collect knowledge like other people collect money', says Christian Wolff. In a recent paper, 'Exploring the genesis of economic innovations: the religious gestalt-switch and the duty to invent as precon-ditions for economic growth', we explain this process in detail.[21]

Out of this changed attitude to knowledge, man's activities moved further and further away from the 'raw' and into the realm of the 'cooked'. Bartering raw materials gave way to the production of manufactured goods, in a process where the value added to the raw materials was imputable to human knowledge – to 'the soul of man' which distinguished him from beasts. Importantly – to the observers of the day – these new and knowledge-based economic activities were seen as bringing more wealth, as being more profitable, than the old resource-based activities. Therefore, in a truly Schumpeterian move, Renaissance economic policy supported the manufacturing industries at the expense of resource-based industries – of encouraging and protecting new knowledge. These economic policies included the establishment of a patent system (in sixteenth-century Venice), of bounties paid to new manufacturers, of the prohibition of export of machinery (in force in England until the 1830s), of the prohibition of migration of skilled workers (in Venice under the penalty of death), on the export duty of raw materials (to increase the value to the producing nation of this inferior good, and to ensure foreign industry a higher price of raw materials than local industry).

One of the earliest bestselling books on economics was *Delle Cause della Grandezza delle Città*[22] written by the Italian Giovanni Botero (1543–1617). The English translation, published in London in 1606, is entitled *The Cause of the Greatnesse of Cities*. What, Botero asks, is more important for making a nation wealthy, the fertility of its soil or industry? No doubt, industry, argues Botero, first of all 'because the things produced by the able hands of man are many more, and have a much higher price, than the things produced by nature.[23] Nature gives the material, but the object . . . is the work of man. Wool is a simple, coarse material of nature. How many beautiful objects, varied in form and shape, the Arts can produce from this.' The best practical example showing the benefits of manufacturing industry over activities based on raw materials was Venice – a city where half of its inhabitants were engaged in manufacturing. A Venetian legislative poster from the eighteenth century fixed the punishment for bringing bread into the city as 'a fine of fifty ducats to be paid immediately and every time and three lashes of the whip'.[24] At roughly the same time the imports of all types of corn into Venice were freed definitely in 1782. The 'raw' could enter freely, the 'cooked' was to be produced nationally. Friedrich List, in my view correctly, saw the repeal of the Corn Laws as just a continuation of this very old policy of protecting 'the cooked' (bread) and letting 'the raw' (corn) have free entry.

Following Venice, England presents the most spectacularly successful use of the strategy of turning a nation's exports from 'the raw' to 'the cooked'. Daniel Defoe describes the English strategy, and praises the Tudor monarchs who carried it out, in his *Plan of English Commerce* in 1728.[25] In the early fifteenth century England was a poor country, heavily indebted to its Italian bankers. The chief export was raw wool. Henry VII, who came to power in 1485, had lived in exile in wealthy Burgundy where English wool was being spun into cloth. The Tudor strategy which started with him was to bring

England into the wealth-creating downstream activities in wool manufacturing that Henry had observed abroad. The English strategy was gradual, starting with import substitution. In 1489 tariffs on cloth were increased and local cloth manufacturing was encouraged. The Crown paid for foreign workers to be brought in and businessmen were paid bounties for establishing textile manufacturing firms. When sufficient manufacturing capacity had been achieved, England prohibited all export of raw wool. As the wave of mechanization extended from wool to other areas of manufacturing, these new industries were in turn given the same preferential treatment initially given to the production of woollen cloth. Friedrich List later put it this way: 'The principle *sell manufactures, buy raw material* was during centuries the English substitute for an (economic) theory.'[26]

The logic of early economic policy seems to have worked by abduction – by a process similar to Kaldor's 'stylized facts'. Everybody could observe that the wool producers in England and the miners in Hungary were poor, just as they could observe that the manufacturers in Venice were rich, as were manufacturers everywhere. In fact, the establishment of the first textile industry in England under heavy protection was based on such a line of reasoning. The English economist Edward Misselden, in 1623, describes very well how economics passes from abductive and intuitive gut feelings to science: 'Wee felt it before in sense, but now wee know it by science.'[27]

In England the conflict between the 'raw' and the 'cooked' is clearly reflected in the main economic debate of the early seventeenth century, in 1622–3 between Gerard De Malynes[28] and Edward Misselden.[29] In the history of economic thought, this debate is interpreted as being about exchange controls and the balance of trade.[30] However, by going back to the sources one finds that the main line of attack by Misselden against Malynes is his 'mechanical' view of man – Malynes has left out man's 'art' and 'soul'. Misselden essentially accuses Malynes of not seeing the difference between 'the raw' and 'the cooked': the difference between stones and timber on the one hand and a house on the other. 'An [sic] House is not an house in respect of the matter whereof it is made; for then all other stone & timber should be a house: but in respect to the *Forme* of it, whereby it is known to be a house', states Misselden. This Forme was the 'cooking process' added by man to the natural 'matter' provided by nature. To Misselden, man creates value by, through his *Mind*, adding *Forme*, not by collecting *Matter*. According to Misselden, Malynes makes a crucial mistake by reducing commerce and economics only to its *matter*, merchandise and money. Without man's art and soul 'there would be no traffique amongst men, not withstanding the materials of trade', states Misselden.[31]

The conflict between the two economists Malynes and Misselden thus anticipates by some 250 years the nineteenth-century German critique of the *Entgeistung* ('the taking away of the human mind') in English classical economics and by some 350 years the present debate on 'physics envy' of neoclassical economics. Misselden argues for a place of *the mind* – what man's creativity adds to the raw materials of nature – in economic theory. His equivalent of *Entgeistung* and 'physics envy' was – and he quotes Aristotle on this – *privation*: 'Privation is not Ens or Beeing, because it is not in the subiect which is made by it.' To Misselden, economics is not in the 'Commodities, Money and Exchange', these are merely 'matters thereof'.

In the late seventeenth century William Petty (1623–87) invents both 'the division of labour' – using a clock factory rather than Adam Smith's pin factory – and 'political arithmetic': 'the art of reasoning by figures upon things relating to government'.[32] Petty, following the trend of virtually all pre-physiocratic and pre-Smithian economics, observes how the relationship between primary production and manufacturing evolves over time: 'There is much more to be gained by *Manufacture* than *Husbandry* . . . Now here we may take notice that as Trades and Curious Arts increase; so the Trade of Husbandry will decrease.' As other English writers of his day, Petty was commenting on the high standards of living in Holland, which he saw as the natural effect of so many Dutchmen being engaged in manufacturing and trade. In a nation involved in manufacturing and trade, agriculture would lose out, since it was everywhere observable that agriculture paid lower wages than manufacturing and trade. He found proof of his thesis in Holland because 'there is little Ploughing and Sowing of Corn in Holland and Zealand, or breeding of young Cattle'. The Dutch imported much of their food.

The 'mechanical' views of Malynes and Locke were soon to win the day through the barter-centred economic theory of Smith and Ricardo. Other than on the intuitive and philosophical level, the early economists contributed relatively little as to explaining why the production of raw materials was an 'inferior' or 'bad' economic activity. The honour of explaining this goes to Antonio Serra.[33] Serra was the first economist who showed the mechanisms through which the nations producing raw materials stayed poor and the nations producing manufactured goods were wealthy. Serra explains the wealth of Venice which had virtually no raw materials and the poverty of Naples which was extremely fertile. The key mechanisms at work in Serra's system are increasing returns to scale in the manufacturing industry of Venice, and diminishing returns and price volatility in the raw materials production in Naples. Serra explains how the volume of manufacturing production in Venice brings costs down and serves to create barriers to entry for other producers. In Serra's system, increasing returns to scale enable the Venetians to sell their products cheaper, while still paying higher wages to their workers than other nations. We shall return to Antonio Serra later in this chapter.

By generally grouping all mercantilists together in the history of economic thought and by reading them almost exclusively secondhand – invariably filtered through the lenses of a neoclassical *Weltanschauung* – we have lost sight of both the process of historical policy formation and of a vast number of valuable insights into our own profession.

COBDEN AND LIST: THE REPEAL OF THE CORN LAWS IN KING'S TAXONOMY

In 1766 Carl von Linné, in the twelfth edition of his book on the natural system, completed his taxonomy of plants and animals by including man, *Homo sapiens*, in the binomial classification system. Linné's taxonomy is still the standard taxonomy in use for the plant and animal kingdoms. Ten years later Adam Smith effectively brought the long-lasting taxonomy of economic activities – of which ones were good and which ones were bad for a nation – to an end in economic theory but not in economic practice. The old taxonomy was, in England, most clearly stated by Charles King in his three-volume work from 1721.[34] Under King's Taxonomy importing raw materials and exporting manufactures was 'good trade' for a nation. Importing manufactured goods and exporting raw materials was 'bad trade', while, interestingly enough, trading by buying and selling manufactured goods with the same foreign nation was also good trade.

This system makes sense under certain assumptions:

- if we associate manufacturing with Schumpeterian historical increasing returns (continuous technical change coupled with increasing returns), that creates a dynamic national rent seeking where the rent is split between capital, labour (which continuously has to upgrade their skills) and government;
- if we associate raw materials with perfect information, perfect competition, diminishing returns and no demand for high levels of human skills.

The world today is still divided into an industrialized First World which, up to and including the Asian Tigers, has been through a successful period of economic policy based on King's Taxonomy, and the Third World, whose poverty is based on specialization in providing the world with raw materials. The support and protection given to innovations and to hi-tech industries in today's industrial countries – what the French call *neo-colbertisme* – is only a proof of the continuing validity of the pre-Smithian taxonomy: economic welfare is increasing only by adding more and more human skills to the 'raw' products of nature. The nations which capture the economic activities where the newest and most sophisticated skills can be profitably employed – at the frontier of human knowledge – become the world leaders.

The repeal of the Corn Laws, which today is generally seen as a victory of the 'new' ideology was, in fact, completely compatible with the old theory based on Charles King's Taxonomy. The repeal of the Corn Laws in England was not the watershed in the history of free trade as we tend to see it today, and as it was sold to the rest of the world by the English of the period. There are two main aspects to this argument:

1   The repeal of the Corn Laws was fully consistent with the trade theory of the *ancien régime*, with Charles King's Taxonomy and the mercantilist tradition of what constituted good and bad trade. On the corn issue, pre-Ricardian trade theory and Ricardo's free trade theories were in complete agreement. One sign of this was that Friedrich List – who in the Anglo-Saxon world tends to be looked upon as a protectionist of the mercantilist school – had argued for many years already that free trade in corn would be in the interest of England.

2   The Corn Laws were seen at the time essentially to be a monopoly of the great landowners, and their repeal was much more a political victory of democracy over feudal privileges of the aristocracy than a victory of free trade. No doubt the repeal of the Corn Laws was used as an argument to open up foreign markets to British manufactures, and this was clearly an issue in the debate. However, French economist Léon Say seems to have pinpointed the essence of Cobden's movement to repeal the Corn Laws: 'Richard Cobden was, above all things, a thorough democrat and his followers trusted before everything else that he would establish democracy upon the ruins of aristocracy, and that he would destroy whatever was left to the great landowners of their feudal privileges.'[35] Say's essay was published exactly 100 years ago, in connection with the fiftieth anniversary of the repeal of the Corn Laws in 1896.

The repeal of the Corn Laws can be seen as representing the decisive confrontation in a Schumpeterian battle, where industrial entrepreneurs, eager to join the upper strata of society, as a byproduct of their own success, came to overturn the old social order.[36] After the repeal 'industrial and commercial success [became] the nearest approach to medieval lordship possible to modern man', in the words of Schumpeter.[37] We shall argue that the repeal of the Corn Laws was primarily a result of this economic and political power struggle, and that the trade theoretical issues were of secondary importance, other than as arguments used by England to make other nations stop protecting their manufacturing industry. In other words: the English used the fact that they no longer protected 'the raw' as an argument for other nations to stop protecting 'the cooked'.

This was seen as a bluff and called such by the most influential German and American economists of the time, but it has convinced mainstream economics of today. We would argue that this represents a major issue behind the continuing poverty of most Third World nations.

Almost forty years after the repeal of the Corn Laws, we find the same issue raised in the US tariff debate. Now King's Taxonomy has achieved a higher level of sophistication: raw materials were, as in the old logic, to enter the country free of duty, but tariffs on manufactured goods were to be gradually increased with increasing skill level of the workers. A very clear statement of this principle is found in a resolution which was passed by the Democratic National Convention in Chicago in 1884:

> First – the abolition of all duties on raw materials, such as wool, iron, and other ores, coal, jute, hemp, flax, dye stuffs, etc., in order that we may compete in home and foreign markets with other manufacturing nations, not one of which taxes raw materials. Second – the adjustment of the tariff, so that manufactures approaching nearest to the crude state will pay a lower rate, and manufactures that are further advanced, requiring more skill and labour, will pay a higher rate of duties.[38]

Eight years later, one author remarks that 'these views . . . [now] form the credo of that party'.[39]

Cobden: free trade in corn in order to achieve cheapness of manufactures

The article on Cobden in the *New Palgrave Dictionary of Economics* strongly emphasizes that 'Cobden's reason [for agitating against the Corn Laws] was peace.' This is certainly one of the reasons, but the main reason was a power-ful economic reasoning which is missed in the Palgrave entry.[40] Going through Cobden's own writings, it is clear that his main economic argument is that free trade in corn would strengthen manufacturing in Britain. Cobden's arguments are in many respects similar to those of Friedrich List. Although today we tend to see them as two opposite extremes, they shared a common pre-Ricardian view on what created national wealth. Both to Cobden and to List, this was not agriculture, not 'the raw', but 'the cooked'.

Cobden views the English economy essentially as a Ricardian corn economy or a Sraffian economy producing 'commodities by means of commodities'. One basic input into English manufacturing was corn to feed the workers for their daily bread. The price of that corn heavily influenced the price of labour. By reducing the price of corn, one would reduce the subsistence cost of labour. For this reason, Cobden says, 'to restrict the import of corn into a manufacturing nation, is to strike at the life of its foreign commerce'.[41]

Richard Cobden pays homage to free trade, not as a lofty human principle, but because were it not for the Corn Laws, the industrialization of the USA and Germany could have been avoided. Cobden sees the high price of corn as the basic reason why England has not been able to hold on to its near-monopoly of world manufacturing: 'The factory system would, in all probability, not have taken place in America and Germany; it most certainly could not have flourished, as it has done, both in these states, and in France, Belgium, and Switzerland, through the fostering bounties which the high-priced food of the British artisan has offered to the cheaper fed manufacturer of those countries.'[42]

In line with Cobden's pro-manufacturing stance for England and his anti-manufacturing stance for the rest of the world, he also favoured the South in the US Civil War. When evaluating any economic theory, we tend to forget the basic ethnocentric bias which I would claim, to varying degrees, underlies all economic theory. Lionel Robbins reminds us to keep in mind that English classical economists were in effect first of all Englishmen, and then economists: 'We get our picture wrong if we suppose that the English Classical Economists would have recommended, because it was good for the world at large, a measure which they thought would be harmful to their own community.'[43]

Today this bias lies in the assumptions of neoclassical theory. One example is that the economic theory of the nations which make their wealth under mass production and increasing returns excludes the possibility that only some economic activities are subject to increasing returns, while others are subject to diminishing returns. This kind of ethnocentrism is in some sense reflected when new trade theory only resurrects one half of Frank Graham's 1923 article,[44] dealing with the effects of increasing and diminishing returns in international trade. Only the half which deals with problems of interest to the industrialized world – increasing returns – is brought back. Using the rather heroic assumption that all economic activities are equally subject to increasing returns, this factor of course becomes yet another argument for universal free trade. Graham, on the other hand, also specifically raises the problem of nations whose exportables are subject to diminishing returns and provides an important clue leading to the understanding of the 'curse of the resources'. In a previous publication I have explained the gap between the First and Third Worlds as a result of increasing and diminishing returns, and of the cumulative effects of uneven learning potential and imperfect competition over time.[45]

Cobden says that 'if a wise modification of our corn laws had been affected at the close of the Napoleonic wars, the official value of our exports would have exceeded by one third its present amount'. And further: 'Under such an assumed state of things, this country, we believe, by this time, would have acquired an increase to its present wealth, to the extent of 350 Millions – nearly one-half the amount of the national debt.'[46] The wealth of the nations clearly lies in manufacturing – in 'the cooked' – corn is only important in order to feed the workers and make their labour cheaper.

Throughout Cobden's writings, he emphasizes the importance of cheapness. Here we find old-fashioned price competition, in contrast to Cobden's contemporary English writer on economics, Charles Babbage, who emphasized not the price of labour, but the role of the use of machinery and of science.[47]

Both Cobden and List sensed the crucial importance of the industrial system. To both of them the industrial system, and the need for change of economic policy which it carried with it, were at the core of their theories: 'The cardinal fact that struck his [Cobden's] eye was the great population that was gathering in the new centres of industry in the North of England ... which the magic of steam had called into such sudden and marvellous being', states Cobden's biographer, John Morley.[48]

Cobden also saw the evils of the manufacturing system, and he was decidedly a man of peace. To quote from his biography: "'But the factory system, which sprang up from the discoveries in machinery, has been adopted by all the civilised nations in the world, and it is in vain for us to think of discountenancing its application to the necessities of this country; it only remains for us to mitigate, as far as possible, the evils which are perhaps not inseparably connected with this novel social element." To this conception of the new problem Cobden always kept very close. This was always to him the foundation of the new order of things, which demanded a new kind of statesmanship and new ideas upon national policy.'[49] Richard Cobden saw, more clearly than most, the demands of the new techno-economic pradigm. By removing the last vestiges of the old feudal order – the duty on corn which subsidized the old nobility – Cobden decisively brought England into the age of industrialism.

At the time of his death there was little doubt that Cobden had achieved his goal of strengthening English manufacturing industry by lowering the price of provisions. On the day after his death, Monday 3 April 1865, his sometime foe, Lord Palmerston, rose in Parliament and 'amidst breathless silence' held a speech in the honour of Cobden. In his speech Lord Palmerston emphasized the great achievements of Mr Cobden: 'in the first place, the abrogation of those laws which hindered the importation of corn, which gave a great development to the industry of the country'.[50]

Both List and Cobden understood the superiority of the manufacturing industry over unindustrialized agricultural pursuits. List, like his US contemporaries, saw clearly that a nation which had reached the stage of manufacturing power of England could 'graduate' to a world of free trade. There was no doubt in List's mind that both Germany and the USA would one day reach a stage where free trade was to their benefit, but only after their level of knowledge and industrial strength were on equal footing with the English.

List's argument can be seen as one where children with the knowledge of second grade education cannot fairly compete with college graduates. Free trade would only be beneficial to both parties when the laggard nation had also received its college degree. The German counterpart of duties for 'infant industry protection' is therefore, in line with this reasoning, *Erziehungszoll* – carrying the double meaning of educational and upbringing duties.

List: why protecting agriculture is entirely different from protecting industry

In 1825 Friedrich List was banned from Germany and went to the USA. List tells us that one important event in his life, which converted him from being a free trader into an advocate of the protection of manufacturing, was the extreme poverty he witnessed in France with the collapse of French manufacturing that followed the fall of Napoleon. The second important event which influenced his view was no doubt his meeting with American political economy, particularly with the thoughts of Alexander Hamilton and, even more, of Daniel Raymond.[51] There are indeed whole passages in List's *National System* which follow, argument by argument, the 1820 book of Raymond.

Two years after his arrival in the USA, on 24 April 1827 List published an article on the English Corn Laws, 'Die englische Kornbill' in the German-language American newspaper, *Readinger Adler*, of which he was editor. In the same year Frederick [sic] List's *Outline of American Political Economy* was published in Philadelphia.[52] In this work List also raises the issue of the English Corn Laws, and asks what would happen to the American farmer if England should open up her corn trade. List foresees a rise in the price of US corn, but already in 1827 is fully in line with Richard Cobden on the main effect of the repeal of the Corn Laws: 'England would increase her manufacturing power immensely, and monopolise the Southern and all other markets.'

List clearly shows that a repeal of the Corn Laws, nineteen years before the event, would be a move which would benefit England, but could hurt American manufacturing. A US dependence on the export of raw materials to England would provide a 'destructive effect' on the USA. England could easily again exclude grain from the USA: 'by giving preference to the produce of Prussia, Poland, etc. etc. as it was the case last year respecting the English possessions in the West Indies. Certain is it that from the day of such an economical dependence the majority of the inhabitants of the United States would have to tremble before every new opening of the English Parliament, having more to fear and to expect from the proceedings and regulations in Westminster than from those in Washington, and that the independence of interest of the Unites States would be lost . . . Would it not be better if we had not sold a single grain of corn to England?'[53] In his articles on this issue List also made a point that the high transportation costs for corn gave the local English producers a big advantage over US farmers. List here presents himself as a forerunner of the *dependencia* school. In List's analysis, however, terms of trade are not the key economic issue, but the inferior nature of depending on the 'raw' rather than the 'cooked'.

In 1830 Friedrich List received his US citizenship and – much to the dislike of some of the German states – President Jackson appointed him Consul General of the USA for Saxony, Bavaria, Hesse-Cassel and Alsace, with a seat first in Hamburg and then in Leipsic [Leipzig]. As a US Consul, List informed his Secretary of State, John Forsyth, about the future development of the English Corn Laws. In a long dispatch dated 'Leipsic, May 15, 1835', List foresees that 'the repeal of the corn laws must become soon one of the principal objects of a reforming ministry, in which they will have to encounter powerful personal interests and prejudices'.[54]

In 1839 List wrote an article on 'The English Corn Laws and the German Protective System' (*Die englische Kornbill und das deutsche Schutzsystem*).[55] List is often not clear about the mechanisms which cause the protection of manufactures to have such a different effect than the protection of raw material. He explains how 'the olive growers will lose out to the machine producers', but his message of why this is so does not always come across completely. Daniel Raymond is in some ways more explicit on how the mechanisms at work under the protection of manufactures raise real wages, in spite of an initial increase in the price of imports. But, in this article, List states his case clearly:

> The Protective System, as we understand it, can only be applied to the cultivation (*Pflanzung*) of manufacturing power. Any limitation on the import of raw materials and agricultural (food) products will in the long run hamper the development of manufactures, and is therefore against the interests of the Protective System. This is the case even if such measures stimulate certain branches of agriculture and certain areas for some time. . . . The development of Manufacturing Power follows completely different laws than the development of Agricultural Power . . . To make this clear, we shall for the moment only outline how differently import duties influence prices of the two branches [manufacturing and agriculture]. When manufacturing is being cultivated, the prices of manufactured goods will rise, but as a result of the growing national manufacturing power and the increased competition resulting from this, the prices will, in time, be lower than they would have been through foreign imports.

Daniel Raymond's 1820 book strongly improves this argument by pointing to the fact that wages will rise considerably more than the prices of manufactured goods. It was an observable fact already since William Petty in the seventeenth century that agricultural wages were everywhere much lower than manufacturing wages. 'Applying import duties to agricultural products, on the other hand, does not have this invigorating power; such duties do not lead to lower prices later on. This flaw in their reasoning (*Denkfehler*), like the mixing up of cosmopolitical with political economy, the [English] school has inherited from the physiocrats.'

The year of the repeal of the Corn Laws was the last year of Friedrich List's life – he died on 30 November 1846. Since 1835 List had spent most of his time in Europe, losing all his US assets in 1837 and leaving the service of the USA. In connection with the repeal in 1846, List made his 'Final Reckoning with the English Free Traders' (*Letzte Abrechnung mit den englischen Freihandelspredigern*).[56] This powerful essay is indirectly directed at Richard Cobden, but more particularly against his *Knecht Freitag* (his slave Friday), that is, James Wilson, the founder of *The Economist*, who had started 'a kind of a crusade' against List: 'Had Mr. Wilson read [our previous publications] he would have found that we have defended the complete freedom of trade with food and raw materials, before any Corn League existed, before one Sir Robert [Peel] was a minister, and before Richard Cobden started protesting against the Corn Laws.'[57] List's frustration lies in the fact that *The Economist* used the repeal of the Corn Laws to convince other nations to give up their protection of manufactured goods.

Again List attacks the barter-based theories of Adam Smith, and their physiocratic nature: 'Adam Smith claims that only work which produces exchangeable value is to be considered productive.' In this system, says List, the person who raises pigs (*ein Schweineerzieher*) is considered productive, the person who raises the level of knowledge of human beings (*ein Menschenerzieher*) is unproductive. In this essay we find the argument of 'the raw' and 'the cooked' again. Superior standards of living can only be achieved by adding productive power to nature. 'Only a harmonious development of the powers of [art and science] can lead to a higher degree of power and civilisation.'[58]

In England we find that List's basic views on what caused human progress were expressed by Charles Babbage,[59] and followed there in practical policy. This made a member of the US Congress, Henry Baldwin, observe that English trade theory 'like most English manufactured goods, is intended for export, not for consumption at home'.[60] A perusal of the works of Richard Cobden confirms that Baldwin's point was well taken. Both Cobden and List argued for the superiority of manufacturing over agriculture – of the 'cooked' over the 'raw'. The arguments behind the repeal of the Corn Laws were not concerning a lofty principle of free trade, but rather that England should get out of 'inferior' agriculture in order to lower the prices of a basic industrial input – corn for the daily bread of its working masses. However, England skilfully used the fact that it no longer protected 'the raw' as an argument for other nations to stop protecting 'the cooked'.

NOTES

1 Valle's works are published as *Obras de Don José Cecilio del Valle*, Ciudad de Guatemala, Tipografía Sanchez & de Guise, 1930, 2 volumes.
2 Roscher's four-volume *Grundlagen der Nationalökonomie* appeared in 26 editions, the first edition in 1854. This work formed a school of thought which was to dominate German economic and industrial policy until World War II. Roscher was the first economist to incorporate increasing returns and mass production in an economic textbook. His dynamic world view formed a platform for later dynamic theories, of economists with such diverse views as Marx and Schumpeter. The quote is taken from one of the two US editions of his textbook: *Principles of Political Economy*, Chicago, Callaghan and Co., 1882, volume 1, p. 137.
3 It can be argued that the last history of economics which gave good coverage of the history of economic policy was Othmar Spann's *Die Haupttheorien der Volkswirtschaftslehre* which first appeared in 1911 and by 1936 had reached 24 editions and a total of 120,000 copies printed in German. The US edition is *The History of Economics*, New York, Norton, 1930. In England the book was published under the title *Types of Economic Theory*.
4 See, for example, Innes, Harold, *Staples, Markets, and Cultural Change. Selected Essays*, Daniel Drache (ed.), Montreal, McGill-Queen's University Press, 1995.
5 This type of thinking was reflected in Brigden, J.B. *et al.*, *The Australian Tariff: An Economic Inquiry*, Melbourne, Melbourne University Press, 1929. Vernon, J. *et al.*, *Report of the Committee of Economic Inquiry*, Canberra, Commonwealth Government Printing Office, 1965.
6 This process is narrated in Hart, Neill, *Increasing Returns and Economic Theory: Marshall's Reconciliation Problem*, University of Western Sydney, Discussion Paper Series no. E9004, 1990.
7 *Rethinking International Trade*, Cambridge, Mass., MIT Press, 1990, p. 4.
8 After King, Charles, *The British Merchant or Commerce Preserv'd*, London, John Darby, 1721, 3 vols.
9 Reinert, Erik S., 'Catching-up from way behind, a Third World view perspective on First World history', in Fagerberg, Jan *et al.*, *The Dynamics of Technology, Trade, and Growth*, London, Edward Elgar, 1994.
10 King, Charles, *The British Merchant or Commerce Preserv'd*, London, John Darby, 1721, 3 vols.
11 These problems are discussed in Reinert, Erik, 'Diminishing returns and economic sustainability: the dilemma of resource-based economies under a free trade regime', in Hansen, Stein *et al.*, *International Trade Regulation, National Development Strategies and the Environment: Towards Sustainable Development?*, Oslo, Centre for Development and the Environment, University of Oslo, 1996.
12 Gerschenkron, Alexander, *Economic Backwardness in Historical Perspective*, Cambridge, Mass., Harvard University Press, 1962, p. 215.
13 Hirschman, Albert O., *The Strategy of Economic Development*, New Haven, Yale University Press, 1959, pp. 109–10.
14 Reinert, Erik, 'Competitiveness and its predecessors – a 500–year cross-national perspective', *Structural Change and Economic Dynamics* 6, 1995, pp. 23–42.
15 Raymond, Daniel, *Thoughts on Political Economy*, Baltimore, Fielding Lucas, 1820. Raymond's work appeared in four editions from 1820 to 1840.

16 Serra, Antonio, *Breve trattato delle Cause che possono far abbondare li Regni d'Oro e Argento dove non sono miniere. Con applicazione al Regno di Napoli*, Napoli, Lazzaro Scorriggio, 1613.

17 Paul Samuelson's factor-price equalization.

18 The most complete account of the economic theory of the slave-owners is contained in *Cotton is King, and Pro-Slavery Arguments*, Augusta, Georgia, Pritchard, Abbot & Loornis, 1860. This is a massive tome of 908 pages, where the core of the economic arguments against the industrialization of the USA is found on pages 19–226.

19 New York, Harper, 1975.

20 Zingg, M., 'The genuine and spurious values in Tarahumara culture', *American Anthropologist* 44 (1), 1942, p. 82. Quoted in Lévi-Strauss, op. cit., p. 336.

21 Reinert, Erik and Daastøl, Arno, Norwegian Institute of International Affairs, Working Papers, no. 540, December 1995. Forthcoming in *European Journal of Law and Economics*.

22 Roma, Vincenzio Pellagallo, 1590.

23 ibid., p. 362. All translations are the author's.

24 'pena di Ducati cinquanta da esser tolto subito ogni volta . . . oltre tre tratti di Corda', Title: *Noi sopra proveditore . . . alle Biaue*, Venice, no date, Stampato per Gio: Pietro Pinelli, Stampatore Ducale.

25 London, C. Rivington, 1728. Palgrave regards Defoe as 'an important authority for economic history'. Higgs, Henry (ed.), *Palgrave's Dictionary of Political Economy* (1926), New York, Kelley, 1963, vol. 1, p. 535.

26 *Das Nationale System der politischen Oekonomie* (1844), Basel, Kyklos, 1959, p. 12. My translation.

27 Misselden, Edward, *The Circle of Commerce*, London, Nicholas Bourne, 1623.

28 Malynes, Gerard, *The Maintenance of Free Trade, According to the three essentiall* [sic] *Parts . . . Commodities, Moneys and Exchange of Moneys*, London William Sheffard, 1622. *The Center of the Circle of Commerce, or, A Refutation of a Treatise . . . lately published by E.M.*, London, Nicholas Bourne, 1623.

29 Misselden, Edward, *Free Trade and the Meanes* [sic] *to Make Trade Flourish*, London, Simon Waterson, 1622. *The Circle of Commerce or the Ballance* [sic] *of Trade*, London, Nicholas Bourne, 1623,

30 Schumpeter discusses the controversy between the two men in his *History of Economic Analysis*, New York, Oxford University Press, 1954, pp. 344–5. See also their respective entries in *The New Palgrave*. In all cases these references are purely to the mechanics of money and exchange.

31 ibid, p. 11.

32 *Political Arithmetick, or a Discourse concerning the Extent and Value of Lands, People, Buildings; Husbandry, Manufacture, Commerce, Fishery, Artizans, Seamen, Soldiers; Publick Revenues, Interests, Taxes, Superlucration, Registries, Banks; Valuation of Men, Increasing of Seamen, of Militia's, Harbours, Situation, Shipping, Power at Sea &c. As the same relates to every Country in general, but more particularly to the Territories of His Majesty of Great Britain, and his neighbours of Holland, Zealand, and France*, London, Robert Clavel, 1691.

33 Serra, Antonio, *Breve trattato delle Cause che possono far abbondare li Regni d'Oro e Argento dove non sono miniere. Con applicazione al Regno di Napoli*, Napoli, Lazzaro Scorriggio, 1613. Serra's remarkable dynamic 'model' shows how wealth is

created without the benefit of natural resources (Venice) on the one hand, and poverty remains in the midst of great natural resources (Naples) on the other. The parallel to modern Japan is interesting.

34 King, Charles, *The British Merchant or Commerce Preserv'd*, London, John Darby, 1721, 3 vols.

35 Léon Say in a speech on 'State socialism in England', 15 January 1884, quoted in *Richard Cobden and the Jubilee of Free Trade*, London, Fisher Unwin, 1896, pp. 131–2.

36 For a description of this, see Schumpeter, Joseph Alois, *The Theory of Economic Development*, Cambridge, Harvard University Press, 1934, pp. 90–94, 156.

37 Schumpeter, ibid., p. 93.

38 Quoted in Schoenhof, Jacob, *The Economy of High Wages. An Inquiry into the Cause of High Wages and their Effect on Methods and Costs of Production*, New York, Putnam's, 1892, p. 5.

39 Ibid., p. 5.

40 Eatwell, John, Milgate, Murray and Newman, Peter, *The New Palgrave. A Dictionary of Economics*, London, Macmillan, 1987, vol. 1, p. 462.

41 *The Political Writings of Richard Cobden*, London, William Ridgway, 1868, vol. I, p. 140.

42 Ibid., vol. 1, p. 150.

43 Robbins, Lionel, *The Theory of Economic Policy in English Classical Political Economy*, London, Macmillan, 1952, pp. 10–11.

44 Graham, Frank, 'Some aspects of protection further considered', *Quarterly Journal of Economics* 37, 1923, pp. 199–227.

45 Reinert, Erik, *International Trade and the Economic Mechanisms of Underdevelopment*, Ann Arbor, University microfilm, 1980.

46 *The Political Writings of Richard Cobden*, London, William Ridgway, 1868, vol. 1, pp. 150–51.

47 *On the Economy of Machinery and Manufactures*, London, Charles Knight, 4th edn, 1835. *Reflections on the Decline of Science in England and some of its Causes*, London, B. Fellowes, 1830. Babbage is best known for his 'calculating machine', celebrated as the first computer.

48 Morley, John, *The Life of Richard Cobden*, London, Chapman and Hall, 1881, vol. 1, p. 96.

49 Ibid., vol. 1, p. 97.

50 Quoted in McGilchrist, John, *Richard Cobden, The Apostle of Free Trade, His Political Career and Public Services. A Biography*, London, Lockwood, 1865, p. 259.

51 Raymond, Daniel, *Thoughts on Political Economy*, Baltimore, Fielding Lucas, 1820.

52 Printed by Samuel Parker. Reproduced in List's collected works in 10 volumes, 12 tomes, *Gesammelte Werke*, Berlin, Reimar Hobbing für die List-Gesellschaft, 1931, vol. II, pp. 96–156. All translations of German texts are mine.

53 *Gesammelte Werke*, vol. II, pp. 146–7.

54 Original in the files of the Department of State, Washington DC. Reproduced in *Gesammelte Werke*, vol. II, p. 326.

55 Reproduced in *Gesammelte Werke*, vol. V, pp. 112–21.

56 Reproduced in *Gesammelte Werke*, vol. IX, pp. 160–64.

57 Ibid., p. 160.

58 Ibid., p. 163.
59 *On the Economy of Machinery and Manufactures*, London, Charles Knight, 4th edn, 1835. *Reflections on the Decline of Science in England and some of its Causes*, London, B. Fellowes, 1830. Babbage is best known for his 'calculating machine', celebrated as the first computer.
60 Quoted in List, *Gesammelte Werke*, vol V, p. 338.

28

COMMENTARY ON CHAPTER 27

Parmjit Kaur

It is easy to agree with some of the basic convictions which seem to have motivated this chapter. There is also, somewhat hidden, an interesting hypothesis which could give direction to a novel investigation of the history of economic thought. That is to say, there is nothing objectionable about the healthy suspicion entertained by Reinert that dominant free trade theory, emanating from the developed world, has a fundamental bias towards the interests of that developed world. Given the fact that in practice less developed countries, under a regime of free trade, persistently lose through unequal international exchange, the theory of trade should indeed not be exempt from critical examination. One can only sympathize, therefore, with an attempt to reassess the historical genesis of trade theory and trade policies, under a working hypothesis like 'have free trade theories always been wielded by more developed countries, while theoretical arguments in favour of protection were put forward by countries with developing industries?'.

Judging by the subtitle of the chapter, one would expect Reinert to test the merits of such a hypothesis by singling out, as a case in point, the opposing views of List and Cobden on the repeal of the Corn Laws. However, the content of the chapter tends to be more diverse in nature than just focusing on this question and as such does not aid the clarity of the arguments posited.

It is true to say that the more conventional histories of economic thought, written by neoclassical economists, are highly selective forays into the rich past of the discipline, too often leading, for example, to a 'lumping together of all mercantilists'. But this very tendency also emerges in the chapter as a few general distinctions are used to carve up the whole history of economic theory and practice into the two camps of barter-based and production-centred theorists.

The way in which a distinction is drawn between 'barter-based economics' and 'production-based economics' is highly questionable for a number of reasons. This dichotomy, which is so paramount in the chapter, needs a greater clarification of the terms used. Presumably in 'barter-centred economics' increases in national wealth are explained as deriving from acts of exchange,

301

while 'production-centred economics' explains the same phenomenon from innovations in production. Understood in this way, if my interpretation is correct, it seems plainly wrong to stamp all classical and neoclassical economists as 'barter theorists'. A great many facts resist such a qualification, for example, in the case of Quesnay or Smith. To name a few, these early theorists were primarily interested in economic growth as recent interpretations have shown. Quesnay believed it to result from technical and organizational improvements in agricultural production, such that the net product or wealth produced was the return to the landlord available for reinvestment. Smith added to this that the same improvements in manufacture would increase the wealth of the nation; neither of them believed that trade created wealth. More generally, the discussion about what activity is productive, that is in which sectors will technical improvements lead to increases in national wealth and which activities will not, pervades for better or for worse the whole of the classical period.

Second, the distinction between 'barter-based economics' and 'production-based economics' is further confounded by the association with two more dichotomies, which are supposed to indicate an altogether more fundamental conflict. Underpinning each type of theory, it is asserted, was a specific philosophical notion of what defines man as a man, or what makes man 'cooked'. 'Production-centred economists' would have assumed that the specific human quality consisted of his ability to produce things in innovative ways, which explains why it was 'oriented around knowledge [mind]'. 'Barter-centred economics', by contrast, would have taken the propensity to 'truck and barter' as the feature which distinguishes man from beast.

The usage of such evocative language can be questionable and does not necessarily contribute to the clarity of the article. Contradictions arise which stem from the fact that the dichotomy needs clearer definition. For example, if in barter-centred theory there is no fundamental difference between raw materials and manufactured goods and if the physiocrats and Smith are examples of barter-centred theorists, how can they at the same time show preference for raw materials.

Apart from these general weaknesses, there are a number of historical observations cited which are too suggestive. Some examples may suffice. It is one thing to argue that some, or even most, protectionist policies of the past were understandable attempts to preserve rare skills or to allow industries to develop. It is another thing to imply that any precise theory 'motivated' these policies, as if dynamic increasing returns, diminishing returns, the slope of the learning curve and the differences between activities profitably to absorb skills and capital have been common concepts for 400 years. Such theoretical principles are, to some extent, formalizations of commonsensical insights which people have arguably possessed for a long time, but to assume that there is little difference between the two leads to historical inaccuracies. For example, the author's opinion that the physiocrats assumed the existence of diminishing returns in agriculture at a time when agricultural production had not been fully exploited is highly questionable.

Do the examples given, in which the trade in grain is seen as 'bad', really demonstrate that it was seen as an activity in which little wealth was generated? A more conventional and credible explanation is, of course, that the precarious nature of the subsistence economies of medieval and early modern Europe with their recurring food shortages compelled the civil authorities to regulate the trade in victuals. In time of shortages, grain exports from the country or region were curtailed to prevent food riots, not because it would be unprofitable. On the contrary, grain merchants were among the professionals who were generally seen as speculators that made large profits at the expense of the poor.

The unduly negative perception of agricultural resources in the production-based tradition, where they are referred to as 'the curse of the resources', is too blatant. Generally, history has shown that technical developments in agriculture precede manufacturing development. The resulting increase in agricultural production has been necessary to liberate excess labour to migrate to towns, thus increasing industrial activity.

To conclude, the chapter adopts a selective reading of economic theory, by use of the barter and production dichotomy in which to frame the arguments. This allows a new look at the resources issues. However, the task is made incredibly difficult by the vastness of the area addressed. Had the realm of the discussion been more limited in scope the examination would have been more focused. It can generally be agreed that Cobden advocated free trade in corn but protection of manufacturing as a way of maintaining a nation's industrial superiority. This notion is just as relevant today, as shown by developed countries aiming to protect their domestic value added through implementation of 'tariff escalation' on imports from developing countries.

INDEX

monopolistic competition 59, 63
Most Favoured Nation status 248
Multifibre Agreement 57, 247
multilateral trade liberalization 247–9
multilateral trade negotiations 126,
    129
multinational enterprises 86, 129;
    effect on trade patterns 86–7; growth
    in 108; subsidiary types 90
Mundell, R. 47–8

national interest 135
national sovereignty 127, 128, 248
new protectionism 119; and labour
    standards 120
new trade theories 39, 41, 292
newly industrialized countries 170, 249
New Zealand 241
non-tariff barriers 107, 128, 240,
    245–6
North American Free Trade Agreement
    (NAFTA) 5, 66, 69, 76–8, 106, 109,
    110, 114–16, 126, 145, 242, 247;
    and repoliticization of trade relations
    116; side accords 117
North–South divide 118–19

oligopolistic industries 169;
    international 173
open economic areas 248–9
open economy 65
optimal currency areas 42, 47–9
optimal tariff 2, 6
Organization for Economic Cooperation
    and Development (OECD) 68–9,
    129, 247
Organization of Petroleum Exporting
    Countries (OPEC) 76

Palmerston, Lord 131, 132, 140
Papua New Guinea 241
Pareto efficiency 13, 14
Peel, R. 1
pegging of currencies 45
Physiocrats 296, 302–3
Poland 217, 218, 221, 225, 237
political economy 105, 125, 186; and
    protectionism 225

price stability and protection 150
prisoner's dilemma 172
product cycle hypothesis 126
product differentiated industries 69, 75
product differentiation 39, 69
product innovation 69, 80
production-centred economics 275;
    versus barter-centred 276–88, 296,
    301–2
productive efficiency 57, 59;
    and international competition 59,
    61–4, 78, 87
productivity 26–7, 29–30, 128, 196–7
protectionism 44, 50, 131; and
    employment 188
protectionist policies 25, 246

quota systems 57, 58; in steel 190

realism 134–5
redistributions caused by trade 19, 24
regional currency blocs 50
regional development 86
regional economic development 101
regional impacts of foreign direct
    investment 88
regional integration 241, 247–8
regional policy 95–6
regional trade areas 5–6
regulation: environmental 107;
    harmonization of standards 5;
    international 106–24; and
    international trade 105; labour
    standards 8, 106–24; as a means of
    channelling political conflict 112;
    purposes of 105; scope of 121;
    selective 105; of services 107; social
    114–24
Reich, R. 28
rents 19, 58, 150, 155–7
research 256–8; and development 91
revealed comparative advantage 39,
    225, 227–8
Ricardo, D. 13, 23, 148, 149, 150–2,
    166, 254, 279, 288; corn theory of
    profit 151
rice duty 239
risk aversion 49